WHAT IF?

Other Books by the Authors

ANNE BERNAYS

Professor Romeo
The Address Book
The School Book
Growing up Rich
The First to Know
Prudence, Indeed
The New York Ride
Short Pleasures

PAMELA PAINTER

Getting to Know the Weather

WHAT IF?

Writing Exercises for Fiction Writers

REVISED AND EXPANDED EDITION

ANNE BERNAYS
The College of the Holy Cross

PAMELA PAINTER
Emerson College
Vermont College

HarperCollins*College*Publishers

Acquisitions Editor: Lisa Moore
Project Coordination: Ruttle, Shaw & Wetherill, Inc.
Design Supervisor: Nancy Sabato
Electronic Production Manager: Valerie A. Sawyer
Desktop Administrator: Hilda Koparanian
Manufacturing Manager: Helene G. Landers
Electronic Page Makeup: RR Donnelley Barbados
Printer and Binder: RR Donnelley & Sons Company
Cover Printer: The Lehigh Press, Inc.

For permission to use copyrighted material, grateful acknowledgment is made to the copyright holders on pp. 506–508, which are hereby made part of this copyright page.

What If? Writing Exercises for Fiction Writers, Revised and Expanded Edition

Copyright © 1995 by Anne Bernays and Pamela Painter

Library of Congress Cataloging-in-Publication Data

Bernays, Anne.
    What if?: writing exercises for fiction writers / Anne Bernays, Pamela Painter.— Rev. and expanded ed.
        p.   cm.
    Includes bibliographical references and index.
    ISBN 0-673-99002-8
    1. English language—Rhetoric—Problems, exercises, etc.
2. Fiction—Technique—Problems, exercises, etc. 3. Creative writing—Problems, exercises, etc.   I. Painter, Pamela.   II. Title.   III. Title: Writing exercises for fiction writers.
PE1413.B47 1995
808'.066813—dc20   94-9793
                                                    CIP

98 99 00 01 -DOC- 11 10 9 8 7

To Our Students

CONTENTS

VII. THE ELEMENTS OF STYLE   139

VIII. A WRITER'S TOOLS   161

IX. INVENTION AND TRANSFORMATION   189

XII. GAMES   269

XIII. LEARNING FROM THE GREATS   275

XIV: A COLLECTION OF SHORT-SHORT STORIES   293

XV: A COLLECTION OF SHORT STORIES 305

PREFACE

When the trade edition of *What If?* appeared in 1990, it was greeted by enthusiastic teachers, students, and fellow writers as the only how-to-write-fiction book that was long on specifics and short on the theoretical material so often found in books about the art of writing. That edition of *What If?* was comprised primarily of exercises introduced by brief but informative essays on the aspects of fiction. There is still no book like *What If?* It's now time for this invaluable tool to find its way into the hundreds of classrooms and workshops where students are learning to write: thus this updated, expanded text edition of *What If?* We view this book as a crucial link in the collaborative effort between the teacher who loves fiction and the student eager to master the craft of writing it.

Because the overall plan and organization of the trade edition works so well, we haven't altered them. Each section of the book, which deals with a separate element of fiction—characterization, dialogue, point of view, etc.—has been retained more or less intact. As before, every exercise is introduced in an opening paragraph. This is followed by instructions for completing the exercise, the "objective" of the exercise, and, frequently, by a student example. All but one of the original exercises are in this new text edition.

Here is what we have added:

- A section each on Style and Revision.
- Expanded sections on Perspective, Distance, Point of View, and Story Elements as a Given.
- Thirty additional exercises.
- Exercises from thirteen first-time contributors, among them George Garrett, Bridget Mazur, Ron Carlson, Richard Bausch, Eve Shelnutt, and Melanie Rae Thon.
- An anthology of twenty-four short stories, with wide-ranging style and subject.

Teachers will find this essentially new book especially useful because it puts the process of writing before any theoretical or abstract consideration. Using this book, the student learns how to write fiction not by thinking about it but by doing it.

In the years since *What If?* was published, we have used it with undergraduate and extension school classes, with graduate writing students in M.F.A. programs, in several four-hour workshops, and with a fourth-grade class. High school teachers use it. People writing at home, alone, use it. Although several exercises may be too advanced for fourth graders, few are too elementary for graduate students.

During our revisions, we have had help, encouragement, and advice from a lot of people. We want to thank all our students who have done the exercises and offered suggestions. We thank the students who contributed their examples—students from Arizona, California, Connecticut, Michigan, Ohio, Tennessee, Utah, Vermont and Paris. They are too numerous to name here, but it has been gratifying to see many of these student examples enlarged to become published stories. We want to thank the teachers of fiction who have used the trade edition of *What If?* and helped us to refine our work, and we particularly thank those who reviewed and made suggestions for this revised and expanded edition of *What If?*—Mona Houghton, California State University, Northridge; Ann Kiernan Davis, Dalton College; David Wojahn, Indiana University; Anne Greene, Wesleyan University; Mary O'Connor, South Dakota State University; Karla Horner, Chattanooga State Technical Community College; Ronald Spatz, University of Alaska Anchorage. We are also especially grateful to those teachers who have contributed their own exercises to this book: Tony Ardizzone, Richard Bausch, François Camoin, Ron Carlson, George Garrett, Perry Glasser, Katherine Haake, Christopher Keane, William Melvin Kelley, Thomas Kennedy, Rod Kessler, William Kittredge, Elizabeth Libbey, Alison Lurie, Robie Macauley, David Madden, Carol-Lynn Marrazzo, Alexandra Marshall, Bridget Mazur, Christopher Noël, Joy Nolan, David Ray, Ken Rivard, Lore Segal, Thalia Selz, Eve Shelnutt, Sharon Sheehe Stark, James Thomas, and Melanie Rae Thon. We thank the students and former students who have granted us permission to print their entire stories in *What If?*: Shelley Hunt, Joseph Connolly, Deborah Joy Corey, Michael J. Ellis, Molly Lanzarotta, Kim Leahy, Mariette Lippo, Matt Marinovich, Christine McDonnell, Barry Peters, Kate Wheeler, and Christopher Winters. We also thank the following people for their editorial and emotional support: Justin Kaplan, Robie Macauley, Hester Kaplan, Anne Brashler, Alice Hoffman, Rick Kot, Lisa Moore, Tom Maeglin, Gina Maccoby, Roberta Pryor, and our colleagues at Emerson, Vermont College, and The College of the Holy Cross.

Anne Bernays
Pamela Painter

INTRODUCTION

ANNE BERNAYS: Good writers know how to do two very different things equally well—write like a writer and think like one.

Writing like a writer is about craft and means gaining absolute control over your material and your tools. It means, for instance, knowing when to use dialogue and when to summarize discourse, learning how to use adjectives and adverbs—that is, sparingly—and concentrating on the specific rather than the vague and abstract. It means anchoring your story in a particular time and place; beginning writers often neglect to supply basic and crucial information: Who are these characters? Where are they? When is this story taking place?

Thinking like a writer is more complex, because it involves the unconscious. You can rely just so much on your five senses; after that you must call on curiosity, imagination, and skepticism—an open attitude not to be confused with cynicism. Skepticism obliges you to look beneath the obvious to get at the true meaning of, say, a smile, a crying jag, or a burst of anger. Things, in other words, are rarely what they seem. The writer must "think" his or her way past *seems* to *is.*

We have included exercises that ask you to assume the voice of the opposite gender, to search for subtext, and to supply several scenarios leading up to the same event—in other words, to enhance that intuitive quality of mind possessed by all good fiction writers.

PAMELA PAINTER: The exercises in *What If?* are also meant to set something in motion. Each exercise is designed to help you to think in new ways, to discover your own material, to enrich the texture and language of your fiction, and to move steadily toward final meaning. And coming full circle, to help you begin again. No matter how widely published a writer is, there is always the need to begin again.

We hope this book will be useful for people who have begun to publish and for those who have never written a word of fiction and are just now taking their first workshop. Our objectives for a workshop are that students will become familiar with: the various techniques for writing fiction, the language used to talk about the creative writing process, and the tools to discuss and criticize each other's work in a supportive and constructive manner. When reading each other's work, it is important to make up your own mind about the effectiveness of a story's beginning, or whether there are missing scenes, or how clear the ending is, etc. The more you hone your critical skills in regard to the work of others, the more you will be able to revise your own work with a cool, discerning eye.

BERNAYS: "Can you *really* teach people how to write?" I have been asked this question more often than any other during almost two decades of teaching. Beneath the question is the implication that being able to write well is a divine gift—either you have it or you don't so no amount of schooling is going to make a difference. Obviously I disagree. Besides, if you alter the question slightly and make it "Can you really de-mystify the process of inventing stories and writing them down?" my answer is "Absolutely."

This book separates and isolates the many elements of fiction, making them a manageable size and shape. Thus broken down and examined one by one, the components of a story or novel are rendered easier to master. This book should help you solve specific writing problems, like finding a good title, deciding on a point of view, discovering where and how to enter a story. Once you feel confident in your ability to exploit these particular skills, it's time to move on and fuse and combine what you have been learning step by step from *What If?*

At the very least you will feel more at ease with written prose and will experience the joy of saying exactly what you want to say the way you want to say it.

PAINTER: To "demystify the process" was the precise intention of *What If?* We didn't set out to write a book about how to write a short story—a write-by-numbers manual—because it can't be done. One of my students, Robert Solomon, spoke to this issue: "The book's value lies in helping me to understand fiction's components and their significance. . . . The exercises serve a preparatory function for when I begin my own true work, when I must deal with various choices and issues in accordance with my own particular vision and the demands it makes."

Writing exercises have long been a part of the learning process for new and established writers. A good many entries in the published notebooks of writers such as Chekhov, Flaubert, Hemingway, Fitzgerald, and Maugham among others, are unlabeled writing exercises—exercises that grew out of analyzing or talking about what these authors were reading at the time. And many entries are tributes to those writers who had shown them by written example how something worked in fiction. Fitzgerald speaks of a "trick" he and Hemingway learned from Conrad (p. 276). John Gardner says of writing that it is a matter of "catching on." In *The Art of Fiction,* he says of exercises, "When the beginning writer deals with some particular, small problem, such as a description of a setting, description of a character, or a brief dialogue that has some definite purpose, the quality of the work approaches the professional." And eventually, for writers who are persistent, the exercises you do here will strengthen your writing as a whole.

BERNAYS: It's possible for one person to be a marvelous storyteller— so long as he or she doesn't have to write it down. Another can form adequate sentences, even whole pages, and yet her story will just lie there, dead on the page.

The exercises in this book should help you sharpen your skills, both in the use of various tools and in the play of your mind. After completing these exercises the raconteur will be able to translate his story into writing and the competent but reticent writer will have learned to exploit her imagination.

You will notice that we make a point of distinguishing and segregating the elements of fiction rather than focusing on The Novel and The Short Story as discrete entities. This is because we believe that the tools and processes are similar for both, as is the emphasis on precision, clarity, and freshness.

PAINTER: We also believe in practice and more practice. Just as every singer, visual artist, dancer, and composer must constantly practice his craft, the writer too must practice. Even though we use language every day in talking, writing letters, or writing notes to "fill up the gas tank and leave the keys in the pantry," or writing memos for our jobs, or ad copy or news-paper articles, this does not mean that we can forgo the practice required in other arts. Practice and persistence are also crucial to a writer. Learn to throw away the flawed sentence, to recast a weak character without feeling a sense of failure. You are growing by making these evaluations of your work. You are practicing the writer's craft. And when you give yourself to your work, immerse yourself in it, you will feel it giving something back to you as if it had a beneficent will and energy of its own.

BERNAYS: If the writer's engine is persistence, then the writer's fuel is the imagination; unlike real fuel, we have an endless supply of it and it costs nothing. Imagination is there in all of us, just waiting to be released.

PAINTER: I became a believer in exercises when I did one for the first time in a writing workshop taught by Tom Bracken, a cofounder of *Story Quarterly.* Bracken gave us disparate elements to combine and weave into a story: banjo music, a penny, and an arresting photograph of two eyes peer-ing through the grainy slats of a boarded-up window. Suddenly, for me, these things were transformed into a story about a lonely teenage girl sit-ting on an orange crate in a country store. She has a penny under her shoe—and knows that only the boy watching her through the boarded-up window has seen her slide it there. Even using the same details, we were amazed at how our stories were totally different from the others. Of course: because each individual imagination—and voice and vision—used these details in a unique, personal way.

Since that time, I have worked with all kinds of exercises. Some are created as a result of reading the work of another writer—I think I will al-ways ask of a particularly effective beginning: what has been set in motion, and how? Some exercises simply appeared out of thin air:"What if?" And others grew out of class discussion as when my student Ben Slomoff asked a question that suddenly illuminated everything. "You mean it's as if every story has its own history?" Yes, yes—that's it. And an exercise was born to convey just that to every class that followed his.

BERNAYS: A boring story is worse than one with rough edges. As a matter of course, I always start off the semester with: "I don't want to see any polite stories." In order to keep you from long-windedness, hot air, and the temptation to stray from the point, we have kept many of these exercises down to a 550-word limit. When you don't have much space, you learn not to waste words. I've found that when a student goes much over the word limit his or her work tends to sound fuzzy and padded. Each exercise is meant, like a well-designed container, to hold the material destined for it.

Either Ms. Painter or I have assigned every one of these exercises to our students (some undergoing revision along the way) at such places as Harvard, Emerson College, Vermont College, Holy Cross, the University of Massachusetts, and numerous summer writing conferences and workshops.

PAINTER: I should say a word here about our "contributors." We've included a number of exercises from friends who are writers who also teach and use exercises in their classrooms. Exercises such as "Ways to Begin a Story," from Robie Macauley and "Changing Your Life," from Joy Nolan, and other exercises from Richard Bausch, François Camoin, Ron Carlson, Elizabeth Libbey, William Kittredge, Alison Lurie, Sharon Sheehe Stark, James Thomas, etc. We are all writers who believe in the power of exercises to demystify writing and at the same time to instill an appreciation for the joy and magic of writing something well.

BERNAYS: The trade edition of *What If?* came out in 1990. Since then our students have published stories in numerous magazines and journals, and many students who contributed the "Student Examples" in the original edition of *What If?* went on to use that beginning or excerpt for stories they eventually published. Others have won various competitions or awards. Still others have gone on to become teachers of writing, making up new exercises for their students. We hope you'll invent your own exercises for particular skills or techniques and paste them onto the white spaces in this book.

PAINTER: Yes, for example, Hemingway is known for his stripped-down dialogue, so you can imagine my delight when a student brought in a superb example of summarized dialogue from one of Hemingway's stories. I first pasted it into my book, and it is now printed in this edition.

BERNAYS: Unlike the trade edition, this textbook incorporates 24 stories by contemporary writers like Ann Beattie, Raymond Carver, Alice Munro. They are here as examples of the art at its best and most powerful, and demonstrate a challenging diversity of subject matter, style, voice, and narrative technique.

The table of contents of this book is a more or less arbitrary arrangement of the various elements and techniques of fiction. Some exercises are more difficult than others but you won't find the easiest is the first in any one section, nor the hardest the last. Don't feel you have to do them in any particular order but complete those that seem to meet your immediate needs. We do suggest that you read the introductions to each section before starting to work.

PAINTER: We made several discoveries while shaping the table of contents. We found that both of us believed in "character-driven" stories as opposed to "plot-driven" stories when we realized that we'd left "plot" as a distinct category out of our first draft. And when asked to add a section on revision, we realized that many of the exercises scattered elsewhere in the book were actually exercises about revision.

We hope you will return again and again to various sections of *What If?*—combining and rearranging the exercises to lead you into your own limitless well of material, to explore that wonderful intersection of biography and fiction, and to realize your potential as a writer. We also hope that you will use the writers whose work we have cited in our examples as a sort of organic reading list. Buy their books and read them; highlight specific passages, write in the margins, type out their sentences. The work of the masters is for the writer the best education, the best inspiration of all.

Interviewer: How do you describe the perfect state in which you can write from early morning into the afternoon?

One must be pitiless about this matter of "mood." In a sense, the writing will create the mood. If art is, as I believe it to be, a genuinely transcendental function—a means by which we rise out of limited, parochial states of mind—then it should not matter very much what states of mind or emotion we are in. Generally I've found this to be true: I have forced myself to begin writing when I've been utterly exhausted, when I've felt my soul as thin as a playing card, when nothing has seemed worth enduring for another five minutes . . . and somehow the activity of writing changes everything.

JOYCE CAROL OATES, *PARIS REVIEW* INTERVIEW

I. BEGINNINGS

First sentences are doors to worlds.

—URSULA K. LE GUIN

Ｎew writers often find beginnings difficult—whether they're starting a story or a novel—because they take the word "beginning" too literally. They cast around for the "beginning" of a story, forgetting that the place where it all began probably showed no hint of conflict, trouble, or complication to come. Your story can begin with dialogue, narrative summary, description, whatever, but it must begin *in medias res,* in the middle of things. You must resist the temptation to give the reader too lengthy an explanation as to how things got to this point. Remember, you are trying to hook the reader's attention, to pull the reader into your story so that he won't wonder, *What's on television tonight?*

Another stumbling block to beginning a story is that new writers think they have to know where their story is going and how it will end—before they begin. Not true. Flannery O'Connor says, "If you start with a real personality, a real character, then something is bound to happen; and you don't have to know what before you begin. In fact, it may be better if you don't know what before you begin. You ought to be able to discover something from your stories. If you don't, probably nobody else will."

The following exercises are designed to encourage you to think about real characters who are involved in situations that are already under way—situations that are starting to unravel because of, or in spite of, the desires and actions of their beleaguered characters. Don't worry about middles or endings yet. Just give yourself over to setting stories in motion—you will soon know which stories capture your imagination and seem unstoppable, which stories demand to be finished. Until that time, begin and begin and begin.

Literature was not born the day when a boy crying "wolf, wolf" came running out of the Neanderthal valley with a big gray wolf at his heels: literature was born on the day when a boy came crying "wolf, wolf" and there was no wolf behind him.

VLADIMIR NABOKOV

1
FIRST SENTENCES:
BEGINNING IN THE MIDDLE

In a *Paris Review* interview, Angus Wilson says, "Plays and short stories are similar in that both start when all but the action is finished." This goes along with Horace's injunction to begin the story *in medias res*—in the middle of things.

Yet, beginners' stories often meander for three or four pages before the story begins to rear its head. One day, out of curiosity, we decided to examine the first lines of stories in big and little magazines, story collections, and anthologies. We discovered that many *first sentences* put the reader in the middle of things. That exploration became the basis for this first exercise.

THE EXERCISE

Consider how many of the opening lines below pull you into the center of the story. What do you know about the story—situation, characters, geography, setting, class, education, potential conflict, etc.—from reading the titles and the following opening lines? What decisions has the author already made about point of view, distance, setting, tone, etc.? Notice how many of the titles are directly related to the first line of the text.

> "The Lady with the Dog"   ANTON CHEKHOV
> They were saying a new face had been seen on the esplanade: a lady with a pet dog.

> "Gesturing"   JOHN UPDIKE
> She told him with a little gesture he had never seen her use before.

> "Exchange Value"   CHARLES JOHNSON
> Me and my brother Loftis came in by the old lady's window.

> "Buried Lives"   BHARATI MUKHERJEE
> One March midafternoon in Trincomalee, Sri Lanka, Mr. N.K.S. Venkatesan, a forty-nine-year-old school-teacher who should have been inside a St. Joseph's Collegiate classroom explicating Arnold's "The Buried Life" found himself instead at a barricaded intersection, axe in hand and shouting rude slogans at a truckload of soldiers.

3

"Everywhere My Father"   ANNE BRASHLER
Gramma said an eight-year old girl shouldn't sleep with her own father,
but my father said that a rolled-up rug down the middle made a double
bed the same as two beds.

"The Remission"   MAVIS GALLANT
When it became clear that Alec Webb was far more ill than anyone had
cared to tell him, he tore up his English life and came down to die on the
Riviera.

"Medley"   TONI CADE BAMBARA
I could tell the minute I got in the door and dropped my bag, I wasn't
staying.

"On Faith Alone"   MELISSA PRITCHARD
For days, Ted Padilla had me bicycling past the dead Indian, bicycling
past a blanket stubbed like a wet cheroot in dirty ditchweed—how did I
know what was or wasn't vital, being new to town.

"A Girl Like Elsie"   KIRAN KAUR SAINI
I tell Mama I waitress in the Village so she don't have to cut me out of
her heart.

"Covering Home"   JOSEPH MAIOLO
Coach discovered Danny's arm when Danny's parents were splitting up
at the beginning of the season.

"Judgment"   KATE WHEELER
When Mayland Thompson dies he wants to be buried with the body of a
twelve-year-old girl.

"Getting an Education"   GLADYS SWAN
Most of the neighbors took in the oddities of Findlay Brightwood the
same way they took in everything else: the domestic quarrels of the
Ryans; the untidy family life of Dr. Kiely—Ear, Eye, Nose & Throat—
whose wife let the kids run wild with neglect; the heavy drinking of the
Pattersons, who partied lavishly on weekends, going through her money
like water, leaving out a full case of whiskey bottles for the garbage man
to cart off the following Monday after their friends had departed in
drunken riot.

"Nickel a Throw"   W. D. WETHERELL
These are the things Gooden sees from his perch eight feet above the
dunking tub at the Dixford Congregational Church's Charity bazaar.

"Appaloosa"   SHARON SHEEHE STARK
My father's girl friend's name was Delores and my mother went by Dusie
because she was one

"The Water-Faucet Vision"   GISH JEN
To protect my sister Mona and me from the pains—or, as they pro-
nounced it, the "pins"—of life, my parents did their fighting in Shanghai
dialect, which we didn't understand; and when my father one day

pitched a brass vase through the kitchen window, my mother told us he had done it by accident.

"Inventing the Abbots"   SUE MILLER
Lloyd Abbot wasn't the richest man in our town, but he had, in his daughters, a vehicle for displaying his wealth that some of the richer men didn't have.

"aw, babee, you so pretty"   NTOZAKE SHANGE
not only was she without a tan, but she held her purse close to her hip like a new yorker or someone who rode the paris metro.

"Bigfoot Stole My Wife"   RON CARLSON
The problem is credibility.

"Rock Springs"   RICHARD FORD
Edna and I had started down from Kalispell, heading for Tampa-St. Pete where I still had some friends from the old glory days who wouldn't turn me in to the police.

"Saturnino el Magnifico"   ALBERTO ALVARO RIOS
The entire circus train fell in the manner of a child's toy into the ravine just outside of town, its cars folding up in the fall so that from a distance they looked like the rough-angled line of teeth on a saw.

"The Blue Men"   JOY WILLIAMS
Bomber Boyd, age thirteen, told his new acquaintances that summer that his father had been executed by the state of Florida for the murder of a Sheriff's deputy and his drug-sniffing German shepherd.

"Woman Hollering Creek"   SANDRA CISNEROS
The day Don Serafin gave Juan Pedro Martinez Sanchez permission to take Cleofilas Enriqueta DeLeon Hernandez as his bride, across her father's threshold, over several miles of dirt road and several miles of paved, over one border and beyond to a town *en el otro lado*—on the other side—already did he divine the morning his daughter would raise her hand over her eyes, look south, and dream of returning to the chores that never ended, six good-for-nothing brothers, and one old man's complaints.

"Another Kind of Nostalgia"   KATHERINE HAAKE
Theo's husband, Frank, was a drop-in center counselor; Theo was a drop-in center bride.

"The Silver Bullet"   JAMES ALAN MCPHERSON
When Willis Davis tried to join up with the Henry Street guys, they told him that first he had to knock over Slick's Bar and Grill to show them what kind of stuff he had.

"Murderers"   LEONARD MICHAELS
When my Uncle Moe dropped dead of a heart attack I become expert in the subway system.

"Jump-up Day"   BARBARA KINGSOLVER
Jericha believed herself already an orphan—her mother was in the
ground by the time she could walk on it—so the loss of her father when it
came was not an exceptional thing.

"The Undesirable"   DAVID HUDDLE
I got over to the side of the road as far as I could, into the grass and the
weeds, but my father steered the car over that way, too.

"Forgiveness in Families"   ALICE MUNRO
I've often thought, suppose I had to go to a psychiatrist, and he would want
to know about my family background, naturally, so I would have to start
telling him about my brother, and he wouldn't even wait till I was finished,
would he, the psychiatrist, he'd commit me.

"The Handsomest Drowned Man in the World"
                              GABRIEL GARCÍA MÁRQUEZ
The first children who saw the dark and slinky bulge approaching
through the sea let themselves think it was an enemy ship.

Now, write ten of your own opening lines for ten different stories.
When you read, look for opening lines that immediately pull the reader
into the story. And if you keep a journal or notebook, consider starting a
new section and adding one first sentence each day—for the rest of your
life.

THE OBJECTIVE

To get into the habit of beginning your stories in the middle of things.
Because you are not obligated to finish these stories, this exercise lowers
the emotional stakes and helps to shake up and surprise the imagination.

STUDENT EXAMPLES

She was trying to tell the joke right but it was his joke and she had to
keep checking with him.   FRANCES LEFKOWITZ

I don't know who found me, or why I was left in a dumpster, but there
was one piece of lore about my rescue that was not forgotten and that
they made sure to hand down to me: written on my chest in navy blue
Magic Marker, my original owner had put the word "Gem," and that is
my real and only name.   BRIGID CLARK

Jason Dyvik's heart, like all bartenders' hearts, was a needy and glutto-
nous muscle.   ERIC MECKLENBURG

Nothing more to say—the storm, son walking further along the cliff than
dad, normal as you please, and the sea reached up and snicked him.
                              PERRY ONION

By the time I was ten I had concluded that death was just a matter of moving furniture.   AMANDA CLAIBORNE, "JEMMA"

My mother explained what sex was the day after I first had it.
                                                  CHRISTY VELADOTA

"In my last life," she said, "I was a telephone pole that stole kid's kites, shorted out whole neighborhoods on Christmas Eve and electrocuted telephone linesmen on their last day before pension."
                                                  ROBERT SOLOMON

Are you my mother's real daughter Rona asked me after Bertha died.
                                                  LYNDA STURNER

Aunt Iris wasn't too steady on her feet, having just shot Uncle Willis through the heart right after breakfast and then having driven 300 miles through mist and drizzle, so when the desk clerk at the Best Western shoved the registration card at her, she was sure she'd give the whole thing away right then and there because dammit, Willis had always filled these things out before.

When the fog rolls into Portsmouth a peculiar, anonymous intimacy descends, taming difficult women and angry men.   JIM MARSH

At Saint Boniface, on the first day of school, Mrs. Riordan found her fourth grade class was nothing more than Sister Mary's third grade from the year before, with one exception: a quiet boy with eyes the color of water, who occupied the front row window seat the way a vacuum takes up space.   BRIDGET MAZUR

Anecdotes don't make good stories. Generally I dig down underneath them so far that the story that finally comes out is not what people thought their anecdotes were about.

                                                  ALICE MUNRO

2

THE STORY'S HISTORY

In "First Sentences: Beginning in the Middle," we illustrate how most stories and novels begin in situation, in the middle of things. But, you might ask, what about the "beginning" of the story itself? Well, a few years ago, during the discussion of a flashback, a student said, "You mean it's as if every story has its own memory, its own history." Yes, that is exactly right. Each story has a history; all characters have pasts; the plots of most stories or novels are affected by something that happened before sentence one on the first page. Yet this history is woven so skillfully into the narrative of the story that most times we don't realize we are actually reading about the past of the story.

It might be helpful to think of the story as a straight line with the first sentence appearing somewhere beyond the start of the line—ideally near the middle. At some point, most stories or novels dip back into the past, to the beginning of the straight line and catch the reader up on the situation—how and why X has gotten himself into such a pickle with character Y. Tolstoy's novel *Anna Karenina* starts off with a household in a flutter over the husband's affair with the governess. Margaret Atwood's novel *Life Before Man* starts *after* someone has committed suicide. Yet these events foreshadow and affect the stories to come. The forward movement of Flannery O'Connor's "A Good Man Is Hard to Find" is so compelling that it is easy to overlook how the grandmother's past informs the action of the story. And the past of Amy Hempel's story "Today Will Be a Quiet Day" is filled with ominous events: children's fights that led the father to say he wanted "Today will be a quiet day" written on his tombstone; the parents' divorce; the boy's friend who told the boy, "never play Ping-Pong with a mental patient because it's all we do and we'll kill you" and who later committed suicide; the kids learning the guillotine joke; the dog that had to be put to sleep—all this before page one. That's good writing.

THE EXERCISE

First, return to a favorite story and make a list of events that occurred before page one. Ask: How do these events affect the story after page one and move the story to resolution? Do this exercise with several stories and novels.

Then look at a draft of one of your own stories. Take notes on your story's history. Does your story have a past? A history all its own? Is the current situation grounded in the history of the story? You might discover that your stories have a case of amnesia—a lack of history that makes the current situation thin or lacking in alternatives and tension.

THE OBJECTIVE

To understand how stories and novels—and the characters in those stories and novels—all have a history that affects their forward movement and resolution.

This discovery of being bound to a particular society and a particular history, to particular sounds and a particular idiom, is for the writer the beginning of a recognition of himself as finite subject, limited, the beginning of a recognition that first puts his work in a real human perspective for him. It is a perspective which shows him his creaturehood.

FLANNERY O'CONNOR

3

WAYS TO BEGIN A STORY

from Robie Macauley

There are many different means a writer might use to begin a story, and the problem is to choose one that most appropriately raises the curtain on the narrative to follow. Ask yourself such questions as these: Do I want my story to open with the sound of voices as people discuss something about their lives? Or do I want to bring one important character forward into the descriptive spotlight and let the reader have a good, long look at her before action begins? Or do I want to begin with an activity—one person, or more than one, engaged in doing something that will be significant for the story to follow? To judge these three possible openings, the writer might then ask questions of the unwritten story: Story, are you going to be about some involvement of people and their attitudes and opinions; are the ways they voice their thoughts going to be important? Or, Story, are you going to concern yourself with the traits, ideas, experiences, and emotions of one person who must seize the reader's imagination at once? Or are you going to be involved with an event—or events—in which the characters take part, and thus you want an opening that shows actions? Here are some of the possible ways of leading off.

With a Generalization

My mother believed you could be anything you wanted to be in America.
AMY TAN, "TWO KINDS"

When people become characters, they cease to be regarded as human, they are something to be pointed out, like the orange tree that President Kruger planted, the statue in the park, or the filling station that once was the First Church hall.
NADINE GORDIMER, "THE LAST KISS"

With a Description of a Person

He was lifting his knees high and putting his hand up, when I first saw him, as if crossing the road through that stringing rain, he were breaking through the bead curtain of a Pernambuco bar. I knew he was going to stop me.
V. S. PRITCHETT, "THE SAILOR"

With Narrative Summary

An unfortunate circumstance in my life has just recalled to mind a certain Dr. Crombie and the conversations I used to hold with him when I was young. He was the school doctor until the eccentricity of his ideas became generally known.

GRAHAM GREENE, "DOCTOR CROMBIE"

The Jackman's marriage had been adulterous and violent, but in its last days they became a couple again, as they might have if one of them were slowly dying.

ANDRE DUBUS, "THE WINTER FATHER"

With Dialogue

"Don't think about a cow," Matt Brinkley said.

ANN BEATTIE, "IN THE WHITE NIGHT"

I'm afraid Walter Cronkite has had it, says Mom.

JAYNE ANNE PHILLIPS, "HOME"

With Several Characters but no Dialogue

During the lunch hour, the male clerks usually went out, leaving myself and three girls behind. While they ate their sandwiches and drank their tea, they chattered away thirteen to the dozen. Half their conversation I didn't understand at all, and the other half bored me to tears.

FRANK O'CONNOR, "MUSIC WHEN SOFT VOICES DIE"

With a Setting and Only One Character

After dinner, with its eight courses and endless conversation, Olga Mikhailovna, whose husband's birthday was being celebrated, went out into the garden. The obligation to smile and talk continuously, the stupidity of the servants, the clatter of dishes, the long intervals between courses, and the corset she had put on to conceal her pregnancy from her guests, had wearied her to the point of exhaustion.

ANTON CHEKHOV, "THE BIRTHDAY PARTY"

With a Reminiscent Narrator

I was already formally engaged, as we used to say, to the girl I was going to marry.

PETER TAYLOR, "THE OLD FOREST"

With a Child Narrator

I don't have much work to do around the house like some girls.

TONI CADE BAMBARA, "RAYMOND'S RUN"

When I was in the third grade I knew a boy who had to have fourteen shots in the stomach as the result of a squirrel bite.

ELLEN GILCHRIST, "VICTORY OVER JAPAN"

By Establishing Point of View

First Person

Since Dr. Wayland was late and there were no recent news-magazines in the waiting room, I turned to the other patient and said: "As a concerned person, and as your brother, I ask you, without meaning to offend, how did you get that scar on the side of your face?"

JAMES ALAN MCPHERSON, "THE STORY OF A SCAR"

There was no exchange of body fluids on the first date, and that suited both of us just fine.

T. CORAGHESSAN BOYLE, "MODERN LOVE"

I'm Push the bully, and what I hate are new kids and sissies, dumb kids and smart, rich kids, poor kids, kids who wear glasses, talk funny, show off, patrol boys and wise guys and kids who pass pencils and water the plants—and cripples, especially cripples.

STANLEY ELKIN, "A POETICS FOR BULLIES"

Third Person

The August two-a-day practice sessions were sixty-seven days away, Coach calculated.

MARY ROBISON, "COACH"

Climbing up with a handful of star decals to paste on the bathroom ceiling, Claire sees a suspect-looking shampoo bottle on the cluttered top shelf.

FRANCINE PROSE, "OTHER LIVES"

THE EXERCISE

This one is in two parts. First experiment with different types of openings for different stories until you feel comfortable with the technique of each. Then see how many ways there are to open one particular story you have in mind. How does the story change when the opening changes from a generalization to a line of dialogue?

THE OBJECTIVE

To see how experimenting with several ways of opening your story can lead you to a better understanding of whose story it is, and what the focus of the story will be.

4

BEGIN A STORY WITH A "GIVEN" FIRST LINE

from William Kittredge

It can be challenging to begin a story with a "given" first line—especially one that starts in the middle. You can use a line from a poem, make one up, or use the one in this exercise. Or ask a friend or fellow writer to give you a first line—this is what Doris Lessing's characters do in her novel *The Golden Notebook*. When we come to the place in the novel where Saul gives Anna the first line "The two women were alone in the London flat," we realize that Anna did write her book, and that *The Golden Notebook,* which begins with that exact line, is Anna's novel.

THE EXERCISE

Begin a story with this line: Where were you last night?

THE OBJECTIVE

The objective is to once more start the story *in medias res*—in the middle of things. Notice how this question begins in the middle of a situation. For example, "last night," the subject of the question, has already happened. If one character asks another this question there are already two people "on stage." And the question will probably produce a conflict. But don't get hung up on making it a line of dialogue—it can be used many different ways.

STUDENT EXAMPLES

Where were you last night was the one thing she couldn't ask him anymore, so they talked about the death of Huey Newton. They were in the kitchen having breakfast, Marcy was eating Special K and Tom, Shredded Wheat. As usual, he had bought two copies of the *Times* and they each came upon the story at the same time. Twenty-three years had gone by since they had met and fallen in love during the height of the demonstrations at Berkeley and now Huey Newton was as dead as their marriage.
LYNDA STURNER

"Where were you last night?" Rob asked.

Eric kicked at the gravel. He knew he'd hear that question as soon as he saw Rob. They had planned to meet under the Grolsch sign by Flanagan's back alley. It was going to be a nice smooth operation. Ski masks, two unloaded guns. In and out before old Flanagan knew what hit him. They had everything planned, including which brand of gin—Gordon's—Rob would grab off the shelf before they ran out of the store. It would have worked perfectly, if Eric had showed up. That was precisely why he hadn't.

Paula A. LaFontaine

Where was I last night and how did I get here? I am lying on the sofa in my old apartment where my ex-boyfriend, Roy, still lives. The afghan I made for him a year earlier is draped over me. I pull it up to my chin. It smells like Roy: Old Spice and Camel filters.

Maria walks out of my old bedroom wearing Roy's blue and white striped Oxford. "You're awake," she says. "Roy says I have to let you stay here as long as you want."

I sit up. My head hurts and my teeth taste like vodka. From Chessy's Bar and Grill. I ran into Roy over by the pinball machines. He made me give him my car keys. They are on the coffee table now, next to my bag and earrings.

"Have a little too much, Janis?" Maria walks past me to the kitchen.

I stand up, holding the arm of the sofa. "Where's Roy?"

Maria puts enough water on for one cup of coffee. "He opens the 7-Eleven on Saturdays. Don't you remember?"

Christy Veladota

"Where you last night?" Tony asked, wiping down the bar in front of me with a gray towel. He doesn't look me in the eye.

"Vegas," I said, fingering an earring, noticing how bald he is, how short. "Where do you think?" Of course, I didn't really spend the night in Vegas or in any place worth mentioning, but when you're forty-one and planted on a bar stool, it's nice to think you still have possibilities, even if you can only reach them in your head.

Bridget Mazur

Here are two other "given" first lines:

I met him on the stairs.

(Note how many different ways the characters could be moving: both up; both down; or passing each other.)

If I went there a second time . . .

(This is the first line of Enid Shomer's poem "First Sunset at Outler's Ranch" from her book, *Stalking the Florida Panther*.)

5

PERSON, PLACE, AND SONG

from Ron Carlson

At the outset of any writing class I always give an assignment. I don't want to see the stories that these writers have in their files—yet. I also don't want to start a class with them talking; they are without exception excellent talkers. They are experts. I want to use that expertise later. Right off, I want them to write. No fears, tears, theory, or clashing agendas. Just a little writing. I want them to take the risk of writing something new—*all of them on an equal footing.*

The assignments I've been making have changed several times, but they're all essentially *prompts*, specific ways of starting. The most recent I simply call Person, Place, and Song. It comes from the second paragraph of Leonard Michaels' story "Viva La Tropicana," which appeared in *The Best American Short Stories 1991.* The paragraph starts:

> The first time I heard mambo, I was in a Chevy Bel Aire, driving from Manhattan to Brooklyn with Zev's son, my cousin Chester. We'd just graduated from high school and were going to a party. To save me the subway ride, Chester came to pick me up. He wore alligator shoes, like Zeb's dancing shoes, and a chain bracelet of heavy silver, with a name tag, on his left wrist. It was a high school fashion, like penny loafers and bobby socks. Chester had spent time in Cuba, but mainly he lived with his mother in Brooklyn and hardly ever saw his father. Uncle Zev, I believe, didn't love Chester too much, or not enough. This accounts for an eccentric showy element in his personality, which distinguished him in high school as a charming ass, irresponsible to girls, obnoxious to boys. As we drove, he flicked on the radio. The DJ, Symphony Sid, began talking to us, his voice full of knowing, in the manner of New York. He said we could catch Tito Puente this Wednesday at the Palladium, home of Latin music, 53rd and Broadway. Then Symphony Sid played a tune by Puente called "Ran Kan Kan."

This paragraph is rich with the specific data that offers clues and sets the tone for the rest of the piece. I could talk about it—all the work it does—for half an hour.

THE EXERCISE

Write a short piece of fiction—about a thousand words. It may be a complete short story and it may be the beginning of a longer piece. But it starts as follows:

The first time I (or Name) heard SPECIFIC SONG TITLE by SPE-
CIFIC ARTIST OR GROUP, I (or Name) was down/up/over at PLACE
and we were doing ACTION.

THE OBJECTIVE

To begin a story simply and specifically. Nothing grand, just close evidence that may lead somewhere. As I have said somewhere else, at greater
length: solve your problems through physical detail.

STUDENT EXAMPLES

The first time I heard the song, "Jesus Loves Me," I was six and sitting
on the grassy shores of Lake Winnebigosh with the rest of my Sunday
School class. Our teacher, Mrs. Henry, waltzed around in front of us, her
guitar hung around her neck, her mouth wide, singing and trying to smile
at the same time. It's an easy song, and we learned quickly—I remember
that. The day was fine and sunny, and the breeze coming off Lake
Winnie ruffled my hair and made me glad to be outside on the grass with
my parents and older brothers. Jesus loved me. I knew it and I sang.

The second time I heard that song it was drifting through the locked
door of my den, where my wife had been lying on the floor the better part
of the night, swathed in afghans and sleeping bags, listening to her Jesus
tapes and denying my ability to be an understanding man. She had holed
up there after another long day of silence, and as I leaned against the
door, I heard the high sweet voices of children singing, Jesus Loves me,
this I know, 'cause the bible tells me so.

"Patty," I said, on hands and knees with my nose wedged between the
carpet and the bottom of the locked door. "Patty, this is ridiculous. Turn
that off. Come out here."

It was ridiculous. It was sad and unfair. We had a good marriage, we
were both smart people—educated, fun I thought—and there was no reason for my wife to be locking me out of my own den, crying into the
down of our sleeping bags, listening to cope-with-the-Lord tapes. I told
her I was perfectly willing to talk it out, whatever it was, but all I got back
was the increased volume of the tinny music seeping through the door,
all those children singing to my wife.

I got up, stiff from my workout that afternoon, and from sitting on the
floor all night, and walked to our livingroom. Our house sits on a hill that
slopes down into the water of Lake Winnie. It has been thirty years since
I sat on the other side, in town, on the shore with my Sunday School
class. The church is over there. Our house is over here. I turned a stuffed
chair around to our tall open windows and watched the water through
our trees. The cool air breezed through the screens and across my bare
arms, over the bare skin of my legs. Since I'd been lifting—it had been a
year now—I could feel the air better and it felt like I was living closer to
my bones. I was looking good and I was proud of the muscles that had
appeared in my arms, that I could tighten up in my legs and roll around
in my back. I could outlift most of the guys at the gym, even the younger

ones from the college who played football but who were mostly fat. I was lean. I thought Patty was proud of me, glad that I'd entered the body-building contest that was coming to town in a few weeks. I guess I was wrong.

I shaved my legs. I didn't need to shave them until the day of the contest, but I'd shaved them this afternoon because I wanted to get the hang of it, didn't want any nicks or cuts on the day of the contest, and besides—I wanted to know how it felt. I liked the smoothness, and the feel of our sheets sliding over my skin. But Patty wouldn't sleep in a bed with a man who shaves his legs. I found that out.

KATHRYN MOHLER

The first time I heard the song, "Let it Be," was on Route 80 near Wheaton, Pennsylvania, three days after my divorce. I was coming cross country in a Pinto wagon with my ex-husband. It was hour number five.

I was leaving New York to be poet-in-residence at Grailville, a women's retreat in Loveland, Ohio. James was moving back to our old hometown in Findlay, to take over his father's medical practice. Pretty separate paths, huh? They should have been separate journeys too, but God must have been bored one day and needed to see a good show, because 48 hours after I said a final goodbye to James, I was saying hello to him on the phone.

He called in a panic. His car had been stolen, his job started in two days, he didn't have any money for a plane ticket because he'd spent it on legal fees for the divorce I had wanted, and he was desperate. Would I please take him with me to Ohio.

I liked the desperate part, so I said yes.

During the first hour I mentally recited the lyrics of every Peter, Paul, and Mary song I knew. Hour number two was occupied with construction tangles and detours. Hours three and four, James drove, and I pretended to sleep. Great mental discipline to pretend to sleep that long. But now, hour five was here—and "Let It Be."

"Good song," I said as the last notes leaked out.

"Yeah."

"Wish you had let me be," I said. I tried to look at him but a grey Lincoln Towne Car was looming in the rear view mirror, and I needed to keep my eyes on the road. I could smell the bagels in the back seat of the car. I'd bought three dozen of them for 36 mornings of bagels and coffee in Ohio. James had eaten two of them for breakfast. The cinnamon raisin ones.

KRISTINA M. ONDER

6

PAIRS OF BEGINNING SENTENCES

from Alexandra Marshall

Sometimes less is more, and sometimes it is just less. But no matter what, writing with a strict economy of purpose can force useful answers to fundamental questions. Even from one sentence you can learn both who the character is and what the story is about. To provide focus, it is helpful to begin by writing sentences in arbitrary pairs with established parameters.

THE EXERCISE

Write the first sentence of a story about a birth. Now write the first sentence about a death. Try other pairs, such as falling in love and filing for divorce. Try pairs that are not in opposition, such as spring and summer. Then invent your own pairs.

THE OBJECTIVE

To write succinct beginning sentence: one that signals the essential "who" and "what" to come.

STUDENT EXAMPLE

A Birth and a Death

1. I won't be doing any bonding with either one of them for quite a while; I knew I shouldn't have gone into the delivery room.
2. "He doesn't look peaceful or tortured or saintly, and no, he doesn't look 'just like himself'; he looks like some dead thing that I never knew, and I don't know why I'm here."

Falling in Love and Filing for Divorce

1. It could have happened to him a dozen times before and with women prettier, smarter, richer, funnier, sexier, even nicer, but it didn't, did it?
2. I don't want to throw her out the window or cheat her out of the money or tell her what a shit she is; I want to thank her for every goddamn day of it.

Spring and Summer

1. All spring means to me is that things change, and if they didn't, I'd never die—but I'd want to.
2. The end of summer stopped having any tangible meaning in his life long ago, but with each year he is still slower to recover from it.

CHRISTOPHER LYNCH

One of the most difficult things is the first paragraph. I have spent many months on a first paragraph and once I get it, the rest just comes out very easily. In the first paragraph you solve most of the problems with your book. The theme is defined, the style, the tone. At least in my case, the first paragraph is a kind of sample of what the rest of the book is going to be. That's why writing a book of short stories is much more difficult than writing a novel. Every time you write a short story, you have to begin all over again.

GABRIEL GARCÍA MÁRQUEZ

7

WHAT WORD COMES NEXT?

from François Camoin

Some narratives are driven by plot, by the idea of what happens next. We visualize a character, a scene, and ask ourselves what happens next. Other narratives are driven by language, by the writer's search for the next word, the next phrase, often without conscious attention to narrative logic. This sort of writing is analogous to a sculptor following the grain of wood with her chisel, seeking what *it* wants to say, and trusting that something recognizable and perhaps interesting will emerge. Instead of asking ourselves what happens next, a writer using this method will ask *what word comes next.* Instead of choosing words to describe something already present in the mind, the writer will let the grain of the language move the narrative along.

THE EXERCISE

Write the first sentence of a narrative. Any sentence will do. Then take two or three words from that first sentence and use them again in the second sentence. Take two or three words from those first two sentences and use them in the third sentence. Go on until the story begins to acquire a logic of its own.

THE OBJECTIVE

To learn to be surprised by what a story has to say, instead of deciding in advance what it must say. To get in touch with that part of ourselves that isn't always immediately available to the conscious mind. Focusing on technique, on a trick, will often allow us to write things we wouldn't otherwise write, things that frighten or disturb us.

EXAMPLES

First Sentence
Frost's lover has a job at the University Hospital; for fifty dollars an hour Cynthia lets medical students practice pelvic examinations on the body which, she tells Frost, she detaches herself from for just as long as it takes the young men to get done with their little explorations.

Second Sentence

She learned the technique of detaching herself from her body, of temporarily allowing herself to float above herself, of not being there except in spirit while she earns her fifty dollars, from Mme. Seroka, her astral flight instructor at the YWCA.

Third Sentence

Astral flight is a science and not an art, she explains to Frost; you push from the inside, against the soles of your feet yourself sliding out of yourself through that little spiritual hole behind your own left ear.

Fourth Sentence

It's a science, because you've learned how you can do it every time, not like making love which you can only do when you're in the mood, and which, she says, touching the most tender part of Frost, is not all that spiritual, though it is something a person can enjoy.

II. NOTEBOOKS, JOURNALS, AND MEMORY

In a cartoon by William Hamilton, a harassed-looking young woman is seated at a desk, holding some manuscript pages. Her typewriter has been pushed momentarily to one side, as she says into the phone, "Frances, can I get back to you? Gordon ran away with the babysitter and I'm trying to see if there's a short story in it."

Of course there's a story in it. Probably several, but now might be a little soon to begin writing about Gordon's flight. Hamilton's young woman needs to take to heart what Wordsworth said about poetry, that it is "emotion recollected in tranquillity."

What this young woman should do, since she is determined to find a story, is jot down in a notebook or journal a few details that she doesn't want to lose. Perhaps Gordon left an odd note? Or one of the children asked if Gordon, who had recently lost his Wall Street job, was going to start a babysitting business. Or perhaps the harassed young wife discovered she was secretly delighted that Gordon was gone?

When she returns to this material at a later time, if she does, she might want to tell the story from Gordon's point of view—a story about a man who leaves his wife because he knows that she will someday leave him. Or from the babysitter's point of view—a story about a babysitter who feels sorry for a husband whose wife begins typing the minute he gets home from work.

The point is, as writers we lead double lives. We live in the world as the people we are—but we also live in the world as writer/observers ready to see a story anywhere, to note a detail that simply couldn't be made up, to record an overheard line of dialogue, to explore our enemies' points of view, and to sift through memory—did we really have a happy childhood? A writer's notebooks and journals are a testimony to this double life. As Socrates said, "The unexamined life is not worth living."

Journals and notebooks function in several ways. One writer may use them as a repository for the raw material for fiction that he will return to for inspiration. Another writer may keep a notebook but never look at what he writes again—for him, the act of selecting and writing something down was the valuable exercise, keeping his writer's ear and eye in shape. And yet another writer may use her journal for deepening stories she's already written.

Our exercises are designed to show you some of the possibilities and rewards of keeping a journal or notebook. It is the perfect place to jot down that odd name you found on a program—"Buck Gash"—a name you'll never legally be able to use, but one you want to remember. Or to make a list of all the places you've ever lived. Or to write a journal entry from the point of view of the babysitter titled "Why I'm running away tomorrow with Mr. Farnham (I call him 'Gordie')."

Fiction gives us a second chance that life denies us.

PAUL THEROUX

8

WHO ARE YOU? SOMEBODY!

Richard Hugo, in an essay titled "In Defense of Creative Writing Classes," recalls the most important lesson he ever learned, "perhaps the most important lesson one can teach. You are someone and you have a right to your life." He decries the way the world tells us in so many ways that "individual differences do not exist" and that "our lives are unimportant." He says, "A creative writing class may be one of the last places you can go where your life still matters." The same thing is true for the writer who sits alone at her desk.

THE EXERCISE

Buy a notebook to use for just this one exercise. Then, on a regular basis, perhaps at the beginning of your writing time or before you go to bed, write for ten to twenty minutes addressing each of the following subjects:

- List in detail all the places you have lived—one place per page. (This is a good way to begin because it gives the entire notebook a concrete grounding in time and place.) You might even want to get very specific, say, by recounting all the kitchens, or bedrooms.
- Next, recall if you were happy or unhappy in those places.
- Consider your parents' relationship, from their point of view.
- List important family members: brothers and sisters, grandparents, uncles and aunts, cousins. What were the dynamics of your nuclear family, your extended family? (Some of these subjects may take several twenty-minute sessions. Leave space for unfinished business.)
- List smells—indoor and outdoor—and the memories they conjure up.
- Do you have any recurring dreams or nightmares? Start a section for dreams.
- Ask yourself, What did I care about when I was five, ten, fifteen, twenty, twenty-five, thirty, etc.? What do I care about now?
- What is your five-year plan?

These are the kinds of questions that help you define who you are. Now make up questions of your own to answer in your notebook. In fact, making up questions to bring back the past, to explore the present, and to voice your hopes and expectations for the future is part of the fun of this exercise.

THE OBJECTIVE

To lead an examined life. Your notebook will become a lifetime companion and an invaluable source of material.

I always write from my own experiences whether I've had them or not.
RON CARLSON

9

PUT YOUR HEART ON THE PAGE

In a letter to a Radcliffe student, F. Scott Fitzgerald wrote of the price she must pay for aspiring to be a professional writer:

> You've got to sell your heart, your strongest reactions, not the little minor things that only touch you lightly, the little experiences that you might tell at dinner. This is especially true when you begin to write, when you have not yet developed the tricks of interesting people on paper, when you have none of the technique which it takes time to learn. When, in short, you have only your emotions to sell.

Too many writers avoid their own strongest feelings because they are afraid of them, or because they are afraid of being sentimental. Yet these are the very things that will make beginning work ring true and affect us. Your stories have to matter to you the writer before they can matter to the reader; your story has to affect you, before it can affect us. William Kittredge says, "If you are not *risking* sentimentality, you are not close to your inner self."

THE EXERCISE

Make a notebook entry on an early childhood event that made you cry or terrified you, or that made you weak with shame or triumphant with revenge. Then write a story about that event. Take us back to those traumatic times, relive them for us through your story in such a way so as to make your experience ours.

THE OBJECTIVE

To learn to identify events in your life that are capable of making you laugh and cry. If you can capture these emotions and put them on paper, chances are you will also make your readers laugh and cry as well.

10

PEOPLE FROM THE PAST:
CHARACTERS OF THE FUTURE

Most of us have an unsettling memory of another child who loomed larger than life as we were growing up. Someone we resented, feared, hated, or envied. It might have been a sibling, a cousin, someone from the neighborhood, or someone from school. Often, that child—perhaps a little older or a little younger—had the power to make us take risks we would never have taken on our own, or had the power to make us miserable. This is the subject of Margaret Atwood's novel *Cat's Eye,* in which artist Elaine Risley is haunted by Cordelia, just such a childhood tormentor and "friend." Well, eventually these children grow up.

THE EXERCISE

First, think about your childhood between the ages of six and twelve and try to recall someone whose memory, even now, has the power to invoke strong, often negative feelings in you. Was that person the class bully, the clown, the daredevil, the town snob, the neighborhood bore, etc? Write down details of what you remember about this person. How she looked and talked. Did you ever have any encounters with this person. Or did you just observe her from a distance?

Next, if you haven't seen this person for ten years or longer imagine what she is doing now, where she lives, etc. Be specific.

If you had a long acquaintance with this person, or still know her, imagine where she will be ten years from now.

THE OBJECTIVE

To understand how our past is material for our imaginations and how writing well can be the best revenge.

STUDENT EXAMPLES

His first name was Frank, or Frankie. We went to a small private day school in California. There were thirteen students in my eighth grade class and all of us were afraid of Frankie who was in the ninth grade. He was the school bully, a mean person, bottom line.

Once when I walked into the locker room, Frankie threw a Japanese Ninja throwing star into the wall just next to me. "Damn, I missed," he said. He talked about how his father had hit him with a 2 × 4 and he'd asked him for more. He bragged that his father had shot and killed a black man. Frankie hated everyone.

I can imagine Frankie in ten years. He'll be a white supremacist living in rural Georgia and working in a factory. He'll be married with three kids. He'll keep loaded shotguns and pistols around the house and will threaten to kill the kids. Before he's 35 he'll be doing time for a murder he committed outside a bar.

HUNTER HELLER

Darlene was two years older than me, heavyset, a great football player. She loved the Dallas Cowboys just like all the guys—although we also liked the cheerleaders. Darlene taught me to ride a bike because she was sick of riding me around on her handlebars. One day, she put me on her Sears ten-speed and pushed me into the street, where I smashed into a parked car. She got mad because I "messed up the paint" on her bike. She says I ruined her first sexual experience one night when all the neighborhood kids were playing "Ring-O-Leveo." According to her, she was under a bush, about to "make her move" on Jeremy Witkins, when I saw her and called out her name and location. We used to smoke Marlboro Reds and drink stolen Budweisers behind the local swimming pool. In the five years I knew her, she never once wore a skirt.

I'll bet Darlene went to Grattenville Trade school—she was tough and good with tools. She probably kept wearing concert-Tee's, denim jackets, and eventually got into heavy metal. I wonder if her teeth got straightened and her acne went away and her breasts got even bigger. I can imagine her dropping out of school, fighting with her folks all the time, and scooping ice cream nine to five at Carvel, or selling 36-shot film out the little Fotomat window. She'll buy takeout most nights. I can see her standing in line for a couple of beers and a slice of pepperoni for her live-in boyfriend, a muffler mechanic named Al, who is too high to deal with the counter person.

DANIEL BIGMAN

I never travel without my diary. One should always have something sensational to read on the train.

OSCAR WILDE

11

AN IMAGE NOTEBOOK

from Melanie Rae Thon

As playwright and actor Sam Shephard traveled cross-country, he kept a notebook which later became *Motel Chronicles,* a book of poems, images, scenes, and snatches of dialogue which evoke the disorienting experience of being continually on the move. A move or arrival at college often has the same effect. It may be difficult to make sense of all that's happening while you're in the middle of it, just as Shephard couldn't make sense of his experiences. But you can render these moments vividly, as Shephard did, put them together, and see what surfaces. This is a good exercise when you're between stories, unsure of where you want to go next. It keeps you writing without pressure and provides a space where material may surface.

THE EXERCISE

For the length of the semester, keep an "image notebook." Every day, record at least one image. (Date these entries.) Use all your senses. Ask yourself: What's the most striking thing I heard, saw, smelled, touched, tasted today? Images begin with precise sensual detail. One day you may overhear a strange bit of conversation, another you may smell something that triggers a memory of a familiar smell. Another day you might find a photograph or take one or do a drawing. You might make a collage of words and pictures from magazines. This assignment is very open. Length is variable. Some days you may write a page, another day a line. Don't get behind. Interesting juxtapositions emerge when you're not conscious of how images are colliding. If you do your week's work all at once, you'll lose this mystery.

THE OBJECTIVE

To learn to pay attention to detail. To gather images for later use. To find interesting juxtapositions to use in stories. To find threads of narrative that lead to stories. To become clearer about what's interesting to you.

EXAMPLES

I think of a white dog in Foot's yard. Big as a husky. White with white eyes, almost white eyes. Leaping to the end of his chain and later running free, dodging cars, but just barely.

I'm remembering the London Tube, the man looking at the punked-out girl as if he wanted to kill her, as if she were disgusting, vile—how the tears welled in my eyes, because I knew how it felt to be looked at that way—but she didn't see. She had spiked, red hair, a lime green miniskirt, torn fishnet stockings, black—a teenager. He was middle-aged, working class? I wonder if he had a daughter of his own. It scared me, the way he looked at her, because I really thought he might leap, might pummel her, might rip her throat.

Down the street the children have made a Snow Snake. This was before the storm. Fifteen feet long, two feet high—sweet-faced serpent. Disappeared now for sure.

There's this point in the perm process where Annette smears gel along the hairline, then wraps cotton under the curlers to keep the solution off my face. It's the gel that gets me. Cool, slick. And I tell her it reminds me of women getting electroshock, how they smeared gel on the head before they applied the electrodes.

Christine tells me this story. Her friend is riding his bicycle but is completely spaced out. He crashes in Harvard Square, runs into a tree. (Where did he find a tree?) Breaks his wrist but doesn't know it. Is just embarrassed. Hops back on the bike. Peddles away. Then the shock hits him and he's down again. When he comes to, he finds himself in a fire-man's arms. Christine and I howl. Make our plans for collapse. To wake that way.

12

CHANGING YOUR LIFE

from Joy Nolan

Art is art because it is *not* nature.
GOETHE

Good fiction has a confluence of detail that real life seldom has. We've all been told "write what you know," and its true that autobiographical material enriches fiction with vivid details. But don't sell your fiction short by sticking to the facts—what you know extends far past the specific incidents of your life. The more flexible and elastic your use of facts and feelings borrowed from life, the stronger your writing will be. Marcel Proust said, "Creative wrong memory is a source of art."

As a writer of fiction, you have to be more loyal to the fiction than to the facts that inspired it. Remembering being chased by a vicious dog as a child may give you just the right flavor of terror to vividly describe a thief's fear while fleeing the police in your story. Or you can invest a fictional event with remembered emotion, or use a real-life scene as a backdrop for your imagination, changing the feelings and consequences entirely.

THE EXERCISE

Choose a central dramatic incident from your life.

- Write about it in first person, and then write about it in third person (or try second person!). Write separate versions from the point of view of each character in the incident.
- Have it happen to someone ten or twenty years older or younger than yourself.
- Stage it in another country or in a radically different setting.
- Use the skeleton of the plot for a whole different set of emotional reactions.
- Use the visceral emotions from the experience for a whole different story line.

32

THE OBJECTIVE

To become more fluent in translating emotions and facts from truth to fiction. To help you see the components of a dramatic situation as eminently elastic and capable of transformation. To allow your fiction to take on its own life, to determine what happens and why in an artful way that is organic to the story itself. As Virginia Woolf said, "There must be great freedom from reality."

Whatever our theme in writing, it is old and tried. Whatever our place, it has been visited by the stranger, it will never be new again. It is only the vision that can be new; but that is enough.

EUDORA WELTY

13

JOURNAL KEEPING FOR WRITERS

from William Melvin Kelley

Everybody has a day to write about, and so writing about the day makes everybody equal. Diary keeping separates the act of writing from creating character and plot. You can write every day and learn certain fictional techniques without having to invent fiction on command.

THE EXERCISE

Write one page a day. Concentrate on observation and description, not feeling. For example, if you receive a letter, the ordinary reaction is to write in the diary, "I received a letter that made me happy." (Or sad.) Instead, describe the size of the envelope, the quality of the paper, what the stamps looked like.

Keep your diary without using the verb *to be*. Forms of the verb *to be* don't create any vivid images. By avoiding its use, you get into the habit of choosing more interesting verbs. You'll also be more accurate. For example, some people will say "John Smith is a really funny guy," when what they really mean is "John Smith makes me laugh." Or "I like John Smith's sense of humor."

Experiment with sentence length. Keep the diary for a week in sentences of ten words or less. Then try writing each day's account in a single sentence. Avoid use of "and" to connect the long sentence; try out other conjunctions.

Switch your diary to third person for a while, so that instead of writing *I*, you can write about *he* or *she*. Then, try mixing the point of view. Start the day in third person and switch into first person to comment on the action. By interspersing first- and third-person points of view, you can experiment with stream of consciousness and the interior monologue.

Try keeping your diary in an accent—first the accent of somebody who is learning how to write English, then the accent of somebody learning to speak English.

Keep it in baby talk: Baby want. Baby hurt. Baby want food. Baby want love. Baby walk.

Try making lists for a diary entry—just a record of the nouns of that day: toothbrush, coffee, subway tokens, school-books, gym shoes.

THE OBJECTIVE

To enhance your powers of observation and description without having to juggle the demands of characterization and plot.

All really satisfying stories, I believe, can generally be described as spendthrift. . . . A spendthrift story has a strange way of seeming bigger than the sum of its parts; it is stuffed full; it gives a sense of possessing further information that could be divulged if called for. Even the sparest in style implies a torrent of additional details barely suppressed, bursting through the seams.

ANNE TYLER, INTRODUCTION TO BASS *1983*

14

THINGS THAT HAPPEN TO YOU

Almost invariably, the beginning writer views his life as dull. The opposite is true—your own life is teeming with incident and emotion. Train yourself to identify and store away for future use the odd, funny, sad, and suspenseful things that happen to you.

THE EXERCISE

Over the period of a week or so write down ten things that made you angry, but don't try to explain why. Over the same time period do the same for ten things that pleased you. Be very specific. Statements like "I felt good when I woke up on Wednesday morning," are too vague to carry any conviction—and this could have happened to anyone. "I ran into Ms. Butler, my third-grade teacher, in the Star Market and she said hello to me by my right name" is specific and could only have happened to you.

THE OBJECTIVE

You may not use most of what you've written down, but you will have practiced viewing your immediate world as a garden full of fictional seeds.

STUDENT EXAMPLE

Things that pleased me

1. Plastic pumpkins and Indian corn at the supermarket checkout.
2. Little girls in winged Viking helmets on Leif Eriksson Day.
3. On Columbus Day, lying in my bed listening to fireworks—muffled explosions which come faster and faster as the show reaches its finale.
4. Jeff's example of slang peculiar to his household: "Week to be" means a person's week off from the chore wheel.
5. Carolyn's new job: painting wooden toys for children.
6. In a cleanly swept fireplace, a little stuffed mouse with red ears.
7. Glancing at my Harmony textbook as I'm getting dressed in the morning, and then suddenly remembering a dream from the night before.
8. A pet rabbit with floppy ears like a dachshund's.
9. After I order a peanut butter frappe with chocolate syrup, the woman in line behind me laughs and says she's going to order the same thing.

10. Jeff's roommate, on a postcard from France, lists the French grammar books he has bought there.

Things that made me angry

1. Heidi walking through the door and then, without saying hello, beginning to complain about the money in the household fund.
2. In the Catholic school playground, kids playing "Duck, duck, goose" while a nun stands watching them.
3. Eric's looking away coldly when Don shakes his hand.
4. Smelling Dunkin' Donuts from half a block away.
5. Learning that *Boston Magazine* readers have an average annual income of $110,000.
6. A smelly man in a dirty sweatshirt browsing near me in the Boston Public Library.
7. The padlocked wooden box where Jeff's neighbor keeps laundry detergent.
8. The bathroom door swinging loose as the pin in the top hinge snaps in half.
9. The teenager in line at Tower Records with a denim jacket covered with buttons from trendy pop bands—Love and Rockets, U2, Talking Heads, and many others.
10. My bedroom window cracking in half in the wind.

MIKE RASHIP

15

CREATIVE WRONG MEMORY

One of the dangers of writing about something that really happened is an urge to stay too close to the literal truth. Because you don't quite trust your memory of it you come up with thin narrative and little texture. Or with details or events the reader may find unconvincing. "It really happened that way." or "It's a true story." is no defense. Also, keep in mind that a recital of just the facts rarely adds up to a satisfying fictional truth.

This is another exercise to show you how to remember what you don't know—how to combine autobiography and imagination to achieve what Proust calls "creative wrong memory."

THE EXERCISE

1. Recall an event or dramatic situation from your childhood and describe the event in one or two sentences at the top of the page.
2. Next, using both words and phrases, make a list of all the things you remember about the event.
3. Now make a list of all the things you don't remember about that event.
4. Finally, begin a story using several details from the list you remember and several from the list you don't remember—details you have made up. One way to make this work is to link important details before you begin. For example: I remember that Uncle Cal and Aunt Marie had a fight, but not what started it.

THE OBJECTIVE

To enlarge and deepen your autobiographical material by making up what you don't remember and adding it to what you do.

STUDENT EXAMPLES

Italics indicate the parts that are "made up."

Notes for First Example

EVENT: death of a classmate (Albert Parsons)

I REMEMBER: my puzzlement about his sudden disappearance. He was dark-haired and serious. It was fall. Shortly afterwards my favorite uncle died and I went to his funeral at the cathedral and cried. I remember lying in bed, knowing my parents would not be there forever, that they would die. I remember at that moment a terrifying fear and sense of loss.

I DON'T REMEMBER: how Albert Parsons died. An illness? I don't remember how I found out. I don't remember how the others in my class reacted. Nor do I remember how my uncle died or how my aunt and parents reacted.

(Here is the beginning of this story.)

It was a crisp, fall afternoon *with both sides lined up on the field for soccer practice when I saw that Albert Parsons wasn't there. Earlier, in the classroom, I hadn't noticed that Albert was missing.* He was a solemn, dark-haired boy who sat quietly *at the back of the first row; he didn't join in any of the recess games.* But soccer was compulsory *and I was worried that our side, Ayre House, was a man shy for the scrimmage. Things weren't in order.*

"Mister Todd," I yelled to our coach, really our fifth grade teacher. He wore a topcoat and bowler hat, *and was eager to blow his whistle to get us started so he could get away to the sideline for a cigarette.*

"Albert Parsons isn't here," I called. *"It's not fair."*

Mr. Todd swung around, taking the whistle from his mouth. "You a coward, Campbell," he barked. *He jerked his head at the other side, Harrington House, whose color was yellow. "You afraid the yellow-bellies over there are going to beat you and you won't end up on the winning side? What's not fair? That you might lose or that Albert Parsons isn't here?"*

His outburst of questions startled me. We were all leary of Mr. Todd. More creepy stories were told about him than any of the other teachers; his class loomed ahead of us like a dragon's cave we would have to someday enter.

DONALD FRASER MCNEILL

Second Example

I know Dick was the first to fire his slingshot at the lamppost near the end of the driveway of the house where the Kirschners had moved out a few weeks before. He missed.

Dick, Tim and I were shooting baskets at the Johnson's house, across the street where Tim lived. We all had our slingshots and after Dick's initial salvo, we started shooting pebbles at the lamppost until Tim hit the glass enclosing the light. The tinkling glass unleashed a frenzy of juvenile deliquency. After missing four shots, I ran up to the post and fired a stone at close range. *The three of us proceeded to demolish the glass around the lamp, not satisfied until the bulb was broken and the filament hung in the air like blades of steel grass.*

Then we went to the back of the house, sneaking around like an imaginary commando unit, firing stones from the woods on the hillside overlooking the garage and back porch. Tim hit the garage window with a lucky shot, creating a hole but not shattering the glass. *We moved in, peppering the window with stones until all the glass had tinkled onto the stone floor inside.*

We moved around front, running past the front door and shooting stones *into the frosted glass on either side of the red double doors, now pretending to be a small Indian war party circling the wagon train.*

Then we went back to shooting baskets, pretending we hadn't stopped at all, trying to act naturally but feeling a rush of excitement at our victory in the war against the Kirschner's windows. *The November day was cool and overcast, but the three of us were sweating heavily.* Once, my sister had caught me in the cellar playing doctor with Lisa and Laurie Kirschner, the twin girls *who were a year younger than I.*

TOM BRADY

16

FAMILY STORIES, FAMILY MYTHS

from Katherine Haake

What I sometimes describe as the "private enduring instinct behind the narrative impulse" is the habit of making things up as you go along. And sometimes I think that "who" I am is just a combination of all the stories I have told about myself, or those others have told about me. And "my" stories are only a fraction of the larger family stories, this enormous mythology about our history and something else as well, something like our fate, that determines who we all are in the intricate interconnectedness of our lives. All four of my grandparents met and married in a small mining town in northern California that was subsequently flooded behind Shasta Dam, which my uncle designed and helped to build. My grandmother decorously lit the wicks of candles before she put them out, while her daughter, my mother, chased neighbors with a pitchfork. My father never speaks of his own father, who died when he was very young. I have a therapist sister who makes up her own stories about my father's silence, my mother's early violence, what went on in the town under the lake, and of course I have my own version of things.

To live in a family, any family, is to participate in the making of myths, and the myths are all different, depending on who is constructing them. Writing, in large part, is a process of translating those myths into language.

THE EXERCISE

Part I

Select a family story, any family story but especially the kind that gets told over and over again—about, say, Aunt Ethyl's one true love, or why the Brewer twins refused to dress alike anymore in high school—and assume the persona of one of the central players. Become Aunt Ethyl herself, or one of the twins, and explain in a letter to another family member (again, not yourself) the "truth" of exactly what happened. That's it. Don't think too much. Just write the way you'd write any letter to someone about whom you care a great deal and whom you suspect won't entirely believe you.

Part II

Select a writing partner and exchange letters. Read your partner's letter, and respond by writing a letter in the persona of the addressee in your partner's original letter.

THE OBJECTIVE

To understand the story-making elements of family life and their relation to writing fiction. To gain some distance on our own mythologies by reading them as other people read them. To discover the unexpected character that lives in the space between letter and response. To be aware of how all written narratives contain, in addition to the narrator, who speaks, a narratee, who listens, and of how each profoundly affects both writing and reading. To see how our families, our pasts, and we ourselves are made and perpetually transformed in language.

I have lost too much by losing, or rather by not having acquired, the note-taking habit. It might be of great profit to me; and now that I am older, that I have more time, that the labor of writing is less onerous to me, and I can work more at my leisure, I ought to endeavor to keep, to a certain extent, a record of passing impressions, of all that comes, that goes, that I see, and feel, and observe. To catch and keep something of life—that's what I mean.

HENRY JAMES, *NOTEBOOKS*, NOVEMBER 25, 1881

17

LET US WRITE LETTERS

Nine-tenths of the letters in which people speak unreservedly of their
inmost feelings are written after ten at night.
THOMAS HARDY

Several writers we know save copies of letters written to close friends as a
sort of journal, and another writer writes a one-page letter every morning
before turning to her fiction. Writing letters can be a form of limbering
up. The exercise "Let Us Write Letters" isn't really an exercise but rather
the suggestion that we all write more letters—to family and friends (and
even to the editorial pages of magazines and newspapers). Robert Watson
makes a good case for this in his poem "Please Write: don't phone."

While there is mail there is hope.
After we have hung up I can't recall
Your words, and your voice sounds strange
Whether from a distance, a bad cold, deceit
I don't know. When you call I'm asleep
Or bathing or my mouth is full of toast.

I can't think of what to say.
"We have rain"? "We have snow"?

Let us write instead: surely our fingers spread out
With pen and paper touch more of mind's flesh
Than the sound waves moving from throat to lips
To phone, through wire, to one ear.
I can touch the paper you touch.
I can see you undressed in your calligraphy.
I can read you over and over.
I can read you day after day.
I can wait at the mailbox with my hair combed,
In my best suit.
I hang up. What did you say?
What did I say? Your phone call is gone.
I hold the envelope you addressed in my hand.
I hold the skin that covers you.

18

LOSING YOUR MIND

from Thomas E. Kennedy

Writers sometimes get trapped in their consciousness, trying to "understand" their story before it even exists, to find "meaning" in every detail, to portray some intellectual idea, to fulfill some preconceived balance—in short, going for an idea rather than for a story, writing from the mind instead of from the heart. This can be a kind of writer's block. This exercise is designed to help you get out of the conscious mind and past the mind police, to enable you to slip into the unconscious and find the source of the imagination there.

THE EXERCISE

Part One

If the mind is the house, the unconscious is the basement. To leave the restricted upper rooms of thought, the writer might descend into the basement where the heat source and water supply originate. Picture the basement of your childhood home or apartment or some other house. Go to it. Is there a door? Open it. Stairs? Descend. Place your hand on the familiar banister, feel its texture against your palm. Smell the dusty fragrance. You see everything there: the quality of light, the texture of the floor and walls. Perhaps you hear the grumble of the oil burner, see the water tank, hear the tick of the gas meter, but . . . behind the tank, in the shadows, is a door you never noticed before, an old wooden door, slightly ajar. You go to it, take the knob in your hand, draw the door open, and the images break free from your mind. Describe them. Write.

Part Two

The imagination can be like a person who has stayed inside too long, alone in his or her house. The house is like a closed mind, a clenched fist; the objective is to open the door and leave. Dusk. You sit on a back porch behind a screen door or on cool cement steps. A breeze through the screen carries the aroma of honeysuckle mixed with the bitter scent of weeds or the smell of the doughnut shop on the corner mixed with the acrid scent of spilled gasoline. At the back of the yard is a weathered picket fence, a rusted barbed wire fence, or a cement wall. And a gate. You rise and cross to the gate. Go through the gate into the dusky shadows. There are people there. What is it? Write.

THE OBJECTIVE

To open the doors and gates into our subconscious minds and let the images flow freely from the surprises beyond.

STUDENT EXAMPLE

Part One

Saturday I invite Lenny Flammerby over, cause he's always got pot. He's three years older than me but doesn't act it. He's out of his skin, crazy as a cat whose tail got run over. We go down into the basement to smoke a joint. Lenny doesn't like it too much, but my mother will never smell it down there with the fumes from the furnace and the smell of old dog shit rotting in the corner.

We're high and it's dark. Lenny's wasted, babbling about some cool radio he bought. I'm not even listening. Then my mother's dog pushes the door open with his nose and sniffs. That mutt is older than me and should've died a long time ago, but he keeps going on, growling as he hobbles up and down the cellar stairs, shitting in peace in the dark like an old man saying his prayers. The dog's wheezing like he's going to have a heart attack any second, but he's been making that noise ever since I can remember. His two feet flop down onto the first step and his nails dig into the wood.

"What's that, man?" Crazy Lenny whispers.

"It's the ghost of my grandfather." I say it soft as possible and hope Lenny will believe me. The dog wheezes some more and jerks himself down another step, feet scratching like firecrackers. The basement is dark as the universe and I can feel Lenny trembling, even if I can't see him.

"He comes around every once in a while to check up on us."

The dog stops and snorts, probably realizing we're there. That's when Lenny passes out onto the cement floor. He makes a pretty loud thud. Then all I hear is that raspy breathing, that dog who never wants to die.

Part Two

Eleanor Schustman wanted her daughter to be happy, but knew that marriage to Patrick Caparozza was not a good idea. Lizzy was twenty-three, Patrick almost thirty. Eleanor might have overlooked it—an Italian, an older man and all that, especially since Lizzy swore she loved him madly. After all he was the boy next door, and that had its romance, its honesty. But there were signs everywhere. Like the fat men nobody seemed to know who wandered around at the wedding reception, smoking cigars, looking serious and evil in white polyester shirts. Like mobsters waiting for a hit. It was unhealthy.

Everyone was dancing in the Caparozza's back yard to Pappy Molo's orchestra, under the green and white striped tent. Patrick and Lizzy in the middle, with the lights and everybody's misty eyes on them. Mrs. Caparozza, her organdy dress green as a pine tree, as though she wanted to match the tent, walked up to whisper in Eleanor's ear, "They look just like dolls on a wedding cake, don't they?" Yes, thought Eleanor, like voodoo dolls, I'd say.

Then somehow the Miller's cat made it through the back fence and out to the middle of the dance floor. Nobody noticed him until he keeled over and died right there, right next to the Millers. It was like he'd come to find them. Mrs. Miller screamed and the music stopped. The cat's tongue was sticking out and its eyes were wide open. Mrs. Caparozza, flustered and hot-looking, said to Eleanor after the Millers took the thing away, "But I always thought cats went off to die alone." All Eleanor said was, "I did too. Isn't it strange?" Then she excused herself and went off to drink a full glass of scotch. Feeling drunk, she remembered something strange, a fly marching slowly across her wedding cake. She and Ted were holding the knife together. Suddenly, twenty-five years later, she could see a faint trail in the icing, the mark of the fly's abdomen. That was before all this.

JOHN B. MITCHELL

III. CHARACTERIZATION

When you meet someone for the first time, you immediately begin to make a judgment about her, an assessment partly conscious and partly instinctive. You take in, for instance, her clothes, her haircut, the type of watch—if any—she wears. When she talks you notice her accent and vocabulary and especially what she says to you. You see if she smiles easily or whether she seems standoffish. These are just a few of the clues you process intuitively.

As a writer, you owe it to your readers to supply your characters with just such a host of clues. The more specific you make these attributes, the more immediate your characters will be. Thus characterization means fleshing out the people who inhabit your fiction by providing them with physical characteristics, habits and mannerisms, speech patterns, attitudes, beliefs and motives, desires, a past and a present, and finally, actions. This last attribute—how your characters act in a given situation—will determine your character's future (as she is further revealed through action) and shape the forward movement and final resolution of your story. As Heracleitus said, "Character is destiny."

Now, where fully realized characters come from is another story. Perhaps it is best summed up by Graham Greene when he says, "One never knows enough about characters in real life to put them into novels. One gets started and then, suddenly, one can not remember what toothpaste they use; what are their views on interior decoration, and one is stuck utterly. No, major characters emerge; minor ones may be photographed." One place that characters can emerge from is your notebooks. For example, read F. Scott Fitzgerald's notebooks to see how a writer's mind works. He even had classifications for notes such as *C*—Conversation and Things Overheard, *P*—Proper Names, *H*—Descriptions of Humanity, etc. Notebooks are a good place to collect names, lines of dialogue, and those details you just couldn't make up—like the guy we saw on the subway who, just before he got off, carefully tucked his wet chewing gum into his ear.

I give characters more moral latitude than I give myself. And when I create characters who transgress on moral codes I possess—they startle me.

EVE SHELNUTT

19

OH! . . . THAT SORT OF PERSON

Carefully chosen details can reveal character in fascinating and different ways. Writer and teacher Ron Carlson calls such details "evidence "—as if you were creating/gathering evidence for/against your character to bring his case (his story) to the reader. Sometimes details tell something about the character described and also something different about the character making the observation.

This is true of Anna Karenina's reaction on seeing her husband, Alexey Alexandrovitch, after a trip to Moscow, during which she patched up her brother's marriage and also met her future lover, Vronsky. Anna returns to St. Petersburg and is met at the train station by Alexey: " 'Oh, mercy! Why do his ears look like that?' she thought, looking at his frigid and imposing figure, and especially the ear that struck her at that moment as propping up the brim of his round hat." We see him as stern and ludicrous and we also feel her dismay as she becomes aware of her feelings toward him for the first time.

In other cases a character reveals more about himself than he suspects. For example, there is a vivid character in *The Great Gatsby* called Meyer Wolfsheim who calls Nick Carraway's attention to his cuff buttons and then boasts, "Finest specimens of human molars." Clearly, Wolfsheim means to impress his listener, but instead of charming Nick (or the reader), this detail has the opposite effect.

In *Rabbit, Run,* John Updike uses physical characteristics to account for Rabbit's nickname. "Rabbit Angstrom, coming up the alley in a business suit, stops and watches, though he's twenty-six and six three. So tall, he seems an unlikely rabbit, but the breadth of white face, the pallor of his blue irises, and a nervous flutter under his brief nose as he stabs a cigarette into his mouth partially explain the nickname, which was given to him when he too was a boy." And clearly, Rabbit is still appropriately called Rabbit, even though he's dressed in a suit and is no longer a boy.

In Pam Houston's story "Highwater" two women tell each other about the men in their lives. Houston writes:

Besides drawing me a picture of Chuck's fingers, Casey told me these things: Chuck used to be a junkie but now he's clean, he had a one-bedroom basement apartment and one hundred and twenty-seven compact disks, and he used moleskin condoms which don't work as well but feel much better. This is what I told her about Richard: He put marinated asparagus into the salad, he used the expression "laissez-faire capitalist" three times, once in a description of himself, he played a tape called "The Best of One Hundred and One Strings," and as far as I could tell, he'd never had oral sex.

The women's early descriptions of apparently dissimilar men are important because by the end of the story, they have each been abandoned by their lover, and Millie says, "I wondered how two men who at one time seemed so different could have turned out, in the end, to be exactly the same."

The first lines of Bobbie Ann Mason's "Shiloh" also bring a character immediately to life. "Leroy Moffitt's wife, Norma Jean, is working on her pectorals. She lifts three-pound dumbbells to warm up, then progresses to a twenty-pound barbell. Standing with her legs apart, she reminds Leroy of Wonder Woman." By the end of the story, Norma Jean is working just as hard at improving her mind—and at not being Leroy's wife.

THE EXERCISE

First work with a story that you've already written, one whose characters need fleshing out. Write the character's name at the top of the page. Then fill in this sentence five or ten times:

He (or she) is the sort of person who _____ .

For example: Meyer Wolfsheim is the sort of person who boasts of wearing human molars for cuff links.

Then determine which details add flesh and blood and heart to your characters. After you have selected the "telling" detail, work it into your story more felicitously than merely saying, "She is the sort of person who . . . " Put it in dialogue, or weave it into narrative summary. But use it.

THE OBJECTIVE

To learn to select revealing concrete details, details that sometimes tell us more than the character would want us to know. Evidence.

STUDENT EXAMPLES

Phillip is the sort of person for whom every transaction in life can be enacted with a Post-it Note.

DINA JOHNSON

He wears ear plugs to bed even when it is sex night.

KIM LEAHY

He is the type of person who once a month calls a travel agency and finds out the prices of flights to places like Tanzania, New Guinea, Bangladesh.

JOHN ROSS

He is the sort of person who opens his groceries and eats from them as he shops; a piece of bread, a finger smeared with peanut butter, a swig of milk. He will let the cashier ring up a pre-priced bag of apple cores.

He saves his hair clippings when he goes to the barber because he is convinced he's going bald and he is determined to create the perfect toupee.

ADRIENNE HEALD

Mary is the sort of person who gets cast as a tree with two lines, and becomes the most interesting part of the play.

JAMES FERGUSON

Emily was the sort of person who was practical in situations where most people were sentimental: when someone died she arrived with toilet paper, paper cups, and a three-pound can of coffee.

BETSY CUSSLER

Will Greene is the sort of person who always has to be the better looking one in a relationship.

ABBY ELLIN

Marlene was the sort of person who would pick up the novel on my bedside table while I was in the shower and read me the entire last page before I knew what was going on.

MATT MARINOVICH

At fifteen, Tony was the sort of person whose chaste heart rejected premarital sex, but whose body was already down at the corner drug store buying condoms.

JOANNE AVALLON

She is the sort of person whose bookshelf is lined with Penguin classics but she has hundreds of Harlequins stacked behind the dresses in her closet.

TED WEESNER, JR.

Willie is the sort of kid who'd make friends by lighting the cigarette of the bully who'd just knocked him on his ass.

ROD SIINO

He was the sort of person who coordinated his outfits by color—
Mondays he wore green, Tuesdays he wore tan, and Fridays, the days he
had to spend with me, he wore black.

KRISTEN CULBERTSON

He's the kind of kid who'd make fun of your lunch.

She was the kind of girlfriend who was always holding other people's babies.

ERIC MAIERSON

I have always regarded fiction as an essentially rhetorical art—that is to
say, the novelist or short-story writer *persuades* us to share a certain view
of the world for the duration of the reading experience, effecting, when
successful, that rapt immersion in an imagined reality that Van Gogh
caught so well in his painting "The Novel Reader." Even novelists who,
for their own artistic purposes, deliberately break that spell have to cast it
first.

DAVID LODGE

20

THE INNER LIVES OF CHARACTERS

We all lead inner lives that run parallel to what we are actually doing or saying. For example, if you are driving west to start a new job, on the way you might make plans, have fears and hopes, and perhaps feel regrets—all this while listening to Miles Davis and traveling at 70 miles per hour on route I-90. You might also be carrying on a conversation with a passenger that divulges none of your misgivings about this move. In dialogue so much goes unsaid, but it needn't go unthought. The same is true of your characters. They are more than descriptions, body language, and dialogue. Every character has an imagination and you as author must respect this imagination (as distinct from yours) and allow her to use it.

Here are some of the ways your characters will lead their inner lives. With their imaginations they will

hope	fear	wonder	yearn
dread	suspect	project	grieve
plan	judge	plot	envy
lie	repress	pray	relive
regret	dream	fantasize	compose
associate	brood	doubt	feel guilt
speculate	worry	wish	analyze

Philip Roth in *Zuckerman Unbound* has his character Nathan Zuckerman project an entire conversation with his ex-wife/estranged wife, Laura, while on the way to see her. He jumps in a cab and heads for the village with "Time enough, however, for Zuckerman to gauge what he'd be up against with Laura. *I don't want to be beaten over the head with how boring I was for three years.* You weren't boring for three years. *I don't please you anymore, Nathan. It's as simple as that.* Are we talking about sex? Let's then. *There's nothing to say about it . . .* " This imagined conversation goes on for several pages until finally Nathan says, "He could only hope that she wouldn't be able to make the case against him as well as he himself could. But knowing her, there wasn't much chance of that." And indeed he has presented her part of the case so well, that Roth doesn't even bring her on stage. Nathan's wife is not home and she never appears in the book, although we feel as if we know her from Nathan's projection of what she might have said to him.

Toni Morrison's Sethe, in *Beloved,* is haunted by the past and laments that her mind just won't stop.

> She shook her head from side to side, resigned to her rebellious brain. Why was there nothing it refused? No misery, no regret, no hateful picture too rotten to accept. Like a greedy child it snatched up everything. Just once, could it say, No thank you. . . . I don't want to know or have to remember that. I have other things to do: worry, for example, about tomorrow, about Denver, about Beloved, about age and sickness not to speak of love.
>
> But her brain was not interested in the future. Loaded with the past and hungry for more, it left her no room to imagine, let alone plan for the next day. . . . Other people went crazy, why couldn't she?

Margaret Atwood's novel *Bodily Harm* ends entirely in the mind of her character Rennie, who says "This is what will happen." She goes on to imagine being saved in passages that alternate with the terrible reality of her situation. Rennie knows there is no real hope—still there is her imagination still hoping in spite of itself.

Alice Hoffman's novel *White Horses* is about a woman who, as a child, was fascinated by her father's tales of Arias. Arias were "men who appeared out of nowhere, who rode white horses across the mesas with no particular destination other than red deserts, the cool waterholes. . . ." Men who weren't lost but "never turned back, never went home, they were always traveling west, always moving toward the sun." She runs away with King Connors, a man she thinks is an Aria—even though her father belatedly tells her, "I don't even know if there is such a thing. I may have invented Arias." No matter, Dina believes in Arias even when her husband turns out not to be one. "When Dina discovered that she was wrong about King, that he was as far from an Aria as a man can be, it was too late, she could never have admitted her error to her father. But these days, Dina felt it had not all been in vain; these days, she was certain her father had been describing someone not yet born." This someone is her son, Silver, whom she describes as "the perfect stranger she had known forever."

John Irving, in *Hotel New Hampshire,* has John, his narrator, imagine a conversation his parents have with a policeman as they walk past the old Thompson Female Seminary and decide to buy it and turn it into a hotel. The novel is in the first person so John, who is in bed, imagines this scene in the conditional.

> "Wutcha *doin'* here?" old Howard Tuck must have asked them.
>
> And my father, without a doubt, must have said, "Well, Howard, between you and me, we're going to buy this place."
>
> "You *are?*"
>
> "You betcha," Father would have said. "We're going to turn this place into a hotel."

Irving takes us into this scene so convincingly that toward the end he drops the conditional.

"Wutcha gonna call it?" asked the old cop.

"The Hotel New Hampshire," my father said.

"Holy Cow," said Howard Tuck.

"Holy Cow" might have been a better name for it, but the matter was decided: the Hotel New Hampshire it would be.

After this, we are back with the narrator who says, "I was still awake when Mother and Father came home . . . "

Charles Baxter's story "Gryphon," which appears on page 323, is told by a young boy fascinated with a substitute teacher's lessons, lessons both true and false—such as her claim that Beethoven only pretended to be deaf to make himself famous. Her lessons grow more and more fantastic and finally she makes a dire prophecy about one of the narrator's classmates. To witness this teacher's imagination at work is an exciting and terrible thing.

The character's imagination is again at work in William Gass's novella "The Pedersen Kid" when the narrator, a teenager, goes down to the crib to see where they found the half-frozen, but still living boy. "Who knows, I thought, the way it's been snowing, we mightn't have found him till spring. . . . I could see myself coming out of the house some morning with the sun high up and strong and the eaves dripping, the snow speckled with drops and the ice on the creek slushing up . . . and I could see myself . . . breaking through the big drift that was always sleeping up against the crib and running a foot right through into him, right into the Pedersen kid curled up, getting soft. . . ." Notice how the narrator speculates in concrete, sensory language.

The narrator in Pam Houston's story "Selway" uses the word "maybe" to explore her motives for making a dangerous highwater trip down the Selway River. She says, "And I knew it was crazy to take a boat through that rapid and I knew I'd do it anyway but I didn't any longer know why. Jack said I had to do it for myself to make it worth anything, and at first I thought I was there because I loved danger, but sitting on the rock I knew I was there because I loved Jack. And maybe I went because his old girlfriends wouldn't, and maybe I went because I wanted him for mine, and maybe it didn't matter at all why I went because doing it for me and doing it for him amounted, finally, to exactly the same thing. And even though I knew in my head there's nothing a man can do that a woman can't, I also knew in my heart we can't help doing it for different reasons." Later in the same story, the narrator wonders if the trip's danger would make Jack propose to her. She says, "Maybe he was the kind of man who needed to see death first, maybe we would build a fire to dry ourselves and then he would ask me and I would say yes because by the time you get to be thirty, freedom has circled back on itself to mean something totally different from what it did at twenty-one."

On your own, look for examples of characters using their imaginations: having dreams or nightmares, looking forward to an event with anticipation or apprehension, or telling the reader how they feel about what is happening at a crucial point in the story. For example, in Theodore Weesner's story "Playing for Money," Glenn has finally won money at pool, but his feelings surprise us and him. "He has never won big before, and the feeling within him now, to his surprise is closer to disappointment than satisfaction. He feels unclean picking up the nickel. Why is it he wonders, that his pride seems shaky and Jim Carr's pride seemed okay?" We would not have known this from only seeing Glenn's actions. The story ends again in Glenn's mind as ". . . he sits hearing the music, looking away, and can see that he is on the wrong side of something, maybe of everything. This is what he can see. Looking for a dream to get started, he thinks. That's what he's doing. Looking for a dream to get started, to have somewhere nice to go." For further discussion of the art of "telling" in a story, turn to "Show and Tell," in Exercise 61.

THE EXERCISE

Have one or more of your point of view characters:

- Wonder about his or her motives for doing something (use the word "maybe").
- Imagine a conversation with another character.
- Imagine an entire scene he or she is not in.

Write a story whose forward movement is propelled by:

- A character's belief in something: a tale such as the one in Alice Hoffman's *White Horses,* a religion, astrology, the *I Ching,* winning the lottery, etc.
- A character's suspicions, guilt, or regrets.
- A character's lie.

THE OBJECTIVE

To respect the minds and imaginations of your characters. To see how a character's imagination can transcend the confines of a limited point of view—as in *Hotel New Hampshire* and *Zuckerman Unbound.* To allow characters to experience the full range of thought of which we all are capable.

STUDENT EXAMPLES

Italics indicate what the character is imagining.

In this passage, a young man is thinking about his girlfriend (the "you") and what she is doing.

> I've been on this train for seven hours and the only interesting thing I've seen is seven drowned, bloated cows. Some guy in the back thought he was having a heart attack near Tuscaloosa, but it was a false alarm and

now he's sending his wife back to the club car for more beer. It's seven o'clock in Boston. Antennas blink on the horizon. *Voices are trying to get to you. Through your television. Through your radio. Even your answering machine is turned off. The cat prowls between your legs. You are reading love poems, pointing to words you love though no one is reading over your shoulder. The crazy lady who lives next door to you is singing in the hallway again, but her own opera is beyond her tonight. The air conditioner clicks on and your lamp dims for a split second.*

You turn another page.

A bag of groceries sits on your kitchen counter. The frozen yogurt is melting and the snow peas are defrosting, but it will be hours before you notice. I want to speak to you. Tell you about the baby in front who is finally asleep, about my damp socks, about the slight delay in Birmingham, and all the other minor details I wish you lived for.

MATT MARINOVICH

In this example, a man has returned home for his father's funeral and imagines what it will be like. After imagining the scene (for himself and for the reader) he decides not to go, but because he has imagined the scene so vividly we feel like we have been there—and indeed it is important for the reader to know what Leonard is missing by not going.

Yet Leonard did not feel pressed for time. He had been deliberately vague with his sisters regarding his return home and knew he was not expected at any specific hour. He imagined the scene awaiting him: *his older sister Carla standing at the door in a business suit would direct the mourners along the receiving line. She would submerge her contempt for her father in a display of sober piety while adjusting her skirt every minute or so. Sandy would resent her sister's command of the situation and sit by their mother, sighing more in frustration than in loss, yet gratified by Carla's increasing weight— stock ammo at family gatherings. Their mother, handkerchief in hand, would sob and shake her head at the flower-encircled casket. Her hair would be up in a bun held in place with a silver pin. Between sobs she would say that her husband had been allergic to flowers and would never allow them in the house, meaning: he never brought any home for her. On her left, Dennis, the youngest, would clasp and unclasp his mother's hands, attempting to console her, though she'd shrug off his hands and ask for Leonard, the very image of his father. Then the siblings would have their moment of solidarity, eyes meeting like lifted glasses, for Leonard would certainly receive the lion's share of the inheritance, and would surely be there soon to take it.*

JONATHAN KRANZ FROM "WAKE" PUBLISHED IN ASCENT

21

NAMING YOUR CHARACTERS

When you name a baby you're taking a real chance, because you have no idea how the little tyke is going to turn out; we all know people whose names seem to belong to someone else. When you name a fictional character you have no excuse for getting it wrong because you should know him better than the members of your own family. The names you choose to give your characters should suggest certain traits, social and ethnic background, geography, and even things that have yet to occur in your story. Think of Vladimir Nabokov's Humbert Humbert and Henry James's Merton Densher—they just *sound* right. Charles Dickens was so adept at this subliminal skill that some of his characters' names have become generic, representing personality types—like Uriah Heep and, most notably, Ebenezer Scrooge. The names you choose have a strong and subtle influence on how your readers will respond to your characters. You may have to rename a character several times before you get it right.

THE EXERCISE

Name the following characters, keeping in mind that you can plant, within a name, a clue to their role in your fiction.

- A petty, white-collar thief who robs his boss over several years.
- An envious, bitter woman who makes her sister miserable by systematically trying to undercut her pleasure and self-confidence.
- A sweet young man too shy to speak to an attractive woman he sees every day at work.
- The owner of a fast-food restaurant who comes on to his young female employees.
- A grandmother who just won the lottery.

THE OBJECTIVE

To recognize that the names you give your characters should not be drawn out of a hat but carefully tested to see if they "work." Sometimes you may want to choose an "appropriate" name (Victoria for a member of the British aristocracy) and once in a while it's a good idea to choose a name that seems "inappropriate" (Bruce for the child of migrant farm workers). In each case, you are sending a message to the reader about who the character is, where he came from, and where he is headed. A name can send a message as powerful as a title.

STUDENT EXAMPLE

Petty thief: Robin Fetter

Bitter woman: Mona Livitts

Shy young man: Tod Humbolt

Lecherous boss: Lenny Salsa

Lottery winner: Nana Shimpkis

JOAN CURLEY

Journalism allows its readers to witness history; fiction gives its readers the opportunity to live it.

JOHN HERSEY

22

WHAT DO YOUR CHARACTERS WANT?

In her superb book *Writing Fiction*, Janet Burroway stresses the importance of knowing what characters *want:*

> It is true that in fiction, in order to engage our attention and sympathy, the central character must *want* and want intensely. The thing that character wants need not be violent or spectacular; it is the intensity of the wanting that counts. She may want only to survive, but if so she must want enormously to survive, and there must be distinct cause to doubt she will succeed.

Sometimes *want* is expressed in terms of *need, wish, hope,* etc.—and it is amazing how many times these words appear in the first two pages of stories.

Study the following examples to learn how *want* can drive a story.

> Mrs. Whipple loved her second son, the simple-minded one, better than she loved the other two children put together. . . .
>
> [She] hated to talk about it, she tried to keep her mind off it, but every time anybody set foot in the house, the subject always came up and she had to talk about Him first, before she could get on to anything else. It seemed to ease her mind. "I wouldn't have anything happen to him for all the world, but it just looks like I can't keep Him out of mischief. He's so strong and active, He's always into everything; He was like that since He could walk. . . . The preacher said such a nice thing once when he was here, and I'll remember it to my dying day, 'The innocent walk with God—that's why He don't get hurt.'" Whenever Mrs. Whipple repeated those words, she always felt a warm pool spread in her breast, and the tears would fill her eyes, and then she could talk about something else.
>
> KATHERINE ANN PORTER, "HE"

In the Gabriel García Márquez story "No One Writes to the Colonel," a colonel has been waiting for a certain letter for almost sixty years. As a young man, he had taken part in a successful revolution and, afterward, the government had promised him and other officers travel reimbursement and indemnities. The colonel's whole life has been a matter of marching in place and waiting ever since. Even though he has hired a lawyer, filed papers, written endlessly, and seen laws passed, nothing has happened. The lawyer notes that no official has ever taken responsibility. "In the last fifteen years, there have been seven Presidents, and each President changed his Cabinet at least ten times, and each Minister changed his staff at least a hundred times." The colonel says, "All my comrades died waiting for the mail"—but he refuses to give up, even though his life has been wasted and he has grown older, sicker, and crankier in the course of time.

The *want* that gives dynamic force to the story can take the form of a strong emotion, such as Mrs. Whipple's protective love; or an obsession, such as the colonel's determination to have his place in history recognized (probably his real motive); or it can be expressed in some specific plan or scheme.

Henry James's novel *The Wings of the Dove* is a good example of an elaborate scheme. Kate Croy, a London woman, knows that her one-time acquaintance Milly Theale, a rich and charming American, is dying of a mysterious disease. The doctors think that Milly's only chance for recovery lies in finding happiness—such as that of falling in love. Kate's scheme is to have her lover, Merton Densher, woo and marry Milly, inherit her money when she dies, and then marry Kate.

In Fitzgerald's *The Great Gatsby*, Jay Gatsby's whole ambition is to recover the past—specifically the idyllic time of his love affair with Daisy Buchanan years before.

Sometimes an ostensible *want* hides or overlays a greater one. Robert Jordan in Hemingway's *For Whom the Bell Tolls* intends to blow up a bridge to halt the advance of Franco's Fascist troops. But as he waits for the strategic moment, an underlying desire to experience the life of Spain and identify with the Spanish people emerges as his real *want*.

Leslie Epstein's *King of the Jews* offers the reader an enigmatic mixture of purposes. I. C. Trumpelman, the Jewish puppet-leader whom the Nazis install as head of the ghetto, wishes to preserve his people from the Holocaust—but he also has a drive to rule, dictate to, and punish them.

Wants in fiction aren't always simple and straightforward things, just as peoples' motives are seldom unmixed. The more complicated and unsuspected—both to her and to us—are a protagonist's aims, the more interesting that character will be and the more interesting will be the unfolding of her story.

THE EXERCISE

Look at the stories you've already written and ask

- What does the central character want?
- What are her motives for wanting this?
- Where in the story is this made clear to the reader?
- How do we learn what the central character wants? Dialogue? Actions? Interior thinking?
- What or who stands in the way of her achieving it?
- What does that desire set in motion?

If you don't know the answers to these questions, perhaps you don't know your character and her desires as well as you should. Aristotle said, "Man is his desire." What your central characters desire will inform the situations and ultimately the elements of the plots in which they are involved.

THE OBJECTIVE

To understand how your central character's desires shape her life. To see characterization as more than description and voice and mannerisms.

23
FUNNY—YOU DON'T
LOOK SEVENTY-FIVE

Readers need to know certain basic facts about your characters. They should have some idea of their appearance and approximately how old they are. A writer can, of course, say something direct, like "Marvin Highsmith, sixty-eight years old, owned a Chevy pickup." But it's more interesting and dramatic to *suggest* a character's age, rather than to present the reader with a naked number. In the following passage from *Memento Mori* by Muriel Spark, an aged woman makes herself a pot of tea; the entire enterprise is made to seem Herculean—as indeed it is for a very old person. Spark never steps in to "tell" the reader that Charmian is in her eighties; it's all done through Charmian's perceptions.

Charmian made her way to the library and cautiously built up the fire which had burnt low. The effort of stooping tired her and she sat for a moment in the big chair. After a while it was tea-time. She thought, for a space, about tea. Then she made her way to the kitchen where the tray had been set by Mrs. Anthony in readiness for Mrs. Pettigrew to make the tea. But Mrs. Pettigrew had gone out. Charmian felt overwhelmed suddenly with trepidation and pleasure. Could she make tea herself? Yes, she would try. The kettle was heavy as she held it under the tap. It was heavier still when it was half-filled with water. It rocked in her hand and her skinny, large-freckled wrist ached and wobbled with the strain. At last she had lifted the kettle safely on to the gas ring. She had seen Mrs. Anthony use the automatic lighter. She tried it but could not make it work. Matches. . . . At last the gas was lit under the kettle. Charmian put the teapot on the stove to warm. She then sat down in Mrs. Anthony's chair to wait for the kettle to boil. She felt strong and fearless.

When the kettle had boiled she spooned tea into the pot and knew that the difficult part had come. She lifted the kettle a little and tilted its spout over the tea-pot. She stood as far back as she could. In went the hot water, and though it splashed quite a bit on the stove, she did not get any over her dress or her feet. She bore the tea-pot to the tray. It wafted to and fro, but she managed to place it down gently after all.

She looked at the hot-water jug. Should she bother with hot water? She had done so well up to now, it would be a pity to make any mistake and have an accident. But she felt strong and fearless. A pot of tea without the hot-water jug beside it was nonsense. She filled the jug, this time splashing her foot a little, but not enough to burn.

When all was set on the tray she was tempted to have her tea in the kitchen there in Mrs. Anthony's chair.

But she thought of her bright fire in the library. She looked at the tray. Plainly she could never carry it. She would take in the tea-things one by one, even if it took half-an-hour.

. . . First the tea-pot, which she placed on the library hearth. Then the hot-water jug. These were the dangerous objects. Cup and saucer; another cup and saucer in case Godfrey or Mrs. Pettigrew should return and want tea; the buttered scones; jam; two plates, two knives, and two spoons. Another journey for the plate of Garibaldi biscuits which Charmian loved to dip in her tea. . . . Three of the Garibaldi biscuits slid off the plate and broke on the floor in the hall. She proceeded with the plate, laid it on a table, and then returned to pick up the broken biscuits, even the crumbs. . . . Last of all she went to fetch the tray itself, with its pretty cloth. She stopped to mop up the water she had spilt by the stove. When she had brought everything into the room she closed the door, placed the tray on a low table by her chair and arranged her tea-things neatly upon it. The performance had taken twenty minutes.

When you start thinking about it you'll realize how many instant calculations you make when you first meet someone, assessing hair, eyes, girth, jawline, and wrinkles. There are literally scores of clues on the human body. There are also indirect clues, like what sort of clothes the person is wearing, her verbal style and idiom; even the way she meets your eyes.

THE EXERCISE

Complete the following sentences to suggest the age of a character, keeping in mind that there are subtle ways to convey this (moral attitude, general psychology, physical surroundings, styles of speech, etc.) as well as the direct (condition of skin and hair, physical mobility, tone of voice, etc.)

1. I figured Carol was as old as my grandmother because
2. We knew it was time for Larry to go into an old folks' home because
3. We knew that Janet was not far from retirement because
4. Although Daphne wouldn't admit being over thirty she gave it away by
5. Tom was obviously approaching the big four-oh because
6. The Harrisons were your unmistakable yuppy baby boomers. They
7. You could tell that Jamie was using a fake I.D. because his
8. It wasn't clear at first, but Michael couldn't have been more than six. Although he talked a blue streak he was

THE OBJECTIVE

To make the best use of your powers of observation. To render important information by indirection and subtlety. To use age in conjunction with characterization; age isn't simply a number—it's also an attitude.

STUDENT EXAMPLE

1. her fingers trembled when she lifted her coffee cup and she made me read Daddy's letter to her twice, all the while accusing me of mumbling.

2. well, it's an awful thing to repeat about someone in your family but he couldn't control his bodily functions any more. It was hard to be around him.

3. management started giving her jobs to other people in the department and she had so many pictures of her grandchildren on her desk there wasn't even room to set down an envelope.

4. ladling on the make-up like a floozy. And when she came back to work after the flu, you could tell she hadn't gone for her weekly touch-up at the beauty parlor.

5. his belly hung over his belt and he complained that the cleaner had shrunk two of his best jackets.

6. had a CD player, a cellular phone, a state-of-the-art Fax, and a bread machine and when I asked them about kids, Marie Harrison said, "thank god the old biological clock is just about to wind down."

7. cheeks were as smooth and pink as a dismissal slip and they flushed when he lowered his voice to ask for a "brew."

8. the same size as most of his class-mates, couldn't tell time and had real trouble tying his shoelaces.

STANLEY MONROE

24

CREATING A CHARACTER'S BACKGROUND, PLACE, SETTING, AND MILIEU

from Robie Macauley

Y ou are what you buy, own, eat, wear, collect, read, and create; and you are what you do for a living and how you live. If somebody broke into your home or apartment while you were away, chances are he could construct a good profile of who you are. You should be able to do exactly that for your characters even when they are "offstage."

THE EXERCISE

Create a setting for one or more of the following and furnish a place with his character—you create the character through observation of the setting. The place can be any kind of locale—house, a specific room in a house, outdoor grounds, an office, a cell, even a bed. The description must incorporate enough characteristic things so that the reader can visualize the absent dweller accurately. Try to avoid stereotypes.

An unsuccessful painter
A former movie star who
    still thinks she's famous
A high school senior about
    to flunk out
A cocktail waitress down
    on her luck
A blind person
A paraplegic

A member of a lunatic fringe
    political group
A foster child
A fugitive from the law
A social climber
A paranoid person
A supermarket checkout
    woman who just won
    the state lottery

THE OBJECTIVE

To be able to select details that will create a character and furnish the world of that character. Note which details indicate the circumstances of the subject—such things as success or unsuccess, social status and habits. Which details indicate emotions, personality, intelligence, character, and outlook on life?

STUDENT EXAMPLE

Jeremy told me that after the accident his mother set up his room like the face of a clock. As I stand in the doorway, at what must be six o'clock, I see what he means.

Straight ahead, against the far wall is Jeremy's bed—twelve o'clock. His mom made the bed with tight hospital corners and his pajamas, black and white striped like a prisoner's uniform, are laid out for him.

His desk is at three o'clock. Braille copies of *A Tale of Two Cities* and *Wuthering Heights* sit next to small cassette recordings of our Psych textbook. Tapes for American History, Econ., and Chemistry are stacked alongside.

I move to five o'clock and touch his empty bookcase. On the third shelf up, his initials, J.M.—Jeremy Malone—are etched deep in the wood. I close my eyes and run my fingers over them. Jeremy made this bookcase a year ago—about two months before his motorcycle accident on Route 9. Jeremy told his parents to take his books away.

The closet door, at nine o'clock, has been scrubbed with Murphy's Oil Soap. His stereo sits at ten o'clock, power off, but the volume turned nearly to its maximum. His posters of *Easy Rider* and the Budweiser girl are gone.

CHRISTY VELADOTA

It's astonishing how accurate intuition and imagination can be when given their heads.

SYDNEY LEA

25

THE HOSPITAL ROOM

from Richard Bausch

The fiction writer must learn to render place so that the physical land-scape reflects the emotional landscape—the human drama—of a story. Describing the look and feel of specific objects *within their dramatic context* is as useful in characterization as action and dialogue. A desperate character may view a small room as a prison while a happy character will view the same room as a comfortable nest.

THE EXERCISE

The room has one large window. It is seven-thirty in the evening, July 3rd, a cool, breezy day, with the vivid colors of clear summer everywhere out-side—trees and grass with late sun on them, blue mountains in the dis-tance. Inside the room are these objects:

A metal-framed hospital bed
A night stand with water glass and plastic pitcher, a bowl of fruit, and small clock radio
A television on an apparatus, supported in the air over the bed
A small trash can with a plastic bag in it
A hardback chair
A box of Kleenex
A pastel of cows standing in a grassy field, with sun and mountains beyond

1. Describe this room from the point of view of a young man who has come to visit his wife, with whom he is very much in love, after the successful and relatively painless delivery of a new baby they both have wanted. She is in the bed, with the baby, and everything is happy, if slightly scary, since they are young and this is a new expe-rience altogether. Deliver what he feels through what you say about how he sees the room.
2. Describe the same room, at the same time of evening, same condi-tions, same light and warmth everywhere, except that now a deeply loved man or woman is dying in the bed, and you are looking through the eyes of that person's offspring. This dying is the natural end sort of dying—the person is quite elderly but loved. Deliver

what the offspring feels through what you say about how he sees the room.

THE OBJECTIVE

To learn to describe physical "props" in a story so that they reflect the particular sensibility of a character moving among them. This exercise is almost limitless, since you can change the situation, and the people, with infinite variety, creating a new challenge each time you do.

26

PUT YOUR CHARACTERS TO WORK

Have you ever worked as a carpenter, cabdriver, janitor, dentist, bar pianist, actor, film critic, drummer, teacher, domestic, waiter, coach, stockbroker, plumber, therapist, minister, policeman, librarian, or mailman? If not any of these, you have probably worked at one or several jobs and have a job now. Have you ever used one of your jobs as background for a story? Or made a job central to the story itself? Better yet: Have you ever put a character to work in a job you've never had?

We have found it remarkable that work seldom finds its way into the stories of beginning writers, although this is fertile ground for harvesting the details of language, setting, socioeconomics, and "machinery." In an interview in *StoryQuarterly,* Grace Paley is asked about her statement that "the slightest story ought to contain the facts of money and blood." Paley replies:

> It really means family, or the blood of ordinary life. . . . As for money, it's just that everybody makes a living. And that's one of the things that students forget entirely. . . . I mean it's not that they have to say what they do at their job . . . it's just that they never go to work. The story takes place between eight in the morning and eight the next morning with nobody ever leaving the room! And those are the things that our life in this world and in this society and in every other society is really made up of. . . . Our family relationships are of the utmost importance, and when they don't exist they're equally important—and how we live, how we make a living. The money in our lives: how we either have it or we don't. . . . If people live without working, that is very important. It's called "Class." And that really is another way of saying that you really DO write about classes, whether you know it or not.

Ethan Canin's first collection of stories, *Emperor of the Air,* is a good example of work as foreground and background. His characters teach astronomy, biology, and English, coach basketball and baseball, sell movie tickets and run the projector, make prints, or play the horn. Other characters are a hospital orderly, a medical student, a grocery store owner, and a retired auto upholstery salesman. Some of these jobs are central to their stories and others are simply what his people do for a living, but each job is given the respect of particularity.

Every writer should have on his bookshelf Studs Terkel's *Working.* It is a gold mine of people talking, explaining, and complaining about their respective jobs. Listen to their talk:

A SPOT-WELDER: "The drill broke. I took it to the foreman's desk. I says, 'Change this as soon as you can.' We were running specials for XL hoods. I told him I wasn't a repair man. That's how the conflict began. I says, 'If you want, take me to the Green House.' Which is a superintendent's office—disciplinary station. This is when he says, 'Guys like you I'd like to see in the parking lot.'"

A DOORMAN: "If tenants came by, you had to stand up. If you were sitting down, you'd stand up. As a doorman then, you couldn't sit like this. When I was first hired, I sat down with my legs crossed. The manager came over and he said, 'No, sit down like this'—arms folded, legs stiff. If tenants came in, you had to stand up quick, stand there like a soldier."

A NURSERY ATTENDANT: "I now work in a greenhouse, where we grow nothing but roses. You can walk in there and the peace and quiet engulfs you. Privacy is such that you don't even see people you work with for hours on end. It is not always pretty. Roses have to have manure put around their roots. So I get my rubber gloves and there I go. Some of the work is rather heavy. . . . The heat in the summer almost kills me. Because there you are under a glass roof where everything is magnified."

A PHARMACIST: "All we do is count pills. Count out twelve on the counter, put 'em in here, count out twelve more. . . . Today was a little out of the ordinary. I made an ointment. Most of the ointments come already made up. This doctor was an old-timer. He wanted something with sulphur and two other elements mixed together. So I have to weigh it out on the scale. Ordinarily I would just have one tube of cream for that."

JOCKEY: "You go to the barn and start as a hot walker. He's the one that walks the horse a half-hour, after he's been on the track for his training, while he drinks water. About every five minutes, you gotta do about two or three swallows. Then you keep with him until he's completely cooled down, until he's not sweating any more. You do this every day. You might walk six, seven horses, which starts building your legs up. We all started this way. There's no short cuts. . . . Willie Shoemaker's the greatest. He has the old style of the long hold. He has a gift with his hands to translate messages to the horse. He has the gift of feeling a horse's mouth. But it's a different style from ninety percent of us. We've gone to the trend of the South American riders. They ride a horse's shoulder, instead of a horse's back."

DENTIST: "Teeth can change a person's appearance completely. It gives me a sense of satisfaction that I can play a role. The thing that bugs me is that you work hard to create, let's say, a good gold bridge. It requires time, effort, and precision. Before I put them in place, I make the patient look at them. An artist can hang his work on the wall and everybody sees it. No one sees mine except me." (Read Jane Smiley's *The Age of Grief*.)

AN INTERSTATE TRUCKER: "Troopers prey on truckdrivers for possible violations—mostly regarding weight and overload. It's extremely difficult to load a steel truck legally to capacity. . . . you have to get around the scales. At regular pull-offs, they'll say: Trucks Must Cross Scales. You pull in there and you find, lo and behold, you're five hundred or a thousand pounds over. You've got to pay a ticket, maybe twenty-five dollars, and you have to move it off. This is a great big piece of steel. You're supposed to unload it. You have to find some guy that's light and break the bands on the bundle and transfer the sheets or bars over on the other truck. Occasionally it's something that can't be broke down, a continuous coil that weighs ten thousand pounds. . . . You wish for the scale to close and you close your eyes and you go like hell to try to get out of the state. You have a feeling of running a blockade in the twenties with a load of booze." (There is almost enough information in this one passage to write a story about a husband/father who is headed home for a family event that he is now going to miss because his load is overweight. He calls home with updates on what is happening, only to be given updates on what is occurring there. Finally he starts down the road, happy to have missed what he is now going toward.)

Books on work make fascinating reading. For example, *Seven Days a Week: Women and Domestic Service in Industrializing America* by David Katzman. Do research for your stories; talk to people about their jobs. Judith Rossner must have spent weeks reading for her novel *Evangeline*. John Updike sent away for manuals on how to run a car dealership when he was writing *Rabbit Is Rich*. Work is at the heart of everyone's day. Faulkner said, "You can't eat for eight hours a day nor drink for eight hours a day nor make love for eight hours a day—all you can do for eight hours a day is work. Which is the reason why man makes himself and everybody else so miserable and unhappy."

THE EXERCISE

Read twenty or thirty pages of *Working*—just enough to whet your appetite for writing fiction. Then write a story in which a character is having a personal problem that is being played out where he or she works. You might want to choose a job that you haven't had so you can bring a fresh eye to its language, its details.

THE OBJECTIVE

To put your characters back to work so we meet them at work—and play.

STUDENT EXAMPLE

The whole thing started when Sparky came unglued in the trunk of my car. That's the number one thing a ventriloquist never does—leave his dummy in ninety-six degree heat in a parking lot. And that's the first thing Lester ever told me. Lester's my older brother and he's a professional ventriloquist. He works the Carmen Miranda room at the Chelsea Hotel on Monday nights. It's the kind of place that keeps its Christmas lights strung up year round. Mondays are slow, but I like to go there and sink down in those plush velvet cushions. I order something ritzy, like a Manhattan, and watch him. Lester's a wizard.

His lips are never more than a quarter inch apart. He can drink a whole glass of water and the Colonel keeps jabbering away. The Colonel's the name of his dummy. The time he spends on that thing. The rack of medals above the Colonel's pocket—those are Dad's medals from WW II, and Dad would be proud to have them on display in such a classy place as the Carmen Miranda Room. It's a shame the place is so slow on Monday nights. Lester says ventriloquism is going to make a comeback, just like everything.

Lester and I live together. When he saw Sparky was falling apart, he really blew his top. He asked me to repeat the most important rule a ventriloquist must remember.

"Keep your buddy clean," I said.

Lester glared at me.

"Sparky is my life-time partner," I said.

Lester's scrunched-up face went back to normal.

We worked on Sparky in silence, gluing the bottom half of his mouth again.

MATT MARINOVICH, FROM "SPOKEN FOR,"
PUBLISHED IN *THE QUARTERLY*

27

SAY IT AIN'T SO

If you think the force of gravity is powerful, try breaking through the defenses of someone committed to denying the obvious. For example, tell the woman who falls for brutish men over and over again that she appears to court cruelty. Tell the man whose son is clearly a screwup, who keeps failing in school and hanging out with the worst crowd, that his son may need help, and the denying father will tell you that his kid is "going through a phase" or "sowing his wild oats." Denial is nearly impregnable; on the other hand, it can be useful in keeping someone from going over the edge.

THE EXERCISE

Write a two-person scene in which one character tries to break through another character's barrier of denial. Make the issue both specific and dramatic. Do this mainly in dialogue but anchor it in a particular time and place.

THE OBJECTIVE

To train yourself to be aware of the unconscious forces in everyday life. People are rarely what they seem; motives are cloudy at best and often almost entirely hidden. Fictional characters, like real ones, ought to incorporate this psychic complexity. Remember that occasionally *no* does mean *yes*.

STUDENT EXAMPLE

The dinner dishes were washed, the dog walked, and Scott, Douglas and Patty Millbrook's fifteen-year-old son, had gone upstairs to watch television.

"Have you done your homework yet?" Douglas yelled after his son. "Remember, no television before homework."

"I've done it, Dad. I did it this afternoon."

"Good boy," Douglas said, and then turned to his wife, who was pouring two cups of coffee. "I have to say, I'm really pleased with how Scott's doing in school. I guess my pestering him all these years has really paid off. I mean, did you see his report card? Three A's and a B+? A lot better than I ever did in school."

"Douglas, we have to talk. I got a call from Mr. Brand this afternoon."

"Who's Mr. Brand?" Douglas asked.

"Scott's English teacher," Patty said.

"Guess he wanted to tell us how great Scott's doing, right?"

"Not exactly," Patty said, sitting down at the table. "Sit down for a minute. Mr. Brand called because he thinks Scott has been cheating." Patty stared at her hands.

"What?" Douglas said, slamming down his coffee. "What did he say?"

"He thinks Scott's grades have gone up so suddenly because he's been cheating. He can't account for it any other way. Of course, I asked Scott, who denied it."

"You asked Scott? You mean you actually believe this Brand guy?" Douglas said. "No son of mine would ever cheat. This is the most absurd thing I've ever heard."

"I don't want to believe it either, but Scott's grades do seem to have jumped suddenly. Last semester he had a C in French and now he has an A. How do you explain that?"

"The boy's smart, Patty. He's finally learned the value of working hard. He's finally listened to me."

"But Douglas," Patty said, laying a hand on her husband's arm, "if anything, Scott's been studying less. Mr. Brand wanted to know if he was under a lot of pressure at home."

"What pressure? The kid's a normal, happy teenager."

"Maybe Scott feels so much pressure to do well that he has to resort to cheating. To please you."

"Great. Now this Brand guy is accusing me. Look, my old man put a lot of pressure on me and I turned out okay, didn't I? I didn't cheat."

"No, but you dropped out of high school, Doug. No one's saying this is your fault, but you *do* put a lot of pressure on Scott."

"You've been brainwashed, Patty. The kid's finally getting it right, and you all think he's cheating. I don't even want to discuss this anymore, and if that Mr. Brand has anything more to say, I'll set him straight. My son doesn't cheat, Patty. He's too smart for that."

HESTER KAPLAN

Fiction is nothing less than the subtlest instrument for self-examination and self-display that mankind has invented yet.

JOHN UPDIKE

28

HE/SHE: SWITCHING GENDER

As a writer of fiction you're seriously handicapped if you can't write convincingly about people unlike yourself. You should be able to assume the voice (or, at least, the point of view) of a child, an old person, a member of the opposite gender, or someone of another race. An accomplished writer assumes as many shapes, sizes, colors, etc., as the fictional occasion demands. This requires you do what actors do when taking on a role: they not only imagine what it's like to be another person, they transform themselves, they get inside their character's skin.

In a *Paris Review* interview, Nadine Gordimer says, "Look at Molly Bloom's soliloquy. To me, that's the ultimate proof of the ability of either sex to understand and convey the inner workings of the other. No woman was ever "written" better by a woman writer. How did Joyce know? God knows how and it doesn't matter." Here is an excerpt from *Ulysses:*

> . . . I smelt it off her dress when I was biting off the thread of the button I sewed on to the bottom of her jacket she couldn't hide much from me I tell you only I oughtnt to have stitched it and it on her it brings a parting and the last plumpudding too split in 2 halves see it comes out no matter what they say her tongue is a bit too long for my taste your blouse is open too low she says to me the pan calling the kettle blackbottom and I had to tell her not to cock her legs up like that on show on the windowsill before all the people passing they all look at her like me when I was her age of course any old rag looks well on you then. . . .

Sue Miller in "Inventing the Abbotts" establishes early in the story that she is writing in the first person from the point of view of a teenage boy when she writes, ". . . at least twice a year, passing by the Abbotts' house on the way to school, we boys would see the striped fabric of a tent. . . ." And here is Doug coming upon his older brother Jacey:

> When I got home that night, I saw the light on in my brother's room. I went in and stood awkwardly in his doorway. He was reading in bed, the lower part of his body covered with a sheet, the upper part naked. I remember looking at the filled-in, grown-up shape of his upper body and momentarily hating him.

In "Gemcrack," Jayne Anne Phillips uses the first person to create a serial killer who was abused by his uncle as a boy. Here is one of his early school memories:

> The girls twirled, seeing how big their skirts became. I lay on the floor inside the circle of chairs. Above me the skirts voluminued like umbrellas. I

saw the girl's legs, thin and coltish. Pale. The ankle socks chopped their calves above the ankle and gave the illusion of hooves. I saw their odd white pants and their flatness. They were clean like dolls. They smelled of powder. They flashed and moved. I turned my face to the hard blond legs of the chairs.

In *A Handful of Dust*, Evelyn Waugh's protagonist, Brenda Last, in the third person, has all the inflections of a woman trying to convince her husband that she's not an adulteress (which she is). Here, she tells her husband over the phone about the apartment she's taken.

Well, there are a good many smells at present and the bath makes odd sounds and when you turn on the hot tap there's a rush of air and that's all and the cold tap keeps dripping and the water is rather brown . . . and the curtains won't pull right across. . . . But it's lovely."

In *Professor Romeo*, Anne Bernays uses the third person to write from the point of view of a man accused of sexual harassment:

"Why do all you girls think you're fat? [Barker asks]" "Even you skinny ones?"

"You really think I'm skinny?"

Barker saw Kathy's teeth for the first time as she grinned at him. He had almost forgotten that bit of magic: tell a female she's thin and she's yours for life.

THE EXERCISE

Write a page in the first person, assuming the voice of someone of the opposite gender. This can be a description, a narrative, or a segment of autobiography. The main point is to completely lose yourself and become another.

THE OBJECTIVE

To learn how to draw convincing verbal portraits of characters different from yourself and to make them sympathetic, rounded, and complex even though you don't especially "like" them or admire what they represent.

STUDENT EXAMPLE

Since I broke my hip I haven't been out of the apartment in three months. A young lady—couldn't be more than sixteen or seventeen— brings in my breakfast and supper. She comes in carrying a tray covered with silver foil. Her name is Debby and she works for the state.

It must have been a shock for Debby first time she saw me naked. It was end of July and hot as blazes. I tried to cover my parts but I wasn't quick enough. She looked away and said, "I've brought you some waffles, Mr. Pirjo, I hope you like them." Then she busied herself getting me my knife and fork. They should have told me she was coming at seven in the morning. Every time Debby comes by I ask her to sit down and have a cup of coffee with me but she says she has five more people on her list, then she's in and out of here so fast, she's like a rabbit you only see the tail of.

JUDITH HOPE

There are three rules for writing the novel. Unfortunately, no one knows what they are.

W. SOMERSET MAUGHAM

29

WHAT DO YOU KNOW
ABOUT YOUR CHARACTERS?

I could take a battery of MMPI and Wonderlic personality tests for each
of my people and answer hundreds of questions with as much intimate
knowledge as if *they* were taking the test.
RICHARD PRICE

In *Death in the Afternoon,* Hemingway said, "People in a novel, not skillfully constructed characters, must be projected from the writer's assimi-
lated experience, from his knowledge, from his head, from his heart and
from all there is of him. . . . A good writer should know as near everything
as possible." Yet students frequently write stories about a major event in a
character's life, although they don't know some of the most elementary
things about that character—information that, if known, most certainly
would affect the character's motives and actions.

Hemingway again speaks to this issue of being familiar with characters.

> If a writer of prose knows enough about what he is writing about he may
> omit things that he knows and the reader, if the writer is writing truly
> enough, will have a feeling of those things as strongly as though the
> writer had stated them. The dignity of movement of an iceberg is due to
> only one-eighth of it being above water. A writer who omits things be-
> cause he does not know them only makes hollow places in his writing.

THE EXERCISE

Work with one of your completed stories that has a character who needs
fleshing out. Take out a sheet of paper and number from one to thirty-
four. At the top of the page, write in the title of your story and the main
character's name—and start filling in the blanks.

1. Character's name:
2. Character's nickname:
3. Sex:
4. Age:
5. Looks:
6. Education:

79

7. Vocation/occupation:
8. Status and money:
9. Marital status:
10. Family, ethnicity:
11. Diction, accent, etc.:
12. Relationships:
13. Places (home, office, car, etc.):
14. Possessions:
15. Recreation, hobbies:
16. Obsessions:
17. Beliefs:
18. Politics:
19. Sexual history:
20. Ambitions:
21. Religion:
22. Superstitions:
23. Fears:
24. Attitudes:
25. Character flaws:
26. Character strengths:
27. Pets:
28. Taste in books, music, etc.:
29. Journal entries:
30. Correspondence:
31. Food preferences:
32. Handwriting:
33. Astrological sign:
34. Talents:

No doubt you will be able to add to this list.

Note: This exercise should be done *after* you have written your story. It is not a way to conceive a character, but rather a way to reconceive a character. It is designed to discover what you know about your characters *after* you have written your story—and what you don't know. For example, one writer, Samuel R. Delany, tells his students to know exactly how much money their characters make and how they make it. And why not apply this list to some of your favorite stories? Note how much is known about the unforgettable grandmother in Flannery O'Connor's story "A Good Man Is Hard to Find" or about the compelling narrator in Peter Taylor's story "The Old Forest."

THE OBJECTIVE

To understand how much there is to know about a character you have created. Of course, it is possible to write a successful story about a character without knowing everything on this list—or perhaps only knowing two or

Bobby D.

three things. On the other hand, beginning writers often don't know more than a character's age or gender—and frequently neglect an essential piece of information that would have greatly informed or shaped their story. You needn't include these details in the story, but their presence in your mind will be "felt" by the reader.

IV. PERSPECTIVE, DISTANCE, AND POINT OF VIEW

Some stories come to us with the point of view already decided and their writing proceeds smoothly to the end. Other stories seem to need a more considered decision about who is going to tell the story and at what distance from the reader; these involve trial and error to get them right. We hope you have both experiences; writing feels like magic when you only have to think "story," but it can also feel powerful when you are compelled to make a more deliberate choice from the wide array of possibilities presented by point of view.

Henry James called the point of view in fiction a "central intelligence." By this, he meant that it operates as the eyes, ears, memory, and understanding through which we receive the story or narrative.

There are various forms of point of view: the first person "I" as in Herman Melville's *Moby Dick,* Margaret Atwood's *The Handmaid's Tale,* J. D. Salinger's *The Catcher in the Rye,* F. Scott Fitzgerald's *The Great Gatsby,* and Molly Keane's *Good Behavior;* the "we," rarely used, as in Joan Chase's *During the Reign of the Queen of Persia;* the second person "you," also rarely used, as in Jay McInerney's *Bright Lights, Big City;* and the third person which has a great deal of latitude.

Within the third person, you can have third person subjective which is very close to first person in that it is limited to one point of view such as Rachel Ingalls's novel *Mrs. Caliban;* or third person objective as in Hemingway's short story "Hills Like White Elephants"; or an omniscient point of view where the author moves from distant description, scene setting, and comment on what is happening to the thoughts of various characters as Tolstoy does in *War and Peace,* Shirley Hazzard in *Transit of Venus,* and Alice Hoffman in *White Horses* and *Turtle Moon.*

The main thing to keep in mind is that you have a story to tell and you must decide how it should be told. To do this, ask yourself two questions: Whose story should this be? Whose vision will be the most effective?

Another important question is: What level of psychic distance do I want to maintain? John Gardner defines "psychic distance" as "the distance the reader feels between himself and the events of the story." In Exercise 31, page 87, we illustrate that often the dilemma is not which POV to choose but which distance to maintain from the reader.

For further discussion of the complex issue of Point of View we suggest that you read Wayne C. Booth's *The Rhetoric of Fiction,* Janet Burroway's *Writing Fiction,* John Gardner's *The Art of Fiction,* Macauley and Lanning's *Technique in Fiction*—and the stories and novels you admire most.

30

FIRST PERSON OR THIRD

When you begin a story, you are faced with the immediate decision of point of view and more often than not, you will choose either the first or third person. For some writers, this decision is a conscious choice involving questions and answers about the most effective "central intelligence." For other writers, point of view is a given—it seems to come with the story they are about to tell.

The first person point of view has the advantage of immediacy and a clear, singular voice—think of John Dowell in Ford Madox Ford's *The Good Soldier,* Captain Charles Ryder in Evelyn Waugh's *Bridehead Revisited,* Benjy, Quentin, and Jason, in William Faulkner's *The Sound and the Fury,* Grendel in John Gardner's *Grendel,* Ruthie in Marilynne Robinson's *Housekeeping,* Antonio in Rudolfo Anaya's *Bless Me, Ultima,* Philip Carver in Peter Taylor's *Summons to Memphis,* Anne August in Mona Simpson's *Anywhere But Here,* and Jing-Mei Woo in Amy Tan's *The Joy Luck Club.* Each of these first person narrators has a special voice that draws us in to his or her world. The limitation of this point of view is that the "I" should be present when most of the action takes place and is the only interpreter, aside from the reader, of what happened.

The third person point of view is a familiar and reliable kind of central intelligence, one that allows the writer greater latitude in terms of distance and the authority to shift point of view. Several novels using third person are: Hemingway's *A Farewell to Arms,* Christina Stead's *The Man Who Loved Children,* Leslie Epstein's *King of the Jews,* and Charles Baxter's *First Light,* whose chapters alternate between a brother and sister's point of view.

The decision whether to use first person or third is often a difficult one. (Anne Bernays wrote her novel *Growing Up Rich* using the third person point of view, then realized it belonged in the first person and rewrote it, starting on page one; it took a year. Changing point of view like this involves a great deal more than simply turning all the she's into I's; the author must step completely away from the story and let the I's voice speak for itself.) Too often writers begin a story in the first person because it makes them feel closer to the story, yet the voice isn't unique enough to warrant first person. In general, if you can substitute "he" or "she" for your "I's," then your story should be in third person.

reread + consider

THE EXERCISE

Begin a story with a third person point of view, making a conscious decision about distance. Write two or three pages. Then begin this same story again using a first person point of view, rewriting the same two or three pages. Do the same in reverse—changing a first person narrative into third.

THE OBJECTIVE

To understand the limitations and powers inherent in both the first and third person points of view. To make you more aware of the choices available to you as author and storyteller.

31

JOHN GARDNER
ON PSYCHIC DISTANCE

In the introduction to this section, we said that understanding and controlling "psychic distance" was as important to fiction as choosing a point of view. John Gardner's superb chapter "Common Errors," from *The Art of Fiction*, illustrates the range of psychic distance in five possible openings for a story:

1. It was winter of the year 1853. A large man stepped out of a doorway.
2. Henry J. Warburton had never much cared for snowstorms.
3. Henry hated snowstorms.
4. God how he hated these damn snowstorms.
5. Snow. Under your collar, down inside your shoes, freezing and plugging up your miserable soul.

Note how the first opening begins at a great distance from the reader in terms of time and space as it places the year of the story and introduces its character as "a large man." Isaac Bashevis Singer often begins his stories at this distance:

It was during the summer of 1946, in the living room of Mrs. Kopitzky on Central Park West.

"THE SEANCE"

In the town of Shidlovtse, which lies between Radom and Kielce, not far from the Mountains of the Holy Cross, there lived a man by the name of Reb Sheftel Vengrover.

"THE DEAD FIDDLER"

Then, like a camera zooming in on a scene, in each of the above stories Singer draws the reader closer to his characters and into their thoughts. At other times Singer begins stories closer in:

Harry Bendiner awoke at five with the feeling that as far as he was concerned the night was finished and he wouldn't get any more sleep.

"OLD LOVE"

I never learned his name.

"TWO MARKETS"

I often hear people say, "This cannot happen, that cannot be, nobody has ever heard of such a thing, impossible." Nonsense!

"ZEITL AND RICKEL"

As you can see, there is enormous elasticity available in distance but it must be carefully controlled—especially since you can change the distance within a story. In general, the distance at which you begin a story or novel is the outer boundary beyond which you cannot go within that story. For example, if you begin a story at say distance 3 as Singer did with Henry Bendiner in "Old Love," you cannot then draw back to the more formal stance of distance 1 by saying "The large man had never slept well." But if you begin at distance 1 as Singer does with ". . . there lived a man by the name of Reb Sheftel Vengrover," you can "zoom in" like a camera within the story, even into a character's thoughts to say "Reb Sheftel was almost speechless with terror, but he remembered God and recovered." Then you can pan back out to "Reb Sheftel was the first to die." and "More years went by, but the dead fiddler was not forgotten."

A careless shift in psychic distance would be to begin with "It was winter of the year 1853. A large man stepped out of a doorway" and move to "God how he hated these damn snowstorms." Although both employ the third person point of view, the psychic shift from one to the other is jarring. Gardner's example of a shift in psychic distance that doesn't work is this: "Mary Borden hated woodpeckers. Lord, she thought, they'll drive me crazy! The young woman had never known any personally, but Mary knew what she liked."

THE EXERCISE

First, go back to Exercise 1, page 3, and read each beginning sentence to determine its psychic distance from the reader—from 1, the greatest distance, to 5 where the psychic distance almost disappears.

Next, begin a new story five times using as your guide Gardner's five beginnings.

Finally, begin a new story at distance 1 or 2 and within 200 words gracefully decrease the psychic distance until you have reached distance 4.

THE OBJECTIVE

To understand how psychic distance works so that you can make conscious decisions about the range of psychic distance to use in each story or novel you write.

32

SHIFTS IN POINT OF VIEW

New writers are often told to use one point of view when telling a story—and for good reason. Shifts in point of view are difficult to do and depend on the writer's absolute control of language, detail, and observation. Four writers who shift point of view are Flaubert in *Madame Bovary,* Shirley Hazzard in *The Transit of Venus,* Alice Hoffman in *White Horses,* and Alice Adams in many of her short stories. Also, shifts in point of view must be warranted. The reader has to learn something from each character's viewpoint that he cannot learn from the perspective and interpretation of one character. Note in Kate Wheeler's story "Under the Roof" how each character has information and perceptions the other characters couldn't possibly know.

Some writers indicate a shift in viewpoint by putting the narrator's name at the beginning of their sections as Faulkner does in *As I Lay Dying,* Anne Tyler in *Celestial Navigation,* and Rosellen Brown in *The Autobiography of My Mother.*

Other writers such as Sharon Sheehe Stark, in *The Wrestling Season,* depend on indications in the narrative for us to know that we are now in a different character's point of view. Chapter 28 ends with Louise: "No wonder she hadn't heard the usual ferocious kabooms of some engine racing before takeoff. He had gone, yes, but not so far. As usual he was camping just outside the thumping, ridiculous mystery of her wifely heart." Chapter 29 begins with Michael: "And Michael woke early to dread. Sometimes that stalled-heart dream of his left him heavy like this, dejected. Yet he was quite certain the night had passed without fatality, dreamlessly indeed."

In Pamela Painter's story "Intruders of Sleepless Nights," the point of view shifts among three characters—a husband and wife pretending to be asleep in their bedroom and a burglar on his way there to steal the wife's jewelry. Each section begins with an observation that tells the reader whose point of view we are in. The burglar is first: "They own no dogs; the maid sleeps out. The catches on the windows are those old-fashioned brass ones, butterfly locks. No alarm system or fancy security." A few sentences later, the wife is next: "Her husband is asleep—finally. His back is to her, his right shoulder high, and now his breathing has slowed to a steady pace like some temporarily regulated clock." After more of the wife's observations, the husband's section is next: "His wife thinks he is sleeping. He knows this by the way she begins to move, adjusting the sheets, almost gaily like a puppet released to live." The story then returns to the original order: the burglar, the wife, and the husband throughout.

Shifts in point of view from paragraph to paragraph, or within the same paragraph, are more difficult to do and few writers attempt this. One writer who does is Alice Adams. For example, her story "The Party-Givers" opens with three people sitting around at the end of a party. In the space of the first two pages, the point of view shifts from Josiah, to his wife, Hope, to Clover, a former lover of Josiah's. Adams writes:

> Josiah liked the party; he smiles to himself at each recounted incident.
>
> Hope, Josiah's small, blond and very rich newlywed wife, during the noisy hours of the party has been wondering if she should kill herself. . . . This is Hope's question: if she killed herself, jumped off one of the bridges, maybe, would Josiah fall in love with Clover all over again? marry her? or would her death keep them guiltily apart?
>
> Clover, a former lover of Josiah's, of some years back, is a large, dark, carelessly beautiful woman, with heavy dark hair, a successfully eccentric taste in clothes. In the intervals between her major love affairs, or marriages, she has minor loves, and spends time with friends, a course that was recommended by Colette, she thinks. This is such an interval, since Josiah who was once a major love is now a friend, and maybe Hope is too; she can't tell yet.

Adams accomplishes her many point of view shifts by skillfully weaving attributions for thought into her narrative: "smiles to himself at each recounted incident," "has been wondering," "this is Hope's question [thought]," "she thinks," and "she can't tell yet."

Graceful transitions are worth all the time and energy you invest in them.

THE EXERCISE

Write a scene involving two or three characters who have secrets from each other—or possess different perspectives on what they are doing or have just done. Or write a story using several points of view. Remember that the point of view shifts must be warranted by the information and perspective each brings to the story.

THE OBJECTIVE

To experience how a shift in point of view works and what conditions of the situation make it necessary.

33

AN EARLY MEMORY, PART ONE: THE CHILD AS NARRATOR

"Write what you know" is by now such a cliché that people tend to ignore it. For the beginning writer it's pretty good advice. Your own life—and your memories of it—have an intensity and immediacy that are useful in creating fiction. It's not just what you know, however, but how you see it, shape it, and enhance it with your imagination. This is the crucial difference between fiction and fact. Fiction is always sifted through a singular set of perceptions, feelings, and wishes, while fact can be recorded by a machine designed for that purpose—a tape recorder or camera. Furthermore, the fiction writer often supplies an implicit rather than an explicit moral attitude.

Keep in mind when doing this exercise that even though you are writing from the point of view of a child or a young adult your audience is still an adult audience. Christine McDonnell, author of the young adult book, *Friends First*, which has a fourteen-year old narrator, makes this distinction:

> In adult fiction, when a story has a child's point of view, usually the child is scrutinizing the adult world, trying to make sense of adult behavior or adult society, as in J. D. Salinger's *Catcher in the Rye*, the childhood chapters in Anne Tyler's *Dinner at the Homesick Resaurant*, the children in Dickens's novels or Susan Minot's *Monkeys*. Children's points of view can add humor—O'Henry—or moral commentary—Mark Twain's Huck Finn. Sometimes, from a child's point of view, the situation seems more frightening or dangerous, as in Robb Forman Dew's *The Time of Her Life*, when the child is caught in her parents ugly, boozy separation, and in Suzanna Moore's *My Old Sweetheart*, about a mentally unstable mother and philandering father. In all of these, the scope of the story is larger than childhood. Children are windows onto a larger picture, and that larger picture is of interest to adults.

The young narrators in Sharon Sheehe Stark's "Leo" and Charles Baxter's "Gryphon" are child narrators trying to make sense of the larger adult world at the point it intersects with their own.

THE EXERCISE

Using the present tense, write an early memory in the first person. Choose something that happened before you were ten. Use only those words and perceptions appropriate to a young child. The memory should be encapsulated in a short period of time—no more than an hour or so—and should happen in one place. Don't interpret or analyze; simply report it as you would a dream. When you can't remember details, make them up; you may heighten the narrative so long as you remain faithful to the "meaning" of the memory—the reason you recalled it in the first place. Limit: 550 words.

THE OBJECTIVE

A fiction writer should be able to present a narrative without nudging the reader or in any way explaining what she has written. The narrative should speak for itself. In using a child's voice you are forced not to analyze but merely to tell the story, unembellished.

STUDENT EXAMPLE

The doorbell rings and I know it's Aunt Judith, the old lady I've been hearing about. She's come to visit us from where she lives, San Francisco, which is very far away. It takes almost a whole day to fly to my house from there in an airplane. She's very old, probably around eighty. I'm peeking through the stair railings when my father answers the door. All I can see is a gray coat and some white hair. She must be deaf because my father's voice is loud when he says hello.

My mother calls, "Come down and meet your Aunt Judith." She's holding her aunt's hand and smiling. I come down and stand behind my mother when I say hello. I don't want her to kiss me. She has more wrinkles on her face than I ever saw. She pats my head and says, "So big for five."

My father says he's going to make some tea. My mother and Aunt Judith and I go into the living room and sit down.

"Come here, Emily, and sit by your old aunt," she says, patting the couch next to her.

I feel funny but I go and sit where she says. She smells like bread in the oven.

"Tell Aunt Judith about school," my mother says.

"I'll be in first grade next September," I say.

My father comes in with the teapot on a tray and some cups. I'm too young to drink tea. I tried it once and it tasted like dirt.

My mother and Aunt Judith are talking about people I don't know. My father looks like he doesn't know them either. I'm staring, but Aunt Judith doesn't mind. She has a mouth that sticks out like a fish with hairs over her top lip. Then I say, "You know what Aunt Judith? You have a mustache." I don't make it up; she does have a mustache; it's just like my grandfather's only not quite so bushy. Aunt Judith gets a funny look on her face. She stands up and says, "Where's the bathroom?"

My mother shows her where the bathroom is and when she comes back she tells me that I shouldn't have said that about Aunt Judith's mustache. "But it's true!" I say.

My mother tells me that just because something's true doesn't mean I have to say it out loud. She looks angry.

Aunt Judith stays in the bathroom a very long time. I want to tell Aunt Judith I'm sorry but I don't know how to. Finally, my mother knocks on the bathroom door. "Are you all right, Judith?" Maybe she thinks she's dead or something.

I can hear Aunt Judith's voice but not what she says. My mother says, "She's okay."

My father says, "Big-mouth Emily."

I'm not staying around any more. I go upstairs but not to my room. I sit at the top where I can hear Aunt Judith when she finally comes out of the bathroom.

EMILY HONIG

In probing my childhood (which is the next best to probing one's eternity) I see the awakening of consciousness as a series of spaced flashes, with the intervals between them gradually diminishing until bright blocks of perception are formed, affording memory a slippery hold.

VLADIMIR NABOKOV

34

AN EARLY MEMORY, PART TWO: THE REMINISCENT NARRATOR

Something crucial to remember: The story doesn't exist until you tell it and the same holds true for when and how your narrator chooses to tell her story. Eudora Welty in *One Writer's Beginnings* speaks of this ordering of time:

> The events in our lives happen in a sequence of time, but in their significance to ourselves they find their own order, a timetable not necessarily, perhaps not possibly, chronological. The time as we know it subjectively is often the chronology that stories and novels follow: it is the continuous thread of revelation.

This is especially true of the reminiscent narrator, a narrator who is looking back and reinterpreting or confronting the past because it has a special pointed meaning for her—a meaning that has often eluded the narrator until this particular telling of the story.

The reminiscent narrator of Peter Taylor's story "The Old Forest" is telling his story from a vantage point of forty plus years. The tone and distance from past events are established immediately with the first line, "I was already formally engaged, as we used to say, to the girl I was going to marry." The narrator goes on to recount events that occurred when he was in an accident with another young woman a week before his wedding. At one point he wonders why these events and the images of Lee Ann's footprints in the snow and of his own bloody hand have stayed with him. "In a way it is strange that I remember all these impressions so vividly after forty years, because it is not as though I have lived an uneventful life during the years since." He goes on to list his World War II experiences, the deaths of his two younger brothers in Korea, the deaths of his parents in a terrible fire, and also the deaths of his two teenage children. As he continues the story, he learns perhaps for the first time to speak of his failures—the most important perhaps was the failure to follow his own heart. He has had a good, long life with the girl he was engaged to. He learned to follow his heart when he left the Memphis social and business community to become an English professor, but it was a lesson he learned through the events of this particular story—and with the help of Caroline his wife.

Alice Munro is another writer who brilliantly employs the reminiscent narrator to tell her story in such stories as "Friend of My Youth,"

"Wigtime," "Hold Me Fast, Don't Let Me Pass," and "Differently"—stories in which the present is informed by the past.

THE EXERCISE

In no more than two pages, use the incident of "An Early Memory, Part One" and tell it from the vantage point of who you are today, that is, inject it with adult vocabulary, insight, subtlety, and comprehension. For example, "My father was obviously confused" replaces "funny look." Change the way the incident is told without altering its content. Use the past tense but keep it a first person narrative. As in the first part of this exercise, try to let the material speak for itself. We draw up out of the well of our unconscious those things that have emotional significance. In contrast to the previous exercise, this one will force you to search—with an adult sensibility—for the underlying "meaning" of the event you simply reported in "An Early Memory, Part One" (p. 91). What have you learned in the interim? What can be gained—or lost—by hindsight?

THE OBJECTIVE

As in many of these exercises, the idea is to empower the writer with the knowledge that he controls the material, and not the other way around. There are countless ways to tell the same story and each way says something and reveals something a little different, not only about what happened but also about how the teller feels about it.

STUDENT EXAMPLE

At the age of five I learned how easy it is to wound someone simply by pointing out to them something obvious to everyone else. I think that I forgot this from time to time as I got older but I certainly learned it in a dramatic way.

My mother's Aunt Judith was then in her late eighties—an old but vigorous childless widow who had helped translate the books of Thomas Mann and lived alone in Berkeley, California. She had come East to visit her brother, my mother's father, and was paying a call at our house. I had never met her and was a timid child anyway, so I hung back until she patted the couch beside her and told me to come sit next to her. I could tell by the expression on my mother's face that she was anxious to have Aunt Judith like and approve of me. I think my mother and she had had an unusually close relationship when my mother was young and lived in New York—where Aunt Judith also lived before she moved to the West Coast.

My father offered to make tea and disappeared into the kitchen. I mainly listened while my mother and Aunt Judith reminisced about people whose names I didn't recognize. But I didn't really mind because I was having such a good time staring at her face. It was a mass of veins and wrinkles—far more than my grandfather had. And she had a black

95

mustache. If you hadn't seen her clothes or heard her speak you might have thought she was a man.

My father came back with the tea and they all drank, Aunt Judith making slurping noises and seeming to enjoy herself except that she really didn't have any idea how to talk to a child as young as I was. She asked me one question—I think it was about school—and then seemed to forget I was there.

But, as I said before, I didn't mind at all; I was a watcher.

Did I know, at some depth, that I should not say what I then said? To this day I'm not certain. But, with no windup, I suddenly said, "You know what, Aunt Judith? You have a mustache."

Her hand flew to her mouth: she looked as if someone had just pierced her lung with a sharp knife. She stared at me, got up, and said, very quietly. "Anne, will you please tell me where the bathroom is?"

My mother was obviously flustered and led her to the downstairs bathroom.

When she came back my mother tried to explain to me that just because something was true did not mean that you had to say it out loud. On my part, I tried to argue but soon gave up because I felt so bad. My father told me I was a bigmouth.

Aunt Judith stayed in the bathroom for fully fifteen minutes. I think my mother was worried that she had fainted. I knew what she was doing: She was studying herself in the mirror, perhaps seeing this horrible mustache for the first time; it must have been a shock.

They were annoyed at me and embarrassed by what I had done (and I can't say I really blame them. A big child but a tactless one). They were nice enough to let me go upstairs. The truth doesn't carry with it its own protection against pain.

EMILY HONIG

Planning to write is not writing. Outlining . . . researching . . . talking to people about what you're doing, none of that is writing. Writing is writing.

E. L. DOCTOROW

35

THE UNRELIABLE NARRATOR

You may find that you want to create a character who says one thing and unwittingly reveals another—for example, a teacher who claims to love all her students, even those with "funny, hard-to-pronounce names and weird haircuts." The unreliable narrator—between whose lines the author invites you to read—is a classic fixture in works of fiction. Eudora Welty's narrator in "Why I Live at the P.O." is a wonderful example of unreliability. So is the narrator of Ford Madox Ford's *The Good Soldier*. And more recently, Stevens, the butler of Kazuo Ishiguro's *The Remains of the Day*, totally deludes himself about the pre–World War II politics of his employer, Lord Darlington, and about his own feelings for another servant, Miss Kenton. And consider the voice of the narrator in Jenefer Shute's acclaimed first novel *Life Size*. Josie has been hospitalized for starving herself and is told that she cannot yet begin psychotherapy because she is "a starving organism" whose brain is "not working the way it should." She thinks to herself, "On the contrary, it's never been purer and less cluttered, concentrated on essentials instead of distracted by a body clamoring for attention, demanding that its endless appetites be appeased. . . . One day I will be pure consciousness, traveling unmuffled through the world; one day I will refine myself to the bare wiring, the irreducible circuitry that keeps mind alive." Were Josie allowed to have her way, she would surely die.

THE EXERCISE

Using the first person, write a self-deceiving portrait in which the narrator is not the person she thinks she is—either more or less admirable. You must give your readers clues that your narrator is skewing the truth.

THE OBJECTIVE

To create a narrator who unwittingly reveals—through subtle signals of language, details, contradictions, and biases—that his or her judgment of events and people is too subjective to be trusted. The reader must thus discount the version of the story offered by the narrator and try to re-create a more objective one for himself.

STUDENT EXAMPLE

A young girl should stand up straight. That's what I told my daughter-in-law, Ruthie. "Don't slouch," is really what I said, "look proud to be with my son." I must say, I've never seen anyone take such offense at a harmless comment.

"You're always criticizing me," Ruthie said. "First you tell me I don't keep the house clean enough, and then you tell me that I'm not feeding your son."

I have to defend myself, don't I? To begin with, I said, "These things you call criticisms—they aren't. They are helpful suggestions, something one woman can say to another. I never said the house wasn't clean enough, it's just that with two small children, sometimes you get too busy to keep house the way you'd like to." The only reason I mentioned the dust balls under the couch was for the children's sake. And, I certainly didn't say that my son wasn't being fed. I only remarked that he was so skinny, that maybe he didn't have time to eat a good meal because of all the work he has to do, being such a nice man to help his wife the way he does. Really, my daughter-in-law is a good girl. She learns fast. I know her mother-she can't help it that she has some bad habits.

And then my son, Geoff, he feels he should protect his wife, so he says, "Ma, quit ragging on Ruthie. Mind your own business, Ma." I understand how he has to take his wife's side so she doesn't get angry at him. But me and Geoff, we have an understanding. I know he agrees with me, so I'm just helping him out a little by mentioning these things, right? He could have had any girl. He's a nice boy to stay with Ruthie and the kids and I just want her to appreciate what she's got.

HESTER KAPLAN

V. DIALOGUE

Dialogue is, basically, two or more characters talking to each other. It is also an ideal, compact way to advance your story by having one character tell another what's happening—to reveal, admit, incite, accuse, lie, etc.

Furthermore, dialogue is an economical way of defining a character, the way someone speaks—accent, vocabulary, idiom, inflection, etc.—tells us as much about what he is like as his actions do.

Dialogue is never a faithful rendering of the way human beings really speak. At its most poetic it is the iambic pentameter of Shakespeare's plays; at the other end is Mark Twain's Huckleberry Finn using the Mississippi Valley vernacular of the 1840s. Both authors omit the hesitations, repetitions, false starts, meanderings, and aborted phrases that make actual human talk so much less compelling. Read a transcript of testimony or of a taped telephone conversation or listen attentively to the next person with whom you have a conversation and you will realize that fictional dialogue is only an approximation of true speech, having been shaped, pointed, and concentrated.

Paradoxically, dialogue is often useful for getting across *what is not said*, what we call the subtext. For instance, if you want to show that someone in a story or novel wants to avoid an unpleasant encounter, you can indicate this by having them talk around the topic uppermost in their mind but never quite touching it. In using dialogue this way, you're asking the reader to read between the lines. This is a tricky maneuver but if you think about how you talk to someone yourself when you're angry at them but don't want to tell them exactly why—by being sarcastic, arch, nit-picky, oversolicitous, etc.—you'll get it right.

It's important, too, to learn when to use direct discourse—*he said, she said*—and when to summarize by indirect discourse. This is partly a matter of what "feels" right and partly of how important the actual words used are to your narrative. For example, forcing character A to answer the phone "Hello," and then having character B say "Hello" back isn't essential. It is flat, and boring—everyone knows how you answer the phone. Far better to cut to the chase: what did character A learn from B's phone call that moves the story along or tells us something crucial about either or both A and B?

> The phone rang. It was George wanting to borrow the jeep. I told him, "Don't bring it back without a full tank of gas."

Dialogue generally goes for the heart of the story, the exchange that matters, the confrontation.

36

SPEECH FLAVOR, OR SOUNDING REAL

from Thalia Selz

Here comes your character. She's Irish—Hispanic—Vietnamese—a Maine congresswoman, a shrimp boatman from Louisiana, or a black professor of English in an Ivy League college who retains traces of her Chicago slum childhood in her speech. Your character is eager to have the conversation that the structure of the story demands. Or maybe she wants to tell the story, as in a first person narrative. Either way, you want that speech to have its own flavor, to suggest the character and background of the person uttering it, without using much phonetic spelling because it can be hard to read. Characters in fiction, like real people, have to come out of a context to be convincing and intriguing—even when that context is imaginary, like postatomic holocaust England in Russell Hoban's *Riddley Walker.*

Chicago
writer

eloquence?

THE EXERCISE

Observe how the following speech fragments convey a sense of accent or national, regional, race, class, or cultural distinctions mainly through word choice and arrangement. Easily understood foreign words or names can help, too. What do these fragments suggest about the individual speakers by conveying the flavor of their speech?

My mama dead. She die screaming and cussing.
ALICE WALKER, *THE COLOR PURPLE*

"'I won't keep you,' I says. 'You must get a job for yourself.' But, sure, it's worse whenever he gets a job; he drinks it all."
JAMES JOYCE, "IVY DAY IN THE COMMITTEE ROOM"

"*Muy buenos,*" I said. "Is there an Englishwoman here? I would like to see this English lady."
"*Muy buenos.* Yes, there is a female English."
ERNEST HEMINGWAY, *THE SUN ALSO RISES*

". . . the working mens one Sunday afternoon taking they only time off. They laying around drinking some moonshine, smoking the hemp, having a cock fight."
PETER LEACH, "THE CONVICT'S TALE"

"My own wife is seven years older than me. So what did I suffer?—Nothing. If Rothschild's daughter wants to marry you, would you say on account her age, no?"

BERNARD MALAMUD, "THE MAGIC BARREL"

"Why me?" she rumbled. "It's no trash around here, black or white, that I haven't given to. And break my back to the bone every day working. And do for the church."

FLANNERY O'CONNOR, "REVELATION"

"Father says for you to come on and get breakfast," Caddy said. "Father says it's over a half an hour now, and you've got to come this minute."

"I ain't studying no breakfast," Nancy said. "I going to get my sleep out."

WILLIAM FAULKNER, "THAT EVENING SUN"

"Copy our sister-in-law," Brave Orchid instructed. "Make life unbearable for the second wife, and she'll leave. He'll have to build her a second house."

"I wouldn't mind if she stays," said Moon Orchid. "She can comb my hair and keep house. She can wash dishes and serve our meals. . . "

MAXINE HONG KINGSTON, THE WOMAN WARRIOR

Now write five of your own speech fragments.

THE OBJECTIVE

In this case, it is threefold: to help reveal character, to convince your reader by making your dialogue sound credible, and to add variety. Differences in speech aren't just realistic; they're interesting and provocative, and they can give vitality to your story. Speech without flavor is like food without savor.

STUDENT EXAMPLES

"Those dipsticks down at work made Ron my boss. What a kick in the butt, huh?" I smiled even though I didn't want to, but Mary Lou didn't smile back, and I'm thinking if *I* can smile—and I feel like hell—why can't she?

BOB PELTIER, "MAKING M1s"

"Who you think you're dealin with, boy? Hoot and holler like that at me again, and there'll be a whoopin' you'll never forget."

PETER BAER

I looked at the Pall Mall. I wondered if he smoked them things without filters so me and my friends wouldn't bum them all away. Tobacco don't taste *that* good. I thought 'bout whether I wanted it bad enough to smoke it anyways, decided I did, took a toke. Tasted like burning rubber boots. "Garbage," I said.

TERY GRIFFIN, "WHERE THE MAN BELONGS"

"Tank you."—"It's *thank* you."—"No *tank* you?—"No. *Thank* you."— "Oh! Sank you."

CYNTHIA HOLLOBAUGH

The wastepaper basket is the writer's best friend.

ISAAC BASHEVIS SINGER

37

DIALOGUE IS ALL ART, NOT TALK

Dialogue has a difficult task in that it must simulate real talk at the same time it must artfully waste no words, reveal character, provide tension, and move the story forward. Kingsley Amis says of dialogue:

> I always try over the phrases, fooling the reader into believing that this is how people actually talk. In fact, inevitably it's far more coherent than any actual talk. . . . but when in doubt I will repeat a phrase to myself seven or eight times, trying to put myself in the place of an actor speaking the part.

This exercise asks you to listen to yourself twice. The first time when you are "acting" out a scene; the second time when you are distilling and writing it—listening for the illusion of real talk.

THE EXERCISE

Have a fellow writer do this exercise with you. Make up situations involving two people who disagree about something—for example, two friends who have planned to shoplift something and one is getting cold feet. Or a landlord and a tenant disagree about the terms of a lease. Next, tape your dialogue as you and your friend "act out" the two "roles" in a scene. Don't decide what you're going to say ahead of time. Improvise, through dialogue, as you go along. Then transcribe the dialogue exactly as it was said.

Here is where your writer's ear comes in. Read over the written account of your scene. How much of the original exchange is useful for your story? How much of the dialogue might you summarize? And are there any "perfect" lines that you would keep? Finally try writing the scene using the transcribe dialogue to give shape to the scene. How much of the original dialogue would you keep?

THE OBJECTIVE

To hear and see how real talk is repetitive, disjointed, and boring. At the same time, to train your writer's ear to transform actual speech into carefully crafted dialogue.

STUDENT EXAMPLE

Two students "acted out" the scenario of a landlord and a tenant renegotiating a lease. When they transcribed their dialogue it went on for three pages. They named the tenant Rita and the landlord Pringle. After they edited it, here is what they kept.

"No new locks, no rent," Rita said.

"I want to see every room, I know I smell a cat."

"What cat?"

"Every room," Pringle said.

"You don't even read your own lease. You have to make an appointment to go through this place. I know my rights."

"Tomorrow. Eight A.M." Pringle turned to go.

"Bring the locksmith. If I did have cats they'd be stolen by now."

"Heard there was a break-in two houses down last week. Getting to be a dangerous neighborhood. You might want to think about moving."

"That's rent-control talk for sure. Locksmith," Rita said and slammed the door.

MIKE GARSON AND KEN BOOTH

38

WHO SAID THAT?

Well, often we're not quite sure because the attribution is faulty or even missing. Yet, it is crucial to know who is saying what to whom because dialogue is central to a scene's drama and forward movement. We need to know whether the wife or the husband says "I've decided to leave—and no further discussion is necessary." Whether the teenager or the parent says, "You're always taking something the wrong way." Whether the mugger or the victim says, "Don't let things get out of hand here."

There are various ways of attributing speech to make it clear to the reader who is talking. The easiest way is to use *he said* or *she said* or the person's name as in the following example:

> "I've decided to leave," George said. "No further discussion necessary."
> "So, no discussion," Mary said. "I'll just list all the reasons I'll be glad to see you gone."
> "Tell it to the dog," he said.
> "That's number one. The dog goes too," she said.

"Said" works most of the time and does not draw attention to itself. Occasionally use "asked" and "replied," but avoid words like "hissed," "trumpeted," "rejoined," "growled," etc. Trust the growl to be inherent in what is said and how the person is described.

Other ways to attribute dialogue to a character are:

■ Use the name of the person being spoken to:

> "Jesus, Benjy, my job's more important than your marathon Monopoly game."
> "Ah mom, you're always taking something the wrong way."

■ Use emotional clues:

> His head was fizzing and he had trouble keeping the gun pointed at the man's tie. Didn't know who was scareder. "Don't let things get out of hand here."
> The man nodded and nodded. "Take it all, you can have it all."

■ Use action:

> She filled a grocery bag with dog food and topped it off with a can of draino. "You getting the picture."

■ Use physical description:

> Benjy's t-shirt said "Death by Doughnuts" and his hair rode his shoul-

ders, Christ-like. "Monopoly is teaching me real estate, banking, investment."

"Just don't get too attached to those dice." Her t-shirts never said anything and her hair had been shorter than his for the past five years.

■ Use thinking by the point of view character:

He should have stuck up some woman first. "Just turn around and start walking."

Attribution doesn't only tell you who is speaking. It also provides a way for pacing a scene, for juxtaposing speech with thought, for slowing the action so the reader can absorb what is going on, for including physical details of the scene, for providing emotional clues, and for adding to the rhythm of the sentences.

Finally, most dialogue important to the drama and forward movement of a story is set off by itself, with its method of attribution. When the speaker changes, you begin a new paragraph as in the above examples. However, sometimes exchanges of dialogue are woven into a paragraph as in the following passage from Anne Tyler's *Celestial Navigation*:

> He held out his hand and said, "Well, goodbye for now, Mrs.—Mary," and she said, "Goodbye, Jeremy," Her hand was harder than his, and surprisingly broad across the knuckles. While he was still holding it he said, "Um, may I come back sometime?"—the final hurdle of the visit. "Well, of course," she said, and smiled again as she closed the door.

Because the dialogue flows along inside the paragraph, the reader is closer to Jeremy's point of view and to his perspective of this parting scene. Below, in a later scene from *Celestial Navigation*, the dialogue is again placed inside a paragraph. Note that what is being said is subordinate to setting the scene: the forest of diapers, the apologetic Mary, the kids playing cards, and the bustle of warm greetings for a surprised and almost speechless Jeremy.

> She led the way to the front of the house. . . . At first all he could see was layers of diapers hanging up and down the length of room. "Sorry," said Mary, "we've had a rainy spell lately, I had to hang them inside." She went ahead of him, parting diapers. He felt like a blind man. It was impossible to tell what kind of room he was in. He smelled laundry detergent and cold, stale air. He heard the children's voices but could see no sign of them. "Seven of hearts," one said. "Eight." "Nine, ten." "Jack. Anyone got the Jack?" "Children, Jeremy's here," Mary said. Then they broke the last diaper barrier and stood in a doorway, looking into a tiny bedroom. The four oldest girls were playing cards on a caved-in double bed. Edward sat beside them stirring up a deck of cards of his own, and over by the window stood Rachel—could that be Rachel?—holding onto the sill and turning to smile up at him, wearing unfamiliar pink overalls and showing several teeth that he had never seen before. "Jeremy," Darcy said. They piled off the bed and came to hug him. He felt a tangle of arms around his chest, another pair around his knees. Everywhere he

reached out, he touched heads of hair so soft it seemed his fingers might have imagined them. "What are you doing here?" they asked him. "Did you come to stay?" "Did you miss us?" He was amazed that they were so glad to see him. After all, they might have forgotten him or never even noticed his absence. "Well, now," he kept saying. "Goodness. Well, now."

When dialogue or what is said is not central to a scene's forward movement, but you still want to include the characters' voices, place the dialogue inside a paragraph. Be sure that we know who is saying what—that it is Mary explaining why the diapers are hanging inside, and that it is the children's voices asking, "Did you miss us." This alternative way of presenting dialogue is an important tool for controlling the pace and shaping the drama of a scene.

THE EXERCISE

Highlight all the dialogue in one of your own stories. Next, find out how many methods of attribution you have used. Remember that attribution contributes a lot more to a scene than just telling us who said what. Then, examine how you have presented your dialogue. Would some lines of dialogue serve your story better inside a paragraph? Are the important lines presented in a dramatic way? Now, rewrite the scene using the tools you have acquired in this exercise.

THE OBJECTIVE

To learn to shape a scene with the tools of dialogue placement and attribution.

39

TELLING TALK: WHEN TO USE DIALOGUE OR INDIRECT DISCOURSE (SUMMARIZED DIALOGUE)

One of the most important decisions a writer must make is whether to use dialogue or to summarize it. Too often dialogue is incorrectly used to provide information that could have been given in indirect discourse. Or else the reader is given the entire scene—for example, the full escalation of an argument—when in fact only the closing lines are important to hear verbatim.

Summarized dialogue allows the writer to condense speech, set the pace of the scene, reveal attitudes, make judgments, describe the talk, avoid sentimentality, and emphasize crucial lines of actual dialogue.

Study the following passages to learn what summarized dialogue accomplishes. Then transform the summarized dialogue into dialogue to understand why the author chose to condense it.

> So this ordinary patrolman drove me home. He kept his eye on the road, but his thoughts were all on me. He said that I would have to think about Mrs. Metzger, lying cold in the ground, for the rest of my life, and that, if he were me, he would probably commit suicide. He said that he expected some relative of Mrs. Metzger would get me sooner or later, when I least expected it—maybe the very next day, or maybe when I was a man, full of hopes and good prospects, and with a family of my own. Whoever did it, he said, would probably want me to suffer some.
>
> I would have been too addled, too close to death, to get his name, if he hadn't insisted that I learn it. It was Anthony Squires, and he said it was important that I commit it to memory, since I would undoubtedly want to make a complaint about him, since policemen were expected to speak politely at all times, and that, before he got me home, he was going to call me a little Nazi cocksucker and a dab of catshit and he hadn't decided what all yet.
>
> KURT VONNEGUT, JR., *DEADEYE DICK*

> She sits in the visitor's chair beside the raised bed, while Auntie Muriel, wearing an ice-blue bed-jacket, cranked up and propped up, complains. They put extra chlorine in the water here, she can taste it. She can remember when water was water but she doesn't suppose Elizabeth can tell the difference. At first she could not get a private room. Can Elizabeth imagine? She had to share a room, share one, with a terrible old woman who wheezed at night. Auntie Muriel is convinced the woman was dying.

She could hardly get any sleep. And now that she's finally here in her private room, no one pays any attention to her. She has to ring and ring, three times even, before the nurse will come. They all read detective novels, she's seen them. The night nurse is from the West Indies. The food is atrocious. She cannot tolerate beets, she always ticks the other vegetables on the menu but they bring beets. Sometimes Auntie Muriel thinks they do things like this to her on purpose. She will speak to Doctor MacFadden, tomorrow. If she has to stay here for a little rest and some tests, which is what he says, the least he can do is make sure she's comfortable. She's never been sick a day in her life, there's nothing really wrong with her now, she isn't used to hospitals.

Elizabeth thinks this may be true.

MARGARET ATWOOD, LIFE BEFORE MAN

That afternoon, Dr. Fish sent a psychiatrist to my bed. He spoke to me kindly in a low voice, and he had a white beard that I found reassuring. He didn't ask about Mrs. O. until the very end. Instead, he inquired about my studies, my parents, my friends. He wanted to know when my headache started and what my other symptoms were. He touched on the subject of my love life with great delicacy and registered my response that it was nonexistent with half a nod. I tried to speak in good sentences and to enunciate clearly. My head hurt, but my breathing was much improved, and I think I convinced him that I was sane. When he finally asked me why I had been screaming at Mrs. O., I told him very honestly that I didn't know, but that at the time it had seemed important to do so, and that I hadn't been screaming but calling. He didn't seem at all shocked by this answer, and before he left he patted my hand. I think I would have enjoyed my talk with him had I not worried about what the conversation was going to cost. He looked expensive to me, and I kept wondering if his sympathy was covered by my insurance.

SIRI HUSTVEDT, "HOUDINI"

Mr. Frazer did not see Cayetano again for a long time, but each morning Sister Cecilia brought news of him. He was so uncomplaining she said and he was very bad now. He had peritonitis and they thought he could not live. Poor Cayetano, she said. He had such beautiful hands and such a fine face and he never complains. The odor, now, was really terrific. He would point toward his nose with one finger and smile and shake his head, she said. He felt badly about the odor. It embarrassed him, Sister Cecilia said. Oh, he was such a fine patient. He always smiled. He wouldn't go to confession to Father but he promised to say his prayers, and not a Mexican had been to see him since he had been brought in. The Russian was going out at the end of the week. I could never feel anything about the Russian, Sister Cecilia said. Poor fellow, he suffered too. It was a greased bullet and dirty and the wound infected, but he made so much noise and then I always like the bad ones. That Cayetano, he's a bad one. Oh, he must really be a bad one, a thoroughly bad one, he's so fine and delicately made and he's never done any work with his hands. He's not a beet worker. I know he's not a beet worker. His hands are as smooth and not a callous on them. I know he's a bad one of some sort. I'm going down and pray for him now. Poor Cayetano, he's having a dreadful time and he doesn't make a sound. What did they have to shoot him for? Oh, that poor Cayetano! I'm going right down and pray for him.

She went right down and prayed for him.

ERNEST HEMINGWAY, "THE GAMBLER, THE NUN, THE RADIO"

Papa-Daddy woke up with this horrible yell and right there without moving an inch he tried to turn Uncle Rondo against me. I heard every word he said. Oh, he told Uncle Rondo I didn't learn to read till I was eight years old and he didn't see how in the world I ever got the mail put up at the P.O., much less read it all, and he said if Uncle Rondo could only fathom the lengths he had gone to to get me that job! And he said on the other hand he thought Stella-Rondo had a brilliant mind and deserved credit for getting out of town. All the time he was just lying there swinging as pretty as you please and looping out his beard, and poor Uncle Rondo was pleading with him to slow down the hammock, it was making him as dizzy as a witch to watch it.

EUDORA WELTY, "WHY I LIVE AT THE P.O."

It was almost three o'clock when Mary Jane finally found Eloise's house. She explained to Eloise, who had come out to the driveway to meet her, that everything had been absolutely perfect, that she had remembered the way exactly, until she had turned off the Merrick Parkway. Eloise said, "Merritt Parkway, baby," and reminded Mary Jane that she had found the house twice before, but Mary Jane just wailed something ambiguous, something about her box of Kleenex, and rushed back to her convertible.

J. D. SALINGER, "UNCLE WIGGILY IN CONNECTICUT"

Not all summarized dialogue occurs in blocks. In the following passage, from "Saul and Patsy Are Getting Comfortable," Charles Baxter summarizes a number of phone calls from Saul's mother before he comes to a particular conversation that he puts into actual dialogue.

Saul's mother, Delia, a boisterous widow who swam a mile a day, played bridge on Tuesdays, tennis on Fridays, called her son every other weekend. When Patsy answered, Saul's mother talked about recipes or the weather; when Saul answered, she discussed life and the nature of fate. In February, after Saul and Patsy had been in Five Oaks for nine months, she said that she had heard from a friend that wonderful teaching jobs were opening up outside Boston, and even closer, right here, outside Baltimore. I heard this, she said, from Mrs. Rauscher. Saul listened to his mother go on for five minutes, and then he stopped her.

"Ma," he said. "We're staying."

"Staying? Staying for what? For how long?"

"For as long as it takes."

"As long as what takes? Honey, you'll never have a normal life as long as you stay there."

"What's normal?"

Alice Munro often intersperses dialogue with indirect discourse. In the following passage from Munro's "Hold Me Fast, Don't Let Me Pass," two people who have just met are dining in a hotel at separate tables. Antoinette owns the hotel.

> Dudley said that he would not eat fish. Hazel, too, had refused it.
> "You see, even the Americans," Dudley said. "Even the Americans won't eat that frozen stuff. And you'd think they'd be used to it; they have everything frozen."
> "I'm Canadian," Hazel said. She thought he'd apologise, remembering he'd been told this once already. But neither he nor Antoinette paid any attention to her. They had embarked on an argument whose tone of practiced acrimony made them sound almost married.
> "Well, I wouldn't eat anything else," Antoinette said.

Another example of dialogue combined with indirect discourse occurs in Munro's story "Differently" when two friends meet at a "hippie restaurant" where they wear "cheap, pretty Indian cotton dresses and pretended to be refugees from a commune. . . ." Munro writes:

> When they weren't playing these games, they talked in a headlong fashion about their lives, childhoods, problems, husbands.
> "That was a horrible place," Maya said. "That school."
> Georgia agreed.
> "They were poor boys at a rich kids' school," Maya said. "So they had to try hard. They had to be a credit to their families."
> Georgia would not have thought Ben's family poor, but she knew that there were different ways of looking at such things.
> Maya said that whenever they had people in for dinner or the evening, Raymond would pick out beforehand all the records he thought suitable and put them in a suitable order. "I think sometime he'll hand out conversational topics at the door," Maya said.
> Georgia revealed that Ben wrote a letter every week to the great-aunt who had sent him to school.
> "Is it a nice letter?" said Maya.
> "Yes. Oh, yes. It's very nice."
> They looked at each other bleakly, and laughed. Then they announced—they admitted—what weighed on them. It was the innocence of these husbands—the hearty, decent, firm, contented innocence. That is a wearying and finally discouraging thing. It makes intimacy a chore.
> "But do you feel badly," Georgia said, "talking like this?"

Note in the first passage how summarized dialogue dispenses in one sentence with the business of Antoinette offering each character fish. And how summarized dialogue allows Hazel to ignore the facts of the argument Antoinette and Dudley are having and instead to describe its tenor as having the "practiced acrimony" of marriage. In the second passage, summarized dialogue summarizes what the women usually talk about before it gives way to specifics in dialogue. It also describes the pace of their talk as "headlong." Notice how words like "agreed," "revealed," "announced," and "admitted" go well with summarized dialogue but are used sparingly with dialogue.

THE EXERCISE

Highlight the dialogue in a story by a writer you admire. Then determine how much dialogue is summarized rather than presented in quotation marks.

Next, set up a situation in which one character is going on and on about something—complaining about grades, arguing with a spouse about the children, or recounting an accident to a friend. Summarize the dialogue, occasionally interspersing it with comments and stage directions.

THE OBJECTIVE

To understand what summarized dialogue accomplishes and how it affects tone, pace, and the shaping of a scene.

STUDENT EXAMPLES

He told me the flypaper was on sale and that even if it wasn't I could walk around town and still not find a cheaper brand. I nodded in agreement but said that what I wanted was a bug light, not flypaper. He rolled his eyes and demanded to know exactly how much I knew about bug lights. Before I could tell him, he pointed his finger at me and explained that the voltage requirements were incredible. A modest bug zapper would cost me five times over what I paid for it during one wet Torville spring and one hot Torville summer. Then there were the outages, which occurred at least twice a summer when everyone was using air-conditioning. No bug protection then, he said. And there was the sheer cumbersomeness of the things. He clapped his hand on my shoulder and brought his mouth close to my ear and said, "They're all made by the Japs. Think what you're doing to this country."

ALEXANDER INGLE

No one could be certain whether Kadi had died by accident or by her own design, yet it was much debated over smoky fires far into the humid West African night, in the manner peculiar to the Fula people. Adulai Embalo, speaker for the village elders, cited the evidence indicating an accident: that Kadi had often slipped at the muddy, sloping edge of the well as she drew water; that she had been up that morning before first light and could not have seen clearly where the bucket-ropes of other women had worn a new incline at the lip of the well; and that her sandals were found nearby, but not her enormous tin washbasin, suggesting that she had been mounting the heavy load on her head when her wet bare feet lost their hold on the slick clay.

The others listened respectfully to this, and paused in silence to consider it in the glow of the dying coals. Mamadu then proposed the facts
that suggested Kadi had taken her own life: that she had quarreled with
her husband Demba the night before; that she had been ashamed not to
have conceived since her third miscarriage the previous rainy season; and
that her rice plot had been damaged by wandering cattle so that her har-
vest would be less than half of what she and Demba needed toward the
purchase of medicine to fertilize her womb, or toward the purchase of a
second wife for Demba. But little could be done about Kadi now, except
to discuss and turn over each point cited by the speakers, which is what
the other village elders did as the fire slowly died, savoring the joy of conversation in the arcane Fulani of older men.

CAMERON MACAULEY, "THE WOMAN AT THE WELL"
PUBLISHED IN PRISM INTERNATIONAL

Recently, I was engaged in a profoundly meaningful conversation in one
corner of a large common room. In the corner opposite somebody was
trying to conduct some silly group discussion. Presently, a young man
strode briskly across the floor and tapped me on the shoulder. "Can you
try and keep it down?" he said. "You can't imagine how your voice carries." . . . It carries. Yes, that's the idea, isn't it? You say what you have
to say the way you have to say it and hope to hell you're bothering somebody.

SHARON SHEEHE STARK, OTHER VOICES

40

THE INVISIBLE SCENE: INTERSPERSING DIALOGUE WITH ACTION

Flannery O'Connor, in her essay "Writing Short Stories," says that in beginning stories,

> dialogue frequently proceeds without the assistance of any characters that you can actually see, and uncontained thought leaks out of every corner of the story. The reason is usually that the student is wholly interested in his thoughts and his emotions and not in his dramatic action, and that is he is too lazy or highfalutin to descend to the concrete where fiction operates.

When you are writing a scene in a story, it might help to think of your characters as being onstage. Your reader will want to know what they look like and what the stage setting looks like. Next, your reader will want to have a sense of how your characters move around and interact with the furniture of their stage world—in other words the stage business, body language, or choreography. Characters live in a concrete world and it is your job as a fiction writer to keep them there.

THE EXERCISE

Write a scene in which a character's body, as well as his mind, is engaged in doing something—stage business. Here are some possibilities:

repairing something
playing solitaire or a game involving other players
doing exercises
painting a canvas or a wall
cutting down a tree
giving someone a haircut

Come up with your own suggestions

Explore how various activities and settings can change what happens within a scene. For example, what happens when characters are planning their honeymoon if they are painting an apartment or one of them is cutting the other's hair. Or what happens when characters are having a confrontation in public—say in a fancy restaurant—rather than in the privacy of their home.

It is also instructive to analyze how a writer you admire handles the interweaving of dialogue and body language. Go through one of your favorite stories and highlight all the body language and choreography. We guarantee this will teach you something.

THE OBJECTIVE

To give concrete life to the scenes our characters inhabit. To understand how action and choreography relate to the objects in the scene and how all of these relate to and help shape dialogue and the engagement of the characters.

STUDENT EXAMPLE

The church was condemned last week, so my sister Marion decided to have the wedding in Mom and Ivan's backyard, in front of the herb garden. I drove by the church yesterday to see the steeple that was sitting on a trailer in the parking lot. Luckily they found that it was rotting and took it down before it fell on people. Marion should take the hint.

An hour ago Mom put me in charge of weeding the old patch of dirt. "It's the least you can do for your sister's special day," Mom said. It had rained last night, so the garden was thick mud. The knees of my new red sweat pants would be stained and I'd need a hairbrush to get it out from under my fingernails.

"Colleen! Where are the car keys?" Marion called, her face pressed against the window screen.

"I put them on the counter," I said.

"They aren't there. Come in here and find them."

I threw another weed on the weed pile and slammed the screen door into the kitchen. Marion's face was pink and her hands shook. "Don't do this to me, Colleen. Mom and I need to leave now." The wedding was two days away and Marion had the whole house preparing. Ivan was at Woolworth's getting new lawn furniture and Mom was at the sink drowning a pot of peeled potatoes.

I wiped my hands on my jeans and pulled the keys from the Union Trust mug next to the sugar bowl. I threw them at her left hand. "Where's Gabe?" Her fiancé lived in the apartment buildings across town. He was nearly thirty, but he still mowed lawns and delivered papers for a living. Instead of a bike, he drove a red Mustang. I figured he should be here weeding the parsley too.

"Shut up, Colleen," Marion said. She bent down to look at her reflection in the microwave door.

"Girls," Mom said, turning off the water hard. She gave me a look and left to get her coat.

KIM LEAHY

41

A VERBAL DANCE: NOT QUITE A FIGHT

Thank God for dialogue. Dialogue is one of the fiction writer's most useful tools. But it's tricky. Good dialogue is not at all the way human beings speak to each other—it's an approximation. Dialogue takes human speech and renders it condensed, highlighted, and pointed. Dialogue is extremely useful when you want to show what a character is thinking and want to avoid the leaden "she thought" formulation. Simply bring on another character and have the two of them hold a conversation. Dialogue reveals character—as anyone who has ever seen a decent play knows. It is also good for breaking up long paragraphs and provides an opportunity to use common idioms. The way a character talks—vocabulary, tone, style, and sense of humor—can tell your readers exactly what you want them to know in a "showing" way that narrative can only "tell."

THE EXERCISE

Write a dialogue between two people who know each other, each taking the opposite side of an issue or problem. This should be a verbal dance, not a shouting match. The issue you choose should be something immediate and particular (like whether to spend money on a vacation or put it in the savings account) rather than abstract (communism is going down the tubes). Keep it simple and emotionally close to the two people involved. The speakers should be equally convincing. That is, you, the author, can't load the argument on one side or the other. Make each person distinctive in her oral style, for example, in vocabulary and tone. Keep in mind that the subtext—what the conversation reveals about the speakers' relationship to each other—is as important as the manifest text. For example, in the what-shall-we-do-with-the-money conversation the subtext is about which of the two speakers has more power—and is willing to exploit it. Limit: 550 words.

THE OBJECTIVE

To learn to use dialogue to reveal character and human dynamics and to understand that speaking style says as much about a person as her behavior does. Incidentally, you should also recognize that dialogue should not be used for the following: for lengthy exposition, to furnish your stage, as a substitute for action, and as a vehicle for showing off your own vocabulary and education. A false line of dialogue can ruin an entire scene.

STUDENT EXAMPLE

"I'm giving up, Jim," Maria said to her husband. "I'm done, finished. No more doctors, no more tests. The end." She pulled the Sunday crossword toward her and looked around the kitchen table for a pencil.

"Maria," Jim said patiently, handing her a red pencil. "I think we should keep trying. You know the doctors say there's still a chance."

"They might say that," Maria said, "but I know there isn't. My body just doesn't want to have a baby. You know how there are some places in the city that just can't make a go of it? A restaurant moves in, people line up, and in six months it's gone. Or a new store moves in, and business is great at first, but then customers stop coming and the business folds? Think of it that way, Jim. My body is a low-rent district for good reason."

"God, Maria." Jim covered his face. "You know I hate it when you talk like this, when you put yourself down. It's beneath you."

Maria tapped the pencil on the table. "I'm not putting myself down. I'm simply stating the fact that I'm not going to get pregnant. And the sooner you admit that, the sooner we can start looking for a baby to adopt."

"No, Maria. We can't adopt. It's not right."

"What do you mean 'right'?"

He was looking at her now. "You know what I mean. Right. Who is the baby's family. Is it healthy? Things like that."

"You mean a baby's parents had to go to Yale?"

He put his hand out to still her tapping pencil. "You know that's not what I mean, Maria. But here we are—well-educated, smart—we could end up with—"

"With what, Jim. A stupid, ugly baby? Someone who wouldn't look too good at your twenty-fifth reunion?" Maria said. She pulled her pencil free.

"You're twisting my words around, and you know it," he said, putting his hand on the partially filled-in puzzle. "You always pretend not to understand what I'm saying. You just never give me what I want."

"What you want?" Maria pushed the crossword away from her and stood up. "Is that it, Jim? I knew there was a reason I wasn't getting pregnant. I guess I just don't want it enough."

"Your sarcasm isn't very productive, Maria." He looked up at her.

"Neither are we, Jim. That's what we're talking about here, isn't it?"

HESTER KAPLAN

42

TEXT AND SUBTEXT: PSYCHIC CLOTHING

Most of us cover the nakedness of our true intentions with layers of psychic clothing. Our smile disguises a grimace; our laugh chokes a sob. The so-called text is right out there; the subtext is what is really going on. The two things don't necessarily have to contradict each other—they may vary only slightly. But it's important for the writer to be aware that subtexts exist, operating on a deeper, hidden level, along with overt action and dialogue.

In John Updike's story, "Still of Some Use," Foster and his former wife are cleaning out the attic of a house they once lived in together and which she is now selling.

> "How can you bear it?" [Foster] asked of the emptiness.
> "Oh, it's fun," she said, "once you get into it. Off with the old, on with the new. The new people seem nice. They have *little* children."

Nothing but pain lies beneath the wife's flippancy.

In Anne Tyler's novel *The Accidental Tourist*, a couple, Sarah and Macon, whose son has recently been killed by a deranged gunman, are riding together in a car.

> Macon sped ahead, with his hands relaxed on the wheel.
> "Did you notice that boy with the motorcycle?" Sarah asked. She had to raise her voice; a steady, insistent roaring sound engulfed them.
> "What boy?"
> "He was parked beneath the underpass."
> "It's crazy to ride a motorcycle on a day like today," Macon said.
> "Crazy to ride one any day. You're so exposed to the elements."

Exposed, just as their son was exposed, as we all are—to whatever "elements" lurk in the world, waiting to finish us off.

THE EXERCISE

Write two very short examples of text, in which the true meaning of the action or dialogue is hidden in a subtext. Under each text explicate the subtext.

THE OBJECTIVE

To learn to use indirection to illustrate the power of hidden meaning. This is something like a double exposure, a photograph that shows two images simultaneously.

STUDENT EXAMPLE

1. My dad is on the telephone. Instead of just talking about work and the weather, as usual, he says, "As you get older, you start to wonder about things—why we're here, or why there's anything at all."

   Subtext: My mom is away in another state visiting my grandmother this week and my dad misses her.

2. When Ellen yells at a truck driver for driving past a parked school bus with its Stop sign out, Mrs. Roche, her nextdoor neighbor, leans out and says, "You should mind your own business." When Ellen explains that what the driver did was illegal and dangerous, Mrs. Roche says, "You just don't understand the situation. You ought to mind your own business."

   Subtext: Mrs. Roche resents having a group of young people living on her block, which she feels belongs only to Irish Catholic families.

   MIKE RASHIP

VI. PLOT

Except for the first two exercises in this section, most have as much to do with characterization as with plot. When we had completed the manuscript for *What If?* and were in the process of creating a table of contents, someone asked, "Where is plot?" Plot was missing. We did have exercises that fit this category, but we had placed them elsewhere. This led us to realize, however, that for both of us plot is subordinate to characterization. In a *Paris Review* interview, William Kennedy speaks to this issue. He says,

> Hemingway's line was that everything changes as it moves; and that that is what makes the movement that makes the story. Once you let a character speak or act you now know that he acts this way and no other. You dwell on why this is so and you move forward to the next page. This is my method. I'm not interested in formulating a plot to which characters are added like ribbons on a prize cow. The character is the key and when he does something which is new, something you didn't know about or expect, then the story percolates. If I knew, at the beginning, how the book was going to end, I would probably never finish.

Thus the forward movement of a story or novel derives from how a character observes—acts or reacts—and the more surprising the better.

In their book *Technique in Fiction*, Robie Macauley and George Lanning suggest that Heracleitus's observation that "character is destiny" should be "written on the wall of every novelist's study." They go on to say that character is only half the dynamics of plot, that a given situation is the other half. How a particular character observes and deals with the circumstances of that situation and chooses to act or not act moves the story forward into plot.

Macauley and Lanning discuss plot in these terms: In the beginning you present a particular character in a situation. The situation should have opposing forces and alternatives, and your central character should have choices—ways of acting or not acting. The situation should grow more complicated, more grave, and finally reach a point of crisis. Thereafter follows the resolution of the crisis—or at the least "something happens." Almost always things will have changed.

Consider how writers have placed certain characters in a situation and set them in motion, from which point they move forward, driven by the force of their own personalities: Isabella Archer in Henry James's *Portrait of a Lady,* Humbert Humbert in Vladimir Nabokov's *Lolita,* Hester Prynne in *The Scarlet Letter,* and Yossarian in Joseph Heller's *Catch-22.*

Once you have placed a character in a situation, our exercise "What If?" is designed to provide you with several organic ways to move your story forward toward complication and resolution. Always, always, with character in motion. In her wonderful book *Mystery and Manners,* Flannery O'Connor recalls lending some stories to a neighbor who when she gave them back said, "Well them stories just gone and shown you how some folks would do." And O'Connor comments, "I thought to myself that that was right; when you write stories, you have to be content to start exactly there—showing how some specific folks will do, will do in spite of everything." And that doing becomes your plot.

43

THREE BY THREE

from William Melvin Kelley

We all know the classic story description: Boy meets girl. Boy loses girl. Boy gets girl. What is implied in those three three-word sentences is that a story has a beginning, a middle, and an end. For example, here is Cinderella:

Cinderella can't go.
She goes anyway.
Cinderella gets Prince.

And here is the Pied Piper:

Man lures rats.
People won't pay.
Man takes children.

Although this story structure won't work for more complicated stories, it is surprising how often it does work, and how full these stories can be.

THE EXERCISE

Break your story idea down into three sentences of three words each. That will give you a beginning, a middle, and an end and help you understand the architecture of the work. By having to choose three verbs, you'll be forcing yourself to consider the three parts of the action.

THE OBJECTIVE

To see if your story, like a good stool, has three legs to stand on.

44

THE SKELETON

The simplest stories are fairy tales and myths in which a central character—who is on some sort of quest or journey—is continually on stage and secondary characters only appear to assist or thwart her. This is what we call a "skeleton" story—you can see its bones. There are no subtleties, motivation is a given, emotions are unanalyzed, and the narrative proceeds in a linear way. In the skeleton the world and its people are viewed in morally black-and-white terms. The temptation to stray will be almost irresistible but if you do, you will drag your reader into thickets of subplots and gangs of minor characters. (The following exercise is based on a suggestion of folklorist Lawrence Millman.)

THE EXERCISE

Write a linear story, in which a strong main character is on a quest for something important and specific (e.g., a shelter for the baby, medicine for a sick mother, or the key to the storehouse where a tyrant has locked away all the grain from a starving populace). The object is a given—don't explain its importance. The main character starts acting immediately. She then meets a (specific) obstacle; finally she triumphs over the obstacle by means of a magic or supernatural element that comes from the outside (like Dorothy's red shoes in *The Wizard of Oz*). You may introduce minor characters but the narrative should never abandon your main character. This story should be told through action and dialogue. Limit: 550 words.

THE OBJECTIVE

Like a medical student who must learn the names and location of human bones before going on to more complex systems, a beginning writer must be able to handle and control basic plot before moving on to more subtle elements like motivation, subtext, and ambiguity. Many of the greatest novels incorporate a quest (*Moby Dick*), a journey (*David Copperfield*), and triumph over an obstacle (*The Old Man and the Sea*). These works also concentrate on one protagonist and end, if not happily, at least on an emotionally satisfying note of resolution.

STUDENT STORY

The Nanny—A Fairy Tale

There was once a young woman who wanted a baby. The urge to produce another life in her own body hit suddenly, like a squall or a virus. Before this, she hadn't particularly liked children. Yet now, without warning, she longed for an infant to nurse, to rock, to carry like a prize in a bundle strapped to her chest.

"A baby?" said her husband. "You don't know a diaper from a linen handkerchief. Babies are loud, they're smelly, and they cramp your sex life. We're fine as we are."

She worked on him. Walking through the park she'd point out babies sleeping like sacks in strollers, crowing and waving from backpacks, or toddling on creased legs. "Let's eat Chinese tonight," he said. If only she could find the secret crack in his heart, the place where the gates would swing open when the magic words were said, letting the idea of their own baby enter like the children of Hamlin.

She took to sitting on playground benches, thinking. She could leave him and find a man who shared her longing. But she loved the fullness of his laugh, the way he sang as he cooked, the curls behind his ears when his haircut was overdue. Maybe she could trick him, pretend her cycle had become unpredictable, blame nature. But she'd never been able to lie well, not even to her mother.

One day as the young woman sat on a bench near a wading pool, a gray-haired nanny sat down beside her, starched uniform gleaming in the sun. "Have any children?" she asked, starting to knit.

The young woman smiled and shook her head.

"Too bad. You'd like a child, wouldn't you? Not married? Men are hard to find these days, they say."

Though partly put off by the nanny's presumptuousness, the young woman shared her problem. "My husband doesn't want children. At least not yet."

"Stalled adolescence," the nanny said. "See it more and more. Want a solution?" Without waiting for an answer, she pulled a pomegranate out of her knitting bag. "Serve him this for dessert tonight and for the next two nights and have some for yourself, too. Be sure he sucks the sweet red part, and doesn't eat the seeds. If he balks, tell him it's better than kiwi."

The young woman did as she was told, carefully watching her husband savor the sharp sweet taste and spit the seeds on his plate. At first she noticed no change in her husband. But on the third day, while sipping cappuccino in an intimate Italian restaurant, he said, "What the hell. You want a baby? What are we waiting for?" And he took her home to bed.

Months later, her stomach as full as a spinnaker, the young woman sat again on the bench near the wading pool, resting her legs. The nanny sat down next to her as she had before, uniform crisp, oxfords firmly tied.

Eyeing the young woman's belly with a smile, she pulled out her knitting and said, "Looking for a nursemaid?"

CHRISTINE MCDONNELL

Fiction has traditionally and characteristically borrowed its form from letters, journals, diaries, autobiographies, histories, travelogues, news stories, backyard gossip, etc. It has simply *pretended* to be one or the other of them.

WILLIAM GASS

45

FROM SITUATION TO PLOT

If you haven't read our introduction to the section on plot, please go back and read it now before doing this exercise. It is important that you understand our preference for character-driven—not plot-driven—stories.

This exercise is designed to illustrate how easy it is to come up with characters in particular situations from only a few given details.

THE EXERCISE

Begin a story using one of the following as your main character:

- A young boy whose father is in jail.
- A waitress who likes her menus to rhyme.
- A policeman with ten cats.
- A 16-year-old in the hospital.
- The driver of a hit-and-run accident.

(Do you see how a policeman with ten cats is a situation in itself just waiting for a little opposition?)

Now, complicate your character's life with opposing forces, with tension and conflict, and offer your character alternatives within that situation. Ask: What does my character want? What would my character do? How will he act or react? How will those actions propel the story forward?

Then experiment with creating your own sets of details involving character and situation. Do ten or fifteen as fast as you can.

THE OBJECTIVE

To understand how the most effective plots are those driven by character. To see how a character within a given of any situation creates his own destiny.

STUDENT EXAMPLES

My dad was the first man in the history of the state of Maryland to be thrown in jail for poor penmanship. An expert came to court and said dad had to have done it. It was all there in black and white, the way he wrote his name. Handwriting analysis, mom called it. A precedent, a landmark case. She's a lawyer and she seemed proud that dad was a part of something with what she calls historical significance, but she doesn't seem to miss him that much.

I miss him, but that's not the worst part. The worst part is learning to write at school. The teachers keep an eye on me like no one else.

RICH PARADIS

STUDENT STORY

Intelligence

I'm eight years old. But I have the mind of a nineteen-year-old. Mom says it's making up for all the wrong Dad did. Today there's going to be a whole camera crew here. They're going to film different angles of me beating myself at chess. Then they want me to walk around the neighborhood in my Eagle Scout uniform. Dad doesn't want to talk to them. So I guess they'll do an exterior of the penitentiary.

Dad called a few hours ago. Mom handed me the phone. She never wants to talk to him. I end up answering all the questions he wants to ask her. He asked me when was the last time Mom talked about him. I told him she said something at the bowling alley because we were having trouble keeping score. Mom doesn't care how much I lie to him because she says he's going to rot in jail. I miss him. But I can't tell him that. Mom would hit the roof and call me a traitor and start that whole thing about who's bringing me up and who's the slob behind bars. With Mom, eventually everything comes down to physical appearances. "It was a choice between your Dad and Henry Lee," she says when she reminisces about marrying Dad. "And Henry Lee had hair on his back."

On the phone, I asked Dad what he made in woodshop, and he asked me if I was eating lots of peas and carrots because the brain is just another muscle and you can't feed it junk. Dad thinks he's grooming me for the Nobel Prize. I made a few reading suggestions. I send him books and tell him to highlight the difficult parts. He's not very easy to explain things to. If he doesn't get it the first time, he gets angry—and when he gets angry, he automatically thinks of Mom and says, "Don't sign anything. Not even your homework. I own the rights to you. Every single cent you make, you freak of fucking nature."

I never hang up on him, no matter what he says.

I wait until he calms down, and then give him an update on how many sparrows have moved into the birdhouse we built.

But it's really sitting in the basement.

The camera crew is here. Taping down cable and knocking over chairs. Mom's on the phone right now because the producer wants a shot of me playing with my friends. I told him I could punch up some people on my computer. But he wants the real thing. So Mom's on the phone, asking Mrs. Milgram if she can borrow her son for the afternoon. That's the same kid who smashed up my invention for the Science Fair last year. The key grip is showing me how to throw a frisbee. The producer is suggesting a shot of me bicycling down Quarry Lane with my dog running after me. But Einstein has arthritis and bleeding gums. He can barely stand up.

The whole neighborhood's watching us. Kids on mountain bikes and skateboards are casing our house, making circles in the road. When Dad was taken away, Mom ran out and aimed the sprinkler at them. Now she's too busy. She's even got a pencil behind her ear.

I tell the producer I know what people want to see. They want to see me in my tiny apron making a white sauce. Or me playing the piano. A little Vivaldi and maybe the camera panning to my sneakers dangling a foot from the floor while my mother turns the pages and presses the pedal. I love it when she steps on the pedal, when the notes run together and take too long to end.

I lower my head and pretend that this is sadness.

MATT MARINOVICH, PUBLISHED IN *THE QUARTERLY*

I guarantee you that no modern story scheme, even plotlessness, will give a reader genuine satisfaction, unless one of those old-fashioned plots is smuggled in somewhere. I don't praise plots as accurate representations of life, but as ways to keep readers reading.

KURT VONNEGUT, JR.

46

WHAT IF? HOW TO DEVELOP
AND FINISH STORIES

W riters sometimes have story blocks—they begin a story easily enough, but then they run into trouble when they try to finish it. Well, one possible reason is that some stories don't have enough forward motion to become a successful story—and these should be abandoned. On the other hand, many story beginnings just need to be examined and explored for their inherent possibilities. As François Camoin says, "A story needs to take a narrative fork."

THE EXERCISE

Look in your files for a story that seems stuck, a story that has a story block. Next, write at the top of a separate sheet of paper the two words *What If*. Now write five ways of continuing the story, not ending the story, but continuing the story to the next event, scene, etc. Let your imagination go wild. Loosen up your thinking about the events in the story. Your what if's can be as diverse as your imagination can make them. More than likely, and this has proved true through years of teaching and writing, one of the what if's will feel right, organic, to your story and that is the direction in which you should go. Sometimes you will have to do several groups of what if's per story, but that's okay as long as they keep you moving forward.

THE OBJECTIVE

To illustrate that most story beginnings and situations have within them the seeds of the middle and end. You just have to allow your imagination enough range to discover what works.

STUDENT EXAMPLE

One writer began a story about a young boy, Paul, who shoplifts with a cousin. The story opens when they take something more expensive than they have ever taken before. This raises the stakes immediately. After writing a superb opening scene of two and a half pages, the writer didn't know where to go with the story. Below are her five what if's for this beginning.

1. Paul decides to admit to shoplifting, but hopes not to implicate his cousin.
2. Paul is excited by shoplifting something more expensive, and talks his cousin into going back again soon.
3. The store security guard notices their theft and decides to set a trap. (Involves some point-of-view issues.)
4. Paul feels brave now and steals something from his stepfather—something Paul has wanted for a long time.
5. There is a time shift to five years later when Paul commits a major burglary.

The writer continued the story with the fourth idea because she felt it was a more interesting and complex development of Paul's situation. If she hadn't explored several alternatives, she might not have arrived at this story line.

Writer's block is only a failure of the ego.

NORMAN MAILER

47

SO, WHAT HAPPENED?

In his introduction to a stellar group of stories, *American Stories: Fiction from the Atlantic Monthly,* C. Michael Curtis says, "Each achieves the sort of transforming moment one looks for in the short story form, a shift in understanding, a glimpse of unexpected wisdom, the discovery of unimagined strength. . . . You will find no minimalism here, no sketches or portraits, no glimpses, merely, of 'things as they are'; these are honest-to-God stories, in which Something Happens." We also feel that *something has to happen* in a story once the original situation has been presented—something in terms of the consequences of situation and action.

In Janet Burroway's discussion of conflict and resolution, she says, "Still another way of seeing the shape of the story is in terms of situation-action-situation. The story begins by presenting us with a situation. It then recounts an action, and when that action is over, we are left with a situation that is the opposite of the opening situation. This formula seems oversimplified, but it is very difficult to find a story it does not describe."

Keep in mind that "opposite" can mean that the narrator at the beginning of the story does not understand her situation, but after a scene or several scenes (action), and by the end of the story, she does. Or she might understand something about another person, an event, or a relationship. Note that Curtis talks about the "transforming moment" in terms of "a shift in understanding," a "glimpse of wisdom," and the "discovery of unimagined strength"—all cerebral transformations. James Joyce calls such a moment the "epiphany."

Burroway goes on to say that the "moment of recognition" must be manifested or externalized in an action, in the concrete world of the story: the prince recognizes Cinderella, and the shoe fits. (See Exercise 61, page 164, "Show and Tell.")

And what of those stories in which "nothing happens." Rust Hills, in *Writing in General and the Short Story in Particular,* discusses the "kind of story that seems at first to be a character sketch." The character seems unaltered at the end of the story—more firmly entrenched in his situation than ever. Yet, what has happened is that his "capacity for change" has been removed. There is no longer any hope for him: that is the change. Janet Burroway uses the metaphor of war to explain this type of story—a story that began with two sides hopeful about victory ends with two survivors, one from each side, grasping the border fence with bloodied fists. "The 'resolution' of this battle is that neither side will ever give up and that no one will ever win; there will never be a resolution." In both instances, possibility and hope are gone. What happens, happens for the reader who has witnessed this failure.

THE EXERCISE

One by one, go through five or six of your stories and look for "what happened" in each story. Mark the moment of transformation, the moment of recognition, the epiphany in each—and then look for the action that makes these moments manifest.

THE OBJECTIVE

To write stories in which something happens.

STUDENT EXAMPLE

(In "Matrimony," the first person narrator finally realizes that she and her ex-husband should stay parted. This is made manifest by the last lines of the story.)

> "So, I guess the key won't exactly work," Phillip said.
>
> "No, I guess it won't work at all."
>
> That night he went back to his apartment, and I played the videotape of our wedding. I watched the whole thing through, and then again as it rewound. I watched as our lips disengaged from our first kiss as husband and wife, as we made frenzied, backward steps down the aisle, and finally walked out of the church at different times, alone.
>
> DINA JOHNSON

48

THE STORY MACHINE

from Perry Glasser

New writers frequently believe "there is nothing to write about" or that "all stories have been told." The "Story Machine" is a heuristic device that mimics what many psychological studies have identified as the chief mechanism of creativity—the juxtaposition of two familiar notions so they are perceived as a single, new notion.

THE EXERCISE

On each of five 3- × -5 index cards, print a vocational label, for example, dentist, truck driver, or fashion model. On each of a second set of index cards, write a mildly strange or unusual behavior. The mistakes here are to be too mundane (brush teeth, clean car) or to be too melodramatic (strangled her lover, drove his flaming truck through the prison walls). Somewhere between lies the quirk of the odd that is interesting: set free the parakeet, pick loose the tennis racket strings, or sew closed his sweater sleeves. Some writers will keep their cards filed for use again and again, and will add to the original pack over time as interesting vocations or actions suggest themselves.

Shuffle each pack of cards (*not* together) and turn over the first pair. The writer may now ask the following question: "Why did Card A do Card B?" "Why did the fashion model pick loose the tennis racket strings?" "Why did the dentist set free the parakeet?" The writer may continue flipping cards until a satisfactory pairing is discovered. If no satisfactory pair develops, reshuffle the cards and repeat the procedure. If you have ten cards in each pack you will have 100 possible pairings; twelve cards per pack will yield 144 pairings.

Bear in mind that the event suggested by the Story Machine should be thought of as the *last* scene of a story. Supply motive for the odd behavior. Supply setting. Supply a conflict that might be resolved by this behavior. Imagine a scene prior to the final scene that demonstrates the severity of the conflict. Imagine a scene that demonstrates the initial difficulty.

This exercise may easily be adapted for a class. Instead of shuffling, students pass cards one way and then another so that no student is left with any of her original cards. The liberating outcome is that if the new pair lacks all resonance for a student, the student has no emotional invest-ment in the product of the Story Machine. No one has made a mistake or performed badly, just some bad luck has occurred. Class discussions of motive and structure can be lively.

THE OBJECTIVE

Retrograde plotting is often a revelation to the beginning writer who has again and again found herself staring off into the space above the type-writer and asking "Now what happens?" Writing toward a conclusion for some writers is easier than exploring the consequences of an imagined premise. One more easily discovers the beginnings of things if one knows the ending. That the Story Machine requires vocational labels gives stu-dents insight to the rudiments of characterization, as such labels suggest education levels and socioeconomic status.

STUDENT EXAMPLE

This student drew three situation cards: (1) A computer salesman audi-tions for a local cooking show, (2) a drug dealer begins work at a homeless shelter, and (3) a teacher sets out to make a three-dimensional map of the city. She chose the computer salesman.

> Marlon has always wondered about the tiny veins that make up romaine lettuce. He is awed that they all build on one another like the networks of minuscule computer bits, pushing information through so many little channels to the ultimate source. Maybe the romaine is packed full of knowledge too.
>
> Lettuce knowledge for other green and leafy vegetables. User friendly.
>
> Marlon's lettuce is to be used as a frame for his star, the elaborate star baby, Seven Cherry Frozen Aspic Salad. The romaine will serve its func-tion, dying prettily across his best china, a bit of standard greenery. His most basic ingredient.
>
> If he wins over the others auditioning today, Marlon will be "Mr. Noon Day Chef," the seventh Channel 7 cook to premiere on "Noon Potpourri." He likes the number seven. Lucky. Marlon needs this job be-cause of layoffs at Computer World's Westgate Mall office where he worked as salesman and chief technician.
>
> Marlon paints his lettuce carefully with two parts Johnson Wax and just a bit of liquid Crisco. Polishing lettuce is a trick he picked up in *Draping Delectables,* a technical photography book he found at a used-book store. His lettuce will never see the inside of anyone's mouth. It will simply make mouths water. Powerful mouths who dominate the studios at Channel 7.
>
> KARLA HORNER

49

PLOT POTENTIAL

The main thing to keep in mind as you're doing plot is that *you're the boss* and not the other way around. It's your story, and you have an infinite number of choices. As a creator of fiction, you should feel supremely at ease in the role of storyteller.

THE EXERCISE

Write five mini-stories (limit: 200 words each) to account for a single event or set of circumstances, such as a man and woman standing on a city sidewalk, hailing a cab. Each story should be different—in characters, plot, and theme—from the others.

THE OBJECTIVE

To loosen the bonds that shackle you to a single, immutable version; to underscore the fact that plot is not preordained but something you can control and manipulate at will, like the strings of a marionette; and to demonstrate once more that there are many ways to skin a cat.

STUDENT EXAMPLE

1. At 2:00 in the afternoon, John, a forty-four-year-old man in a business suit, and Dawn, a twenty-two-year-old woman in a tight skirt and high heels, came out of the Hancock Building. While John stood in the street trying to hail a cab, Dawn stayed on the sidewalk, sobbed, and blew her nose. When John finally managed to get a cab, he helped Dawn in and then got in next to her. John is Dawn's boss and she is his secretary. At 1:45 she'd gotten a call from the hospital; her mother had a heart attack and was in intensive care. When Dawn went in to tell John why she had to leave so suddenly, he looked as though it was his mother who was in the hospital. Dawn could not understand why he was so concerned, why he was getting a cab for her, and now going with her to the hospital. He'd never been very nice to Dawn or interested in getting to know her and this show of sympathy was out of character. John held Dawn's hand in the cab and said, "Oh God, oh God." And he wondered how he was going to tell Dawn that he was her mother's

lover, that they'd fallen in love the night Dawn brought her mother to the company Christmas party.

2. As usual, Pauline had been totally humiliated by her father, and now he was making a fool of himself trying to hail a cab. Pauline thought that if she stood on the sidewalk and looked like she was waiting for someone, no one would connect her with her father. He'd insisted on coming to her interview with her. He insisted on sitting in the waiting room while she was in with the personnel director, and he pestered the receptionist with stories about how cute Pauline had been as a child and how smart she was as an adult. Pauline knew he did it with good intentions—he wanted her to be safe in the city, but it was driving her crazy. As he flailed his arms and tried to whistle down a cab, she took a few steps backward, and then ran. When she reached the subway station she decided to ride to the end of the line.

3. Maggie hated the city, the people in it, the noise, the dirt, and especially that man who had stepped out in front of her and was trying to flag down the cab she had been waiting for. When a cab finally pulled up and he put his hand on the door, she bounded off the sidewalk and banged him so hard with her hip that he fell to the street. "Get your own cab, buster."

"Maggie?" he said, still on the ground. "Maggie Pillbox? Is that you?"

"Wow," she said. "It's you, Doctor Pantry. Gosh, if I'd known it was you, I never would have hit you so hard."

"Still hostile, eh?" he said. Doctor Pantry had been Maggie's psychiatrist. She helped him up, and for the next fifty minutes, they stood on the sidewalk, Doctor Pantry listening carefully and taking notes as Maggie told him all her life's woes.

4. The man and woman trying to hail down a cab, the ones dressed like an insurance salesman and his secretary, had just pulled off their greatest crime to date. It wasn't the big time and they knew it, but eleven wallets, a watch, and a solar calculator weren't bad for five minutes' work. Once in the cab, they put the loot on the seat and started going through it, unaware that the cabdriver was watching in his rearview mirror. The woman talked about how they could finally afford Cindy's braces. The man said he could now pay the rent, and the cabdriver took them on a circuitous route to the police station.

5. Joe had been driving a cab for only two weeks and still found the job intoxicating. He liked best trying to figure out what each person was like before they got into his cab. He'd readily admit that he was usually wrong about people. He'd thought the couple he'd picked up that morning was going to scream at each other, but they were

silent and held hands. His last fare had turned out to be a transves-
tite so convincing that he'd almost asked him/her out on a date.
Now this couple, the man in the three-piece suit waving him down
and the much younger woman on the sidewalk, worked together
and were lovers dying to get away for an afternoon of hot passion.
Why else the unlikely pair? "Forest Lawn Mortuary," the man said
as he got into the car. "And step on it. We don't want to be late."

TERRY FRENCH

A story isn't about a moment in time, a story is about *the* moment in
time.

W. D. WETHERELL

VII. THE ELEMENTS OF STYLE

Style is the feather in the arrow, not the feather in the cap.

—GEORGE SAMPSON

Titles cannot be copyrighted, and so we have stolen for this section the title of one of the most important books on writing, E. B. White and William Strunk's *The Elements of Style*. Mr. White, always exact and eloquent on the subject, said during an interview, "I don't think style can be taught. Style results more from what a person is than from what he knows." He went on to say that there are a "few hints that can be thrown out to advantage. They would be the twenty-one hints I threw out in Chapter V of *The Elements of Style*. There was nothing new or original about them, but there they are, for all to read." Everybody should have a copy of this book on his shelf, but as a reminder we have listed the chapter headings of Chapter V below:

1. Place yourself in the background; 2. Write in a way that comes naturally; 3. Work from a suitable design; 4. Write with nouns and verbs; 5. Revise and rewrite; 6. Do not overwrite; 7. Do not overstate; 8. Avoid the use of qualifiers; 9. Do not affect a breezy manner; 10. Use orthodox spelling; 11. Do not explain too much; 12. Do not construct awkward adverbs; 13. Make sure the reader knows who is speaking; 14. Avoid fancy words; 15. Do not use dialect unless your ear is good; 16. Be clear; 17. Do not inject opinion; 18. Use figures of speech sparingly; 19. Do not take shortcuts at the cost of clarity; 20. Avoid foreign languages; 21. Prefer the standard to the offbeat.

Strunk and White is a good place to begin, but it isn't the whole story of style in fiction. What would John Barth be without his instructional presence; Didion without Didion; Vladimir Nabokov without his complicted, high style; Alice Adams without her qualifiers; Laurie Colwin without her breezy manner; Russell Hoban without his unorthodox spelling; Nicholson Baker without his explanations; Flannery O'Connor without her inventions in dialect; Joseph Conrad without his opinions; John Updike without his figures of speech; Thomas Mann and Sandra Cisneros without their foreign languages; and Donald Barthelme without the upbeat?

Begin with Strunk and White, but as you grow more experienced in writing and life, you will grow into a more individual style.

Cyril Connolly also speaks of style as an integral part of who the writer is when he says, "Style is manifest in language. The vocabulary of a writer is his currency, but it is a paper currency and its value depends on the reserves of mind and heart which back it. The perfect use of language is that in which every word carries the meaning that it is intended to, no less and no more."

The exercises in this section are designed to make you more aware of the elements of style, style in language—sentence structure, word choice, diction, tone, etc.—in your own work and the work of writers you admire. And what we said in Exercise 9 "Put Your Heart on the Page" is worth repeating here: Know yourself. Write from the heart. Ellen Glasgow said, "Style should be [like] a transparent envelope which changes color in response to the animation within."

50

STYLE: THE RIGHT WORD

from Rod Kessler

Students often ask what they can do to develop a style of their own. Most writers would agree that style as such can't be taught, and that the best thing students can do is write honestly and write a lot. Trying too hard to have a writing style is like trying too hard to have a particular style in your personality—you run the risk of seeming affected. In *The Elements of Style* E. B. White says, "Every writer, by the way he uses the language, reveals something of his spirit, his habits, his capacities, his bias. . . . No writer long remains incognito." Still, writers who develop an awareness of style and learn to understand the components of other writers' styles are in a better position to perceive and shape their own writing.

THE EXERCISE

Part I

Read the passages below by Toni Morrison, Kurt Vonnegut, Jr., John Updike, Henry Miller, Ann Beattie, William Faulkner, and Amy Hempel, paying attention to what makes them distinctive.

Beloved   TONI MORRISON

Outside a throng, now, of black faces stopped murmuring. Holding the living child, Sethe walked past them in their silence and hers. She climbed into the cart, her profile knife-clean against a cheery blue sky. A profile that shocked them with its clarity. Was her head a bit too high? Her back a little too straight? Probably. Otherwise the singing would have begun at once, the moment she appeared in the doorway of the house on Bluestone Road. Some cape of sound would have quickly been wrapped around her, like arms to hold and steady her on the way. As it was, they waited till the car turned about, headed west to town. And then no words. Humming. No words at all.

Cat's Cradle   KURT VONNEGUT, JR.

Miss Pefko wasn't used to chatting with someone as important as Dr. Breed and she was embarrassed. Her gait was affected, becoming stiff and chicken-like. Her smile was glassy, and she was ransacking her brain for something to say, finding nothing in it but used kleenex and costume jewelry.

Rabbit Is Rich   JOHN UPDIKE
Then he sees it, behind the barn, where the woods are encroaching upon
what had once been a cleared space, sumac and cedar in the lead: the
tilted yellow shell of a school bus. Its wheels and windows are gone and
the snub hood of its cab has been torn away to reveal a hollow space
where an engine was cannibalized; but like a sunken galleon it testifies to
an empire, a fleet of buses whose proprietor has died, his widow left with
an illegitimate daughter to raise. The land under Rabbit seems to move,
with the addition of yet another citizen to the subterrain of the dead.

Henry Miller's Book of Friends   HENRY MILLER
The reason our relationship was on the cool side was twofold. Jimmy was
a wop and a Catholic and I was a product of that one hundred percent
American white collar Protestant tribe which seems to dominate
America. Jimmy's friends were all of the lower or lowest class. They were
all good fighters—some were already getting to be well-known in amateur boxing circles. But perhaps the thing that I could stand least in
Jimmy was his pride and ambition. He wanted to lead in everything.
What's worse, he *believed* these myths and legends about our heroes. One
could never convince him that George Washington was a real pain in the
ass or that Thomas Jefferson had several children by his Negro slaves.

"Marshall's Dog"   ANN BEATTIE
Mrs. Anna Wright. She signs her name to a note she has written Mary's
homeroom teacher—an excuse for Mary's absence from school on
Monday and Tuesday. She writes so many notes. She feels obliged to offer details now. In this note she mentions a specific drug given to Mary
by the doctor: penicillin. Rainy, cold weather, a sore throat, a tendency
toward strep, penicillin. Her husband has told her to stop writing notes,
but what is she supposed to do?

"A Rose for Emily"   WILLIAM FAULKNER
Alive, Miss Emily had been a tradition, a duty, and a care; a sort of
heridatary obligation upon the town, dating from that day in 1894 when
Colonel Sartoris, the mayor—he who fathered the edict that no Negro
woman should appear on the streets without an apron—remitted her
taxes, the dispensation dating from the death of her father on into perpe-
tuity. Not that Miss Emily would have accepted charity.

"Going"   AMY HEMPEL
There is a typo on the hospital menu this morning. They mean, I think,
that the pot roast tonight will be served with buttered noodles. But what
it says here on my breakfast tray is that the pot roast will be severed with
buttered noodles.
    This is not a word you want to see after flipping your car twice at sixty
per and then landing side-up in a ditch.

Part II

Read the unidentified passages below by the same writers. (A passage by a
well-known seventh writer has been thrown in to make this more challenging.) Then match up these unidentified passages with the appropriate

writer, and in each case make a list of the components of style that you relied on for your answer.

A _____ : This weekend Sarah and Julie are visiting. They came on Friday evening. Sarah was one of George's students—the one who led the fight to have him rehired. She does not look like a troublemaker; she is pale and pretty, with freckles on her cheeks. She talks too much about the past, and this upsets him, disrupts the peace he has made with himself. She tells him that they fired him because he was "in touch" with everything, that they were afraid of him because he was so in touch.

B _____ : Then he was moving, running, outside the house, toward the stable; this the old habit, the old blood which he had not been permitted to choose for himself, which had been bequeathed him willy nilly and which had run for so long (and who knew where, battening on what of outrage and savagery and lust) before it came to him. I could keep on, he thought, I could run on and on and never look back, never need to see his face again. Only I can't. I can't, the rusted can in his hand now, the liquid sploshing in it as he ran back to the house and into it, into the sound of his mother's weeping in the next room, and handed the can to his father.

C _____ : The first three days are the worst, they say, but it's been two weeks, and I'm still waiting for those first three days to be over.
One day into the program, I realized the only thing that made me smart was nicotine. Now I can't plan a trip from the bed to the bathroom. I don't find the front door fifty percent of the time. In my head there's a broken balcony I fall off of when I speak.

D _____ : It is a beautiful woman who has come to look at the apartment. An American, of course. I stand at the window with my back to her watching a sparrow pecking at a fresh turd. Amazing how easily the sparrow is provided for. It is raining a bit and the drops are very big. I used to think a bird couldn't fly if its wings got wet. Amazing how these rich dames come to Paris and find all the swell studios.

E _____ : But her brain was not interested in the future. Loaded with the past and hungry for more, it left her no room to imagine, let alone plan for, the next day. Exactly like that afternoon in the wild onions—when one more step was the most she could see of the future. Other people went crazy, why couldn't she? Other people's brains stopped, turned around and went on to something new, which is what must have happened to Halle. And how sweet that would have been: the two of them back by the milk shed, squatting by the churn, smashing cold, lumpy butter into their faces with not a care in the world. Feeling it slippery, sticky—rubbing it in their hair, watching it squeeze through their fingers. What a relief to stop it right there. Close. Shut. Squeeze the butter.

F _____ : David stopped, blocked by a grimy window at the end of a blind alley. All he knew was that he'd never been there before, that his memory had blown a gasket, and that the deer was not on the payroll. The air in the alley was thick with tango music and the stench of scorched insulation. David scrubbed away some of the crust on the window with his handkerchief, praying for a glimpse of something that made sense.

Inside were ranks of women at benches, rocking their heads in time to the music, and dipping soldering irons into great nests of colored wires that crept past them on endless belts. One of them looked up and saw David, and winked in a tango rhythm. David fled.

G _____ : He did not want any consequences. He did not want any consequences ever again. He wanted to live along without consequences. Besides he did not really need a girl. The army had taught him that. It was all right to pose as though you had to have a girl. Nearly everybody did that. But it wasn't true. You did not need a girl.

H _____ : The taxi took him straight to the airport; Carson saw nothing of the city but the silhouettes beside the highway and the highway's scarred center strip. For an instant after takeoff, a kind of map spread itself underneath him, and then was gone. Yet afterwards, thinking back upon the farm voices, the distant skyscrapers, the night visits of the nurses, the doctors with their unseen, unsullied homes, the dozens of faces risen to the surface of his pain, he seemed to have come to know the city intimately; it was like, on other of his trips, a woman who, encountered in a bar and paid at the end, turns ceremony inside out, and bestows herself without small talk.

THE OBJECTIVE

To train writers to recognize components of style: sentence length, sentence structure, verb tense, imagery, diction, and tone. The ability to discuss components of style helps writers to address their own work with a knowledgeable eye. (For the answers, turn to Rod Kessler's bio note.)

51

A STYLE OF YOUR OWN *refer to after completing draft*

from Rod Kessler

Students are often surprised to discover patterns within their own writing styles. Sometimes the patterns reveal strengths of style, but sometimes the patterns uncover easy-to-fix problems, such as "having the as's"—using too many "as he was walking" constructions.

THE EXERCISE

Make a photocopy of a page from a story you've already put into final form. This can be the opening of the story or a page from the middle, it doesn't matter—but be sure the page is typed neatly. Also bring in a copy of a page from a fiction writer you admire. Analyze your page for:

1. Sentence length. From the top of your page count down ten sentences. Make a list indicating the word length of each sentence. How varied in length are your sentences? Do you have a mix of short and long, or are your sentences around the same length?

   Next, add up all the words in your ten sentences and divide by ten—which gives you your average sentence length.

   Now perform the same counts on the page from the writer whose work you admire—writer X. How varied are these sentences compared with your own? What is the writer's average length?

2. Modifier density. On your own writing sample, mark all of the adjectives and adverbs you've used in the first 100 words and add them up. This gives an approximate percentage of modifiers. (If you counted 5, that's 5 out of 100 or 5 percent).

   Perform the same count on the page from writer X. How do your styles compare?

3. Sentence structure. Does each of your paragraphs contain a mixture of simple, complex, and compound sentences? Or are they all of the same structure? How many times do you begin, say, with participial phrases (Running to the station, Jack. . . . Looking up at the sky, Joan. . .)? How many times do you use "subject-verb" constructions? How many times do you use "as" as a conjunction? (Jerry turned to go as the bell chimed.) (Read John Gardner's discussion of "The Sentence" in *The Art of Fiction* in which he teaches the lesson of the sentence by example.)

4. Diction. How many of the first 100 words exceed two syllables? Three syllables? More than three? (Again, read Gardner's section "Vocabulary," same book.)

5. Verbs. What percentage of your verbs are forms of the boring verb "to be"? How often do you use the passive voice?

THE OBJECTIVE

To enable students to regard their own prose style objectively and decide if they need to make changes—perhaps vary their sentences or cut out an obvious mannerism. Some students might want to go beyond 10 sentences and 100 words to do a closer study of their "natural" prose.

Sometimes you have to play a long time to play like yourself.

MILES DAVIS

52

TABOOS: WEAK ADVERBS AND ADJECTIVES

Voltaire said the adjective is the enemy of the noun and the adverb is the enemy of the verb. Thus war ensues on both—with the object of banishing adjectives and adverbs forever. Banishing them precipitously and unfairly. John Gardner said, "Adverbs are either the dullest tools or the sharpest tools in the novelist's toolbox." Adverbs are not meant to augment a verb—as in walked *slowly*—but to create friction with the verb or alter its meaning. For example, pair the following adverbs with different verbs to see how they change those verbs: relentlessly, conscientiously, chastely, uncharacteristically, reluctantly, gratuitously, erroneously, furtively, and inadequately.

Adjectives may seem to bolster nouns when in fact they often weaken them. Yet some adjectives have everything to do with style and meaning. The following are examples of adverbs and adjectives when they are used well:

She had been to Germany, Italy, everywhere that one visits *acquistively*.
ELIZABETH BOWEN, *THE LAST SEPTEMBER*

Within the parson's house death was *zealously* kept in view and lectured on.
ISAK DINESEN, "PETER AND ROSA"

She jammed the pedal to the floor, and like something huge and prehistoric and pea-brained, the Jeep leapt *stupidly* out of its stall.
SHARON SHEEHE STARK, *A WRESTLING SEASON*

I have always enjoyed gestures—never failing to bow, for example, when I finished dancing with a woman—but one attribute I have acquired with age is the ability to predict when I am about to act *foolishly*.
ETHAN CANIN, *EMPEROR OF THE AIR*

She reached again for the door and kept her eyes on him, like a captive who edges *watchfully* towards escape.
SHIRLEY HAZZARD, *THE TRANSIT OF VENUS*

So closely had we become tied to the river that we could sense where it lay and make for it *instinctively* like cattle.
W. D. WETHERELL, *CHEKHOV'S SISTER*

When Sula first visited the Wright house, Helene's *curdled* scorn turned to butter.

TONI MORRISON, *SULA*

147

With a *bladdery* whack it [the boat] slapped apart and sprang away.
SHARON SHEEHE STARK, *A WRESTLING SEASON*

Charmian sat with her eyes closed, attempting to put her thoughts into *alphabetical* order.
MURIEL SPARK, *MEMENTO MORI*

Hank was not accepted at Harvard Law School; but *goodhearted* Yale took him.
JOHN UPDIKE, "THE OTHER"

On the far side of the room, under the *moiling* dogs the twins are playing.
FRANÇOIS CAMOIN, "BABY, BABY, BABY"

THE EXERCISE

Circle all the adverbs and adjectives in a published story and decide which ones work. Then, exchange all weak adverbs and adjectives for strong ones of your own. Consider omitting them altogether. Now do the same exercise with one of your own stories.

THE OBJECTIVE

To be alert to the power—and the weakness—of these verbal spices. To avoid them except when they can add something you really need.

STUDENT EXAMPLES

Hunched over, scissors clasped in her hands, the old woman passed like a shadow behind a screen of young birch and stepped *possessively* into her neighbor's garden.
COLLEEN GILLARD

I clatter Sparkey's mouth and make him laugh *demonically,* or have him insult the guy who is sitting too near the stage.
MATT MARINOVICH

Magdalen was the woman who'd managed to turn her passion *sacred.* She was the saint who turned the flesh *Divine.*
MARIETTE LIPPO

53

WORD PACKAGES ARE NOT GIFTS

A word package is a group of neutral words strung together into a hackneyed phrase. Word packages are used by lazy writers searching for an easy way out of a difficult or slippery thought. (Frequently they are found at the beginnings of sentences.)

THE EXERCISE

Stay away from the following word packages. They signal to the smart reader that you lack freshness and are an uninteresting writer.

Better than ever
For some curious reason
A number of. . .
As everybody knows
She didn't know where she was
Things were getting out of hand
It came as no surprise
It was beyond him
Needless to say
Without thinking
He lived in the moment
Well in advance
An emotional roller coaster
Little did I know
To no avail

THE OBJECTIVE

To learn to write without word packages until your use of them is absolutely deliberate and to some purpose.

54

BOXCARS AND MECHANICAL STYLISTICS

from David Madden

The functional usefulness of conjunctions and connectives is obvious. Their mechanical and clumsy use in first drafts, even by the most skillful writers, is not so obvious. The effect is to drug the reader's responses. Phrases pass before the reader's eyes like boxcars hooked together, rather than a flowing stream.

THE EXERCISE

In the revision phase of the creative process, make a raid on your story to arrest the overuse of conjunctives and connectives such as "but," "and," "as if," "which," "when," "or," "so," "nor," "yet," "for," "after," "because," "if," "since," "where," "while," "as," "although," "unless," "until," "also," "finally," "however," "therefore," and "moreover."

THE OBJECTIVE

To maximize the sense of experience happening now, to sustain a sense of immediacy. The words cited above, when overused or used too mechanically, call attention to the fact that you are constructing sentences—as if you were, in the lingo of a lawyer, only dealing out facts to reach a verdict.

55

CUTTING TO THE BONE

from David Ray

W hen Hemingway was asked if he revised much, he answered by handing across a story and telling his interviewer to take it home and read it
carefully and tell him the next day if he had found a single word that could
be cut. The interviewer decided that this was Hemingway's way of telling
him that the story had undergone many revisions.

THE EXERCISE

Take a passage of your work and read through it at least three times, questioning each word. Then cross out every word possible. The adverbs will,
no doubt, be the first to go, then most adjectives. See if prepositional
phrases can be omitted or replaced by a single word. Is description excessive? Ask if a word, a sentence, a paragraph, or even a page can be cut.

THE OBJECTIVE

To make the writing as spare and trim and essential as Hemingway's or
Chekhov's. Recall Chekhov's advice about spare description, "very brief
and relevant . . . one ought to seize upon the little particulars, grouping
them in such a way that, in reading, when you shut your eyes, you get a
picture." He regarded it as an insult to overdescribe; the writer gives just
enough detail to evoke the reader's knowledge of life. He also suggested,
of course, that one write a beginning, middle, and end, then cut the beginning and the end. The story is what's left. It is remarkable how often
that advice is just what is needed. The challenge to every word will make
the writer aware of her tolerance for fat!

56

SUIT YOUR SENTENCE
TO ITS MEANING

from Thalia Selz

Many stories are unconvincing because the writer is using the wrong kinds of sentences for the material and mood. A string of short subject-verb-object sentences can sound infantile instead of sounding excited like the Robert Boswell passage below. Or a stream-of-consciousness passage may merely list scattered details instead of using them to create scene and mood like the montage by Dos Passos.

"All fiction has style," says Stephen Minot in *Three Genres*. "But it is important to examine just what your style is and then to judge whether it is the best possible approach for a particular story." Both Minot and John Gardner, in *The Art of Fiction,* carefully examine the sentence as an element of style, and their observations can help any writer.

THE EXERCISE

Read the following passages to see how the writers convey information while shaping our attitudes and emotions.

In Ernest Hemingway's *The Sun Also Rises* an obscure character is killed by a bull being taken to the bullring in a Spanish town. The first brief sentences deliver the objective facts almost as coolly as a newspaper obit. The final two sentences are longer and have a more complex structure (why?), and the string of ten short prepositional phrases that ends the passage not only mimics the rhythm of the train wheels but creates a poetic, lulling, hypnotic effect, suggestive of a chant.

> Later in the day we learned that the man who was killed was named Vicente Girones, and came from near Tafalla. The next day in the paper we read that he was 28 years old, and had a farm, a wife, and two children. . . . The coffin was loaded into the baggage car of the train, and the widow and the two children rode, sitting, all three together, in an open third-class railway-carriage. The train started with a jerk, and then ran smoothly, going down grade around the edge of the plateau and out into the fields of grain that blew in the wind on the plain on the way to Tafalla.

In *The Big Money,* John Dos Passos describes Rudolph Valentino's progress through a city.

the streets were jumbled with hysterical faces, waving hands, crazy eyes; they stuck out their autographbooks, yanked his buttons off, cut a tail off his admirably tailored dress suit . . . his valets removed young women from under his bed; all night in nightclubs and cabarets actresses leching for stardom made sheepseyes at him from under their mascaraed lashes.

Cynthia Ozick's short story "The Shawl" takes place in a concentration camp during World War II. The child Magda is so attached to her shawl that she can be hidden away from the guards inside it.

> She tangled herself up in it and sucked on one of the corners when she wanted to be very still.
> Then Stella took the shawl away and made Magda die.
> Afterward Stella said: "I was cold."
> And afterward she was always cold, always. The cold went into her heart . . .

And from Robert Boswell's "The Darkness of Love":

> She stood. They held each other, afraid to talk. Louise led him out of the living room into the hall. She opened the door to the walk-in closet and spread the comforter.

Now rewrite a passage of your own trying to make the words, the length of the sentences, and their syntactical rhythms express as nearly as possible both the information you want to convey and the attitudes and emotions you want your reader to feel.

THE OBJECTIVE

To shape sentences to do your bidding. Sentences aren't just snowshoes to get you from the beginning to the end of your story. They are powerful tools with which to carve a story that wasn't there until you decided to create it.

STUDENT EXAMPLES

Notice how these students combine sentence length and rhythm with meaning.

> "It's tonight."
> "Who?"
> "Hoffman."
> "How?"
> "We suicide him. Booze and pills."
>
> BOB PELTIER

Jeannie's hands drew Ferris-wheel circles in the air, turning an invisible car back over front, front over back, the invisible car larger than the metal Matchbox cars Tim had played with as a child and smaller, smaller, smaller than the silver Honda in which he had died.

TERY GRIFFIN, "HOLDING ON"

You're wasting time sitting in a doctor's office when you could be traveling or meeting famous people. Really sick kids always get to meet famous people. But you know you aren't dying because you feel and look fine. How can anything serious be wrong if you look fine?

GAIL FEINBERG, "A COMING OF AGE STORY"

I held the seat of the bicycle, aiming it into the alley, and headed down the grayness toward home.

DOUG LLOYD, "FEWER HAPPY ENDINGS"

I don't feel that it's plot that is moving my stories along from the start to their finish. I know it's not plot. It's language largely . . . and the characters' observations.

AMY HEMPEL

57

PARODY AS TEACHER

A writer's voice combines tone, emotional stance, vocabulary, inflection, typical sentence structure, even paragraphing—in a word, style. Some writers achieve a style so distinctive that it readily lends itself to parody. The verbal equivalent of a visual caricature, parody heightens and exaggerates a writer's stylistic traits—both good and bad. Henry James, Virginia Woolf, William Faulkner, and Ernest Hemingway are four writers whose singular and unmistakable voices seem to beg for parody.

THE EXERCISE

After you have read *A Farewell to Arms* write a parody of Hemingway, specifically a scene that emerges from the following circumstances: Catherine did not die in childbirth and her baby survived. Lt. Henry brought her back to the United States, where they are now living together. Their baby is a year old and the honeymoon is definitely over. Try to imitate Hemingway's voice, tone, rhythms, and mood, using exaggeration and humor.

THE OBJECTIVE

Parody is not mere flattery or, as often thought, ridicule; it's also a demonstration of how deeply the parodist understands the work imitated, how clearly the author's voice comes through. A successful parody not only complements the original; it should stand on its own good-natured and witty feet.

STUDENT STORY

A Fond Farewell

Catherine woke up alone. Frederic's side of the bed showed no signs of having been slept in. Through the open door to the adjoining room, Catherine heard little Ernest starting to move around in his crib. She threw on her silk robe, picked up the baby and went downstairs to the kitchen. She put Ernest in his high-chair, and spooned apple sauce into his mouth. Catherine heard noises trickling through the closed door to the guest bedroom down the hall. A minute later the door opened and Frederic came out, followed by a stunning young woman with red hair, dressed entirely in white.

"Good morning, honey," Frederic said. "Sleep well?"

"Pretty well, thanks."

The woman sat down and began playing with the baby.

"Do you love me?" Catherine asked.

"Of course," Frederic said, patting her on the head. He got a bowl from the cabinet, filled it with cornflakes, and poured white wine over the cereal. He sat down next to the woman and started eating.

"Sweetie-pie," Catherine said. "Who is this?"

"Oh, I'm sorry, Catherine, this is Laura Sullivan. Laura, this is my wife Catherine."

"It's a pleasure to meet you," Laura said, extending her hand. Catherine shook it.

"You have a lovely home. How kind it was of Freddie's grandfather to die and leave it to you."

"I'm still hungry, Catherine. Make me an omelette."

"Yes dear." Catherine opened the door to the refrigerator. In it there were eggs and there was milk in a glass bottle and there was beer and there was wine and there was lettuce and there was American cheese and there were carrots and there were onions and there was a rutabaga.

The baby started to cry. Frederic grabbed a bottle, filled it with grappa, and handed it to the little tyke. Ernest took the bottle from his father, popped the nipple in his mouth and began to suck. "Barely a year old and I'll bet his liver is already shot."

"Do you love me?"

"You betcha. Just keep cooking."

"But if you love me, why do you need her?" Tears slipped down Catherine's cheeks.

"I didn't plan any of this, Catherine. It just sort of happened. Remember last week, when I got so drunk I had to go to the hospital and have my stomach pumped? Well, that's where I met Laura. She's a nurse, just like you."

"I couldn't help falling in love with him," Laura said, interrupting. "The way he smelled of alcohol, the way he couldn't string three coherent words together, and that cute little gagging noise he made when I stuck the tube down his throat. He was irresistible."

"What does she have that I don't have?" Catherine said, still crying.

"A mind of her own, for one thing."

"I could have had a mind of my own if you'd told me to."

"I want you to move out by the end of the week."

"But we're married!"

"Well, no, not really. You wouldn't let us get married—remember? I've been meaning to thank you for that. You can have most of the furniture. But I'll need the double bed. Is my omelette ready yet?"

Catherine served him his egg, then she got dressed and left the house, still weeping. She didn't even notice the rain.

MICHAEL J. ELLIS

58

PRACTICE WRITING
GOOD, CLEAN PROSE

from Christopher Keane

Too often new writers think in terms of story, rather than in terms of words—of building a story with words. As a result, their early efforts are often overwritten and flowery. The following exercise will challenge your use of language—and it might change the way you write.

THE EXERCISE

Write a short story using words of only one syllable.

THE OBJECTIVE

To make you conscious of word choice.

EXAMPLE

Fire

I see her in a red dress, a red bow in her hair. She would have on black shoes and white socks. The socks would be up to her knees. She would have been, say, five years old at the time the fire broke out. It would have still been dark; it would have been cold.

She would be in her room at the time.

She would have waked from a deep sleep as if pushed or shoved. She would have known what to do. She was that way, they tell me. She was that kind of child.

I see her leave her room, stand at the top of the stairs in the front hall, smell the smoke. She would be dressed; she put on her clothes when she climbed out of bed. When she smelled smoke she would scream a fire scream that would start at the base of her throat, pass through her lips in a howl. The howl would wake those in the rest of the house. It would curl through the rooms, ride the smoke that climbed the stairs, seep through doors, cloud the glass.

The man got up first and woke his wife. They heard the child's howl filled with smoke, and they raced to the cribs of the twins, they raced to their room. Flames licked the closed doors, climbed the walls.

The man and his wife crept down the back stairs. They heard the girl's scream but there was no way to reach her. There was no time. They did not want to leave the house, but they had to. While there was still time. They must save at all cost what they had in their arms. Each held one of the twins that they took from the cribs. The twins slept on. They slept a dead sleep, safe in the arms that held them.

I see her red dress. I see a red bow in her hair. She would be told she saved them all, and she would be glad. She would have scars on her face and arms. The scars would hurt. The fire would be with her through life.

She would see the red dress and the red bow in her dreams, the white socks up to her knees. In her dreams, she would stand at the top of the stairs in the front hall. She would smell smoke and start to howl. The scars would not have come yet, nor the pain.

ANNE BRASHLER, EDITOR, *STORYQUARTERLY*

The difference between the right word and the nearly right word is the same as that between lightning and the lightning bug.

MARK TWAIN

59

READING YOUR WORK ALOUD

John Updike says that the best way to get the kinks out of your prose is to read it aloud. Reading aloud what you have written reveals its flaws in the same way a magnifying glass reveals blemishes on your skin.

Keep in mind that the eye and ear are connected and that what the reader sees will somehow be transmitted to his inner ear. Too many sentences with a similar construction will make your reader yawn. You should always read your work aloud before showing it to anyone. Doing this will help you avoid monotony, repetition, flatness, unintentional alliteration, and other impediments to smooth, fluid prose.

The following passage from Mavis Gallant's story "The Four Seasons" is an example of prose that sings when read both silently and aloud. "The sea was greener than anything except Mrs. Unwin's emerald, bluer than her sapphire, more transparent than blue, white, transparent glass. Wading with a twin in each hand, she saw their six feet underwater like sea creatures. The sun became white as a stone; something stung in its heat, like fine, hard, invisible rain."

THE EXERCISE

Write a description in which the sentences are variously built. The subject should not always be the first word; some sentences should be longer than others. Read aloud the work of an author you admire and see how he or she accomplishes this. It's all right to imitate.

THE OBJECTIVE

Prose is both utilitarian and decorative. Unless you're deliberately reaching for a flat, monotonous tone, you should try for variation in the sound of your prose.

STUDENT EXAMPLE

In this part of the world winter strips the trees early. Close to the sea, to the bay, they turn gray in late October while the ground beneath them hardens, then freezes. The sky above the outer Cape is often cloudless and blue, blue the shade of Sandwich glass. The gentle hills frost over. The birds have fled. Hidden during summer months, vistas of dune and distant houses suddenly open out, as if a swath had been cut through lo-cust and maple and evergreen. You can see for miles. As for the wind, it's an almost constant companion, often blowing to hurricane speed, whistling through the house, cutting under sill and window pane, with a noise like that at sea; it can drive you mad.

JANET McINTYRE

In conversation you can use timing, a look, inflection, pauses. But on the page all you have is commas, dashes, the amount of syllables in a word. When I write I read everything out loud to get the right rhythm.

FRAN LEBOWITZ

VIII. A WRITER'S TOOLS

As we said in the introduction, to produce good fiction you have to think like a writer—be open, skeptical, curious, passionate, and forgiving. The other, equally important, requirement is to master the techniques of the craft and, not incidentally, get rid of bad habits.

What we call "tools" includes matters such as handling the problems of time and pace, bringing abstract ideas to life, learning to show and tell, mastering transitions, and naming everything from diners to dogs. Finally, we ask you to write badly—on purpose.

A few fortunate people who have never written anything seem to be able to sit down and write and make it sing; most of us, however, have to go through a long apprenticeship of trial and error. These exercises were designed to provide you with company along the way. The techniques you use over and over again—being as ruthless as the toughest editor—should take you from the uncertainty and disarray of a first draft to controlled and quite possibly exciting works of fiction.

60

HANDLING THE PROBLEMS
OF TIME AND PACE

from Robie Macauley

The traditional rule is that episodes meant to show important behavior in the characters, to make events dramatic as in theater, or to bring news that changes the situation should be dealt with in the scenic, or eyewitness, manner. Stretches of time or occurrences that are secondary to the story's development are handled by means of what is called a narrative bridge. Dialogue is the direct report of speech; indirect discourse is the summary of what was said. Some examples:

Scenic
Now they were at the ford, the rain was still falling, and the river was in flood. John got out of the jeep and stared at the white violence of the water they must cross to reach the place where the muddy road picked up again.

Narrative Summary
The journey to Punta Gorda took two days by near-impossible road. At one point, they had to cross a raging river and follow a muddy track that only a jeep could manage.

Dialogue
"Now how are we going to get across this monster?" Lisa asked.

"Easy," said John. "We take the rope over, get it around that big tree and use the winch to pull the jeep across."

"But who swims the flood with the rope?"

"Well, I can't swim," he said, "but you're supposed to be so good at it."

Indirect Discourse
When they came to the swollen river, John suggested that they put a rope across and then use the jeep's winch to pull the vehicle to the farther bank. Because Lisa had talked so often about her swimming ability, he suggested ironically that she be the one to take the rope over.

THE EXERCISE

Here are the events that might make a long short story. Write a scenario in which you indicate

- Where you would place a full scene or incidental scene.
- Where you would use summaries, either narrative summaries or summarized scenes and indirect discourse.

In her final year in medical school in the 1970s, Ellen fell in love with a young intern at the teaching hospital. His name was Gamal and he came from Lebanon. Although Gamal was not political himself, his younger brothers were involved in radical Arab politics.

Ellen's New England Jewish family had always been liberal. Her father, Mark, was a lawyer who had defended Black Panthers in the 1960s and antiwar activists in the 1970s. Her mother, Sarah, a writer, was equally liberal. They were both fervently pro-Israel.

When Ellen brought Gamal home for the winter holidays, the situation grew very tense as one by one, Israel, religion, politics, and child-rearing practices seemed to crop up in their conversations. Although Ellen was uncomfortable at times, she felt that love was more important than politics.

Mark and Sarah were meticulously polite and tolerant in Gamal's company, but they worried in private. They'd always supported Ellen's decisions, but now, they thought, she was about to ruin her life.

The wedding was set for June at the parents' house in Connecticut. It would be a small affair because relatives on both sides would refuse to come. But Mark and Sarah rationalized a lot and put the very best face on it.

The day came. Everything was ready. There was going to be a civil ceremony—a compromise—and then a garden party at Ellen's home.

When Mark got up that morning, he turned on the television news. The lead story was about the bombing and destruction of a TWA plane in Greece by terrorists. Gamal's two brothers had been arrested as prime suspects. Mark and Sarah confronted Ellen and Gamal.

Now you resolve the story.

THE OBJECTIVE

To learn to identify which parts of a story should be presented in a scene and which parts of a story should be summarized. To develop an understanding of pace.

61

SHOW AND TELL: THERE'S A REASON IT'S CALLED STORYTELLING

from Carol-Lynn Marrazzo

Flannery O'Connor observed that "fiction writing is very seldom a matter of saying things; it is a matter of showing things." In other words "show don't tell." There is a difference, however, between "saying" and "telling" and the wise writer is not afraid to tell. As the following story excerpts illustrate, O'Connor and other fine writers blend telling and showing in their stories and novels—and for good reason. When a writer depends solely on showing and neglects the narrative that artfully shapes, characterizes, qualifies, or in some other way informs the character's actions, the reader is abandoned to extrapolate meaning based upon what is observed—for example, a character's sweating palms or nervous twitch—and the reader then, rather than the writer, creates the story.

Contrary to what you may think or have been led to believe, writers tell their stories and even O'Connor tells plenty. In "Good Country People," the main character, Joy, a cripple and self-cultivated cynic, is transformed by a moment of vulnerability with a Bible salesman. O'Connor shows the action, but tells Joy's transformation. In this and examples that follow, first read the plain text, then read the complete passage including the narrative in italics.

She sat staring at him. *There was nothing about her face or her round freezing-blue eyes to indicate that this had moved her; but she felt as if her heart had stopped and left her mind to pump her blood. She decided that for the first time in her life she was face to face with real innocence. This boy, with an instinct that came from beyond wisdom, had touched the truth about her.* When after a minute, she said in a hoarse high voice, "All right," *it was like surrendering to him completely. It was like losing her own life and finding it again, miraculously, in his.*

Very gently he began to roll the slack leg up.

The sentence that begins "There was nothing" explains why the "show, don't tell" rule so often fails. We are told that we cannot know through observation alone what is happening within Joy. If you are unconvinced, read just the showing alone again. Ask: Is there any indication Joy has changed? In this passage, telling not only heightens the moment, it reveals it is a moment of rapture.

164

"Good Country People" and other stories prove that a complementary interplay between telling and showing at the transforming moment in the story is often crucial to the reader's understanding. Here is a key passage from Eudora Welty's "Livvie is Back." This is the story of a girl married to a sickly old man named Solomon. When Livvie holds and kisses Cash, a young laborer, Welty tells the reader exactly what Livvie realizes about herself and marriage.

> She gathered the folds of his coat behind him and fastened her red lips to his mouth, and *she was dazzled at herself then, the way he had been dazzled at himself to begin with. In that instant she felt something that could not be told—that Solomon's death was at hand, that he was the same to her as if he were dead now.* She cried out, and uttering little cries, turned and ran for the house.

Here the reader is told Livvie's thoughts and feelings about Solomon—"that he was the same to her as if he were dead." Welty chose not to leave the moment to showing alone.

Another quick example. In Jane Smiley's story "Lily," Smiley tells in one word what Lily experiences when she betrays her good friend:

> Lily broke into a sweat the moment she stopped speaking, *a sweat of instant regret.*

Lily's response is characterized as "regret." The whole story would be changed if Lily reacted with a "sweat of" confusion or triumph.

There is nothing economical or reticent about James Joyce's telling in "The Dead" during Gabriel's epiphany, the moment when he internalizes that all with his wife is not as he thought—she was loved once by a boy, a love Gabriel knew nothing about. The physical manifestations of Gabriel's new awareness are, in contrast, quite modest.

> "He is dead," she said at length. "He died when he was only seventeen. Isn't it a terrible thing to die so young as that?"
> "What was he?" asked Gabriel, *still ironically.*
> "He was in the gasworks," she said.
> *Gabriel felt humiliated by the failure of his irony and by the evocation of this figure from the dead, a boy in the gasworks. While he had been full of memories of their secret life together, full of tenderness and joy and desire, she had been comparing him in her mind with another. A shameful consciousness of his own person assailed him. He saw himself as a ludicrous figure, acting as a pennyboy for his aunts, a nervous well-meaning sentimentalist, orating to vulgarians and idealizing his own clownish lusts, the pitiable fatuous fellow he had caught a glimpse of in the mirror. Instinctively* he turned his back more to the light *lest she might see the shame that burned upon his forehead.*
> *He tried to keep his tone of cold interrogation but* his voice when he spoke was humble and indifferent.

Telling is also used to good effect in Amy Hempel's Story "In The Cemetery Where Al Jolson Is Buried," in which the first person narrator is visiting a dying friend in the hospital. Hempel writes:

"I have to go home," I said when she woke up.

She thought I meant home to her house in the Canyon, and I had to say No, *home* home. *I twisted my hands in the time-honored fashion of people in pain. I was supposed to offer something. The Best Friend. I could not even offer to come back.*

I felt weak and small and failed.

Also exhilarated.

Hempel's narrator tells exactly how she feels—conflicted.

A wonderful example of balanced and complementary interplay between showing and telling is the transforming movement in Peter Taylor's "The Gift of the Prodigal." In order to appreciate how remarkable the telling is, first read only those portions of the passage that are NOT italicized.

I say to myself, "He really is like something not quite human. For all the jams and scrapes he's been in, he's never suffered any second thoughts or known the meaning of remorse. I ought to have let him hang," I say to myself, "by his own beautiful locks."

But almost simultaneously what I hear myself saying aloud is "Please don't go, Rick. Don't go yet, son." *Yes, I am pleading with him, and I mean what I say with my whole heart.* He still has his right hand on the doorknob and has given it a full turn. Our eyes meet across the room, *directly, as they never have before in the whole of Ricky's life or mine. I think neither of us could tell anyone what it is he sees in the other's eyes, unless it is a need beyond any description either of us is capable of.*

Presently Rick says, "You don't need to hear my crap."

And I hear my *bewildered* voice saying, "I do . . . I do." And "Don't go, Rick, my boy." My eyes have *even* misted over. But I still meet his eyes across the *now too silent room.* He looks at me *in the most compassionate way imaginable. I don't think any child of mine has ever looked at me so before. Or perhaps it isn't really with compassion as he is viewing me but with the sudden, gratifying knowledge that it is not, after all, such a one-sided business, the business between us.* He keeps his right hand on the doorknob a few seconds longer. Then I hear the latch click and *know he has let go.* Meanwhile, I observe his left hand making that *familiar gesture,* his fingers splayed, his hand tilting back and forth. I am out of my chair now. I go to the desk and bring out two Danlys cigars from another desk drawer, which I keep locked. He is there *ready to receive my offering when I turn around.* He accepts the cigar without smiling, and I give it without smiling, too.

Now ask: If only the "showing" portion of this passage were available, would a reader have any idea what subtle understanding has transpired between father and son? Study the passage carefully and observe Taylor's strategy as he grounds the passage through the father's keen senses (showing) and at the same time gives the reader access to the father's most intimate thoughts (telling)—all while the action keeps moving forward.

THE EXERCISE

Choose a story in which you think the transforming moment is effectively rendered. Underline the telling portions of that moment and read the passage without the underlined portions. Do this for a number of stories.

Then, turn to a story draft of your own in which you think the transforming moment is not yet effectively rendered. Underline the telling portions of that moment. If you have no "telling," add some, but try to balance the showing and telling to their best combined effect. If it seems impossible to tell anything, then you might not know your characters well or know what your story is about.

THE OBJECTIVE

To be able to both show and tell. To experiment with different combinations of showing and telling to enhance your narrative technique and to illuminate the final meaning of your story.

STUDENT EXAMPLE

Peter pointed at both Caro and me. "You know, he gave so much, and it's like we all wanted to punish him when he wasn't perfect. I forgave him his faults a long time ago and I only wish you two had done the same."

Caroline stabbed out her cigarette. "Okay, I admit I was a shit."

"I guess you were, considering he did pay for your school and all your clothes," Peter said.

I bit my lip to stop it trembling, but I couldn't keep my eyes from filling up. *I had wanted perfection and when my parents hadn't fit the bill, I had turned to Mike, then lost faith in him when he hadn't measured up. Mike had never betrayed me, he had just done the best he could.* His bookshelves were dark, implacable; *they watched me, and I thought of the night I found the photographs—a night a confused child had carried into foolish adulthood.*

I stood up and said I was going outside. I followed the sound of voices. Everyone was still gathered around the water garden. I sat in one of the iron chairs that faced the reflecting pool. Around me, the trees we planted years ago had matured and *I thought about Colin at the airport, saying it really is a short life. Suddenly, I wanted a part of him and* fished around in my purse for his ring. It glinted red in the sun and as I slipped it on my finger, I caught my father's wavering reflection in the water. I turned. *I hadn't really looked at him in a long time.* He was standing alone by the sundial, one hand relaxed in his pocket, the other bringing a cigarette to his lips. *It had been good of him to come, I realized.* He noticed me watching and motioned for me to join him. He was tentative, but *I could see he really wanted to know about my studies, about the Viking Adventure exhibit, about me.*

I've heard that once you have children, you always love them. No matter what you do, no matter what they do. You can't help it. There's always something there. I thought about that when I suggested he might visit Colin and me in Ireland and my father put his arm around me and said he'd come anytime, all I had to do was say the word.

MARYANNE O'HARA, FROM "THE WATER GARDEN"

62

THE POWER OF "SEEMED" AND "PROBABLY"

New writers often think that they have to go into the heads of all their characters in order for the reader to know what they are thinking. They forget that people can reveal themselves in a myriad of ways: dialogue, body language, and so forth. They also forget that in reality no one has access to another person's thoughts and that, in addition to listening to what those close to us say and observing how they act, we are constantly assuming, suspecting, projecting, and imagining what they think.

Learn to give your characters (especially the point-of-view character) the same imagination that you have. An example of this occurs in a Bartholomew Gill mystery novel, *McGarr and the Politician's Wife*. The entire plot turns on the word *seemed*. A man, Ovens, has a head injury and is lying in a coma. The detective goes to see him and needs to know if he might have just fallen or if there was foul play. He asks the doctor if Ovens can speak and the doctor says not for another forty-eight hours.

The author writes, "Ovens' eyes, however, seemed to contradict the assessment of the insouciant young doctor. Dark brown, almost black, they told McGarr that Ovens knew the score: that his was not merely a medical problem that a favorable prognosis could eliminate, that whoever had done this to him had a very good reason, and those eyes, suddenly seeming very old, realized his troubles weren't over." So McGarr doesn't have to wait forty-eight hours. He starts his investigation immediately.

Ann Beattie's use of the word *probably* in her story "Afloat" indicates that the story is not third person from the point of view of the 16-year-old child who is introduced at the beginning of the story. Beattie writes, "When she was a little girl she would stand on the metal table pushed to the front of the deck and read the letters aloud to her father. If he sat, she sat. Later, she read them over his shoulder. Now she is sixteen, and she gives him the letter and stares at the trees or the water or the boat bobbing at the end of the dock. It has probably never occurred to her that she does not have to be there when he reads them." The "probably" is a clue that someone else is making this conjecture. Sentences later, after the letter is presented, the first person narrator comes in with "he hands the letter to me, and then pours club soda and Chablis into a tall glass for Annie and fills his own glass with wine alone."

THE EXERCISE

Write a scene that involves two characters. Now allow the point of view character to suspect or imagine what the other character might be thinking. Or have your point of view character imagine something that is probably true.

THE OBJECTIVE

To show how your characters can use their imaginations to interpret the behavior and dialogue of other characters.

STUDENT EXAMPLES

She *probably* expects me to keep on mowing her lawn and trimming her hedge all summer even though I told her there was no way that dog and me were going to be friends. She *probably* thinks it's something we can work out, me and the dog, like I got time for throw and fetch.

JACK NEISSEN

Benny *seemed* uneasy about leaving her right after their fight, packing his duffle slowly, two things in and one thing back out, and Darl appreciated this, but she had a whole weekend of plans made—repainting their bedroom anything but black and packing up and dragging his collection of beer cans down to their storage bin somewhere in the basement. Might as well not make up before the next fight.

PATTY SINCLAIR

She *probably* has no idea her son's the one stealing people's spare tires, and I sure ain't going to tell her unless he hits me twice in one year. I figure the neighborhood owes it to her—her husband a cop shot down in the line of duty.

JOHN SANTINO

63

BRINGING ABSTRACT IDEAS TO LIFE

One of the principal problems in writing stories is to make abstract ideas come to life. It is not enough to talk of poverty or ambition or evil, you must render these ideas in a concrete way with descriptive sensory details, similes, and metaphors. Examine how growing old is handled in Muriel Spark's *Memento Mori*, poverty in Charles Dickens's *Bleak House* and Carolyn Chute's *The Beans of Egypt Maine*, racism in Ralph Ellison's *Invisible Man*, growing up in Frank Conroy's *Stop-Time*, ambition in Theodore Dreiser's *An American Tragedy*, and evil in William Golding's *Lord of the Flies*.

THE EXERCISE

Make several of the following abstractions come to life by rendering them in concrete specific details or images.

racism	poverty
injustice	growing up
ambition	sexual deceit
growing old	wealth
salvation	evil

THE OBJECTIVE

To learn to think, always, in concrete terms. To realize that the concrete is more persuasive than any high-flown rhetoric full of fancy words and abstractions.

STUDENT EXAMPLES

Racism

not sitting next to a minority person on the subway

SANFORD GOLDEN

referring to others as "you people"

FRED PELKA

Poverty

checking for change in the telephone booth

SANFORD GOLDEN

a young boy carrying water to an abandoned building where his family is living

MOLLY LANZAROTTA

Sexual deceit

splashing on Brut to cover the smell of a woman's perfume

SANFORD GOLDEN

keeping a pair of clean underwear in your pocketbook

SUSAN HIGGINS

Growing old

not making it across street before light flashes "Don't Walk"

SANFORD GOLDEN

the stairs become a place of treachery

JIM MEZZANOTTE

Evil

"Let's sell tickets to the rape."

FRED PELKA

purposely running down animals on the road

SANDY YANNONE

Prejudice

Victoria slipped the camphor between her skin and her undershirt before opening the library door. Her mother made her wear it from Rosh Hashanah to Passover, a guard against winter colds. "In Poland it was colder," she always said, "yet we never got sick in the winter." It was useless for Victoria to point out that one aunt and uncle had died in Polish winters despite their health charms.

She placed her bag of books on the library's high stone counter where "Returns" was written in a beautiful penmanship. "I hope you didn't tear any of these," Mrs. Holmes said, pausing in her friendly chat with a woman who looked like Betty Crocker. One by one she checked in the ragged copies of kids' classics saying that sometimes it looked as if Victoria had eaten her dinner on these books. She smiled to the woman. "Everything turns into rags in their hands, you know."

Victoria went to sit in the children's section of the library. Three new books were displayed on the table. She might get through by closing time. She knew Mrs. Holmes wouldn't let her take out these books till yellow tape obscured some of the words. She wondered if it might make a difference if Mrs. Holmes knew that she was the best reader in the whole fifth grade.

BARBARA SOFER

64

TRANSPORTATION: GETTING THERE ISN'T HALF THE FUN—IT'S BORING

This isn't strictly an exercise: It's more of a reminder. When moving characters from one place to another write about how they got there only if it's crucial. Think of the movies—rarely do we see a character on a bus or in a train *unless the trip itself tells us something we absolutely need to know about the story or the character.* The lovers are in bed; next thing we see they're in a little bistro, smooching over a glass of Pernod. Who cares how they got from bed to bistro? Avoid stairs, sidewalks, subways, planes, trains, and automobiles if you can tell your story as completely without them.

A short story is like a flare sent into the sky. Suddenly and startlingly, it illuminates one portion of the world and the lives of a few people who are caught in its glare. The light is brief, intense, and contrasts are likely to be dramatic. Then it fades quickly and is gone. But, if it is worth its moment of brilliance, it will leave an afterimage in the mind's eye of the beholder.

ROBIE MACAULEY

65

NAMING THE DINER, NAMING THE DIET, NAMING THE DOG

In an earlier exercise, "Naming Your Characters" (p. 58), you learned how to choose a character's name with care and respect for the essence of that character.

Likewise, during the course of writing stories set in counties and towns with restaurants and mortuaries, stories in which characters play in rock bands, buy race horses, play on football teams, or found new religions, you are going to have to name it all. Think of William Faulkner's Yoknapatawpha County, Thomas Hardy's Wessex, Willa Cather's Red Cloud, Marilynne Robinson's Fingerbone Lake, Anne Tyler's Homesick Restaurant and travel guide series, *The Accidental Tourist,* and Oscar Hijuelos's Mambo Kings. Names matter.

THE EXERCISE

In your notebook, keep a list of unusual names for potential characters. In fact, every writer should have a collection of old yearbooks, benefit programs, phone books, and so forth to browse through when he needs to name a character. And don't stop there. Keep lists for things you might need to name sometime in a story. Remember that tone is important, so when naming the following things choose an earnest name and a farcical one.

Name the following things. Imagine stories they might go in.

a desert town	a football team
a race horse	a diner
a literary magazine	a new religion
a new disease	a new planet
a rock band	a polluted river
a summer cottage	a poetry collection
triplets	a chihuahua
a liqueur	a burglar
a beauty salon	a bar
a new diet	a lipstick color
a soap opera	a yacht

THE OBJECTIVE

To loosen up your imagination by naming things you wouldn't ordinarily have to name—never mind "own."

STUDENT EXAMPLES

Clearly, the students had more fun with the farcical names.

Desert town
Drymouth   NOREN CACERES

Racehorse
Running Scared   CHRISTY VELADOTA
Windpasser   SAM HALPERT
Race Elements   JAY GREENBERG

Literary magazine
Listen   GREG DUYCK

New disease
Afluenza   MOLLY LANZAROTTA

Rock band
Wake-up call   GREG DUYCK

Summer cottage
Bric-a-brac   KARLA HORNER

Triplets
Holt, Rinehart, and Winston   ROBERT WERNER

Liqueur
Velvet Elvis   MOLLY LANZAROTTA

Beauty salon
Tressed for Success   E. J. GRAFF

Diner
Crisco   DAVID ZIMMERMAN

New religion
People of the Tree   KARLA HORNER

Planet
Pica   DAWN BAKER

Polluted river
Floop River   DANIEL BIGMAN
Fever Stream   SANDY YANNONE

Chihuahua
Bruno's Lunch   KAREN BROCK

Burglar
Nick Spieze   GREG DUYCK

Diet
Body Carpenter   DAVID ZIMMERMAN
The Remote Control Diet   SANDY YANNONE

Soap opera
On Borrowed Time   JAY GREENBERG
The Rammed and the Damned
(on cable T. V.)   SANFORD GOLDEN

Lipstick
Screaming Salsa   EVE BAKER

Yacht
Waves Goodbye   MOLLY LANZAROTTA

66

TRANSITIONS: OR WHITE SPACE DOES NOT A TRANSITION MAKE

Often in the course of a story or novel you need a transition to indicate a flashback, a movement in time, a movement in space, or a movement from scene to narrative summary. Many writers have trouble with transitions. They either treat them too elaborately so that they jar the reader out of what Gardner calls "the vivid and continuous fictional dream," or they ignore them altogether and use white space to indicate that some shift has occurred. In either case, writers neglect the very medium they are using—language—to do it for them, and do it gracefully.

Here's Ray Carver, in "Where I'm Calling From," moving from the present to the past:

> ". . . If, if you ask for it and if you listen. End of Sermon. But don't forget. If," he says again. Then he hitches his pants and tugs his sweater down. "I'm going inside," he says. "See you at lunch." "I feel like a bug when he's around," J. P. says. "He makes me feel like a bug. Something you could step on." J. P. shakes his head. Then he says, "Jack London. What a name. I wish I had me a name like that. Instead of the name I got."

WHITE SPACE

> Frank Martin talked about that "if" the first time I was here.

Notice how Carver not only uses "first time I was here" to indicate that there has been a shift, but he also reuses the "if" to make it graceful. Here's another example from the same story where Carver moves from past to the present *without* white space:

> Then I noticed a bunch of us were leaning over Tiny, just looking at him, not able to take our eyes off him. "Give him air!" Frank Martin said. Then he ran into the office and called the ambulance.
> Tiny is on board again today. Talk about bouncing back.

Notice how he brings us back to the present with the word "today" tucked into the sentence that focuses on Tiny's return.

Robert Taylor, Jr., in his story "Colorado," signals a movement from scene to narrative summary with white space, but he doesn't neglect language:

I want to go right away, said Janie.

WHITE SPACE

Want, Want, Want. Was there ever a family with so many wants.

In Alice Munro's "Differently," there is a time shift after a woman lies to her babysitter:

> "My car wouldn't start," she told the babysitter, a grandmother from down the street. "I walked all the way home. It was lovely, walking. Lovely. I enjoyed it so much."
> Her hair was wild, her lips were swollen, her clothes were full of sand.

WHITE SPACE

Her life filled up with such lies.

In the same story, the narrator moves from remembering the past with her ex-husband, Ben, to the present scene with Raymond by using white space *and* language:

> People make momentous shifts, but not the changes they imagine.

WHITE SPACE

> Just the same, Georgia knows that her remorse about the way she changed her life is dishonest.

Sometimes it is more efficient to use phrases to indicate a shift in time or place. Here are several phrases that Carver uses in his story "Fever": "all summer, since early June," "In the beginning," "in the livingroom," "That evening, after he'd put the children to bed," "After he'd hung up," "After Eileen had left," "This was the period when," "Just before the incident with Debbie," "Over the summer," "But a few hours later," Once, earlier in the summer," "The next morning," "In a little while," "For the first time in months," "During first-period art-history," "In his next class," "As he moved down the lunch line in the faculty dining room," "That afternoon," "That evening," "It was the middle of the fall term," and "The next time he awoke." All of these phrases are used to move the story along in space and time. Note how the school day is gracefully moved along from "first period art-history" to "next class" to "the lunch line."

THE EXERCISE

Turn to a third or fourth draft of a story and examine your transitions. Is what is happening clear? Do your transitions employ language or are you depending on white space and your reader's imagination? Do your transitions gracefully connect the sections being bridged? Now rewrite your transitions, using language as a bridge to lead the reader from here to there to there.

THE OBJECTIVE

To be able to lead the reader gracefully over and around unnecessary parts of the story and to bridge skillfully the shifts in time, memory, and space.

STUDENT EXAMPLE

BEFORE: Her voice was soft. "I don't suppose she drives a pickup truck."

WHITE SPACE

At Brady Pontiac, I park in front of the showroom window, which displays a banner that reads, No Credit? No problem!

AFTER: Her voice was soft. "I suppose she was the reason for all those deliveries."

WHITE SPACE

I can see my mother in a different light now. Back then, I couldn't see anyone else's hurt—otherwise, I would have had to face my own. I suppose that's typical of adolescents. Brady Pontiac's spotlights shine through the beginning snow and I pull in, parking in front of the showroom window. I'm still feeling curiously distanced. A banner stretching across the window reads, No Credit? No Problem! Typical.

BEFORE: I lean over and lay my ear against the quick rise and fall of his back. I am struck by how fragile life is, and how responsible I am for his.

WHITE SPACE

When I was growing up, my father sold pacemakers and pumps for Bohran & Capley Medical Supply.

AFTER: I lean over and lay my ear against the quick rise and fall of his back. I am struck by how fragile life is, and how responsible I am for his.

WHITE SPACE

Alex is lucky. I don't think anyone ever felt particularly responsible for my life. When I was growing up, my father sold pacemakers and pumps for Bohran & Capley Medical Supply.

MARYANNE O'HARA, FROM "THE GHOST CHILD"

67

THE JOURNEY OF
THE LONG SENTENCE

The following exercise came from a conversation with the poet Richard Jackson, who uses exercises and always does each exercise with his students. He tells his class to write a poem that is one sentence long. He says the sentence should keep pushing and gain momentum. Even in the midst of suspension and qualification, the sentence has to move forward—not just repeating—but adding new information and achieving new emotional levels to finish on a different emotional note at the end. He says that what goes along with this assignment is the assumption that the sentence should radiate out (beyond the concerns of the mere lyric self, or the narrator or story per se) to embrace more of the world, of the complications surrounding details and events and observations and feelings. Then the details become a part of an intricate set of relationships, giving and taking from that set.

Below is the poem, printed with permission without its line breaks from *Alive All Day*, that Jackson wrote for this exercise:

THE OTHER DAY

I just want to say a few words about the other day, an ordinary day I happen to recall because my daughter has just given me a yellow flower, a buttercup, for no reason, though it was important that other day, that ordinary one when the stones stayed stones and were not symbols for anything else, when the stars made no effort to fill the spaces we see between them, though maybe you remember it differently, a morning when I woke to find my hand had flowered on the breast of my wife, a day so ordinary I happened to notice the old woman across the street, hips so large it's useless to try to describe them, struggle off her sofa to pull down the shade that has separated us ever since, her room as lonely as Keats' room on the Piazza di Spagna where there was hardly any space for words, where I snapped a forbidden photo that later showed nothing of his shadow making its way to a window above Bernini's fountain, a shadow that hesitated as if to open one of Fanny Brawne's letters before deciding to take them to the grave unread, who knew how little his own death must mean to the boys playing in the Piazza below, a shadow that I later understood as my own, indecipherable, but I just wanted to tell you about that other day, the ordinary one, when the drunk turned over under the local papers beneath a bush in the park, when another in a T-shirt, tatooed, picked up the paper to check the lottery number, then put it down, secure it was just another ordinary day, that happy day in which nothing left my shadow, that sorrowful day in which nothing entered, while I took my mother to the clinic at noon to burn away the spot on her lungs not nearly as large as the one Keats fought, walked along the river alone, bought broccoli for my favorite soup, and good wine, hummed a pitiful song unconsciously, on that day when a few million cells in each living thing died and were replaced perfectly, when I wrote a few words, crossed them out, wrote others, that day, I can tell you now, when someone left a bunch of yellow flowers, buttercups, on a grave of a nameless child burned forty years ago in a circus fire, leaving also the child's name, Sarah, which is why I remember that other day, because it seems if her story could be known thousands of other ordinary days that belonged to her might also be known, and I could tell my daughter why I have this sudden desire to weep all day, why I weep for the names of the dead continuing, Samir Sayah, 16, shot in the stomach by soldiers, Amyad Nafea, 18, shot in the chest by soldiers the moment, perhaps my cat scratched the door, while the cicadas began their afternoon thrumming on that ordinary day where I found myself powerless and guilty once again, a day so ordinary the descendents of the very lice that bothered Christ began their work in the hair of the boy trying to outrun the soldiers, an ordinary day, yes, when it was not so impossible to go looking for the dead, though I must say that of all the deaths that inhabit me the one the other day was the least noticed lately, so small that I imagined myself alive all day, holding a yellow flower, just one, just to remember, a day I can almost forget except for its likeness to today, a day I must call ordinary because if it is not so ordinary then Christ, we are pitiful for our poor laments, the deaths so small we must imagine ourselves alive all day.

The opening paragraph of William Kennedy's *Quinn's Book* is one long wonderful sentence:

I, Daniel Quinn, neither the first nor the last of a line of such Quinns, set eyes on Maud the wondrous on a late December day in 1849 on the banks of the river of aristocrats and paupers, just as the great courtesan, Magdelena Colón, also known as La Última, a woman whose presence turned men into spitting, masturbating pigs, boarded a skiff to carry her across the river's icy waters from Albany to Greenbush, her first stop en route to the city of Troy, a community of iron, where later that evening she was scheduled to enact, yet again, her role as the lascivious Lais, that fabled prostitute who spurned Demosthenes' gold and yielded without fee to Diogenes, the virtuous, impecunious tub dweller.

For other examples of long sentences intrinsic to a writer's style, turn to the work of William Faulkner, Henry James, Julio Cortazar, and Marcel Proust, all of whom wanted to explore and express continuing action with qualification and complication. Jamaica Kincaid's story "Girl," on page 296, is all one sentence.

THE EXERCISE

Begin a story with a long sentence that follows the directions that Richard Jackson gives his class. Or write a short short story that is only one sentence long.

THE OBJECTIVE

To develop a sense of how syntax can qualify, develop, and provide an expansive context for our observations in much the same way the brain does, finding a linear order for what are often simultaneous aspects of an observation.

STUDENT STORY

Molly Lanzarotta's short short story "One Day Walk Through the Front Door" received honorable mention in the World's Best Short Short Story Contest of 1992.

One Day Walk Through the Front Door

It got so the only place I could cry was the freeway since traffic jams and the absence of curves made driving and crying less dangerous, unlike surface streets which scattered the pile of flyers on the passenger seat, jumbling the printed images of my sister's face and frightening me beyond tears with the sight of a life slipping out of reach as I pulled into gas stations, cafés, rest stops, a mad woman slapping flyers on walls, in people's faces, blurting *Have you seen her?* . . . until soon I only made calls from phone booths, avoiding the empty apartment I shared with her, talking to police, friends, reporters, even giving phone interviews so sometimes it was my own voice on the news as I drove, *I just hope she's safe, I want her home,* other times my voice shouted back at the radio, *say her name, don't drop the story, oh Jesus, please,* then I'd cry more and believe how alone I felt, surrounded by hundreds of people encased in tinted-glass worlds that could neatly hide any individual horror, until I could only whisper, *please even just her body,* because I had to know or I'd be stranded in this moment forever and I'd never sleep again, but wait, always wait to see her one day just walk through the front door . . . then, finally, my last hope was to hear it from our priest, but it was the car, detached reporting from that radio on the fifth day: they'd found a body, floating in the bay.

MOLLY LANZAROTTA

68

TITLES AND KEYS

A title is the first thing a reader encounters, and the first clue to both initial meaning and final meaning of the story. Look back to the sentences in the exercise "First Sentences." Notice how many first lines play off the title of the story.

Titles can also be a way of finding stories. Blaise Cendrars once said in an interview, "I first find a title. I generally find pretty good titles, people envy me for them and not only envy me but quite a few writers come to see me to ask for a title."

And until your book is in galleys, you can still change the title. Below are the titles of some famous novels, along with their original titles.

War and Peace—All's Well That Ends Well, by Leo Tolstoy
Lady Chatterley's Lover—Tenderness, by D. H. Lawrence
The Sound and the Fury—Twilight, by William Faulkner
The Great Gatsby—Hurrah for the Red, White and Blue, by F. Scott Fitzgerald
The Sun Also Rises—Fiesta, by Ernest Hemingway

New York Magazine has published a competition for many years. One example is a game in which you were asked to change some famous (and successful) title just enough to make it a loser rather than a winner. The difference between the true ring of the real title and the false note of the parody suggests how good titles are the ultimate test of the exact word, *le mot juste.* Here are some examples.

A Walk on the Wild Side, by Nelson Algren: *A Hike Through Some Dangerous Areas*
One Hundred Years of Solitude, by Gabriel García Márquez: *A Very Long Time Alone*
Girls of Slender Means, by Muriel Spark: *Minimal-Income Young Women*
The Naked and the Dead, by Norman Mailer: *The Nude and the Deceased*
A Farewell to Arms, by Ernest Hemingway: *A Good-bye to War*

The best titles convey some immediate picture or concept to the reader and they do it with an exciting, tantalizing juxtaposition of words.

Finding the ideal title might take time—and effort. Ernest Hemingway says, "I make a list of titles after I've finished the story or the book—sometimes as many as a hundred. Then I start eliminating them, sometimes all of them."

THE EXERCISE

Part I

Have a place in your writer's notebook where you play around with titles and start a list of possibilities for future stories.

Part II

When you need a title for a new story or novel, make a list of possible titles from inside the story and from just thinking about the story. (Try for a hundred.) Then start eliminating titles you know you won't use and see what is left. Chances are that the title you choose will not be the first one that occurred to you or the "working" title of the story.

THE OBJECTIVE

To learn how titles can lead you to stories and to sharpen your instincts for a good title.

STUDENT EXAMPLES

Restaurant Thanksgiving
Company Time   ANNE SPALEK

False Starts   JONATHAN KLEIN

Sunday Funnies   ELLEN TARLIN

For Your Own Good
In Place and On Time   THERESA GOMEZ

This Silence Between Songs
        FRANK BACH, FROM "CURES," A POEM BY DAVID RIVARD

The Nights Take Care of Themselves
        LAINA JAMES, FROM "THE SATISFACTION COAL COMPANY,"
                                   A POEM BY RITA DOVE

Below is the list of titles Ellen Tarlin compiled for a story. Note how one title leads to another, and how "Throwing Things Out" leads to "The Things You Keep" which became the title of Ellen's story, which was published in the *Santa Clara Review.*

Titles I pulled out of the text	*Titles I pulled out of my head*
1. Out There	1. Locking Yourself In
2. Nobody Notices	2. Locked Up
3. Disappointment	3. Locked In
4. Everything You Own Out the Window	4. Alone in His Room

5. Alone in His Room
   for Three Days
6. Three Days Now
7. Man of the House Now
8. Alone in his Room
9. His Sartre and Nietzsche

10. Everything Out
    the Window
11. He Didn't Throw
    the Furniture
12. Through the Window

13. STP
14. Off the Record
15. Six Hundred Records
16. Family Album
17. Back Story
18. Come Home
19. Aeschylus, Euripides
    and Peter Brady
20. The Lost Weekend
21. The Tossed Weekend
    (I actually sent it out
    to someone with this
    title! Yuk!)
22. Hungry
23. Unbearably Hungry
24. How Deranged Do You
    Have to Be?
25. Not Deranged Enough
26. Too Much Competition
    in New York
27. Ghost of Someone's
    Tragedy
28. Throw Everything Away
29. Another Drunken Episode
31. Begrudged Insanity
32. The World Should
    Come to Him
33. Three Days Worth of
    Red Hairs
34. Reel Grease

5. Throwing Things Out

6. Out the Window
7. Tony Treadwell
8. Here's the Story
9. Nobody Notices (this was my
   second choice—I used this title
   for a while)
10. Throwing Things Away

11. Throwing Things Out

12. The Things You Keep (this is
    the title of the final published
    story)
13. The Things You Hold Onto
14. The Things You Throw Away
15. The Things You Get Rid Of
16. Throwaways
17. A Throwaway
18. Tossed Out
19. Out of It

20. Staying In
21. Going Out

22. Coming Out
23. Staying Away
24. Staying Home

25. Out the Window
26. Not Crazy Enough

27. Who He Is

28. Tony
29. Tony's Father
31. American Family
32. Dorm Life

33. Life of a Student

34. Here's the Story of the
    Treadwell Family

35. Crazy in New York   35. Reaching Out
    (title of the rough draft)
36. Not Crazy in New York   36. Reaching In
37. Off the Record
38. Pigeon Man

Writing is a hard way to make a living, but a good way to make a life.

DORIS BETTS

69

WRITING BADLY—ON PURPOSE

from Bridget Mazur

Some people think that the more you learn about writing, the easier it is to write. Actually, the opposite is probably true. It's easy to write when no one's warned you about pitfalls like the Passive Voice or the dreaded Dialogue-Done-in-Confounding-Dialect or the Cliché. A writer who is consciously trying to sustain a particular point of view, avoid "adjective overload," and write good, clean prose all at the same time is a writer who may find herself staring in despair at a blank piece of paper or computer screen.

In his essay "Writing in the Cold," Ted Solotaroff describes one of the writer's most "fundamental" and "enabling" rights—". . . the right to write uncertainly, roughly and even badly. A garden in the early stage is not a compelling place: it's a lot of arduous, messy noisome work—digging up the hard ground, putting in the fertilizer, then the seeds and seedlings." And remember, Ernest Hemingway said, "The first draft of anything is shit." For writers too frightened by the list of literary pitfalls to commit a single thing to paper, these are helpful reminders. What if you do slip into the passive voice? What if you do let an uneducated character use a five-syllable word? What if you mix a metaphor or concoct a run-on sentence? That's what early drafts are for: you need to write the story out to see what you have story-wise, and what you need to fix.

The truth is, writing badly can be fun, especially if you know better. It's like kicking off those cruel siletto heels you've been wearing and donning a pair of really ugly, comfortable slippers. Go ahead—try it. Your feet—and your muse—will thank you.

THE EXERCISE

Part I

Begin a story or scene you've thought about before, but give yourself permission to write badly. In fact, try to write badly, violating "rules" of style and fiction as they occur to you: use clichés, dangle those modifiers, mix those metaphors, and haphazardly shift point of view.

Part II

Exchange stories with another writer doing the same exercise. Then correct the errors each of you has made.

THE OBJECTIVE

To send that Horribly Tedious Internal Editor (who comes alive inside most writers the minute they sit down to write) out for a drive so you can exercise your right "to write uncertainly, roughly, even badly." You probably won't write as badly as you think—you might even be surprised at how good some of your writing instincts are, even when you are trying to write badly.

The second part of this exercise gives the Horribly Tedious Internal Editor in you something to do so she doesn't feel left out. Also, because of the humorous writing this exercise tends to produce (intentionally or unintentionally), it's fun to share with your writing friends.

IX. INVENTION AND TRANSFORMATION

"Invention and Transformation" could have been the title of this book. All writing is either inventing something new or a new way of saying something familiar, or transforming what is there into how it is there individually for each writer.

But because "Invention and Transformation" isn't the title, we are using it as a sort of catchall for exercises that didn't fit into a more specific category such as dialogue—exercises that defied categorization. For example, the last exercise in this part, "The Terrain of Your Stories," asks you to look at your work as a whole and identify the imagined terrain of your existing fiction, and then allow it to generate and inspire new stories.

Another exercise challenges you to inhabit the mind of your enemy. This exercise underlines something that Rosellen Brown once said in an interview: "Fiction always has an obligation to the other side, whatever it is. Finding an adequate angle of vision is the hardest thing about writing it. It's frightening to imagine the inner life of an 'enemy.' But what is more worthwhile."

In the exercise "Go Ahead, Yawn," you are challenged to affect the reader physically—although "yawning" is not what you want your reader to do. How about making your reader laugh?

The exercise "It's a Laugh" asks you to think of something in the past that wasn't funny when it happened, but now seems to have the makings of a hilarious tale—because of how you tell it. And then there's the exercise on writing compelling sex scenes. (Remember the endless scene in Scott Spencer's *Endless Love* that completely ignored the sense of smell?

Didn't believe it, right?) Is "being explicit" necessary? To answer that, read John Fowles's *The Ebony Tower*.

But enough of this introduction. On to transforming your own material and experiences into fiction, on to inventing strange new worlds.

70

THE ENEMY'S LIFE

from Lore Segal

Your first job as writer of a story is to make up the people to whom your story will happen. Not one character, but several, many, all of whom live inside their own bodies, look out of their own eyes at a different world.

THE EXERCISE

Week One

Write a scene that brings to fictional life someone you hate. Make the reader hate her. It might be someone who annoys you—someone whose manner you can't stand, whose voice grates on you. Or it might be some-one who has offended you or done you some harm, or someone to whom you have done some harm—there are many reasons to hate people. If you have the courage, take on someone who is evil on the grand scale. It can be someone you know, someone you know about, or, best of all, invent a real nasty.

Week Two

Write the same scene, from the point of view of the nasty, and write it in the first person.

THE OBJECTIVE

Story and only story is the peaceable kingdom where you and I and the next fellow can lie down on the same page with one another, not by wip-ing our differences out, but by creating our differences on the page. Only on the page of a story can I look out of your and my and the other fellow's eyes all at the same time.

STUDENT EXAMPLE

Week One

"Doctor" Andrews, as he styled himself, was one of those white men who can be taken seriously no place in the world except an obscure bush country in Africa. He was a Canadian health program administrator, trained as a nurse, with a minimal knowledge of medicine, yet blessed with a kind of bureaucratic power in the Republic of Songhai by virtue of his control over the medical aid program provided by a generous Canadian government. He was a plump, rosy, voluble, man with tiny white teeth in an insincere smile.

I met him when he arrived one day to inspect my clinic. He bustled around, looked over the shoulder of one of my Mandinka aides who was sewing up a gash in a boy's leg and said superciliously, "Not very sterile, you know. But I suppose they've never heard of the concept." I mentioned that we did use antiseptics, kept the surgery room as clean as possible, and did scrub before even minor procedures, but he paid no attention.

He inspected my three shelves of medicines and sniffed. "What do you call this?" he asked.

I took the opportunity to put in my oft-frustrated request. "We have lots of infections here," I said, "and one of the things we could use is a supply of penicillin. I know the Canadian program has a steady supply and I wonder if you could spare me some from time to time?"

He turned and looked at me as if I had demanded his wallet. "Really!" he said. "You do have grandiose ideas about practicing in the bush. I think you should realize that we need every gram of medication we have for the government hospital in the city. For the kind of patient who counts."

Week Two

The first day I met him in a remote Mandinka village, he was asking for penicillin. The American hadn't even been here a month yet, and already he thought he could set our whole health care system on its head and shake miracles out of its pockets. I knew he would blunder ahead and upset the Africans with his persistent demands; Peace Corps is full of self-important American youngsters who little realize the damage they're capable of inflicting on fragile, carefully constructed development projects like ours—initiated a decade before anyone even thought of inviting the USA in.

The Canadians make a point of sending qualified people here, and of briefing us meticulously. But the American knew little about the health care system over which he raged; he couldn't see the impossibility and the dangers of shipping penicillin out to a bush clinic where the natives had never even seen a Band-Aid; he thought that just because he had arrived, we would scramble to meet his every need—he had no notion of how hopelessly overworked we are, and will be for many years to come, in the involved process of establishing this system. If Peace Corps had courteously offered his services to us in advance, instead of flinging him pointlessly out into the bush, he could have become a useful member of our team. Now he's no more than a gadfly—another obstacle to be worked out. It wouldn't take much to get him transferred—or better yet, deported.

I still wonder why we didn't go ahead and get rid of him.

CAMERON MACAULEY

A good title should be like a good metaphor: It should intrigue without being too baffling or too obvious.

WALKER PERCY

71

TAKING RISKS

One of the great pleasures of writing fiction is letting your imagination and fantasies take off anywhere they want to go. Most people feel guilty when they think of doing something awful to someone they dislike; writers can invent a story and in it fling a hated character from a moving car or have him go blind. Another fantasy you can play out is doing something the very idea of which terrifies you—like parachuting from a plane or sailing across the ocean solo. As a fiction writer you're at a serious disadvantage if you can't write about an experience you're unlikely ever to know firsthand. This is not as easy as it seems, because you must sound not only plausible diving to the depths of the Aegean, you've also got to know what you're talking about—all those details about the scuba gear have to sound absolutely authentic. This is why a lot of novelists spend so much time in libraries—they're making sure they get it right.

THE EXERCISE

Using the first person, describe an event or action you are fairly sure you will never experience firsthand. Be very specific—the more details you incorporate the more likely it is that your reader will believe you. Include your feelings and reactions.

THE OBJECTIVE

"Write what you know" is all very well but it certainly does restrict most of us within narrow confines. You must also be able to write what you don't know, but can imagine. This is what your imagination is for. Let it fly.

STUDENT EXAMPLE

I've been a missing person for ten days and the novelty is starting to wear off. My girlfriend's losing her patience, and my wife is on the eleven o'clock news.

"How can you just lie there and watch her cry like that?" Maura says.

"I left a note for Chrissakes. She's trying to humiliate me," I say. Every day, all over America, guys leave their wives and nothing happens. Mine calls the FBI and reports me as missing.

Joe Shortsleeve, WBZ-TV's intrepid reporter, is asking my wife if I was involved in any illegal activities.

"No," she says gloomily. Her eyes are puffy. "He's the most normal person in the world."

"You can have him back," Maura shouts at the television. She's furious that I'm getting all this attention. The camera is following a helicopter as it circles above some wooded area. I can't figure out why they're searching for me there. I hate forests. The camera cuts to a German shepard dragging a fat cop around a cemetery. The dog stops and wags its tail. The cop waves something in front of its nose.

"That's my *sock*," I say. Maura doesn't care. She's lying next to me like a big white corpse. Naked. I wish she'd cover herself after sex. I already feel like I know her too well.

Tomorrow I'll go home and become the biggest joke in Massachusetts. They'll probably arrest me for conspiring to remain invisible or something.

I tell Maura I'm going to take a walk, and I put on my Celtics cap. It's one of the items I was wearing when my wife last saw me. I might as well be conspicuous, now that things have been decided.

My first stop is the Store 24, where I buy the Boston Herald and a scratch ticket. I let the little Pakistani guy behind the counter get a real good look at me. He points to something on the front page and smiles. That's it, I say to myself, it's all over.

"Beel Clin-Ton," he says and shakes his head in mock disgust.

I wind up at Mister Donut. There's a cute girl there who works the late shift. It's starting to snow and we're talking about skiing. She tells me she gets homesick every time it snows because she grew up in Vermont. I sip my coffee but save my jelly stick for later. I don't like eating donuts in front of good-looking women because crumbs get stuck in my moustache. I watch her as she mops between the tables. I can't be sure if she likes me or she's just a nice person, but I have the secret that might tip the scales. I want to confess.

"I'm a missing person," I say as she squeezes the water into a grimy yellow bucket on wheels.

"Listen," she says. "I know the feeling."

Matt Marinovich

72

SEX IS NOT ALL IT'S CRACKED UP TO BE—IT'S MORE

from Christopher Noël

Anatole Broyard writes that

> sex almost always disappoints me in novels. Everything can be said or done now, and that's what I often find: everything, a feeling of generality or dispersal. But in my experience, true sex is so particular, so peculiar to the person who yearns for it. Only he or she, and no one else, would desire so very much that very person under those circumstances. In fiction, I miss that sense of terrific specificity.

THE EXERCISE

With this caution and exhortation in mind, write a sex scene for a story in which you know your fictional characters well.

THE OBJECTIVE

To gain access to this rich material indirectly so that this universal experience can feel singular, as though coming to be for the first time in history.

STUDENT EXAMPLES

> So this was sex. This is what she had been waiting for. Her eyes began to water from her allergy to the feather pillows his mother had bought him for college. "Don't cry," he said, as if confident that she was overwhelmed by the moment. And when she looked up at him she remembered what had first attracted her: the little bursts of gold in his dangerous gray eyes. She could tell he was worldly, and that he could teach her things.
>
> On top of her, though, right now, he was no more than dead weight. Twice he poked her in the ribs with his elbow; his feet felt like ice against the tops of her ankles. He could have trimmed his toenails. She bit her bottom lip and tried not to move. She counted the squares of acoustic tile on the ceiling to keep her mind off what he was doing: poking around somewhere between where he was supposed to be and the inside of her right thigh. As soon as she noticed that the roof had once leaked right

above their heads—the faded stain the size of an orange was the give-away—something else occurred to her: he had lied. This was his first time, too.

MARIETTE LIPPO

"Ever feel eggs?" I say, slipping my hand into the bowl, six golden yolks gracefully avoiding my fingers. I catch one up and hold it out to her. She steps back against the stove, but I know it's the reverse of what she meant to do. "See?" I stroke the full, slick globe with one finger of my dry hand, resistance quivering the sac so slightly it could be alive. "If you're careful, they don't break. Feel how perfect," I say, and place her hand atop mine, cupping egg and risking everything in one small motion. For a moment, we don't move; we're seeing, feeling, tasting with our fingers. With the flat, pink palms of our hands. Then she butts a forearm up against my chest and pushes me aside, reaching behind me on the counter for the bowl. Dipping in, she spreads her fingers and pulls up a yolk, a fat one.

"Ever taste eggs?" she says, sliding it inside my mouth before I can resist. The taste is slippery and thick, and my tongue moves without my wanting it. Around the other yolk, the first one, our hands are still together. "Don't break it," she says, laughing, and I hold on, my free hand slipping up beneath her sweater where I find more and more fragile flesh I want to hold, sustain, and burst at the same time. Then she pushes into me like we are dancing, her legs apart, her lips close enough to kiss and I can't stop. The yolk between our tongues, we meet around it, over, under, and I am reaching up between her legs with one desperate, free hand when suddenly she pulls back, thinking twice. Inside my mouth, all yellow goes to liquid and my hopes—so thick—drip sadly down my chin, my throat, hesitating in their viscosity like the tears you hold back, blinking, like everything in the whole world, chickens, girlfriends, omelet dinners depend on you not breaking down.

BRIDGET MAZUR

If we had to say what writing is, we would define it essentially as an act of courage.

CYNTHIA OZICK

197

73

MY PET

from Alison Lurie

The following exercise works best if it is done first and discussed and analyzed afterward.

THE EXERCISE

Write a composition on the subject "My Pet." The only requirement is that this must be a pet you have never owned. It can be anything from a kitten to a dinosaur, from a fly to a dragon. Describe what your pet looks like, how you acquired it, what it eats and where it sleeps, what tricks it can do, and how it gets on with your family, friends, neighbors, or the people at work.

NOTES FOR DISCUSSION

We are, we are told, a nation of pet lovers, and more than half the households in America include an animal, bird, or fish. What are the motives for keeping a pet? Possible suggestions are need for protection, need for affection (a creature you can love and/or one that will love you), aesthetic appreciation (the beautiful pet as interior decoration), parental feeling (a child substitute), sadistic impulses (something to maltreat), etc. What is the function of the pet in your exercise?

A portrait of a pet is also one way of creating a portrait of its owner. What does this exercise tell us about the pet's owner (for instance, that he is kind, timid, affectionate, loves beauty, etc.)?

It has also often been remarked that some people come to resemble their pets, or vice versa. Why does this happen? In other cases, the pet is extremely different from the owner; possibly it may express impulses that its owner does not want to or cannot express (for example, the actively aggressive dog with an apparently passive and peaceful owner). Is the pet in your composition like or unlike its owner, and how?

Animals can play an important part in fiction, and not only in so-called animal stories. Some classic examples are Balzac's "A Passion in the Desert," Kafka's "The Metamorphosis," D. H. Lawrence's *The Fox*, and Ursula K. Le Guin's "The Wife's Story." What is the character and function of the pet in your exercise? What is its relation to its owner? How could this description be the basis for a short story?

THE OBJECTIVE

To expand your conception of characters and relationships.

Appealing workplaces are to be avoided. One wants a room with no view, so imagination can meet memory in the dark. When I furnished this study seven years ago, I pushed the long desk against a blank wall, so I could not see from either window. Once, fifteen years ago, I wrote in a cinder-block cell over a parking lot. It overlooked a tar-and-gravel roof. This pine shed under trees is not quite so good as the cinder-block study was, but it will do.

"The beginning of wisdom," according to a West African proverb, "is to get you a roof."

ANNIE DILLARD

74

IT'S ALL IN YOUR HEAD

Avoiding the obvious when writing about extreme states of mind is a real challenge for any writer. Resorting to such clichés as "his heart was in his mouth," "she was on cloud nine," and "he flew off the handle" is far easier than figuring out what is really happening to someone scared, happy, or angry. You must translate the emotion or feeling into fresh, interesting language, rendering precisely or metaphorically what is taking place within the character. Here is Mrs. Dalloway, in Virginia Woolf's novel, experiencing pleasure. "The cook whistled in the kitchen. She heard the click of the typewriter. It was her life, and, bending her head over the hall table, she bowed beneath the influence, felt blessed and purified, saying to herself, as she took the pad with the telephone message on it, how moments like this are buds on the tree of life."

THE EXERCISE

Write three short paragraphs, the first "fear," the second "anger," and the last "pleasure" without using these words. Try to render these emotions by describing physical sensations or images. If you want, write mini-stories, dramatizing these emotions. Try to make your language precise and fresh.

THE OBJECTIVE

To learn to render emotional states without a falling back on tired and imprecise language.

STUDENT EXAMPLE

Fear
Melville found himself abruptly awake and aware of human noises coming from downstairs—the quiet closing of the front door, a step or two in the hallway. His ears rang with concentration as he lay perfectly still. The footsteps came up the stairs, crossed the landing, then moved toward his room. His breath emerged in short, loud gasps. He tried to swallow but his tongue was too dry. The pulse of his heart made loud popping sounds in his ears. Sweat gathered in his armpits. Melville had not moved so much as a finger when he saw the doorknob being slowly turned from the far side of the door. He opened his mouth and attempted to scream but

no noise came from his throat. He began to shake violently while his blood slowed within icy veins and arteries.

Anger

A silver Camaro cut in front of Malaver's car, forcing him to slam on the brakes and throwing his body against the steering wheel. At the next light the Camaro was still in front of him; Malaver could see two people sitting so close together they looked as if they were both driving.

"Effing teenagers," Malaver said aloud. "Shouldn't give kids like that licenses." He massaged his neck where it had been hurt and watched sourly as the couple in the Camaro kissed. He tightened his hands on the steering wheel. They kissed again. That's it! He'd had it with these damn kids. He undid his seat belt with trembling fingers, got out of his car and walked up to the driver's side of the Camaro. The girl and boy, wearing twin leather jackets, the girl's yellow hair frizzed as if electrified, returned his stare with clear disdain.

"Bug off, grandpa," the boy said, as the light turned green. The car took flight, burning rubber as it went.

Malaver walked back to his car, got in and began to drive again. All the muscles in his neck and upper body felt as if they were going to rip and shred like wet paper. His head hurt dully. He was sure that if he saw these two again he would do something terrible and violent to them.

Pleasure

Jillie thought the ice cream sundae was beautiful just to look at, and she let it sit in front of her for a minute before starting to eat. The ice cream made her think of being rolled in soft blankets, and the whipped cream was like the clouds outside. The cherry looked like her cat's nose. She took her first spoonful, and as the hot fudge and ice cream made her mouth both hot and cold, she shut her eyes. She curled her toes and moaned. The second bite was even better and she moaned again and giggled. A trickle ran from the corner of her mouth because she was smiling so much. It hung off the side of her chin, and she thought of it as an ice cream tear. She wanted to give everyone she loved a taste, her mother, her father, and her brother, but it was her seventh birthday and she didn't have to share. After another bite, she couldn't control herself any more, and as loud as she could, she screamed, "Oohh, I just love this." When it was all gone, she wiped the inside of the dish with her finger and stuck it in her mouth. She rubbed her stomach and shut her eyes and hummed to herself.

BRIAN FOSTER

75

GO AHEAD, YAWN

An article in the *San Francisco Examiner* by John Flinn began with the challenge, "Try, just try, to read all the way through this article without yawning. Bet you can't. . . . If you're normal, the very mention of the subject has set in motion the powerful and uncontrollable urge to stretch those jaw muscles copiously, throw back your shoulders and arms and inhale deeply." (Have you yawned yet?)

Fiction is capable of having the same effect on the reader; we don't mean when it is boring, but when it sets out to do more than just draw the reader's intellect and emotions into the story. Several reviewers of John Updike's *Rabbit at Rest* said that it was not for the literally faint of heart because the passages of Rabbit's death from a heart attack were so well written. And in a *Paris Review* interview, Kurt Vonnegut speaks to this issue of reader involvement.

> When I used to teach creative writing, I would tell students to make their characters want something right away even if it's only a glass of water. Characters paralyzed by the meaninglessness of modern life still have to drink water from time to time. One of my students wrote a story about a nun who got a piece of dental floss stuck between her lower left molars, and who couldn't get it out all day long. I thought that was wonderful. The story dealt with issues a lot more important than dental floss, but what kept readers going was anxiety about when the dental floss would finally be removed. Nobody could read that story without fishing around in his mouth with a finger.

THE EXERCISE

Include in one of your stories a passage that physically affects the reader in the way the dental floss does in Vonnegut's anecdote.

THE OBJECTIVE

To learn to create a physical world that makes a believer of the reader and pulls her into the tangible, felt life of the story.

STUDENT EXAMPLE

After a few seconds the gravestone seemed especially hard and inflexible and I couldn't stop being aware of the cold marble. The way your tongue becomes intolerable, heavy and dumb, once you start thinking about it. Eddie did it to me, he said one day, right before art history, which is the ultimate clockwatching period, "Aren't tongues stupid? Just sitting there. Who's holding them up? They're like cheese bricks." Then the whole period while tickticktick Frazier pointed her chalk at the pull-down screen, I both stared at my watch and tried to find space for my thickening tongue. The gravestone was the same—suddenly unnatural, too upright. I pushed against it with my back, hoping God wouldn't notice, or worse, Elizabeth Wood Colter, 1799–1812. It wouldn't move, like a moldy Greyhound bus seat, stuck from all the years of back and forth and back. I pressed harder, sliding up the stone, pushing off with my feet. Finally it slanted backwards about five inches and I slid to the ground.

MARY SALIBA, "EVERYTHING REPLACEABLE"

76

FARAWAY PLACES

Many writers have written about places they have never been—Franz Kafka about America in *Amerika,* Saul Bellow about Africa in *Henderson the Rain King,* Thomas Pynchon about postwar Germany in *Gravity's Rainbow,* W. D. Wetherall about the Crimea in *Chekhov's Sister,* and Hilding Johnson about India in her story "Victoria"—yet their descriptions of these places persuasively transport the reader there. Below are passages from a novel and a short story.

> Finally one morning we found ourselves in the bed of a good-sized river, the Arnewi, and we walked downstream in it, for it was dry. The mud had turned to clay, and the boulders sat like lumps of gold in the dusty glitter. Then we sighted the Arnewi village and saw the circular roofs which rose to a point. I knew they were just thatch and must be brittle, porous, and light; they seemed like feathers, and yet heavy—like heavy feathers. From these coverings smoke went up into the silent radiance.
>
> SAUL BELLOW, *HENDERSON THE RAIN KING*

> Flowers stayed tight in the bud, drying in crisp pods and rattling to the ground one by one in the still night.
>
> The bearers brought half as much water, then still less. The children on the wards slid from whining into torpor.
>
> A sacred cow wandered into the hospital courtyard and could go no further. It was chalky, white, fleshless, its loose dry hide scarred in random constellations, a dessicated wreath of twisted flowers digging into its neck. It stood, eyes closed and head nearly to the ground, for a day and night. Early the next morning I came upon Richard holding a bucket of water beneath the animal's nose.
>
> I said, "We don't have much of that."
>
> "It's what I was allotted for shaving."
>
> I shrugged. "Suit yourself."
>
> In the afternoon the cow knelt, shuddered and died. The sweepers came with great hooks and dragged it out of the courtyard, leaving thin trails of scarlet in the pale dust.
>
> At supper, Richard said, "If they think so much of the beasts, how can they let them suffer?"
>
> "To them they're gods. In general, people don't care much about the suffering of a god. You should know that by now."
>
> HILDING JOHNSON, "VICTORIA"

THE EXERCISE

Choose a country where you have always longed to go but haven't yet been and set a story there. Read old and new Fodor's guides as well as other recent travel guides and *National Geographic;* buy a map; study the country's politics, religion, government, and social issues; read cookbooks—always, always looking for the persuasive detail, something you would almost have to be there to know.

THE OBJECTIVE

To write with authority and conviction about a place to which you have never been.

STUDENT EXAMPLE

One of the reasons Tess had come to Japan was to visit the fish auction by the Sumidagawa River, where her father probably went during his business trips when he wanted to feel at home. He'd run an auction in the back parking lot of St. Leonard's Church till Tess was ten. Near the marketplace, she knelt on the slick pavement and pulled heavy trash bags around each of her yellow sneakers. The auctioneers had already begun and the wholesalers were placing their bids. She spotted another tourist with plastic bags up to his knees. He was kneeling in a puddle and snapping pictures with an old Polaroid. A brochure had advised wearing the bags because hoses would continually be pumping water over the pavement, washing away stray bits of raw sea food. Tess wove in and around the people and crates of tuna and crab. She took in small breaths through her mouth. Jake should have come with her to see this.

Jake was the first stranger Tess spoke with on her vacation. Her friend, Marlene, had worked late last night, so Tess had made her way to a sushi bar with a large fish tank at its center. She was wondering if the tank was in place of a printed menu. That was when Jake came up and asked if she'd like to join him. He was in Tokyo for three days on business.

The fish they ordered that night was sliced ribbon-thin, and shaped like roses. Jake used one chopstick to push some raw tuna into the green smudge of wasabi. He choked and rubbed his tongue on his sleeve. Tess shifted on her pillow.

"That's a nasty little paste," he said. He coughed and took a long drink of beer.

She looked at the paper lanterns over the bar. Her father used to attach one yellow balloon to a wooden sign that read "The Everything Auction." "It's horseradish," Tess said.

KIM LEAHY

77

IT'S A LAUGH

Humor is emotional chaos remembered in tranquility.
JAMES THURBER

Styles of humor seem to change shape and kind more quickly than any other form of writing. From Ring Larder through James Thurber, S. J. Perelman, Ogden Nash, Nathanael West, Joseph Heller, John Kennedy O'Toole, and Woody Allen, we have American humor that ranges from gentle reminiscence to the grimmest shade of black. It may be true partly because one man's meat is another man's poison (or, as Ogden Nash said, "One man's Mede is another man's Persian"), and it's hard to get any large number of people to agree on what's a laugh. So, the writer of humor has to depend largely on her own sense of what is funny about life. As E. B. White said, "Humor can be dissected as a frog can, but the thing dies in the process and the innards are discouraging to any but the pure scientific mind."

Just as humor defies analysis, it seems to defy any rules—rules of tolerance or good taste. One of the classics of English satire is Jonathan Swift's cruel "A Modest Proposal"; W. C. Fields made fun of marriage, sobriety, and family values; Lenny Bruce relied heavily on racial slurs and intolerance to amuse his audiences. Some writers and comedians even risk scatology—traditionally the most despised form of humor.

All of which is to say that if you take a sardonic view of the world ("the world is a comedy to those who think, a tragedy to those who feel") and can express it with humor and wit, you should do your own thing. Read Lawrence Sterne, Kingsley Amis, Dave Barry, P. G. Wodehouse, Nicolai Gogol, Kurt Vonnegut, Lorrie Moore, Ilf and Petrov, Mark Twain, Michael Frayn, Evelyn Waugh, Somerville and Ross, Molly Keane, Oscar Wilde.

The main thing a writer should remember is that written humor is quite a different thing from comedy on the stage or that delivered by a stand-up comedian. Oral humor largely depends on timing, tone of voice, body language, and the infection of laughter in an audience. Written humor depends on language alone—words create the joke. Thus the writer of fiction should not imitate—in fiction—what came off so uproariously or wittily on the stage, in a movie, or on TV. His nuances, allusions, surprises, parodies all come from verbal skill and shrewdness. Good narrative, fresh language, succinct expression, hitting the point—these are the heart of written humor. Or, as Shakespeare said it better, "Brevity is the soul of wit."

THE EXERCISE

Write about something that happened to you that didn't seem funny at the time, for example, the day you were stuck in a traffic jam and a bee flew in through the car window or the time your tenant set your stove on fire and the firemen wrenched it from the wall and tossed it into the backyard. Bring the incident under the humor spotlight and transform it so as to emphasize things that will make your reader smile or laugh. Pacing is important, as are crucial surprising details, and your own confidence that the story does not need analysis or authorial nudging. Limit: 550 words.

THE OBJECTIVE

Because humor resides largely in the attitude you assume toward your material, you must be able to discover and exploit those elements that highlight the comic, the exaggerated, and the unlikely. Keep in mind that you could just as easily take the bee story and make it tragic (bee bites driver, driver crashes into another car, killing infant in back seat).

STUDENT EXAMPLE

In the 1970s, boys wore their hair long, over their ears and down the backs of their necks. I was thirteen and my mom and dad used to make me babysit my two younger brothers, Jimmy and Peter. Mom paid me fifty cents an hour. To keep the kids from killing each other, I parked them in front of the TV set until it was time for Peter—who was six that year—to go off to bed. Jimmy was eleven and he hit his little brother every time I turned my back or went to pee or anything.

This one night I got an inspiration. "Who wants to make cookies?" I said.

"I do, I do," Peter said.

Jimmy said, "That's girl stuff."

I told him to suit himself and Peter and I went out to the kitchen to round up the ingredients. Peter asked if we could make chocolate chip cookies and I said sure we could. I got out the stuff we needed and plugged in the Mixmaster Dad got Mom for Christmas. Pete dragged a chair over to the counter and stood on it so he could see what was going on.

Pretty soon Jimmy joined us and even asked if he could help. Pete said no but I said yes and since I was the boss what I said went. We measured out the flour, and poured in all the chips in the bag, and then the other things and dumped the dough into the electric mixing bowl. "Okay," I told Peter. "Ignition."

He pushed the button and the blades began to move through the dough. When I went to check on the oven, Peter must have leaned way over because the next thing I heard was him screaming bloody murder. "Help, hey, it's got my hair, hey turn it off!"

I gasped: Peter's head was practically inside the bowl and one long lock of his hair was being twisted around the knob holding the blades, pulling him closer and closer to the blades. Just like James Bond.

Jimmy shrieked, "Yikes! It's eating Peter. The mixer's eating Peter!"

But was he doing anything about it? No way. I rushed over and turned it off. Peter wrenched his head away, fell off the chair, and landed on the floor, holding his head and screaming bloody murder. For some reason, there was no blood but he had a bald spot the size of a large mixing spoon.

We had to throw away the cookie dough—it was full of Peter's hair. He wore his Red Sox cap day and night for the next three weeks. Mom never figured out why.

TERRY FRENCH

78

TOTAL RECALL

from Alison Lurie

The following exercise works best if it is done first and discussed and analyzed afterward.

THE EXERCISE

This exercise should be done with two or more people; one to read the instructions aloud while the others concentrate on recalling the experience. Read slowly and pause between sentences and paragraphs; the whole process should take at least five minutes.

Shut your eyes. Go back in your mind to some summer or part-time job you had in the past. Look at the surroundings in which you were working. See the place in which you worked: factory, schoolroom, restaurant, hospital, store, library, whatever. Or perhaps it is an outdoor scene: beach, road, garden, construction project, ranch, café. Notice the shapes and colors of what is around you. Look at the materials with which you are working, note their shapes and colors.

Now look at the other people who are present in this scene: coworkers, boss, customers in the restaurant or shop, children at camp, or a babysitting job. Choose one person and observe her closely; notice what she is wearing and the expression on her face. What is she doing as you watch? What gestures is she making?

Now begin to hear the sounds that belong to this scene. The clank of machinery, the sizzle of hamburgers cooking on the grill, the splash of water in the pool, the ringing of phones, the thump and hum of music, whatever it may be. Listen to the voices: what are they saying? Perhaps you will hear a line or two of dialogue. What is the person you especially observed saying, and what do you or someone else say in reply?

Now allow yourself to experience the smells that belong to this scene: food cooking, fresh-cut grass, motor oil, sweat, flowers, disinfectant, whatever. If you are working in a restaurant or bar, or eating on the job, you may want to become aware of taste too: the lukewarm bitterness of instant coffee in a plastic cup, the sugary chocolate slickness of a candy bar hidden in your desk drawer.

Look around you at this point and become aware of the climate of your surroundings. Is it winter or summer? If you are working outdoors, what is the weather like? What time of day is it? If you are indoors, is the air stuffy or fresh, smoky or clear? What can you see out the window?

Next, become aware of the sense of touch, of the textures of the things you are working with: soft or rough, smooth or fuzzy, wet or dry. Notice heat and cold: the damp, icy feel of a glass of soda, the warm silky texture of a child's hair; the hot oily parts of a broken lawnmower.

Now turn your sense of touch inward; become aware of the motions you are making and the sensations in your muscles: the strain of lifting sacks of dirt or cement, the pleasure of stirring cake batter round a big stainless-steel bowl, the weight of a tray of drinks on your shoulder.

Finally, notice your emotions. Do you like this job or hate it? Are you interested in what is going on around you or bored? Are you tired and depressed or in good spirits? Where will you go when work is over for today?

Do you like or dislike the people around you? What do you feel about the person you chose to observe? What do you think she feels about you? What would you like to say to her? If you said it, what would this person probably say or do?

When all these things are clear in your mind, but not until then, open your eyes and record them as rapidly as possible. Write in the present tense. Don't bother about legible handwriting, complete sentences, or spelling words correctly: the point is to get this material down on paper while it is still fresh and vivid in your memory. You are not composing a story, only making notes.

NOTES FOR DISCUSSION

Writers differ in their sensitivity to the world. Some especially notice shapes, some smells, some colors, some textures; some see gestures, others see clothes or facial expressions. James Joyce, whose eyesight was poor, perceived the world mainly in terms of words and sounds; Thomas Wolfe, a large man with an even larger appetite, was famous for his awareness of the tastes and odors of food.

As you look over your notes, ask yourself whether there are kinds of perception you are neglecting in your writing, or passing over too rapidly. Do you habitually describe scenes and people in black and white, for instance? If you are doing this exercise in a group, read your notes aloud and ask the other people present what they noticed about your strengths and weaknesses of recall. Once you are aware that you don't always remember to include colors, smells, sounds, texture, or whatever, you can make a conscious effort to do so, and your writing will become more vivid.

If this exercise worked especially well for you, perhaps it could be turned into a story. Suppose the two main characters were you and the person you observed and spoke to, what might happen between them? What change in them or in their relationship might take place?

No matter what you are writing, you can use this technique. If you like, you can concentrate on people rather than scenes; visualize them in detail, see what they are doing, hear their words, etc. Once you become really familiar with the process, it is not even necessary to go back in imagination to a real scene or a real person; you can call up an invented character or event in the same way.

THE OBJECTIVE

To make some experience as vivid as possible, to recall it in full sensual and emotional detail before you begin to write.

I want stories to startle and engage me within the first few sentences, and in their middle to widen or deepen or sharpen my knowledge of human activity, and to end by giving me a sensation of completed statement. The ending is where the reader discovers whether he has been reading the same story the writer thought he was writing.

JOHN UPDIKE, INTRODUCTION TO *BASS 1984*

79

THE TERRAIN OF YOUR STORIES

from Eve Shelnutt

When writers, just beginning, have accumulated a handful of stories, they begin to realize that each story contains a miniature "world." What they sometimes don't understand is that a whole town, region, sometimes even a country, is in the process of being created. It lies as an unsurveyed terrain shrouded in the mist of the writer's vision and will emerge only slowly, story by story. But an exercise can help beginning writers grasp the breadth of his or her imaginative territory and even seed it with new outposts of civilization.

THE EXERCISE

Reread all of the stories you've written to date, noting in particular their locales. Note the types of dwellings you've put your characters into; the roads they travel on; the trees that surround their houses; the weather.

On a large sheet of paper, draw a "map" of the places the characters inhabit. Ask: How far does character X in one story live from character Y in another story? What lies in between the places where they live?

When the "map" has been completed ask: Under what circumstances might character X and character Y meet? Add to the map the envisioned locale of the meeting. Do this with as many characters as you have populating your stories. Ask: During what season might they meet? Why that particular season?

When the imagined "meeting" of two characters inhabiting separate stories interests you, consider writing a story in which the two interact. Or consider writing a story in which why they would never meet is explored, asking what has happened irrevocably to prevent these characters from meeting.

THE OBJECTIVE

Stories can "feed" other stories. This exercise not only shortens the time in which it takes a writer to understand that she is probably tied to an imagined terrain in fiction, but it can also expand the writer's imagination in such a way that new stories beg to be written.

X. STORY ELEMENTS AND FORMS AS A GIVEN

Writers get their ideas for stories or novels from inside their heads, from memory, from what they see and hear around them—including the daily newspaper, the tragedy next door, the overheard conversation, the arresting image. Joan Didion began *Play It as It Lays* after seeing a young actress being paged in a Las Vegas casino. Didion says, "A young woman with long hair and a short white halter dress walks through the casino at the Riviera in Las Vegas at one in the morning. She crosses the casino alone and picks up a house telephone. . . . I know nothing about her. Who is paging her? Why is she here to be paged? How exactly did she come to this? It was precisely this moment in Las Vegas that made *Play It as It Lays* begin to tell itself to me." Other writers start with a situation (e.g., a person taking a shower hearing a strange noise beyond the bathroom door). Although we don't especially endorse it, some writers begin with an abstraction—injustice, war, divorce, child abuse, etc.—and proceed to make up the story and characters that dramatize the idea.

The exercises in this section are here mainly to help the beginning writer recognize effective fictional triggers. Here is a situation—now compose a story growing directly out of it. While some of these triggers are general (e.g., "Sunday") others are quite specific and ask for different "versions" or "accounts" of particular incidents. One exercise asks the writer to use a small unit of time as the story's "given" form. Another exercise from James Thomas limits the length of the story to 750 words, and still another from Ron Carlson asks the writer to use the letters of the alphabet to structure the story—from A to Z. In other words, these exercises are imagination stretchers and should help writers who feel they don't know what to write about or how to recognize fictional potential.

Often, seemingly difficult guidelines are more liberating than being able to write about anything. Relax, have fun. It's all out there, floating free, waiting for you to pull it down and anchor it in story.

80

SUNDAY: DISCOVERING
EMOTIONAL TRIGGERS

Most of the time it doesn't matter on what day of the week you set your action—unless it's a Sunday (remember the movie *Sunday Bloody Sunday?*). Most people feel at loose ends on this day, even those who spend the morning in church. Instead of using the freedom wisely, a lot of us tend to overdo it—overeat, oversleep, overreact. Sundays bring out the worst in people. Children grow anxious as the weekend draws to a close and they realize they haven't done their homework. During football season, another possible area of tension opens up. Then there is the obligatory trip to grandma and grandpa's house for a large heavy meal and some equally heavy recriminations. Things happen on Sundays that wouldn't happen on weekdays. So if you want to examine domestic dynamics close up, set some action on a Sunday and let her rip.

THE EXERCISE

Title it "Sunday." Write 550 words.

THE OBJECTIVE

Certain words and ideas, such as *retirement, in-laws, boss, vacation, pneumonia,* and *fraud,* serve as triggers for stories or scenes in fiction. *Sunday* is one of these. Try to think of others.

STUDENT EXAMPLE

On Sunday mornings, walking to the bathroom, I'd be treated to the sight of my roommate, Abby, in bed with a man, yet another man I didn't recognize. Every Sunday, I'd tell myself I needed to get my own apartment, or at least install some doors in this one. I used to love Sundays before Abby moved in. I'd sit in the sunny spot in the kitchen and drink cup after cup of coffee. I'd read the newspaper—first travel, then arts, weddings, the news—and then my mother would call. We'd talk about Sundays that we'd spent together—going to the planetarium, buying bras, cooking barley. Sundays, I didn't touch my students' papers I'd brought home. I didn't get dressed until 11:00 A.M. I didn't mind feeling lonely.

Now, when I was halfway through the arts section, a shirtless man came into the kitchen. I pulled my robe tighter.

"Geez, I hate Sundays," he said. "They're endless. Give me a Saturday night any day. Hey, I'm Stan," he said, putting out a hand. I shook it. Abby trailed in after him.

"Hi, gorgeous," she said to me. "Met Stan?"

"Sure did," I said, smiling and turning back to the paper. Go away, I thought. Go back to bed. Leave me to my Sunday. The phone rang, and shirtless Stan twisted to pick it up.

"Good morning," he said. "Oh. . . . It's for you," he said, handing me the phone.

"Her mother," Abby said. "Every Sunday. Kind of like church, I guess."

"No, Mom," I whispered into the phone that I'd dragged out into the hall. "No, Mom. That was not my boyfriend. . . . No, he's not a burglar. . . . No, I don't know who he is. . . . No, I don't let strange men into my apartment at all hours." And on it went. My head throbbed.

When I got off the phone, I went back into the kitchen. Stan was sitting in my chair. Abby was sitting on Stan's lap twirling his chest hairs.

"Hey, gorgeous," Abby said. "We're going to grab a bagel and then go to the planetarium. Half-price on Sundays. Want to come?"

"Better than sitting around here moping," Stan said. "Ouch. Stop pulling my hairs." He slapped Abby's hand away.

HESTER KAPLAN

81

FIVE DIFFERENT VERSIONS:
AND NOT ONE IS A LIE

We tell stories every day of our lives. But *how* we tell the story is often determined by who we are telling the story to. Think of the range of people in one's life—parents, spouse, children, friends, lovers, priests, rabbis, in-laws, social workers, parole officers (come on—use your imagination), doctors, claims adjusters, lawyers, judges, juries, therapists, talk show hosts, astrologers—the list goes on and on. And as we tell these people our story, we add or subtract, exaggerate or play down, tolerate or condemn, depending on the identity of the person to whom we are telling our tale.

THE EXERCISE

Here is the situation: You have just come out of the movie theater around seven in the evening and you are mugged—a person asks for your money, then knocks you to the ground before running away. Or make up your own situation.

Next, pretend you are telling the account of this event to five different people:

    your mother
    your best friend
    your girlfriend or boyfriend (or wife or husband)
    a therapist
    a police officer

THE OBJECTIVE

To become conscious of how we shape and shade the stories that we tell to each other according to the listener. Your characters also tell stories to each other and make selections about content according to whom they are telling the story, the effect they want the story to have, and the response they want to elicit from the listener. A lot of dialogue in fiction, in real life, is story telling—and there is always the story listener who is as important to the tale as the tale itself.

STUDENT EXAMPLE

Telling My Mother

So I'd been to the bathroom 'cause I knew I wouldn't get to go before I made it home and no, I wasn't wearing my black mini! You don't wear leather in early autumn. Anyway, I'd asked this guy—some kid from school—what time it was and he told me 7:10. Don't worry. He wasn't the mugger—I did not ask the mugger the time. It was Johnny Something Or Other from my morning Lit. 121. Anyway, I'm just walking down the sidewalk, heading for the car and it happened. Johnny Whozit must have heard it. He's a big kid, probably a football player or something, and that's all I could think about there, sitting sprawled all over the ground. That kid could've helped me out.

Telling My Best Friend

After that last scene where Sonny Bono's wife's hair blows up and the fat girl gets to dance, I decided to just go ahead and leave early. I took a detour by the john and left out the side door, stopping just long enough to remind this student of mine about something. I wasn't out that door five minutes when I got a whiff of the nastiest smell, something like urine and chocolate all mixed together. And it kinda came on me hard and I lost it, I think, just about then. Next, I felt this thing take ahold of my purse, straightaway, lift it off my arm. And then I sat on the ground trying to remember seeing anybody at all.

Telling My Boyfriend

Listen, I have never, not once, taken anything so hard. They found me sitting on the sidewalk in front of the Tivoli, my dress up around my bottom, crying, you know. Just out of my head. The policeman told me I was going to have to calm down, tell him some facts. But I couldn't even remember what film I'd been to. (I'd gone to *Hairspray* again for the third time. I know you think that's silly, but I've got this thing about John Waters.) I don't remember a thing past losing my pocketbook. You'd think we were in New York City or something.

Telling My Therapist

I have this thing about smells. Dirty smells. Like for instance, my mom tells the story how I'd whip off my diapers the very second they filled up, and well, that's sort of the way I am today. And you can imagine how I felt when this dirty, stinking body—and that's all I can recall about it— pulls into my personal space and attacks. All I could think about was: I am going to get sick, right here, right in front of all Broad Street.

Telling a Police Officer

I was just minding my business, leaving a little early. School tomorrow. I teach, you know, and he must have come out from one of those cars over there because I didn't see him in the building. He was real big, lots of muscles. I didn't get a good look at his face, but he was dressed like a street person and smelled like one. Strong, you know, in more ways than one.

KARL HORNER

While short stories often tell us things we don't know anything about—and this is good of course—they should also, and maybe more importantly, tell us what everybody knows but what nobody is talking about. At least not publicly.

RAYMOND CARVER, INTRODUCTION TO *BASS 1986*

82

SUDDEN FICTION OR
THE SHORT-SHORT STORY

from James Thomas

In our introduction to *Sudden Fiction,* Robert Shapard and I recount how we solicited responses to our working first title, "Blasters," and were amazed at the "uproar." Writers not only had opinions about the word for the short-short story, but also about their traditions, their present developments, the motives for writing and reading them, how they compare to sonnets, ghazals, folk tales, parables, koans, and other forms.

Almost no one agreed entirely on anything. These responses, collected in *Sudden Fiction's* Afterwords make lively reading, but we prefer to let you have the final word for this exercise: to write a story of less than 1500 words. Highly compressed, highly charged, insidious, protean, sudden, alarming, tantalizing, these short-shorts do confer form on small corners of chaos, and, at their best, can do in a page what a novel does in two hundred.

Other anthologies of short-short stories include Irving and Ilana Wiener Howe's *Short Shorts,* with its informative introduction; Robley Wilson's *Four Minute Fictions* which were first published in *North American Review;* and Shapard and my *Sudden Fiction International.*

Question: What is shorter than "sudden fiction?"

Answer: "Flash fiction."

These even shorter stories (all under 750 words) are collected in *Flash Fiction,* edited by Tom Hazuka, Denise Thomas and myself. Then there is the World's Best Short Short Story Contest, run by Jerome Stern at Florida State University at Tallahassee, whose winners and finalists appear in *Sundog: The Southeast Review.* Will anyone forget the "big wind" or "moiling dogs" from the 1991 winning story, "Baby, Baby, Baby," by François Camoin.

THE EXERCISE

Read, read, read these shortest of stories with joy and amazement at their range and multiplicity of form.

Then write one—under 750 words.

THE OBJECTIVE

To create a world, give it shape—all of a sudden, in a flash.

STUDENT STORY

Scrabble

Until I was ten, Dad was a kind man with gray hair and crinkly blue eyes. He never went to college, but he taught me to play Scrabble and even let me win a few times. Mom never understood why I bothered. She kept telling me Dad was being easy, that he could beat me even when I *was* using a dictionary. Dad always smiled and said it was the thought that counted. Then we'd keep playing.

When I was eleven my father was a domineering lawyer who would play obscure Latin words and then show me his legal dockets to prove he was right. I never won and I almost quit.

When I was thirteen he was a factory worker from Pittsburgh who played half a game, then threw the board on the fire. Mom said good riddance, but I got another. So did she when I was sixteen—a fast-talking insurance salesman who palmed the Z before we drew letters. Mom and I both caught him cheating, and we didn't miss him.

When I was nineteen he was a dozen or so faceless beer-smells who rarely said a word to me, much less put any on the board. I did crosswords, and Mom said she was glad I turned out normal.

After that, Mom gave up on men. By that time I was thirty and Dad was three letters, five points, on a double word score which made ten.

CHRISTOPHER WINTERS

A story is a way to say something that can't be said any other way, and it takes every word in the story to say what the meaning is.

FLANNERY O'CONNOR

83

ACCOUNTING: HOW DID WE GET HERE?

In her wonderful essay "Mr. Bennett and Mrs. Brown" Virginia Woolf talks about her sources of inspiration. She writes, "I believe that all novels begin with an old lady in the corner opposite" [in the train]. That is, the moment she sees a stranger she begins to make up a story about her. When you try this you'll find that some of your stories lead nowhere; others keep on growing. Most experienced fiction writers do this constantly—always making up who that person is and why he's sitting there in the rain. Or what those two people are talking about while waiting in line to buy their tickets. If you don't already have this habit, cultivate it. Start accounting for things, explaining who, what, why, and how. Write your ideas down, read them over.

THE EXERCISE

Imagine you are in a line of traffic driving away from the country at nine o'clock on a Sunday morning in August. This line of traffic is much heavier than you anticipated. Who are these people and why are they leaving the beach instead of going in the opposite direction? Account for the occupants of the six cars in front of you. (For example, the man in the Chevy is going back to town because he just found out his doughnut shop there was broken into at 3:00 A.M. He is pissed.)

THE OBJECTIVE

To train yourself to take off from what you see and hear and create an instant story out of it. To encourage speculation and explore motivation.

STUDENT EXAMPLE

Only a completely macho dude would drive a car like that—a silver Corvette—so it's obvious why he's going back to the city early instead of staying and working on his tan. Clearly, things didn't work out so well with the girl he'd met last night. He'd been hoping that she'd ask him to spend the day with her, but after that shameful performance last night, he just wants to get away as quickly as he can.

Just like the commercial, the family in the wood-paneled station wagon had their money stolen while they were buying flip-flops, and they had to call their weekend short. The boy and girl in the backseat are sucking on McDonald's shakes bought with the little bit of change they found on the car floor, and the husband and wife aren't talking to each other. Each blames the other.

The young woman in the yellow Honda is working the noon-to-five shift today in Filene's men's shirt department and had to leave the party early. She is chewing her nails and hopes she makes it back in time; otherwise, this will be the third time this month she's been late to work.

The old man driving the Oldsmobile is the teenage boy's grandfather. They've just come back from visiting the old man's daughter (the young man's mother) in the insane asylum the day before. They spent the night in a cheap motel. The boy stayed up watching television until 3:00 A.M., while the old man snored. They both couldn't wait to get away from the crazy woman.

The five Chinese people, three men and two women, who are crammed into the K-Car, are trying to see as much of the USA as they can in two weeks, before they all have to go back to the University of Utah where they are doing postdoctoral work in the fusion lab. They saw the mountains and then turned around to keep on schedule.

The man and woman in their thirties are lovers and have just spent their first romantic weekend together where they have discovered some things about each other they don't like; he spends too long in the bathroom, she talks about her ex-husband too much. Now they are each feeling a little guilty for lying about having to be back home early.

AMY JENNINGS

223

84

PSYCHO: CREATING TERROR

Y̶ou like scary? Here's an exercise students have so taken to heart that they report terror-filled, sleepless nights. Many writers shy away from extremes when in fact it's those very tense situations and moments that give fiction its excitement and singularity. You should be able to handle violence, passion, and terror as easily as you do two people having a friendly conversation over a couple of burgers.

THE EXERCISE

You're taking a shower in your house or apartment. You are not expecting anyone and the front door is locked (the bathroom door is not). You hear a strange noise in a room beyond the bathroom. Now, take it from there for no more than two pages. This can be in either the third or the first person. Don't spend any time getting into the shower; you're there when the action begins.

THE OBJECTIVE

To tell a convincing story centered on speculation and terror.

STUDENT EXAMPLE

Ajax, my cat, must have crawled on top of the refrigerator again and knocked over the basket of onions. And now he's playing with the onions—that's the scraping noise—and when I get out of the shower they're going to be all over the floor. Sometimes when Ajax sees another cat he starts to moan and howl, like he's doing now—but he sounds strange. Maybe he's hurt himself.

I pull back the shower curtain and stick my head out to listen. The noise has stopped but I think I just saw something move in the hall. I can't see much from here, but I'm sure a shadow darted past the door. I let the water run over my head again and shut my eyes as the soap runs by, and all of a sudden I feel a draft of cold air. I open my eyes through the soap and hold my breath; the soap stings my eyes. Everything is quiet. All I can hear is the sound of the water, but again I think I see a shadow change. I turn off the water and now I'm breathing fast. I'm standing on the bath mat and Ajax comes in and rubs against my wet legs and then the moaning starts again but it's not the cat, who jumps in fright. I clutch a towel to my chest. I don't know whether to look out into the hall or shut the door. I freeze. Things are crashing in the kitchen, glass breaks; a chair is moved. I slam the bathroom door and manage to lock it even though my fingers are trembling. I'm whimpering. Ajax is hunched in the corner, behind the toilet. The moans grow louder; they're coming closer.

What can I use as a weapon? A disposable razor? A tube of shampoo, a toilet brush, a bottle of Fantastik? I hold this bottle like a gun, my finger on its trigger. I've dropped the towel and I get into the other corner, making small sobbing noises. The moans stop abruptly; then the pounding on the door begins.

HESTER KAPLAN

I don't invent characters because the Almighty has already invented millions. . . . Just like experts at fingerprints do not create fingerprints but learn how to read them.

ISAAC BASHEVIS SINGER

85

THE NEWSPAPER MUSE:
ANN LANDERS AND
THE NATIONAL ENQUIRER

In her essay, "The Nature of Short Fiction; or, the Nature of My Short Fiction," Joyce Carol Oates says that she is "greatly interested in the newspapers and in Ann Landers' columns and in *True Confessions* and in the anecdotes told under the guise of 'gossip.' Amazing revelations!" She says she has written a great number of stories based on "the barest newspaper accounts . . . it is the very skeletal nature of the newspaper, I think, that attracts me to it, the need it inspires in me to give flesh to such neatly and thinly-told tales, to resurrect this event which has already become history and will never be understood unless it is re-lived, re-dramatized."

THE EXERCISE

Collect Ann Landers columns, gossip columns, and stories from *Weekly World News* or *True Confessions* that seem to you to form—either partially or wholly—the basis for a story. Often, these newspaper accounts will be the "end" of the story and you will have to fill in the events leading up to the more dramatic event that made the news that day. Or perhaps the story leads you to ask what is going to happen to that person now.

Clip and save four or five items. Outline a story based on one of them, indicating where the story begins, who the main characters are, what the general tone (that is, the emotional timbre of the work) will be, and from whose point of view you elect to tell the story. These articles can be used for shorter, more focused exercises. For example, describe the car of the person in the article, or the contents of his wallet. Or have the person from the article write three letters.

THE OBJECTIVE

The objective is threefold. One is to look for an article that triggers your imagination and to understand how, when you dramatize the events, the story then becomes *your* story. The second is to increase the beginning writer's awareness of the stories all around us. And third to practice deciding how and where to enter a story and where to leave off.

STUDENT EXAMPLE

One writer used an article from *Weekly World News* about a Japanese moving company that specializes in moving people at "odd times of the day." The service was popular with debtors avoiding creditors and with girlfriends leaving boyfriends. In one case, a woman took her boyfriend to dinner, while the moving company removed her possessions from their apartment.

When I went for the job interview, I found the owner in a garage-office, seated at his desk, which wobbled on three legs and a stack of cinder blocks. He was writing in a ledger and stuffing a jelly doughnut into his mouth between calculations.

I cleared my throat and he turned to boom a "Hi there, kid" at me, then wiped his fingers on his shirt and shook my hand. We sat down on the ripped red vinyl of an old car seat and Jake lit up a Marlboro. In between drags, he tried to explain how he'd founded the business, but he kept getting interrupted by calls from potential customers. He'd put each caller on hold, telling them he'd have to check with the personnel department or ask the mechanics about the truck fleet. Then, winking at me, he'd hang the phone over his shoulder and tap his cigarette in the general vicinity of the ashtray, and finally get back on the line to finish the call. When I asked what all that was about, he said he wanted people to think his company was some kind of big deal outfit.

"Impresses the hell out of most of them." He glanced out the door at the company truck—the "fleet" that he'd mentioned on the phone—parked by the curb. "There's another gag I pull. Y'know what people always ask me?" When I shrugged he said, "They ask, 'Where's Darkness Falls?'"

I wanted the job so I humored him. "So what do you say?"

"I tell them it's just south of Northboro. Sometimes I say just east of Westboro. I want them to think that we're a really mysterious outfit."

"What's so mysterious about moving stuff?"

His cigarette ashes fluttered down on my jeans as he leaned toward me. "It's not that simple, Kerry. Let's say you want to be moved with no questions asked, any time of night. Maybe your business wasn't cutting the mustard, so you figure you better move your equipment before the bank moves it out for you. Who do you call? The Darkness Falls Moving Company," he said, grinning. "When you want to make a sudden move, we're the move to make."

Everyone else who interviewed me had given me the look of death when I said I had to quit in September, but Jake just shrugged and said he could use me about four nights a week. "Be prepared to work anytime between dusk and dawn," he said. "I'm the Robin Hood of the moving business."

SCOTT WEIGHART, THE DARKNESS FALLS MOVING COMPANY

86

WRITE A STORY USING
A SMALL UNIT OF TIME

Some short stories employ a small, contained unit of time or center on a single event that provides the story with a given natural shape. For example, in Nicholson Baker's short story "Pants on Fire," the narrator puts on a shirt and takes the subway to work, nothing else happens. Raymond Carver's story "Cathedral" takes place in one evening when an old friend comes to visit the narrator's wife. And Sharon Sheehe Stark's story "The Gift" tells of a family's car ride to a relative's wedding, achieving a unity of time and place.

THE EXERCISE

Make a list yourself of things that are done in small units of time. Here are several suggestions: Naming a pet or a child, breaking up with someone, playing a game such as Risk or Monopoly, washing a car, stealing something, waiting or standing in line for something, packing to go somewhere, changing the message on an answering machine, cleaning a refrigerator, having a birthday party, etc.

Now write a four- to seven-page story staying within the confines of a particular time unit. For example, a birthday party story would probably last only a few hours, or an afternoon or evening.

THE OBJECTIVE

To recognize the enormous number of shaped time units in our lives. These units can provide a natural substructure and shape for a story and make the writing of a story seem less daunting.

STUDENT EXAMPLES

One student wrote a five-page story using the time unit of changing a bicycle tire. Another student wrote a story using the time unit of wrapping Christmas presents.

STUDENT STORY

The Smell of Garlic

The day I left Ian, I made him a bacon and garlic omelet. Banana pancakes were my specialty he once said, but the smell of warm bananas never lingered after the last plate was in the dishwasher. I smashed garlic with a meat tenderizer and separated three cloves which I chopped with a steak knife. We never bought a garlic press.

Ian wasn't home yet. He said he was going bowling the night before. I caught up on my reading—percentage of women who are dissatisfied with their thighs? 72, said a report in *Allure,* and "For people born before 1930, memories of youth were aroused by odors of pine and hay, while people born between the 30s and 70s were reminded of youth by Play-Doh, Vicks Vaporub, and Pine Sol."

The bacon was spitting so I brought the flame down and cracked eggs. Before I packed, I went around the house to find the good smells. The soles of his hiking boots smelled like cut grass from the backyard we cleared six years ago. His Bruins cap was the smell of camping, when we spent two hours assembling the green tent, or when we lost seven hamburgers in the fire and ate marshmallows for dinner. The bad smells were the bowling shoes still in his closet, and the perfume on his shirts that wasn't mine.

When he came home, he found the omelet warming in the oven. By then I had tried to scrub the garlic off my fingers for the third time in the bus station bathroom.

KIM LEAHY, HONORABLE MENTION, WORLD'S BEST
SHORT SHORT STORY CONTEST 1992

87

NOTES AND LETTERS

The first novels in the English language were in the form of letters—so-called epistolary novels, like Samuel Richardson's *Pamela* and *Clarissa*. Recent epistolary novels are Hal Dresner's *The Man Who Wrote Dirty Books*, Lee Smith's *Fair and Tender Ladies*, and Alice Walker's *The Color Purple*. And then there are the novels that employ letters. Herzog in Saul Bellow's novel by that name writes letters to Spinoza; to Willie Sutton, the famous bank robber; and to presidents. In Ann Beattie's novel *Love Always*, Lucy Spenser receives and replies to letters as Cindi Coeur, the Miss Lonelyhearts of a magazine called *Country Daze*. Sam Hughes, a feisty 17-year-old girl in Bobbie Ann Mason's *In Country*, meets the father, who died before she was born, in the diary he kept in Vietnam and his letters home. Tucked into the narrative of a work of fiction, a letter allows the author an especially intimate tone—somewhat like talking into the reader's ear. It's also useful at crucial moments in a plot—in it things get told economically and with a sense of urgency. A letter is often a quick way of delivering exposition, characterization, and voice.

THE EXERCISE

Here are several situations and the letters they might engender. You're a senior in college writing home to tell your parent(s) that you're dropping out of school. You want them to understand, if not exactly approve of, your reason(s) for leaving. Make these specific and persuasive. Then write the answer, either from one or both of the parents. Or, you're writing a letter to your landlord to tell him you are withholding the rent until he addresses problems in your apartment. Or you are leaving behind a note for your spouse explaining why you are leaving him or her. Or you are writing literary graffiti on the walls of a toilet stall in the Library of Congress. Limit: 500 words.

THE OBJECTIVE

To get inside the head of another person, someone you have invented, and assume her voice to vary your narrative conveyance.

STUDENT EXAMPLE

Cher Mom and Dad,

I hope you two know how to speak a little French, because I have some news for you that's going to knock your berets right off. Remember

I told you that I was taking French this semester? Well, I didn't tell you that my teacher's name was Mademoiselle Pipette and I didn't tell you that I had a crush on her. It turns out that she had a crush on me too, and now we are madly in love. We want to get married so little Pierre or little Gigi will have a dad when he or she arrives at the end of May. I'm going to be a *père!* (That's "father" in French.)

Jeannette can't support us on her teaching salary, so I'm dropping out of college. You've always taught me to be responsible for my actions and this seems like the correct thing to do. I'm going to get a job to support my family and make a home for us. Someday I'll go back to school. The dean assured me I can reapply later and finish my degree.

You two are going to be grandparents! I'm sure you're as excited by all this as I am. College seems unimportant at the moment in the face of these great changes. I know you'll love Jeannette and she sends a *bonjour* to you.

Avec amour (that's "with love"),
Teddy

Dear Teddy,

Forget it. No son of mine is going to drop out of college and get married just because a schoolboy crush on his French teacher went a little too far. I think I know better than you when I say that a twenty-one-year-old boy has no conception of what it means to be a responsible father and husband. And what kind of job do you imagine yourself getting? Who's going to hire a boy whose only work experience was mowing his parents' lawn?

I, too, talked to the dean. At the end of the semester, your Mademoiselle Pipette will say good-bye to teaching and to you. I have arranged for her go back to France and have the baby there. I have also gotten her assurance that she and you will have no more contact.

I've spared your mother the news of this mindless mess. It would only make her sicker. Though you don't think so now, you will thank me in years to come for getting you out of this situation. In the meantime I suggest you get back to your studies and work hard toward that all-important degree.

Fondly,
Dad

BRIAN FOSTER

Memo from *Atlantic* editors

Subject: Articles and stories we do not want to read or edit:

Short stories which ask the reader to blame society for misfortunes inflicted on the characters by the author.

88

STIRRING UP A FICTION STEW

from Sharon Sheehe Stark

When you don't have a story pushing to be written, it is still a good idea to write anyway, to exercise language and story. This is especially true for beginning writers who sometimes have to be shown they can "wing it" without knowing exactly where they are going.

THE EXERCISE

Begin a story from random elements such as two characters, a place, two objects, an adjective, and an abstract word. If you are not in a class, give this list to someone and have them provide you with the words so you will be surprised by them. If you are in a class have the class make up a random list. Then everyone must use these elements in the first two pages of a story.

THE OBJECTIVE

To exercise your imagination, to prove to yourself that all you need is a trigger to get you started writing. And if you care about the story you start, the finish will take care of itself.

STUDENT EXAMPLE

Below are the words students chose in a workshop and one student's story written from this list.

pyromaniac	skycap
all-night diner	tuna fish
bowling pin	gardenia
polyester	infinity

Next to the airport: DANTE'S DINER, OPEN 24 HOURS, red neon sign blinking on and off. Red's a cheerful color.

I been night cook here at Dante's for twenty years. Dante, he died last March. House burned down; some pyromaniac lit it. Hell of a thing. Dante's kid owns the place now. Never seen her. But her lawyer came by yesterday—skinny guy, in one of those crummy polyester suits. Asking a

232

lot of questions, sticking his pointy nose into everything. Told me she wanted to sell.

What does she care? So I'm out of a job—so what's it to her? They'll turn the goddamn place into a Lum's or a Hardee's or something. Progress. Premade frozen burgers—premeasured milk shake mix—packaged pie. Progress? Hey, this is a diner: a *diner,* with diner food: hot beef sandwiches, real mashed potatoes, rice pudding, tuna on rye with potato chips and a pickle, and my lemon meringue pie.

I like the people who come in here: skycaps, tourists, kids on dates, hippies, businessmen. Last night a bowling league came in from a tournament over at Airport Lanes. All of them in satin jackets with big bowling pins embroidered on the backs, eating and talking and looking at a couple of pretty girls in the back booth, girls with long hair, shiny pink lips and perfume like gardenias.

I like night work. It's my time. The nights stretch on forever—what's that word? Infinity. The dark outside, all blue, the red neon blinking. Jukebox going. The way I slap my spatula down on the grill, the way I flip eggs over. The way people look when they come in—hungry, tired, and when they leave, they look fed. I get so I'm almost sorry when it's morning. Especially now with that lawyer ruining my day.

GINA LOGAN

89

SOLVING FOR X

from Ron Carlson

The following exercise works best if it is done first and discussed afterward.

THE EXERCISE

Write a short story with the following conditions: It is exactly 26 sentences in length. Each sentence begins with a word which starts with one of the letters of the alphabet—in order. For example:

All the excuses had been used. By the time the school doctor saw me, he'd heard everything. Coughing, I began to tell him about the lie which I hoped would save us all. AND SO FORTH.

Also, you must use one sentence fragment. Oh, and one sentence should be exactly 100 words long and grammatically sound.

THE OBJECTIVE

The objective here is initially obscured by how confused everyone is to have such a strange mission. Tell them to get over it. What the assignment illuminates is form's role in process. Since the imposed form has nothing at all to do with the writer's real agenda, the exercise becomes a fundamental exploration of our sense of story, narrative rise and fall, and process—process most prominently. What a challenge and a comfort knowing how that next sentence begins! The discussions we've had over these ABC stories are some of the strongest and most central, and the issues that arise follow us all semester.

To make a more dramatic point about structure and its relationship to process, divide any group of writers in two and assign only half the above exercise to the first group. Assign the second group the same exercise but make it clear that the twenty-six sentences do not have to be in alphabetical order. Any bets on who has the more difficult task?

STUDENT STORIES

Arnie's Test Day

Arnie Watson, facing five tests on a spring Friday of his junior year at Riverdale High School, sat in his bedroom at five a.m. and wrote all over his clothes. Beneath the bill of his Chicago Bulls cap, Arnie wrote in

Spanish—twenty vocabulary words from a list that he was provided by Señora Martin on Monday and told to memorize by Friday. Certainly Arnie would have memorized those words, just as he had done with vocabulary lists all year, had he not been on the phone for two hours Thursday night trying to convince Marilou Spencer not to break up with him. Dismayed when Marilou slammed the phone in his ear, Arnie couldn't concentrate on his Español the rest of the night. Exasperated, he rose early on Friday and meticulously wrote those twenty words and shorthand definitions in fine black ink on the underside of the cap's red bill.

Frankly, Arnie didn't have the chance to study history that week, either. Gus Finley and Arnie were going to meet at the Riverdale Library on Tuesday and study the amendments to the Constitution, but Arnie got stuck in the house after a fight with his parents. How are you going to get into a real college, they yelled, a Michigan or a Duke or a Stanford, if you fall out of the top five percent of your class, if you bring home any more eighty percents in your honors classes? Just you wait and see, Arnie retorted, storming upstairs to his bedroom.

Knowing that he couldn't leave the house after such a scene, Arnie didn't meet Gus at the library, which is why on that Friday morning before school, Arnie wrote abbreviated versions of the amendments on the inside collar of his Reebok polo shirt, actually needing to write on the inside of the shirt itself, repealing Prohibition just above his heart.

Luck ran against Arnie that week in English, too. Mr. Phelan, the Riverdale basketball coach, told his players they had better be at spring conditioning OR ELSE. Naturally, Arnie wanted to stay on Phelan's good side for his senior season, so Arnie ran and lifted weights with the rest of the team after school that week, precluding him from reading all but the first chapter of *The Great Gatsby*. On Friday morning, then, Arnie wrote "Jay Gatsby" and "Nick Caraway" and "Tom Buchanan" and "Daisy Buchanan" on the tanned inside of his belt along with a very brief synopsis of their literal and metaphorical roles in the novel; on the pale blue inside waistband of his jeans, Arnie elaborated on Fitzgerald's symbolism, even drawing a pair of spectacles overlooking a map of the East Egg and West Egg, Gatsby's mansion, a heap of ashes and a skyscraper representing New York City, praying that the information he had gleaned from *Cliff's Notes* would be useful on Mrs. Schenck's in-class essay.

Possibly the most difficult test for Arnie would be physics. Quantum theory was hard enough for Arnie to understand during lectures and labs; finding time to memorize formulas for Friday's test was another problem.

Right when he opened his notebook on Wednesday night, Arnie's grandmother called to say that Grampa had been admitted to Riverdale Hospital with chest pains. So Arnie and his parents spent three hours at the hospital, where Arnie read *People* magazine instead of *Introduction to Physics* while waiting for the doctors to report Grampa's condition. They said Grampa would have surgery on Friday—Arnie's test day—only a few hours after Arnie wrote quantum physics formulas on the outside of his polyester white socks.

Unusual as it was, Arnie faced a fifth test that Friday in trigonometry. Vindicating himself for being required to attend Riverdale Lutheran Church choir practice last night—after basketball conditioners and before his devastating phone call to Marilou Spencer, after lying to his parents that no, he did not have any tests on Friday, after answering countless questions from other choir members about his grandfather's impending heart operation—Arnie wrote trigonometry notes on the bottom white soles of his Air Jordan basketball shoes. Why me, Arnie thought, and next to the silhouette logo of Michael Jordan flying above the world, Arnie charted trigonometic patterns. X-axis: the function of pressure is on the rise. Y-axis: the probability exists that Arnie will be forced to use his crib notes. Z-axis: the arc of trouble in Arnie's life increases at an extremely sharp angle, the black line speeding unheeded toward infinity.

BARRY PETERS

Giving It Away

All I wanted at the time were dining chairs for the refectory table, something oak but not too precious, late teens or twenties maybe, t-backs, with new tapestry covered seats. But Xaviera was thinking bigtime, she was into Shaker and Stickley and thwarting industrialization and alienation. Capitalism nosediving, an Arts and Crafts revival, all this and more she flung at me on Saturday mornings when we drove the valley, hitting yard sales and estate sales hopefully ahead of the antique dealers; or, if the dealers beat us there, they would be after depression glass or Roseville and not the chairs stacked high under the tarp in the garage, where I would spot them, and where I would measure their turned legs with my eye, flip them over one by one and check for planing, gouges, clicking at the sad state these lovely pieces had fallen to—white spiders nesting in the joints, the seats worn and faded.

"Don't give anything away," Xaviera said, meaning I looked too eager, meaning I should hold out for the real thing, meaning I have a face that anyone could read, and, after having done so, would raise the price, or decide not to sell.

Every Saturday morning that spring she was at my door by seven-thirty, classifieds in hand, the ads highlighted and color-coded by location. Fluorescent orange, the Avenues. Green, the east bench, from Holladay to Sandy. Hot pink, Sugarhouse. I sometimes dragged her to Rose Park, even though she had tried to educate me in the ways of things, of antiques—that nothing good could be found west of Trolley Square—but Xaviera, I said, these people have grandmothers and great aunts who ordered mission furniture from the Sears catalogue and bought Fiesta place settings at Woolworth's, and she shrugged.

"Junk," she said, "is relative; but if all you have are grandmother's pearls and her turkey platter, would you let them go?"

"Keeping a thing is also relative," I said. "Like that woman in Sugarhouse who said her therapist told her selling her mother's oak sideboard might help her clean up her internal house and live in the here and now.'"

"Might," Xaviera said. "Not that I haven't thought about it myself, cutting everything loose and starting over—you have to admit it's tempting. People start to expect certain things from you after a while, like you only collect thirties flatwear, or you would never wear black or vote a straight party ticket or would drop everything and start over, wham, just like that. Quicksilver, presto-changeo."

Right now, I thought, when Xaviera was snapping her fingers and looking determined, right now is not the time to be saying these things to me; right now I want chairs that are not all business, chairs I can bring to life with orange oil and steel wool; right now I want to look like I am putting down roots, thinking of remodeling, maybe putting in a bay window on the east side of the dining room or a skylight in the bathroom—I want this now. Starting again, (*startling again,* my mother once said, adding an *l,* propping the black phone receiver up to her ear with her shoulder while she sprinkled the laundry on ironing day, *morning is always that way for me, a new beginning, rise and shine—so why should this be any different?*), no thank you, not me—what I want is continuity.

"Think about it," Xaviera said, and I was, that was the problem, that's all I have ever done, my one big problem, *you think too much*—always I weighed possibilities and probabilities against each other. Until that spring with Xaviera I had shrugged it all off and kept on. Very much as always, Xaviera saying turn here, don't turn there, and then that one day she yelled stop stop! and jumped out of the car before I had even complied, and I stopped thinking and took notice.

"Why here?" I asked, but Xaviera wasn't listening, she was heading for a house that sat back a bit from the street, a house with odds and ends stacked up high on the porch and on the lawn, a house that wasn't highlighted on our list.

Xaviera said, "Oh jeez, oh lord, sweetie look at this," and she unrolled a rug that was all over rose trellises and blue hyacinths and yellow birds, a Victorian copy from the twenties, I guessed, and Xaviera was crouched down, resting her chin on her knees, remembering something, from the look on her face.

"You're giving it away," I said, and the woman standing in the open doorway thought I was talking to her and jumped and called out a price that was too high, and Xaviera turned to me and whispered *please, please, how much can you help with this?*

Zip, I thought, zero, nothing will help this, but I gave her what she needed anyway.

SHELLEY HUNT

90

THE END FORETOLD

Few readers are tempted to turn to the end of a novel to find out "what happens," because the journey to the end is one of the pleasures of being inside that particular story. However, some writers tell future events at the beginning of their story or novel, trusting their story-telling abilities to keep the reader reading. Early on in his story "White Angel" Michael Cunningham writes about two brothers, the younger of whom adores his older brother, Carlton. "I was, thanks to Carlton, the most criminally advanced nine-year-old in my fourth-grade class. I was going places. I made no move without his counsel." The next sentence begins, "Here is Carlton several months before his death, in an hour so alive with snow that earth and sky are identically white." And we continue reading on for that "hour so alive"—alive even more so in the face of Carlton's impending death.

Rudolfo Anaya also foretells events in his novel *Bless Me, Ultima*. In the first pages his narrator tells us, "The attic of our home was partitioned into two small rooms. My sisters, Deborah and Theresa, slept in one and I slept in the small cubicle by the door. The wooden steps creaked down into a small hallway that led into the kitchen. From the top of the stairs I had the vantage point into the heart of our home, my mother's kitchen. From there I was to see the terrified face of Chavez when he brought the terrible news of the murder of the sheriff; I was to see the rebellion of my brothers against my father; and many times late at night I was to see Ultima returning from the Llano where she gathered the herbs that can be harvested only in the light of the full moon by the careful hands of a curandera." Note how murder and his brothers' rebellion are woven into a sentence that brings us through to his adored Ultima.

In the beginning of *Stones for Ibarra*, Harriet Doerr writes, "Here they are, a man and a woman just over and just under forty, come to spend their lives in Mexico City and are already lost as they travel cross-country over the central plateau. The driver of the station wagon is Richard Everton, a blue-eyed, black-haired stubborn man who will die thirty years sooner than he now imagines. On the seat beside him is his wife, Sara, who imagines neither his death nor her own, imminent or remote as they may be."

Other works of fiction that foretell their endings are Elizabeth Jane Howard's "The Long View" and Gabriel García Márquez's *Chronicle of a Death Foretold*.

THE EXERCISE

Select one of your own stories that has an ending that is final—a story in which someone leaves a place or person forever, someone dies, or something irrevocable and irreparable takes place. Now move this "news" to the beginning of your story. Be brief. Then read your story again to see if the journey through the story is rewarding in itself.

THE OBJECTIVE

To put pressure on the story—sentence by sentence—by "giving away" the ending. To understand that chronology is fluid and sometimes irrelevant to the experience of the story.

XI. REVISION: REWRITING IS WRITING

Revision is just that: a chance to reenvision your work, to revise your story or chapter until it feels finished. Often the difference between a good story and a publishable story is revision. Ted Solotaroff, in his essay "Writing in the Cold," says:

> Writing a first draft is like groping one's way into a pitch dark room, or overhearing a faint conversation, or telling a joke whose punchline you've forgotten. As someone said, one writes mainly to rewrite, for rewriting and revising are how one's mind comes to inhabit the material fully. In its benign form, rewriting is a second, third, and nth chance to make something come right, to 'fall graciously into place', in Lewis Hyde's phrase. But it is also a test: one has to learn to respect the misgiving that says, This still doesn't ring true, still hasn't touched bottom. And this means to go back down into the mine again and poke around for the missing ore and find a place for it and let it work its will.

We didn't understand the reluctance of beginning writers to rewrite—and in fact ascribed it to a lack of commitment—until one student wrote in her class evaluation: "The most important thing I learned this semester was that rewriting is writing. Although I understood in theory the importance of revising work, somehow I felt guilty unless I produced something new—and preferably something good—the first time. Rewriting felt like cheating." When we brought this up in subsequent classes, most students admitted that they mistrusted the degree to which established writers say they revise. "Surely Saul Bellow doesn't have to rewrite!" Yet Saul Bellow rewrote *Herzog* twenty times. "The first chapters of Gish Jen's novel flow so smoothly that they must have come right the first time." Yet Gish Jen rewrote her opening chapters forty times. From that class on, we have made it a point to show students that *rewriting is writing* and that revising a story or novel—two, ten, or forty times—is part of the pleasure of writing. When William Faulkner was asked what advice he would give to young writers, he said:

> At one time I thought the most important thing was talent. I think now that the young man or the young woman must possess or teach himself, training himself, in infinite patience, which is to try and to try until it comes right. He must train himself in ruthless intolerance—that is to throw away anything that is false no matter how much he might love that page or that paragraph.

We have found that students often lose interest in revision because they merely go back over a story from start to finish—making a few changes as they go. They fail to see that an early draft is in a fluid state and can be totally redrafted and/or rearranged: the final scene might be moved to the beginning; the first person might be changed to third; present tense might be changed to past; characters might be dropped or invented; language, scene length, imagery, body language, description, etc., all are evaluated—often separately.

We chose not to include sample pages from a work in progress or examples of successive drafts because how something finds its way on to the page or is changed or deleted is a mysterious, complicated, and always personal process. The most successful "reproductions" of the revision process appear in Janet Burroway's *Writing Fiction* and David Madden's *Revising Fiction*. The exercises in this section are designed to take you through various aspects of the revision process, and to help you discover how revision works best for you. Bernard Malamud said, "Revision is one of the true pleasures of writing."

The only way, I think, to learn to write short stories is to write them, and then try to discover what you have done. The time to think of technique is when you've actually got the story in front of you.

FLANNERY O'CONNOR

91

EXPLORING THE CREATIVE WRITING PROCESS

from Tony Ardizzone

When I talk to students about the writing process and how they might become more productive and even happier writers, I tell them it's best to write in stages. It's like washing a linoleum floor, I say. Then I describe the process step by step.

I say start in one corner and clear off a small section, not too much, maybe the top four tiles and the next four down. Sweep these sixteen tiles thoroughly. Then prepare a bucket full of warm, soapy water and wash the sixteen tiles until they're clean. Wait for the sixteen tiles to dry. After they're dry, check to see if dirt from the other tiles has gotten on them, and if so sweep the dirt off. Then pour on the polish. Wait for the polish to dry. Then buff the polish until it shines. Then move onto the next section of sixteen tiles.

By this time students are shaking their heads. They tell me that's no way to wash a floor. You'd go crazy washing floors like that, they say. You're repeating every little step. The way to wash a floor, they say, is to do it in big stages: to clear the floor entirely of furniture, to sweep the tiles all at once, then wash the entire floor, wait for it dry, then polish the entire floor, wait for the polish to dry, then buff and shine it.

Do it in big stages, they say, not in a series of repetitions that attempts to perfect each and every little thing as you go along.

I agree with them. Then I add that I was really talking about writing by describing the way how *not* to write.

THE EXERCISE

Read one of the many volumes of *Writers at Work: The Paris Review Interviews,* and take notes on the sections in which writers talk about the process they follow as they write. Then look at your notes for similarities, as well as differences, in the writing processes they describe. Consider which writer works most like the way you write. Which writer works most differently from you? Discover ways that you might change how you go about writing fiction in order to work more happily and successfully.

THE OBJECTIVE

To learn that while there is no single correct way to write fiction, there is a series of stages that most writers inevitably follow. These stages begin with a spark or germ and then include *discovering* the preliminary or first draft, *exploring* further possibilities of character and action in one or more middle drafts, then *editing and polishing* the work in a satisfying manner. Most successful writers do what is more or less appropriate to the stage they are working on. Writers who attempt to do too much too soon often end up feeling frustrated. There is a time to discover and take risks and explore unforseen possibilities, and another (usually later) time to polish the work's syntax and diction.

92

OPENING UP YOUR STORY

When stories are in an early draft they sometimes feel thin, in need of more texture—in need of something. This is the precise time when your story is most flexible and capable of being opened up; successive drafts weave the sentences ever more tightly together. At first glance this exercise on opening up your story might seem the most artificial, the most intrusive foray into your work. Keep in mind, however, that even when suggestions come from "outside" the story, your own imagination is still in control of selecting the material, the details, the language, to make many of these suggested additions absolutely organic to your story.

THE EXERCISE

Choose a story to work with that is still in an early draft form. Read it through so you are thoroughly familiar with it and with the characters. Then find a place in the story to complete and insert the following sentences (change the pronoun as necessary).

The last few nights she had a recurring dream (or nightmare) about

_____.

Her mother always warned her that _____.

The one thing I couldn't say was _____.

The telephone rang. It was a wrong number but the caller refused to hang up. Instead, she _____. (Have at least five or six exchanges.)

Something seemed different _____.

The last time he had worn this _____ was when _____.

If someone said make a wish, she would wish for _____.

As for God, _____.

People were probably saying _____.

This time last year she was _____.

Five years from now he'll be _____.

Secretly, I collected _____.

Outside, it was _____. (Make the weather do something, for example, play off the inside atmosphere. Choose a season.)

Suddenly, she remembered she had forgotten to _____.

On the TV (or radio or CD player) _____ was _____.

She suspected that _____.

The smell of _____ brought back _____.

As a child, he had learned _____.

Now come up with some of your own inserts.

THE OBJECTIVE

To experience how your semiconscious imagination is capable of conjuring up material that is absolutely organic to your story for each "fill-in" from the above list. Writers who do this exercise are always amazed at how something so seemingly artificial can provide them with effective additions to their stories.

STUDENT EXAMPLES

Last night Bobby had *the dream* again that Albert was down in the basement, he had all the bodies in the basement, everyone strapped to a chair in a big circle, and the washer was going, rumbling and ticking like there were rocks in it, and Albert was in the middle of the circle with a beer in his hand and he was singing, spinning around and singing to each body, bending, bowing to each one and Bobby yelled to him Albert what the fuck, what the fuck Albert and Albert sang to him too, sang get your own beer, get your own beer brother Bobby, and that's when he realized what the bumping noise was, it was their shoes, all of their shoes, Albert was washing their shoes in the washer, all their feet were bare, purple, and Albert was still singing to him, singing now I'm cleaning their shoes.

JIM MEZZANOTTE, "BROTHERS"

That night I dreamed that the dolls I'd knitted around the spare rolls of toilet paper were twirling on a dance floor. Their skirts weren't my knitted ones, but the toilet paper itself, unwinding in strands like the trains of wedding gowns.

JANET TASHJIAN

The one thing I can't say is that I have a feeling we might not make it. A negative attitude in the mountains is a taboo. There were two guys who got lost in a snowstorm on this same mountain just a week before and froze to death. But Donnie knows what he's doing.

TOM BRADY

The one thing I couldn't tell my brother about was the night Nelson pushed his way into the bathroom of the trailer while I was pulling up my pants.

Nelson didn't say a word. He shoved me back into the hard sink and pressed against me, and all I could see was his shaved head, up close the stubble of dark hair just beginning to cover the scabs sliced into his scalp. Momma called out for me to help with dinner, and next thing I'm in the kitchen trying to explain what nearly happened. When things happen that quickly, it's easy to be convinced of anything else.

"Winnie," Momma said, "Nelson only went to wash his hands."

Later on, all the proof you have is a fear that shoots through you every time you smell a certain kind of bathroom cleanser, and that's nothing you can explain to a brother.

CHRISTINE FLANAGAN

The caller refused to hang up, instead she kept asking me if I knew where Joey was. I told her there was no one here by that name.

"Just tell him it's Maria," she said. "He'll know."

"But there's no Joey here."

"Did he tell you about me?" Her voice rose. "He told me about you, you little slut."

For a second I wondered if this Maria somehow knew me, or she knew Billy, or Samantha, or even my mother. "I'm hanging up," I told her. "Sorry." After I hung up I realized I had apologized, and that she had only called me the name I had been afraid to say all night.

BARBARA LEWIS

He was calling for a Mrs. Patterson to tell her that she might win a million dollars in a vacuum cleaner-catalogue-sweepstakes. I said, "There is no Mrs. Patterson here."

"Can I talk to your mom?" he asked.

"No," I said. "Her name's not Mrs. Patterson."

He said, "Your mother must be Mrs. Luckman. She promised she'd call me back." My mother was Mrs. Luckman but what the man didn't know was that my mother was always promising everyone everything. She had no time for all her promises. I tried not to hurt his feelings. "Mr.," I said, "Promises are easy to forget when there's more important things to be remembered." Later I often wondered if he understood me.

DORY ELZAURDIA

Something seemed different, Solomon stopped showing us magic tricks, and drank a lot more, and Mom and he stayed up later, ever since he discovered it was cucumbers he had planted and watered and worried over and weeded and not the mush melons that were so dear to his heart.

ERIC MECKLENBURG

As for God, he got invoked so often by both sides that I finally told those dickheads God was sitting this one out. I said they better get the hymns picked and the body buried and hope the devil wasn't the one that wrote the will.

CAROLL THOMAS

"Let's go," the girl said and the boy took the keys from her, still looking at my brother. *She was probably thinking* we came from some sick family, and this wasn't our fault.

CHRISTINE POSTOLOS

That summer we saw twelve movies. We went on two-mile walks. We ate out at least one meal a day, sometimes two. *Secretly I collected* paper menus from the restaurants, stacking them neatly underneath the coloring books in my suitcase. I circled the food I ate, adding up the calories. If it was breakfast I usually ordered two poached eggs (160 calories), dry whole wheat toast (140), and a glass of orange juice (100 to 120). Then I highlighted the foods I wanted to eat, but couldn't.

ABBY ELLIN

Secretly I'd taken all the engraved matchbooks from the tables—Lorraine and Gregory, April 29, 1952—and smuggled them out of the reception in the pockets of my coat, in my purse. They were stacked, one up one down, in a box of Totes on the top of my closet.

JANET TASHJIAN

Outside, it's what you'd expect when everything else is going wrong— freezing rain and a travel advisory that will keep me and Clive together one night longer than we planned.

DAVID STEINER

The cloying smell of lakewater *reminds me* of my running route at home, along a river.

ANNE L. SEVERSON

The smell of fresh coffee *always brings back memories* of teacher's lounges where we'd try to relax between classes, exchanging stories about students and complaints about the principal. We pretended we were friends, but I truly wonder if we ever were.

CHRISTOPHER HORAN

As a child he'd learned the trick of being the lightning rod to his parents' arguments and he wondered now if they would thank him or even remember what for him had been dinners in hell.

ANDREW ORNSTEIN

93

GIFTS TO YOURSELF

In addition to bringing your characters and story alive, details are first and foremost gifts to yourself as a writer, something to be used and reused, and quite possibly something that will determine the course of the story. Flannery O'Connor speaks to the mystery and power of the telling detail. "I doubt myself if many writers know what they are going to do when they start out. When I started writing that story ["Good Country People"], I didn't know there was going to be a Ph.D. with a wooden leg in it. I merely found myself one morning writing a description of two women that I knew something about, and before I realized it, I had equipped one of them with a daughter with a wooden leg." And that wooden leg became central to the story.

It is true that a story's powerful details often take on symbolic significance, but we never encourage students to insert symbols into their stories. A symbol is something that stands for something else—usually smaller and more mundane than the larger truth it represents. Symbols can arise from a number of things—real details, personal attitudes, habits, acting, and so on. The important thing to remember is that significant detail adds to the texture of the story. It makes the story a more interesting (or surprising) account of what-if reality. A symbol should be a subtle hint about the author's ultimate meaning for the fiction. Do not confuse the two uses. Details, when used and reused well, have a way of becoming symbols without the writer's self-conscious effort to make them so.

THE EXERCISE

Make a list of the important details in an early draft of a story. Then consider if there are any details—gifts to yourself—that have unexplored potential for opening up your story, for taking plot in a different direction. Can you delete superfluous details?

THE OBJECTIVE

To learn what Flannery O'Connor means when she says, "To say that fiction proceeds by the use of details does not mean the simple, mechanical piling-up of detail. Detail has to be controlled by some overall purpose, and every detail has to be put to work for you. Art is selective."

STUDENT EXAMPLES

Christopher Horan says: "I don't know what possessed me to have the narrator scrubbing the toilet bowl and wearing rubber gloves when his landlord shows up at the door, but when I had to decide what the narrator had invented, I didn't have to look very far."

> That afternoon the landlord appeared at my door and said he'd waited long enough. I took off my rubber gloves (for the first time in months I'd been scrubbing the toilet bowl) and shook his hand. I thanked him for his patience, told him that of course I sympathized with him and understood that he, too, had bills to pay. Fortunately, I assured him, lightly punching his upper arm, he wouldn't have to wait much longer. By the end of the week I expected to receive the first payment for my invention, which would make me solvent enough to give him a year's rent if he liked. He massaged the bridge of his nose between his thumb and forefinger, closed his eyes, and let out a deep sigh. Then, as if he knew he would later regret it, he repeated the word "invention." So I told him, trying desperately to sound as if I weren't making it up on the spot, about my patent—my patent for the self-cleaning toilet bowl.

Janet Tashjian says: "In my story, 'Objects in Mirror Are Closer Than They Appear', I made my main character a toll collector on the Mass Pike. Because of the repetitive motion of the job, her doctor prescribes special gloves for her carpal tunnel syndrome. As the story progresses, these constricting gloves begin to represent everything that has been re-pressing her (her mother, religion, etc.). And I use them to end the story."

> The gloves slowed me down a bit but Dr. Larson insisted I wear them all day, every day, to help my throbbing wrists. They reminded me of the way my mother used to tie a long piece of yarn to each of my mittens, thread it through the sleeves of my winter jacket, behind my neck then down the other sleeve.
>
> (The story's last sentence is: I hung the gloves on the handle of my door and fastened the straps. They immediately filled with the wind and exhaust of the highway, like the automatic reflex of hands, waving good-bye or hello.)

PUBLISHED IN MASSACHUSETTS REVIEW

94

A LITTLE GARDENING,
A LITTLE SURGERY

When a story or novel isn't working, it often helps to look at it in a new way—not just on your computer screen or even in hard copy manuscript—but with scissors and tape and a conference table or floor.

In her book *The Writing Life*, Annie Dillard says she has often "written" with the "mechanical aid of a twenty-foot conference table. You lay your pages along the table's edge and pace out your work. You walk along the rows; you weed bits, move bits, and dig out bits, bent over the rows with full hands like a gardener."

Novelist E. L. Doctorow, formerly an editor, when asked about the relationship between editing and the craft of writing, said, "Editing taught me how to break books down and put them back together. . . . You learn how to become very free and easy about moving things around, which a reader would never do. A reader sees a printed book and that's it. But when you see a manuscript as an editor, you say, Well this is chapter twenty, but it should be chapter three.' You're at ease in the book the way a surgeon is at ease in a human chest, with all the blood and the guts and everything. You're familiar with the material and you can toss it around and say dirty things to the nurse." Thus, one method for revising, or "reenvisioning," a story is to become very self-conscious about its shape, its components, when it is laid out in front of you in pieces.

THE EXERICSE

Choose a story that doesn't seem to be working and cut it apart into the separate components of scenes and narrative passages and flashbacks. Number each piece in the order in which it appears in your story. Then lay these story pieces out on a large table or on the floor and absorb what is in front of you. Ask:

- How many scenes are there? Are there too few or too many?

- Does each scene accomplish something? Can some be combined? Deleted?

- Are there any missing scenes? Unexplored territory?

- Is the material from the "past" in the right places?

- What would happen if you rearranged the sequence of events?

■ What would happen if you begin with the ending scene and use it to frame the story?

As you ask yourself these questions, pace back and forth and move your story pieces around. Play with them. Experiment. If you have missing scenes, add a piece of paper that says "add scene about _____." Then, when you are satisfied with the order of your story, number the sections again—ignoring the original numbers. Then compare the old order—and numbers—to the new order. Chances are 9 might now be 3 and 2 and 4 might be combined. Finally, instead of doing "block moves" on your computer, retype the story again from scratch—using your new arrangement. Feel the difference, the power of the revised word.

THE OBJECTIVE

To see an early draft of a story as something that isn't etched in stone. Not only are the words and lines capable of being revised, but the story structure itself is often still fluid enough to rearrange and analyze for the questions listed above.

STUDENT EXAMPLES

One student had a 12-page story that wasn't working, and when she cut the story apart, was astonished to discover that although it was a short story, it had seventeen separate scenes. She eliminated eight of those scenes by summarizing or omitting them altogether and ended up with a publishable story.

I asked one class to write about this "scissors and tape" process and below are several responses:

> This was a good learning process. I saw the story as a whole, laid out on the floor, while also seeing how individual sections fit into the whole. I then asked myself, truthfully this time because the separated pages were staring me in the face, if the order was the best it could be? I discovered I hadn't been nearly as truthful or careful as I could have been.
>
> KIM REYNOLDS

> I discovered that Gladys, my incorrigible housekeeper, is not introduced until page 18. In class, Kim Reynolds suggested that I drop Gladys, but I wanted to keep her. Now, I see what Kim means. I could remove all of Gladys' components without affecting—at all—the heart of the story. It's hard to see a scene objectively until you separate it from the rest of the story and dare it to stand on its own. Cutting up a story liberates you; it gives you a kind of "fuck it" attitude when you see how easy it is to shape and move things around.
>
> LEE HARRINGTON

> I thought cutting things apart and switching them around would somehow damage my overall story. I thought it was pretty close to perfect the

way I had it. (I was sort of embarrassed by this attitude because I'd never considered myself a "touchy artist" type, but that's a subject for another paper.) Then I saw that one scene took up fourteen of seventeen pages. Other sections were much too short and one section repeated everything I had written in another section. The second draft isn't exactly flying along at the speed of sound, but I'm happy about the way it's coming together now.

MICHAEL SUMMERS

Mainly I learned that any story is fluid. I will do this for every story now. I've also cut up other stories—in particular, a couple of Alice Munro's, since many of her stories dip into the past. I'm amazed at how long some of her sections of the past really are (like mine!), but in hers every word counts.

MARYANNE O'HARA

Cutting the story up brought me into the story. I'd felt distant from it even though I was constantly picking it up and reading it. Now after looking at my story piece by piece the task of filling it out seems more managable.

JACKSON HOLTZ

95

DYNAMIC SCENING

from Thalia Selz

The playwright Harold Pinter writes about creating drama from the "battle for positions." He pointed out that threat—and thus the necessary tension—arises from having people in a confined space battling over dominance and over "what tools they would use to achieve dominance and how they would try to undermine the other person's dominance." Pinter's scene dynamics work not only for plays but equally well for scenes in short fiction and novels.

THE EXERCISE

Examine a scene you are having trouble with, one that (1) demands action, although not necessarily physical action, and (2) provides a turning point in your story. If you don't yet have such a scene in your story, try writing one. Make it at least three pages long, although five pages will give you a greater chance to develop the personal dynamics and show how the balance of power can keep changing. Tish, discovering that Mort has cheated her in a business deal, confronts him with evidence that would stand up in court, forcing him to return funds he has stolen. Alycia, a charming jewel thief, is caught in the act by her intended victim—an attractive diamond merchant—and seduces him, ensuring both his silence and the gift of a handsomely insured necklace.

THE OBJECTIVE

To show that by the time the scene is over the position of dominance has changed while the characters remain consistent and credible throughout.

96

MAGNIFYING CONFLICT

from David Ray

Low-energy writing has, in some circles, become fashionable, but it will probably not remain so for very long. Great fiction is tense with conflict—between characters, within characters, between characters and forces opposing them. We need only think of Ernest Pontifex's struggles with his father in the Victorian classic *The Way of All Flesh* or the custody battle of *Kramer vs. Kramer* or Raskolnikov's struggle between his fixation on murder and his impulse to love and remain loyal to his family and its values in *Crime and Punishment*—or more accurately, his struggle between sanity and insanity. We might recall the heroine of *Pamela*, struggling against the wiles of her employer-seducer. Or we might think of Huck Finn, in his perplexity and struggle against the racism he's been taught and his more trustworthy intuition and loyalty to his friend Jim, a runaway slave. In *Moby Dick* there is conflict on many levels, but primarily between hunter and hunted, malefic force and the innocent violence of nature. Any solid work of fiction will provide ready examples. The Japanese poet Kobayashi Issa found a storm of raging conflict even within a dewdrop, the most peaceful thing he could find in nature when he sought a retreat from his grief. The writer who loses touch with his responsibility to energize his fiction with conflict will probably have a very limited or temporary audience.

THE EXERCISE

Take a story you have completed and go through it and intensify the conflict, magnifying the tension and shrillness at every turn, even to the point of absurdity or hyperbole. Add stress wherever possible, both between characters and within them as individuals. Exaggerate the obstacles they face. Be extreme.

THE OBJECTIVE

To create an awareness of the need for a high level of tension while encouraging a healthy regard for how easily it can become excessive. This exercise is not meant to "improve" the story, although it often provokes new and more dynamic descriptions and dialogue. It raises the writer's consciousness about the need for conflict in fiction.

Interviewer: How much rewriting do you do?

Hemingway: It depends. I rewrote the ending to *Farewell to Arms,* the last page of it, thirty-nine times before I was satisfied.

Interviewer: Was there some technical problem there? What was it that had stumped you?

Hemingway: Getting the words right.

WRITERS AT WORK

97

WHAT'S AT STAKE?

from Ken Rivard

W hat's at stake in your story? What is in jeopardy in your story? What is at risk? What do your characters stand to win or lose—custody of the kids, a place on a starting line-up, the approval of a tyrannical boss?

Once you can answer that question, then ask if your stakes are high enough to keep readers reading. When they are too low, the story fails to move us. The survival of a tenuous relationship, a minor personal insight, getting through one more day at a tedious job—it's difficult to make such familiar scenarios come alive. You have to overcome the reader's skepticism that the lousy husband, crappy job, or minor realization is worth all the fuss and bother in the first place. Why not create a dilemma that immediately snags and holds our attention? Consider the following situations:

- A 6-year-old boy disappears for a few hours. Eventually, he's discovered, unharmed, a few blocks from his home, with no memory of what has happened to him. Years later, as a university student on vacation, he drives by the street where he disappeared, notices a young boy, and acts on an irresistible compulsion to lure him into his car. (Ruth Rendell's "The Fallen Curtain")
- An eccentric substitute teacher subverts the $2 + 2 = 4$ universe of her fourth-grade students by introducing them to "substitute facts" (such as $6 \times 11 = 68$), Egyptian cosmology, and the curse of the Hope diamond. One afternoon she explains the use of Tarot cards, and predicts the early death of a particular student. (Charles Baxter's "Gryphon")
- For years, a reticent working-class white woman has allowed a devil-may-care friend to talk her into "adventures" without their husbands' knowledge, including slipping away once a week to go tea dancing. At the ballroom, they make the acquaintance of a young black man who becomes their regular dance partner. When the more daring woman dies, her friend screws up her courage for one last afternoon of escape. This time, their dance partner begins communicating gentle, but unmistakable signals of sexual interest. (William Trevor's "Afternoon Dancing")

Inexperienced writers often forget that readers are essentially voyeurs, peering through the window of a story into its characters' lives. If the view is uninteresting, readers will look elsewhere. Though quite different in structure and style, each of the three stories involves us in circumstances full of promise for events to come from which it is impossible to turn away. How strange will the substitute teacher get before the school administration finds her out? Will the adult kidnapper remember what happened to him as a boy, and is he doomed to replay some dreadful scene? What will the woman do, confronted with possibilities for new adventure, now that her spunky friend isn't there to encourage her—what will she win or lose?

Beginning writers often agree in principle that high stakes are good, but balk when it comes to actually upping the ante in their own stories. This natural inclination to avoid tension and/or conflict (always inherent in high-stakes situations), and to avoid putting anything at risk or in jeopardy, is a survival skill in the real world, but a death knell to fiction. In order to create a story with high stakes you must make a leap of imaginative faith—that some things, at least for your characters, are unambiguously worth fighting for. Getting the lady is worth the risk of getting the tiger. In the three stories mentioned, the stakes are high and what is lost or won matters enormously.

THE EXERCISE

Part I

Examine some of your favorite stories and novels and ask: What's at stake? Force yourself to identify the devices the author uses to show his characters risking something in order to pursue what they desperately want.

Part II

Examine your own fiction and ask: What's at stake? If you can't answer then you don't know enough about your characters or their lives yet to revise the story. If, on the other hand, your answer takes more than a sentence or two, then, again, you probably don't know, or the stakes are too diffuse.

Another question: Is what's at stake inherently interesting?

The answer to this question involves a certain latitude for taste. But there is no shopworn situation that cannot, in the right hands, become fresh and new. However, the overfamiliarity of some situations makes them especially difficult to bring to life. It's often more interesting, for reader and writer, to work on the credibility of an extraordinary situation than it is to try to pump life into a tired one.

THE OBJECTIVE

To understand that compelling stories are about characters motivated to take risks, to put something in jeopardy, to gamble for high stakes, in order to get what they want. And to incorporate a sense of urgency into your own fiction.

98

WRITING OUTSIDE THE STORY

from Elizabeth Libbey

Sometimes a story feels as if it hasn't reached its full potential. You know it isn't finished yet, but you are not sure how to proceed in revising it. Another draft doesn't seem to be the answer, nor do you want to put it aside for a while. This is the time when "writing outside" the story might be the way to return to working inside it.

There are different ways to write outside a story. Some of the methods have to do with exploring the inner life of your main character through diary entries, letters to other characters, dreams, or lists. Or you might try writing a missing scene or a scene that occurred before the beginning of the story. Or perhaps you avoided a confrontation scene or stopped your story too soon. Even if you don't use this material in the story, it will, as Hemingway said, make itself felt.

THE EXERCISE

Pull out one of your stories that doesn't feel finished. Have your main character do the following exercises—as if she had her own notebook. For example, maybe you write with a number 2 pencil, but your character prefers to use a Rapidograph pen. Go with the pen. Remember, your character is doing this exercise—not you, the author!

So, as your main character:

- make a diary entry for the time of the story
- make a diary entry for the time preceding the story
- write a letter to someone not in the story about what is happening in the story
- write a letter to someone in the story

Or you might explore places in the story that you haven't either dramatized or summarized. Examples:

- Have your characters avoided a confrontation? (This is a natural reaction— we are all nonconfrontational and, therefore, we often allow our character to avoid the very scenes and confrontations that we would avoid.) Does your story have missing scenes?
- What events happened before the beginning of the story? Before page one?

Try writing scenes of those events that most affected the beginning of the story. Maybe you started the story later than you should have.

■ Write past the ending. Maybe your story isn't really finished. Perhaps you are avoiding the confrontation scene because you aren't sure what your characters would say to each other.

THE OBJECTIVE

To explore aspects of a story that may seem, at first, to be on the periphery, but at closer look can deepen or open it up. Nothing is ever lost by more fully knowing the individual world of each story. And it's better to let your characters speak for themselves.

I try to leave out the parts that people skip.

ELMORE LEONARD

99

THE FIVE-HIGHLIGHTER EXERCISE

from David Ray

Good writers must, of course, be good readers, aware of texture and the orchestration of sense impressions that make vivid fiction. Really powerful writing is memorable for visual sweep or for tactile detail, for near-palpable sensations of touch or near-audible music. Memories of taste are cited when readers speak of Proust. Indeed, great fiction has the power of poetry. A. E. Housman described that power as recognizable "by the symptoms which it provokes in us . . . when I am shaving . . . if a line of poetry strays into my memory, my skin bristles so that the razor ceases to act." We need to evoke this power to move readers physically.

A look at the beginning of Stephen Crane's "The Open Boat," for example, reveals a vivid passage dominated by visual imagery. Alice Munro's "How I Met My Husband" starts with auditory and kinetic energy, followed by a dash of color and a scream: "We heard the plane come over at noon, roaring through the radio news, and we were sure it was going to hit the house, so we all ran out into the yard. We saw it come in over the treetops, all red and silver, the first close-up plane I ever saw, Mrs. Peebles screamed." The following passage from Nelson Algren's *The Man with the Golden Arm* is typical of that writer's command of a full palette:

> This time she was protected against the light, standing in her fresh white dress and the little blood-red earrings against the sallow olive of her cheeks and the midnight darkness of her hair. The hair that swept down over her shoulders as if touched by the wind that drove the curtains aside when the long Els stormed overhead. She was looking less careworn since John had left her.
>
> "I just thought you'd like to see a dog that drinks beer," Frankie apologized, "you told me to get one of my own to kick."
>
> "I didn't say nothin' about a beer-drinkin' one, Frankie," she protested as gravely as a child. "But if you want we'll try him out." Rumdum, at first listening only listlessly, picked up suddenly and hauled Frankie forward into the room.
>
> "The smell of Budweiser makes him powerful," Frankie explained. Before she could get the saucer filled Rumdum had licked the saucer dry and Frankie had to clamp his snout with both hands, the great hound whimpering brokenheartedly, till she could get it filled again without losing a finger.

"He ain't had a drink all day." Frankie sympathized with all dry throats. "Fact is, I ain't neither." He pulled the bottle off his hip with feigned surprise at finding it there. "Look what some guy stuck in my pocket!"

"I'll stick to beer," Molly told him cautiously. "I been on the wagon since John's gone." She turned to the little combination record player on the dresser while he drank.

"Everythin' is movin' too fast," the record complained drowsily.

THE EXERCISE

Using five different-colored highlighters, mark a text with a different color for each sense impression, for example, blue for visual, red for auditory, green for taste, etc. Synaesthesia would, of course, be indicated by more than one color. Writers vary greatly in terms of the dominance of one sense or another. The goal, though, is to find passages using all five senses—then to write such passages.

THE OBJECTIVE

To heighten awareness of the need for a full repertory of sense evocations in good writing. Ideally you should call forth all five senses as well as synaesthesia. The writer thereby evokes from the reader a full range of responses.

100

WITH REVISION
COMES FINAL MEANING

Meaning isn't something you start from: it's something you work toward through successive drafts of your story or novel. Chances are if you tell a story to present some general principle, some truth about life, then your story is never going to come alive with specific characters living their specific lives. In *Mystery and Manners,* Flannery O'Connor says, "A story is a complete dramatic action—and in good stories, the characters are shown through the action and the action is controlled through the characters, and the result of this is meaning that derives from the whole presented experience."

So it's okay to write the first draft of a story without knowing what the story is about. Again, O'Connor says it best. "In fact, it may be better if you don't know what before you begin. You ought to be able to discover something from your stories. If you don't, probably nobody else will."

Stanley Elkin has an effective method for finding out what a story means. He suggests that after five or six drafts, you should write what the story means in one sentence. Then use that sentence to cut, revise, add, adjust, or change the next drafts. Use that sentence as a filter, or a window, to the whole piece.

THE EXERCISE

Write one sentence for a story that is in its fourth or fifth draft. Then revise the story to heighten and illuminate this final meaning.

THE OBJECTIVE

To make you aware of how you come to final meaning slowly, slowly, as you revise a story. To bring you through this process to what you intend the story to mean and what you want to convey to the reader. And finally, to make everything in the story accrue to this final meaning.

101

IT AIN'T OVER TILL IT'S OVER

When men and women began telling tales around evening campfires, surely the most frequent words from their audience were "and then what happens"? Perhaps the only assurance these storytellers had that their story was truly over was someone in the audience saying "tell us another one." It is this last response—"tell us another one"—that you want from your readers at the end of your story or novel. If your reader is still saying "And then what happened?" clearly your story isn't over and hasn't achieved the emotional resolution necessary in most stories.

A complete short story should be like a suspended drop of oil, entire unto itself. Or, viewed another way, it should be psychically "resolved." That is, when the reader gets to the last sentence she will understand that the story ends here—she doesn't have to know what happened to the characters beyond this final moment.

THE EXERCISE

Examine each of your stories carefully to make sure it has this psychic resolution. Read them to a friend or fellow student and ask if they think it's finished. One of the hardest things to learn is how to judge your own work; it's eminently reasonable to try it out on a sympathetic—but objective—listener.

THE OBJECTIVE

To master the art of tying up narrative and thematic threads.

102

IN-CLASS REVISION

In spite of good intentions, writers often don't put enough time into revising a story, so they never learn to trust the process, and their stories'
potential remains unexplored. This exercise suggests ways to revise and
shows you how to relax into the revision process. Ideally, the exercise
should be done in a workshop or class over a period of three or four hours.
Although all questions and suggestions for revision will not apply to all
stories, enough will speak to each writer's individual story to make the
session rewarding and even fun.

THE EXERCISE

Bring to class a first or second draft of a story—a story you care about
enough to spend three or four hours revising. (Caring about the story is
crucial to this exercise's success.) Also bring several highlighters, scissors,
and tape. The teacher or workshop leader will ask questions, give instructions, and direct you to various exercises. You will probably find questions
and problems that can't be answered or resolved during this session; jot
down notes as reminders for the next time you revise this particular story.

- Underline the first interesting sentence in your story—interesting for language, characterization, setting, atmosphere—for something. (It should be
  the first or close to the first sentence.)

- Is your beginning the best way to start your story? See Exercise 3, "Ways to
  Begin a Story."

- Whose story is it? How does the story reflect this? Is the point of view right
  for the story?

- What does your main character want? Where do you indicate this in the
  story? How does this drive the story? See Exercise 22, "What Do Your
  Characters Want?"

- Do your characters have an inner life? See Exercise 20, "The Inner Lives of
  Characters."

- What does the reader learn about your main characters in the first third of
  the story? Is any crucial information withheld from the reader? Do Exercise
  29, "What Do You Know About Your Characters."

- What is the situation of your story? See the Introduction to Plot on p. 121.

- Does your story start in the right place—in the middle? What is the story's "history?" See Exercise 2, "The Story's History."

- What is at stake in your story? What is at risk? What can be won or lost? See Exercise 97, "What's at Stake?"

- Does your story have tension, conflict? See Exercise 96, "Magnifying Conflict."

- How many scenes does your story have? See Exercise 94, "A Little Gardening, A Little Surgery." Now for the scissors: cut your story apart into its components and spread it out somewhere to peruse.

- Does your dialogue serve the story well and move the plot along? Do you use indirect discourse where needed? See Exercise 39, "Telling Talk."

- How well have you choreographed your scenes? Highlight the body language in your most important scenes. See Exercise 40, "The Invisible Scene."

- How felt is the tangible world of your story? How many senses are brought into play? See Exercise 99, "The Five-Highlighter Exercise."

- Have you developed your story's gifts to yourself? Make a list of the significant details and check to see if you have reused them. See Exercise 93, "Gifts to Yourself."

- Does your story have enough texture? Open up your story with Exercise 92, "Opening Up Your Story." This exercise should take a while to do. Spend about four minutes each on six to eight "inserts." Have students suggest other "inserts."

- Is the language of your story interesting? See the Introduction to "The Elements of Style," p. 139.

- Do your adjectives and adverbs enhance your nouns and verbs? Circle all the adjectives and adverbs in the first two pages. See Exercise 52, "Taboos: Weak Adjectives and Adverbs."

- Do your sentences vary in length and complexity? See Exercise 51, "A Style of Your Own."

- Does something happen in your story? Something that is significant, that carries everything? Is there a change? See Exercise 47, "So, What Happened?"

- Do you know how your story ends? Are there unanswered questions? See Exercise 101 "It Ain't Over Till It's Over."

- Does your story both show and tell, especially toward the end of the story? See Exercise 61, "Show and Tell: There's a Reason It's Called Storytelling."

- What final meaning are you working toward in your story? See Exercise 100, "With Revision Comes Final Meaning."

- Was your title thrown at the top of the page or chosen with care? Make a list of 50 or 100 possible titles—take some from within the story. See Exercise 68, "Titles and Keys."

You've accomplished a lot in the past few hours. Now, think about what you have discovered about this story and sometime in the next day or two return to this story for further revision. Then bring a new draft in to the next class. Include a page or two in which you discuss the revision process and how it worked for you. How will you proceed in the future?

THE OBJECTIVE

To relax into the revision process and give your story your undivided attention. To see the process as a fluid one—made up of components which are variable, manageable, and fun.

XII. GAMES

We have included three games with words partly for your amusement and partly as a demonstration that the combination and recombination of the twenty-six letters of the alphabet don't always have to end in so-called deathless prose. Words are magical playthings as well as instruments of persuasion, entertainment, enlightenment, social change, and uplift. These games are more fun than going to the movies, watching television, or playing poker.

103

LEARNING TO LIE

Beginning writers often resist their imaginations as something childish, exotic, or out of reach when in fact everyone has at some time told a lie. So for this exercise think of writing fiction as telling a lie. (This exercise is actually a variation on a late-night parlor game and is particularly good for the first session of a class or workshop.)

THE EXERCISE

In two or three sentences, write down three unusual, startling, or amusing things you did or that happened to you. One thing must be true, the other two must be lies. Use details.

Here is what one writer used for herself.

Elvis Presley wrote me a two-sentence letter after I sent him a poem I'd written about him and a picture of my younger sister in a bikini.

The first time I heard him play, Buddy Rich threw me a drum stick during a drum roll and never missed a beat.

I asked Mick Jagger to sign a program for me, but he said he'd prefer to sign my left white shoe. And he did.

Now everybody do one.

Then one by one read them to the group. The group is allowed to ask questions pertaining specifically to the details. For example, someone might ask the above person, "Why did you send your sister's photograph instead of your own?" Or "What was Buddy Rich playing?" Or "Do you still have your shoe and if so, where is it?" The "author" has to be able to think on her feet, to make up more convincing details, to "lie." Then ask for a vote as to which story is true and which stories are fictions. It is surprising how many people are already good storytellers, capable of finding the concrete persuasive detail. (The second "lie" is true.)

THE OBJECTIVE

To understand how we can exaggerate events in our lives, appropriate the lives of others—friends, enemies, strangers—or just plain out-and-out lie. All these are ways of using what we see and experience to produce fiction.

STUDENT EXAMPLE

I once stole a pair of diamond earrings from Saks Fifth Ave. After I found out they were cubic zirconia, I took them back and slipped them into the display counter. Why get in trouble for *faux* anything?

I have tried to get my cat, Frosty, on David Letterman's Stupid Pet Tricks for the past three years. I've gotten into the semifinals, only to have Frosty pee all over everyone who tried to coax her into doing her tricks.

When I was young, I was convinced that my two older brothers were plotting to kill my mother. I remember it so vividly that I still can't eat Christmas dinner without worrying about the carving knives.

CLAIRE ISRAEL

(The third "lie" is true.)

104

THE DICTIONARY GAME

In one sense, all fiction writing is artifice: dialogue isn't like real speech: stories are, for the most part, invented; singing prose is as carefully crafted as a glass bowl. The following calls on you to exercise pure inventiveness, pure craft.

THE EXERCISE

A game for four to six players. Using a standard English dictionary, each player takes turns being *it*. The *it* finds a word that none of the other players knows the meaning of (everyone is on his honor to tell the truth about this). The *it* then writes down the real definition, while the other players invent and write down a definition they hope will be construed as the real one. They then pass their papers in to the *it*, who gives each definition a number, making sure they are all legible. The *it* reads each one in turn. The players make up their minds about which definition is real and then they vote by holding up the number of fingers corresponding to the number of the definition they choose. You may not vote for your own definition. Scoring: You get one point for each player who thinks yours is the correct definition. If you guess the real definition you get one point. If no one guesses the real definition, the *it* gets one point.

THE OBJECTIVE

Words are what it's all about. You can play around with them in much the same way you play around with plot and with ideas.

105

FICTIONARY: A VARIATION OF DICTIONARY

It can be fun to try to invent sentences that another writer might have written. This game is played using the books of writers who are fairly well known to all the players—say books by Philip Roth, Henry James, Virginia Woolf, Saul Bellow, Bobbie Ann Mason, Isaac Bashevis Singer, etc. Choose writers with a very distinct style.

THE EXERCISE

Choose one sentence, preferably one with four to ten words, from a story or a novel. Next, call out the first letter for each word in the sentence. For example, if you were to use this sentence from John Gardner's *Grendel*, "Pick an apocalypse, any apocalypse," you would call out P A A A A. Then ask the players to make up a sentence containing words beginning with those letters. After that, the same rules apply as those for Dictionary (see page 272).

THE OBJECTIVE

To have fun with language and try to imitate or outwrite the published author.

XIII. LEARNING FROM THE GREATS

The great guides were the books I discovered in the Johns Hopkins library, where my student job was to file books away. One was more or less encouraged to take a cart of books and go back into the stacks and not come out for seven or eight hours. So I read what I was filing. My great teachers (the best thing that can happen to a writer) were Scheherazade, Homer, Virgil, and Boccaccio; also the great Sanskrit taletellers. I was impressed forever with the width as well as the depth of literature—

—*JOHN BARTH*

We hope this book will take you in two directions: first, into your own well of inspiration, your own store of forgotten or overlooked material, and into your own writing and, second, back to the greats who are your true teachers.

F. Scott Fitzgerald is one of these teachers, and he names his own teachers in the following passage.

By style, I mean color. . . . I want to be able to do anything with words: handle slashing, flaming descriptions like Wells, and use the paradox with the clarity of Samuel Butler, the breadth of Bernard Shaw and the wit of Oscar Wilde, I want to do the wide sultry heavens of Conrad, the rolled gold sundowns and crazy-quilt skies of Hichens and Kipling as well as the pastelle [*sic*] dawns and twilights of Chesterton. All that is by

275

way of example. As a matter of fact I am a professional literary thief, hot after the best methods of every writer in my generation.

In a letter Fitzgerald again pays homage to a "teacher." He says, "The motif of the 'dying fall' [in *Tender is the Night*] was absolutely deliberate and did not come from the diminution of vitality but from a definite plan. That particular trick is one that Ernest Hemingway and I worked out— probably from Conrad's preface to *The Nigger* [*of the Narcissus*]." Madison Smartt Bell echoes this sense of learning tricks from a master in his dedi- cation for *The Washington Square Ensemble*. He says, "This book is dedi- cated to the long patience of my parents with a tip of the trick hat to George Garrett."

The exercises in this next section are meant to show you how to read for inspiration and instruction. Study the letters and journals of writers to discover how they grappled with problems you will encounter in your own fiction. For example, Flaubert worried about the "lack of action" in *Madame Bovary*. In a letter to Louise Colet he says, "The psychological development of my characters is giving me a lot of trouble; and every- thing, in this novel, depends on it." And he immediately comes up with the solution, "for in my opinion, ideas can be as entertaining as actions, but in order to be so they must flow one from the other like a series of cas- cades, carrying the reader along midst the throbbing of sentences and the seething of metaphors."

And read what writers say about writing, for example John Barth's *Lost in the Funhouse*, Elizabeth Bowen's *Collected Impressions*, Raymond Carver's *Fires*, Annie Dillard's *Living by Fiction* and *The Writing Life*, John Gardner's *The Art of Fiction* and *Becoming a Novelist*, E. M. Forster's *As- pects of the Novel*, William Gass's *On Being Blue*, Henry James's prefaces to his novels, Flannery O'Connor's *Mystery and Manners*, Eudora Welty's *The Eye of the Story*, and Virginia Woolf's *A Room of One's Own*, among others. And now on to our exercises for learning from the greats.

106

FINDING INSPIRATION
IN OTHER SOURCES—
POETRY, NONFICTION, ETC.

A writer is someone who reads. We recommend that you read the letters and notebooks of writers, biographies and autobiographies, plays and poetry, history and religion. Reading for writers has always engendered a cross-pollination of ideas and forms. For the writer, everything is a possible source for an epigraph, a title, a story, a novel.

Below are some well-chosen epigraphs.

Charles Baxter, *First Light*

Life can only be understood backwards; but it must be lived forwards.

SØREN KIERKEGAARD

F. Scott Fitzgerald, *The Great Gatsby*

Then wear the gold hat, if that will move her;
    If you can bounce high, bounce for her too,
Till she cry "Lover, gold-hatted, high-bouncing lover,
    I must have you!"

THOMAS PARKE D'INVILLIERS

John Hawkes, *The Blood Oranges*

Is there then any terrestrial paradise where, amidst the whispering of the olive-leaves, people can be with whom they like and have what they like and take their ease in shadows and in coolness?

FORD MADOX FORD, *THE GOOD SOLDIER*

Nadine Gordimer, *Burger's Daughter*

I am the place in which something has occurred.

CLAUDE LÉVI-STRAUSS

Amy Hempel, *Reasons to Live*

Because grief unites us,
like the locked antlers of moose
who die on their knees in pairs.

WILLIAM MATTHEWS

Joyce Carol Oates, *Them*

. . . because we are poor
Shall we be vicious?

JOHN WEBSTER, THE WHITE DEVIL

Sharon Sheehe Stark, *A Wrestling Season*

Life's nonsense pierces us with strange relation.

WALLACE STEVENS

THE EXERCISE

Read widely for inspiration and then use an original text as an epigraph for your own story or novel. For example, think of Stanley Kunitz's wonderful line: "The thing that eats the heart is mostly heart." This would make a superb epigraph to a story, collection, or novel titled "Mostly Heart." Begin a story with this line in mind. Or write a story that illustrates this line from John le Carré's *Tinker, Tailor, Soldier, Spy:* "There are moments that are made up of too much stuff for them to be lived at the time they occur."

Choose several of your favorite poems and reread them with an eye toward finding a title or using a line as an epigraph to a story. Or choose a sentence from an essay or popular song.

Read, read, read. Then write, write, write. Sometimes in reverse order.

THE OBJECTIVE

To absorb what we read in a way that allows it to spark our own creativity, to use it as inspiration for our own writing. To build on what has gone before.

Mary McCarthy once lost the only manuscript copy of a novel. Interviewer Bob Cromie said to her, "But it's your novel, you can write it again." McCarthy replied, "Oh, I couldn't do that—I know how it ends."

107

PLACES WITHOUT PEOPLE

Very few good short stories or novels float in time and space; they are firmly anchored in a particular year, or years, and in a singular place—whether it's a rooming house, region, or country. Place matters. You can't for example, imagine *The Catcher in the Rye* taking place in third-century Rome or even the American Southwest at the beginning of the twentieth century. It must be post-World War II New York. Place is thematically almost as important as characters or plot.

THE EXERCISE

Look at the work of the following authors and try to analyze how they managed to give their settings so much power and personality: William Faulkner (a mythical Southern county), Nathaniel Hawthorne (a severe New England town), Herman Melville (the sea and ships), Evelyn Waugh (London), John Cheever (suburbia), Toni Cade Bambara (Atlanta), and Jay McInerney (New York City). These are just a few authors among many who recognize that characters must not float in space but be anchored to a particular place in a particular time.

THE OBJECTIVE

To learn that setting and place are crucial elements in narrative. Where you set your story has to reflect—or create tension with—the overall theme and plot of the work.

108

THE SKY'S THE LIMIT: HOMAGE TO KAFKA AND GARCÍA MÁRQUEZ

from Christopher Noël

In a *Paris Review* interview, Gabriel García Márquez says,

> At the university in Bogotá, I started making new friends and acquaintances, who introduced me to contemporary writers. One night a friend lent me a book of short stories by Franz Kafka. I went back to the pension where I was staying and began to read *The Metamorphosis*. The first line almost knocked me off the bed. I was so surprised. The first line reads, "As Gregor Samsa awoke that morning from uneasy dreams he found himself transformed in his bed into a gigantic insect . . ." When I read the line I thought to myself that I didn't know anyone was allowed to write things like that. If I had known, I would have started writing a long time ago. So I immediately started writing.

THE EXERCISE

For inspiration read Kafka's story, or perhaps García Márquez's "A Very Old Man with Enormous Wings." Then if you are part of a group, each member should write a fantastical first line and then pass it to the left (or right). Each person, receiving a first line from her neighbor should then try to make good on its implicit riches, to open up a world from this seed, one that is different from the everyday world but nonetheless full of concrete detail and clear and consistent qualities, rules of being.

Next, write a story of your own.

THE OBJECTIVE

To loosen up your thinking, to countenance a greater range of possibilities, and to see that sometimes even the most apparently frivolous or ludicrous notions, completely implausible even for the slanted implausibility that writers use, can turn out to be just the ticket. What's strange can be made to seem necessary in a story; you can work to solidify the strangeness if, while you're writing, you keep a sort of grim faith at those pivotal moments—whether the first line or the third chapter or the final paragraph—when it seems you are betraying or trivializing your authentic vision of the world.

STUDENT EXAMPLES

I scream each time I see that the house is surrounded, and I know this makes Carmen's patience wavery, like the heat mirages. Carmen has always lived in this desert and tells me that it is the normal way for Joshua trees to behave. But how am I to get used to them, all standing there with their arms raised each time I pass the window and forget not to look out. The Joshua trees are moving closer every day, and to me this is ominous, Carmen or no Carmen.

This house, this desert, are supposed to be for my health. Carmen, too, is supposed to be for my health. The doctor in Boston told my son so. Warm climate, a companion, and the old lady will be all set. Well, that doctor didn't know about the ways of the desert. I watch as the Joshua trees group and regroup like some stunted army, never quite making up their minds that they are going to advance. Bradford gets upset on the phone if I talk about the Joshua trees, how they are preparing for some sort of final march. Carmen can see it in the moon, although I don't tell Bradford this lest he think Carmen a bad influence.

MOLLY LANZAROTTA,
"RUNNING WITH THE JOSHUA TREE"

When Rene returned from the army, I felt at first that we should not contradict him, although the letter that had come weeks before clearly stated he was dead.

And sure enough, my cousin Rene did not at all wish to discuss the manner of his dying, which had been described in great detail in the letter from his friend in the army, how he had been dismembered by the rebels in the mountains, how he'd been skinned and scalped, his eyes gouged out and any number of things, to the point that there was nothing left to send home of him, nothing for us to mourn but the letter. I was practiced at this, this sudden grief with no ceremony, and wondered whether soon I would be the last one of this family, too, just one young girl left from so many.

And then Rene wandered in on a night that was gray with the glow of distant explosions, gray himself, covered with the dirt of the mountains and the dust of the desert our town has become. Little Yolanda shrieked when he pulled back the burlap we'd hung over the door of our collapsing home, and, of course, none of us could finish our meal. Rene sat down and ate everything on each of our plates, while his brother Evelio shouted, paced the room and questioned him, and his mother, Luisa, wept and kissed him and pulled on her rosary until it snapped, showering us all with tiny black beads. It seemed that they had cut the voice out of Rene as well, when they killed him, because he did not want to talk at all.

MOLLY LANZAROTTA, "THE DEATH OF RENE PAZ,"
FROM *CAROLINA QUARTERLY*

If it hadn't been for my long serpentine tail, I wouldn't have lost my job as a cabdriver. It wasn't that management objected so much, God knows good help is hard to find these days, but eventually passengers complained, especially when I became agitated, say, in heavy traffic and whipped my tail into the backseat. I even struck a passenger once, but not on purpose or forcefully, and no permanent damage was done. I apologized afterward. I didn't get many tips.

I tried to make a virtue of my tail by decorating it on holidays, tying bright ribbons around its circumference until it looked like a barber pole, or the lance of a medieval knight. Things seemed to be working, at least until that incident with the motorcycle cop.

"Believe me, Melvin, it's not you," the dispatcher said. "Well, actually, it is you, in a way. But it's not personal," he pleaded, larding his voice with concern to avoid a class action suit. "Insurance is eating me up, man. That pedestrian you hit the other day. . . "

"I can explain that. I was giving a left turn signal. . . "

"Melvin, go to a doctor. Get it taken off. You're a good driver. You got a future."

"But it's part of me. It kind of gives me something to lean against."

He shrugged his shoulders toward the picture of the near-naked woman embracing a tire on the Parts Pups calendar on the wall. "He likes it," he said, as if to her. Then he looked at me. "Okay, Mel, you like it. You live with it. But not here."

And so I was out of a job.

Gene Langston, "Fired"

I read Shakespeare *directly* I have finished writing. When my mind is agape and redhot. Then it is astonishing. I never yet knew how amazing his stretch and speed and word coining power is, until I felt it utterly outpace and outrace my own, seeming to start equal and then I see him draw ahead and to things I could not in my wildest tumult and utmost press of mind imagine.

Virginia Woolf, A Writer's Diary

109

LEARNING FROM THE GREATS

Most writers can look back and name the books that seemed to fling open doors for them, books that made them want to go to the typewriter and begin to write one word after another.

When asked if one writer had influenced her more than others, Joan Didion replied,

> I always say Hemingway, because he taught me how sentences worked. When I was fifteen or sixteen I would type out his stories to learn how sentences worked. . . . A few years ago when I was teaching a course at Berkeley I reread *A Farewell to Arms* and fell right back into those sentences. I mean they're perfect sentences. Very direct sentences, smooth rivers, clear water over granite, no sinkholes.

THE EXERCISE

Choose a writer you admire, one who has withstood the test of time. Type out that writer's stories or several chapters from a novel. Try to analyze how the sentences work, how their vocabulary differs from your own, how the structure of the story emerges from the language, how the writer intersperses scene with narrative summary. Feel in your fingers what is different about that prose.

THE OBJECTIVE

To understand how another writer's sentences work. To learn to analyze what succeeds in the fiction of a master and *how* it succeeds.

110

IMITATION: SINCERE FLATTERY— AND LEARNING

Once you have typed out the words, sentences, and paragraphs of other writers, you will know a lot more about the way their prose works. So why not put this knowledge to use and actually try to imitate them—not in your own stories but in their stories.

THE EXERCISE

In a story or novel by a writer you admire, find a place between two sentences that seems like a "crack" that could be "opened up." Next, write your own paragraph or scene and insert it into this place. Now read the entire story including your addition.

THE OBJECTIVE

To understand just how much you need to know to really understand another person's story and how it works—and then add to it. The answer: everything—characterization, plot, tone, style, etc.

STUDENT EXAMPLES

Two consecutive sentences from "A Very Old Man with Enormous Wings," by Gabriel García Márquez:

> The Angel was no less stand-offish with him than with other mortals, but he tolerated the most ingenious infamies with the patience of a dog who had no illusions. They both came down with chicken pox at the same time.

Two students inserted the following additions between the above two sentences.

> The child would build, over days, leaning castles of shells and stray sections of wire against the Angel's unmoving body. Mornings after the old man had shifted during sleep, the child would run out of the hot house, sweating already, to scream at him. The child had not learned the patterns of the old man, his times of stillness and the moments of earthquake movement that bent the chicken coop wire.

Pelayo would take the child fishing every week. After these trips, the two would walk up to the chicken coop with their string of catch and hold them up for the Angel. But he would not turn and look at them and Pelayo came to doubt the Angel's sailor origins. The wise neighbor told Pelayo and Elisenda that the child would be an altar boy if only he kept a safe distance from the Angel, however, the child continued to play in the chicken coop, and began to call the old man the hen-man.

GREG DUYCK

The child hung dried crabs and lizards off the fallen Angel's wings, climbed onto his back to grasp the crow feathers in his tiny hands. The child tried to pull the enormous wing wide, imagining they were flying as the chickens ticked his muddy toes. He thought of the Angel as a great, broken doll and spent hours tying colored rags around his dried fig of a head, hanging rosaries around his neck and painting the crevices of his face with soot and red earth, the Angel all the while mumbling in his befuddled sailor's dialect.

When the wise neighbor woman heard words of the Angel's language coming out of the child's mouth, she shook her head and threw more mothballs into the chicken coop. She told Elisenda, "Your child will grow wings or be carried off. He will disappear into the heavens." For a while, Elisenda tried to keep the child in the garden and Pelayo repaired the broken wires of the chicken coop. But the child continued to play on the other side of the wire and the Angel remained so inert that Elisenda ceased to believe it was the Angel's tongue her child spoke at all, but his own made up child's language. Soon the child was once again playing inside the coop, flying on the back of the old man.

MOLLY LANZAROTTA

Two consecutive sentences from *Lost in the Funhouse,* by John Barth:

Ambrose's former archenemy.

Shortly after the mirror room he'd groped along a musty corridor, his heart already misgiving him at the absence of phosphorescent arrows and other signs.

One student inserted this between the above two sentences.

Ambrose wanders aimlessly, loses sight of Peter as Magda chases him beyond the mirrors, into the darkness of the next room. Their laughter echos and he cannot tell the direction from which it comes. He will not call out to them. He is not lost yet. He will find his way out on his own. The smudges of hand prints on the mirrors reassure Ambrose that he is not the only one to follow this path through the funhouse. In one of the reflections, his arm is around the waist of an exquisite young woman with a figure unusually well developed for her age. He is taller, wearing a sailor's uniform. The image moves away, but Ambrose remains. Glass. *Not a mirror.* Sentence fragments can be used to emphasize discoveries or thoughts that suddenly occur to a character. The point is communicated to the reader without saying "he thought. . . " The fragmented thought may be used in combination with italics to create a feeling of urgency. Ambrose tries creating a path parallel to the one taken by the others but is constantly forced to change direction as the mirrors obscure his goal. At an unordained moment he reaches out to touch what he thinks is another mirror, but turns out in fact to be a passageway.

ZAREH ARTINIAN

I can't write without a reader. It's precisely like a kiss—you can't do it alone.

JOHN CHEEVER

111

STYLE: ONE SIZE FITS ALL

from George Garrett

All writers, except for those few, lucky or unlucky, who are stuck with one obsessive personal style (not to be confused with voice), work hard at finding a style that fits the subject of a work of fiction, a style that is appropriate. One way of teaching and learning about the possibilities of style is by working within the boundaries of what may seem to be a radically inappropriate relationship between style and subject, thus form and content. This can be a very liberating experience for the writer. One of the best and easiest exercises is to take something written in a fairly distant past for other purposes and to try to "update" the material in a contemporary style. This hardly ever works, but failure can teach as much or more than success.

THE EXERCISE

Reread Book II of *The Faery Queene*. Then translate some of the action from the sixteenth century to here and now. Write part of it in prose and in the style and manner of, for example, the early essays of Tom Wolfe.

THE OBJECTIVE

To cause the writer to think, if only in a state of disconnection, about the relationship and tension between style and content, how style can support or subvert content.

112

BORROWING CHARACTERS

Authors have been borrowing characters from other author's works for years. Some well known examples are Jean Rhys's wonderful novel *Wide Sargasso Sea,* which provides an account of the early life of Mrs. Rochester, the wife of Mr. Rochester in Charlotte Brontë's *Jane Eyre.* George Macdonald Fraser uses Tom Brown and Flashman from Thomas Hughes's novel, *Tom Brown's School Days.* And there have been any number of continuations of the adventures of Sherlock Holmes. Nicholas Meyer's *The Seven Percent Solution,* Rick Boyer's *The Giant Rat of Sumatra* and Sena Jeter Nasland's *Sherlock in Love* are three of the best. John Gardner wrote a novel titled *Grendel* about the beast in *Beowulf.* Joseph Heller brought King David once again to life in *God Knows.*

THE EXERCISE

Take an antagonist or a minor character from a story or novel by someone else—a character who has always intrigued you. Make that person the protagonist in a scene or story of your own. For example, what would Allie Fox's wife say if she were to tell her version of Paul Theroux's *Mosquito Coast,* or write a story about their courtship? And what would Rabbit's illegitimate daughter, from Updike's *Rabbit* novels, say if she could tell her story?

THE OBJECTIVE

To enter into the imaginative world of another writer, to understand that particular world, and to build from it.

113

WHAT KEEPS YOU READING?

In *The Eye of the Story,* Eudora Welty writes, "Learning to write may be part of learning to read. For all I know, writing comes out of a superior devotion to reading."

Part of the apprenticeship of being a successful writer is learning to read like a writer, discovering how a particular story catches your attention and keeps you involved right straight through to the end.

THE EXERCISE

Halfway through a story ask yourself several questions: What do I care about? What has been set in motion that I want to see completed? Where is the writer taking me? Then finish reading the story and see how well the writer met the expectations that she raised for you.

THE OBJECTIVE

To illustrate how the best stories and novels set up situations that are resolved by the time you finish the story or close the book. To learn how to arouse the reader's curiosity or create expectations in the first half of your story or novel, and then to decide to what degree you should feel obliged to meet those expectations.

114

THE LITERARY SCENE
CIRCA 1893, 1929, 1948, OR?

from George Garrett

The year 1929 saw the publication of major books (in the present view of things) by Faulkner, Fitzgerald, Thomas Wolfe, and others. The Pulitzer Prize, and the lion's share of review space, went to Oliver LaFarge for *Laughing Boy*. Another example: Throughout the 1920s one of the most productive and interesting American novelists, widely reviewed and praised, was Joseph Hergesheimer. One of the very few reviews of a work of fiction by the young William Faulkner was devoted to Hergesheimer and indicates not only that Faulkner took his work very seriously, but also that Hergesheimer influenced Faulkner's own art.

THE EXERCISE

You are given (or draw out of a hat) a year, say 1929. You are responsible for knowing the literary history of this year as it saw itself. That is, on your honor you do not use books or histories to learn about the literary scene in 1929. You use only the newspapers and magazines of that year. In due time you report on that year to the rest of us. (To make it a bit more interesting, the student who chose 1929 might do a book report on LaFarge's *Laughing Boy*, discovering thereby that it is an excellent novel.)

THE OBJECTIVE

Year after year, to your surprise and to ours, you will report on all kinds of once-famous writers none of us has ever heard of. You will discover that many now acclaimed masters were ignored or given short shrift in their own time. Thus learn a basic truth—that they did not know or accurately judge their own era and neither can we. It follows that the writer's business is to write. Reputation, or the lack of it, is out of your hands. Persevere. Endure. Maybe prevail.

115

COMMITTING PROSE
AND POETRY TO HEART

Students have heard teachers say "every word matters" so often that these very words have almost lost their meaning. It became a challenge to find a way to make every word matter to each student individually.

While teaching at several writing conferences, I noticed that fiction writers tend to remember what other writers have said about writing—and said eloquently as illustrated by the writers quoted in this book—while poets have memorized the poem itself. "Not memorized," the poet Christopher Merrill says, quoting one of his students, "Committed to heart."

This exercise is designed to demonstrate to students that every word does matter by asking them to choose a poem or an excerpt from a story, essay, or novel and to commit their chosen selection to heart. The simple feat of memorization is less important than the act of absorbing some example of a masterful use of language. The style and cadences of the Bible verses Abraham Lincoln learned as a boy emerged in his "Gettysburg Address." Taken into memory, some piece of eloquence will always be there when you need it, silently saying that you can be eloquent too.

THE EXERCISE

At the beginning of the semester, have the class number off 1-2-1-2; the first week the 1's are responsible for reciting to the class something they have committed to heart, the week after the 2's recite, and so on. Each student should choose their excerpt a week ahead of time. And each student should choose something that they want to carry in their hearts forever.

EXERCISE VARIATION

From Christoper Merrill

Each week give students a poem or an excerpt from a story or novel to commit to heart. In Class, ask students to write the piece in their notebooks and then follow with discussion.

THE OBJECTIVE

To instill in students an appreciation for language that can only be learned by committing language to heart.

The end of a piece of fiction might be an ambivalent stare or a shattering showdown. What matters is keeping your work true to itself. You start writing the ending when you write your first word.

JEROME STERN

XIV. A COLLECTION OF SHORT-SHORT STORIES

20/20

Linda Brewer

By the time they reached Indiana, Bill realized that Ruthie, his driving companion, was incapable of theoretical debate. She drove okay, she went halves on gas, etc., but she refused to argue. She didn't seem to know how. Bill was used to East Coast women who disputed everything he said, every step of the way. Ruthie stuck to simple observation, like "Look—cows." He chalked it up to the fact that she was from rural Ohio and thrilled to death to be anywhere else.

She didn't mind driving into the setting sun. The third evening out Bill rested his eyes while she cruised along making the occasional announcement.

"Indian paintbrush. A golden eagle."

Miles later he frowned. There was no Indian paintbrush, that he knew of, near Chicago.

The next evening, driving, Ruthie said, "I never thought I'd see a Bigfoot in real life." Bill turned and looked at the side of the road streaming innocently out behind them. Two red spots winked back—reflectors nailed to a tree stump.

"Ruthie, I'll drive," he said. She stopped the car and they changed places in the light of the evening star.

"I'm so glad I got to come with you," Ruthie said. Her eyes were big, blue, and capable of seeing wonderful sights. A white buffalo near Fargo. A UFO above Twin Falls. A handsome genius in the person of Bill himself. This last vision came to her in Spokane and Bill decided to let it ride.

GIRL

Jamaica Kincaid

Wash the white clothes on Monday and put them on the stone heap; wash the color clothes on Tuesday and put them on the clothesline to dry; don't walk barehead in the hot sun; cook pumpkin fritters in very hot sweet oil; soak your little cloths right after you take them off; when buying cotton to make yourself a nice blouse, be sure that it doesn't have gum on it, because that way it won't hold up well after a wash; soak salt fish overnight before you cook it; is it true that you sing benna in Sunday school?; always eat your food in such a way that it won't turn someone else's stomach; on Sundays try to walk like a lady and not like the slut you are so bent on becoming; don't sing benna in Sunday school; you mustn't speak to wharf-rat boys, not even to give directions; don't eat fruits on the street—flies will follow you; *but I don't sing benna on Sundays at all and never in Sunday school;* this is how to sew on a button; this is how to make a buttonhole for the button you have just sewed on; this is how to hem a dress when you see the hem coming down and so to prevent yourself from looking like the slut I know you are so bent on becoming; this is how you iron your father's khaki shirt so that it doesn't have a crease; this is how you iron your father's khaki pants so that they don't have a crease; this is how you grow okra—far from the house, because okra tree harbors red ants; when you are growing dasheen, make sure it gets plenty of water or else it makes your throat itch when you are eating it; this is how you sweep a corner; this is how you sweep a whole house; this is how you sweep a yard; this is how you smile to someone you don't like too much; this is how you smile to someone you don't like at all; this is how you smile to someone you like completely; this is how you set a table for tea; this is how you set a table for dinner; this is how you set a table for dinner with an important guest; this is how you set a table for lunch; this is how you set a table for breakfast; this is how to behave in the presence of men who don't know you very well, and this way they won't recognize immediately the slut I have warned you against becoming; be sure to wash every day, even if it is with your own spit; don't squat down to play marbles—you are not a boy, you know; don't pick people's flowers—you might catch something; don't throw stones at blackbirds, because it might not be a blackbird at all; this is how to make a bread pudding; this is how to make doukona; this is how to make pepper pot; this is how to make a good medicine for a cold; this is how to make a good medicine to throw away a child before it even becomes a child; this is how to catch a fish; this is how to throw back a fish you don't like, and that way something bad won't fall on you; this is how to bully a man; this is how a man bullies you; this is how to love a man, and if this doesn't work there are other ways, and if they don't work don't feel too bad about giving up; this is how to spit up in the air if you feel like it, and this is how to move quick so that it doesn't fall on you; this is how to make ends meet; always squeeze bread to make sure it's fresh; *but what if the baker won't let me feel the bread?;* you mean to say that after all you are really going to be the kind of woman who the baker won't let near the bread?

CONFIRMATION NAMES

Mariette Lippo

We studied the saints, slipped the boys in through a break in the hockey field's fence, and led them to the woods the nuns had deemed "off-limits."

Vicky let a boy read her palm there. He told her her lifeline was short, that she'd better learn reverence for the moment. She cried for weeks before choosing the name Barbara, patron saint of those in danger of sudden death.

Susan said she would only go "so far," but no one knew what that meant. Boys went nuts trying to find out. They loved to untie her waist-long hair, to see it fan underneath her. She loved their love letters, the way they'd straighten up whenever she walked by. She chose Thecla, who'd caused the lions to "forget themselves;" instead of tearing her to shreds, they licked her feet.

Jackie couldn't wait for anything. The nuns told her impatience was her cross. Even the lunches her mother packed would be gone before ten, and she'd be left sorry, wanting more. She'd chosen Anthony, "the Finder," in a last-ditch effort to recover what she'd lost. But the nuns gave her Euphrasia, the virgin, who'd hauled huge rocks from place to place to rid her soul of temptation.

Before mass, we'd check her back for leaves.

None of us, of course, chose Magdalen, the whore. She was the secret patron whose spirit, we believed, watched over us from the trees. She was the woman who'd managed to turn her passion sacred. She was the saint who turned the flesh Divine.

YOURS

Mary Robison

Allison struggled away from her white Renault, limping with the weight of the last of the pumpkins. She found Clark in the twilight on the twig-and-leaf-littered porch behind the house.

He wore a wool shawl. He was moving up and back in a padded glider, pushed by the ball of his slippered foot.

Allison lowered a big pumpkin, let it rest on the wide floorboards.

Clark was much older—seventy-eight to Allison's thirty-five. They were married. They were both quite tall and looked something alike in their facial features. Allison wore a natural-hair wig. It was a thick blond hood around her face. She was dressed in bright-dyed denims today. She wore durable clothes, usually, for she volunteered afternoons at a children's day-care center.

She put one of the smaller pumpkins on Clark's long lap. "Now, nothing surreal," she told him. "Carve just a *regular* face. These are for kids."

In the foyer, on the Hepplewhite desk, Allison found the maid's chore list with its cross-offs, which included Clark's supper. Allison went quickly through the day's mail: a garish coupon packet, a bill from Jamestown Liquors, November's pay-TV program guide, and the worst thing, the funniest, an already opened, extremely unkind letter from Clark's relations up North. "You're an old fool," Allison read, and, "You're being cruelly deceived." There was a gift check for Clark enclosed, but it was uncashable, signed, as it was, "Jesus H. Christ."

Late, late into this night, Allison and Clark gutted and carved the pumpkins together, at an old table set on the back porch, over newspaper after soggy newspaper, with paring knives and with spoons and with a Swiss Army knife Clark used for exact shaping of tooth and eye and nostril. Clark had been a doctor, an internist, but also a Sunday watercolorist. His four pumpkins were expressive and artful. Their carved features were suited to the sizes and shapes of the pumpkins. Two looked ferocious and jagged. One registered surprise. The last was serene and beaming.

Allison's four faces were less deftly drawn, with slits and areas of distortion. She had cut triangles for noses and eyes. The mouths she had made were just wedges—two turned up and two turned down.

By one in the morning they were finished. Clark, who had bent his long torso forward to work, moved back over to the glider and looked out sleepily at nothing. All the lights were out across the ravine.

Clark stayed. For the season and time, the Virginia night was warm. Most leaves had been blown away already, and the trees stood unbothered. The moon was round above them.

Allison cleaned up the mess.

"Your jack-o'-lanterns are much, much better than mine," Clark said to her.

"Like hell," Allison said.

"Look at me," Clark said, and Allison did.

She was holding a squishy bundle of newspapers. The papers reeked sweetly with the smell of pumpkin guts.

"Yours are *far* better," he said.

"You're wrong. You'll see when they're lit," Allison said.

She went inside, came back with yellow vigil candles. It took her a while to get each candle settled, and then to line up the results in a row on the porch railing. She went along and lit each candle and fixed the pumpkin lids over the little flames.

"See?" she said.

They sat together a moment and looked at the orange faces.

"We're exhausted. It's good night time," Allison said. "Don't blow out the candles. I'll put in new ones tomorrow."

That night, in their bedroom, a few weeks earlier in her life than had been predicted, Allison began to die. "Don't look at me if my wig comes off," she told Clark. "Please."

Her pulse cords were fluttering under his fingers. She raised her knees and kicked away the comforter. She said something to Clark about the garage being locked.

At the telephone, Clark had a clear view out back and down to the porch. He wanted to get drunk with his wife once more. He wanted to tell her, from the greater perspective he had, that to own only a little talent, like his, was an awful, plaguing thing; that being only a little special meant you expected too much, most of the time, and liked yourself too little. He wanted to assure her that she had missed nothing.

He was speaking into the phone now. He watched the jack-o'-lanterns. The jack-o'-lanterns watched him.

NO ONE'S A MYSTERY

Elizabeth Tallent

For my eighteenth birthday Jack gave me a five-year diary with a latch and a little key, light as a dime. I was sitting beside him scratching at the lock, which didn't seem to want to work, when he thought he saw his wife's Cadillac in the distance, coming toward us. He pushed me down onto the dirty floor of the pickup and kept one hand on my head while I inhaled the musk of his cigarettes in the dashboard ashtray and sang along with Rosanne Cash on the tape deck. We'd been drinking tequila and the bottle was between his legs, resting up against his crotch, where the seam of his Levi's was bleached linen-white, though the Levi's were nearly new. I don't know why his Levi's always bleached like that, along the seams and at the knees. In a curve of cloth his zipper glinted, gold.

"It's her," he said. "She keeps the lights on in the daytime. I can't think of a single habit in a woman that irritates me more than that." When he saw that I was going to stay still he took his hand from my head and ran it through his own dark hair.

"Why does she?" I said.

"She thinks it's safer. Why does she need to be safer? She's driving exactly fifty-five miles an hour. She believes in those signs: 'Speed Monitored by Aircraft.' It doesn't matter that you can look up and see that the sky is empty."

"She'll see your lips move, Jack. She'll know you're talking to someone."

"She'll think I'm singing along with the radio."

He didn't lift his hand, just raised the fingers in salute while the pressure of his palm steadied the wheel, and I heard the Cadillac honk twice, musically; he was driving easily eighty miles an hour. I studied his boots. The elk heads stitched into the leather were bearded with frayed thread, the toes were scuffed, and there was a compact wedge of muddy manure between the heel and the sole—the same boots he'd been wearing for the two years I'd known him. On the tape deck Rosanne Cash sang, "Nobody's into me, no one's a mystery."

"Do you think she's getting famous because of who her daddy is or for herself?" Jack said.

"There are about a hundred pop tops on the floor, did you know that? Some little kid could cut a bare foot on one of these, Jack."

301

"No little kids get into this truck except for you."

"How come you let it get so dirty?"

"'How come,'" he mocked. "You even sound like a kid. You can get back into the seat now, if you want. She's not going to look over her shoulder and see you."

"How do you know?"

"I just know," he said. "Like I know I'm going to get meat loaf for supper. It's in the air. Like I know what you'll be writing in that diary."

"What will I be writing?" I knelt on my side of the seat and craned around to look at the butterfly of dust printed on my jeans. Outside the window Wyoming was dazzling in the heat. The wheat was fawn and yellow and parted smoothly by the thin dirt road. I could smell the water in the irrigation ditches hidden in the wheat.

"Tonight you'll write, 'I love Jack. This is my birthday present from him. I can't imagine anybody loving anybody more than I love Jack.'"

"I can't."

"In a year you'll write. I wonder what I ever really saw in Jack. I wonder why I spent so many days just riding around in his pickup. It's true he taught me something about sex. It's true there wasn't ever much else to do in Cheyenne.'"

"I won't write that."

"In two years you'll write, 'I wonder what that old guy's name was, the one with the curly hair and the filthy dirty pickup truck and time on his hands.'"

"I won't write that."

"No?"

"Tonight I'll write, 'I love Jack. This is my birthday present from him. I can't imagine anybody loving anybody more than I love Jack.'"

"No, you can't." he said. "You can't imagine it."

"In a year I'll write, 'Jack should be home any minute now. The table's set—my grandmother's linen and her old silver and the yellow candles left over from the wedding—but I don't know if I can wait until after the trout à la Navarra to make love to him.'"

"It must have been a fast divorce."

"In two years I'll write, 'Jack should be home by now. Little Jack is hungry for his supper. He said his first word today besides "Mama" and "Papa." He said "kaka."'"

Jack laughed. "He was probably trying to finger-paint with kaka on the bathroom wall when you heard him say it."

"In three years I'll write, 'My nipples are a little sore from nursing Eliza Rosamund.'"

"Rosamund. Every little girl should have a middle name she hates."

"'Her breath smells like vanilla and her eyes are just Jack's color of blue.'"

"That's nice," Jack said.

"So, which one do you like?"

"I like yours," he said. "But I believe mine."

"It doesn't matter. I believe mine."

"Not in your heart of hearts, you don't."

"You're wrong."

"I'm not wrong," he said. "And her breath would smell like your milk, and it's kind of a bittersweet smell, if you want to know the truth."

VISION OUT OF THE CORNER OF ONE EYE

Luisa Valenzuela

It's true, he put his hand on my ass and I was about to scream bloody murder when the bus passed by a church and he crossed himself. He's a good sort after all, I said to myself. Maybe he didn't do it on purpose or maybe his right hand didn't know what his left hand was up to. I tried to move farther back in the bus—searching for explanations is one thing and letting yourself be pawed is another—but more passengers got on and there was no way I could do it. My wiggling to get out of his reach only let him get a better hold on me and even fondle me. I was nervous and finally moved over. He moved over, too. We passed by another church but he didn't notice it and when he raised his hand to his face it was to wipe the sweat off his forehead. I watched him out of the corner of one eye, pretending that nothing was happening, or at any rate not making him think I liked it. It was impossible to move a step farther and he began jiggling me. I decided to get even and put my hand on his behind. A few blocks later I got separated from him. Then I was swept along by the passengers getting off the bus and now I'm sorry I lost him so suddenly because there were only 7,400 pesos in his wallet and I'd have gotten more out of him if we'd been alone. He seemed affectionate. And very generous.

Translated by Helen Lane

XV. A COLLECTION OF
SHORT STORIES

HAPPY ENDINGS

Margaret Atwood

John and Mary meet.
What happens next?
If you want a happy ending, try A.

A.   John and Mary fall in love and get married. They both have
worthwhile and remunerative jobs which they find stimulating and challenging. They buy a charming house. Real estate values go up. Eventually,
when they can afford live-in help, they have two children, to whom they
are devoted. The children turn out well. John and Mary have a stimulating and challenging sex life and worthwhile friends. They go on fun vacations together. They retire. They both have hobbies which they find stimulating and challenging. Eventually they die. This is the end of the story.

B.   Mary falls in love with John but John doesn't fall in love with
Mary. He merely uses her body for selfish pleasure and ego gratification of
a tepid kind. He comes to her apartment twice a week and she cooks him
dinner, you'll notice that he doesn't even consider her worth the price of a
dinner out, and after he's eaten the dinner he fucks her and after that he
falls asleep, while she does the dishes so he won't think she's untidy, having all those dirty dishes lying around, and puts on fresh lipstick so she'll
look good when he wakes up, but when he wakes up he doesn't even notice, he puts on his socks and his shorts and his pants and his shirt and his
tie and his shoes, the reverse order from the one in which he took them
off. He doesn't take off Mary's clothes, she takes them off herself, she acts
as if she's dying for it every time, not because she likes sex exactly, she
doesn't, but she wants John to think she does because if they do it often
enough surely he'll get used to her, he'll come to depend on her and they
will get married, but John goes out the door with hardly so much as a
good-night and three days later he turns up at six o'clock and they do the
whole thing over again.

Mary gets run-down. Crying is bad for your face, everyone knows that
and so does Mary but she can't stop. People at work notice. Her friends
tell her John is a rat, a pig, a dog, he isn't good enough for her, but she
can't believe it. Inside John, she thinks, is another John, who is much

nicer. This other John will emerge like a butterfly from a cocoon, a Jack from a box, a pit from a prune, if the first John is only squeezed enough.

One evening John complains about the food. He has never complained about the food before. Mary is hurt.

Her friends tell her they've seen him in a restaurant with another woman, whose name is Madge. It's not even Madge that finally gets to Mary: it's the restaurant. John has never taken Mary to a restaurant. Mary collects all the sleeping pills and aspirins she can find, and takes them and a half a bottle of sherry. You can see what kind of a woman she is by the fact that it's not even whiskey. She leaves a note for John. She hopes he'll discover her and get her to the hospital in time and repent and then they can get married, but this fails to happen and she dies.

John marries Madge and everything continues as in A.

C. John, who is an older man, falls in love with Mary, and Mary, who is only twenty-two, feels sorry for him because he's worried about his hair falling out. She sleeps with him even though she's not in love with him. She met him at work. She's in love with someone called James, who is twenty-two also and not yet ready to settle down.

John on the contrary settled down long ago: this is what is bothering him. John has a steady, respectable job and is getting ahead in his field, but Mary isn't impressed by him, she's impressed by James, who has a motorcycle and a fabulous record collection. But James is often away on his motorcycle, being free. Freedom isn't the same for girls, so in the meantime Mary spends Thursday evenings with John. Thursdays are the only days John can get away.

John is married to a woman called Madge and they have two children, a charming house which they bought just before the real estate values went up, and hobbies which they find stimulating and challenging, when they have the time. John tells Mary how important she is to him, but of course he can't leave his wife because a commitment is a commitment. He goes on about this more than is necessary and Mary finds it boring, but older men can keep it up longer so on the whole she has a fairly good time.

One day James breezes in on his motorcycle with some top-grade California hybrid and James and Mary get higher than you'd believe possible and they climb into bed. Everything becomes very underwater, but along comes John, who has a key to Mary's apartment. He finds them stoned and entwined. He's hardly in any position to be jealous, considering Madge, but nevertheless he's overcome with despair. Finally he's middle-aged, in two years he'll be bald as an egg and he can't stand it. He purchases a handgun, saying he needs it for target practice—this is the thin part of the plot, but it can be dealt with later—and shoots the two of them and himself.

Madge, after a suitable period of mourning, marries an understanding man called Fred and everything continues as in A, but under different names.

D. Fred and Madge have no problems. They get along exceptionally well and are good at working out any little difficulties that may arise. But their charming house is by the seashore and one day a giant tidal wave approaches. Real estate values go down. The rest of the story is about what caused the tidal wave and how they escape from it. They do, though thousands drown, but Fred and Madge are virtuous and lucky. Finally on high ground they clasp each other, wet and dripping and grateful, and continue as in A.

E. Yes, but Fred has a bad heart. The rest of the story is about how kind and understanding they both are until Fred dies. Then Madge devotes herself to charity work until the end of A. If you like, it can be "Madge," "cancer," "guilty and confused," and "bird watching."

F. If you think this is all too bourgeois, make John a revolutionary and Mary a counterespionage agent and see how far that gets you. Remember, this is Canada. You'll still end up with A, though in between you may get a lustful brawling saga of passionate involvement, a chronicle of our times, sort of.

You'll have to face it, the endings are the same however you slice it. Don't be deluded by any other endings, they're all fake, either deliberately fake, with malicious intent to deceive, or just motivated by excessive optimism if not by downright sentimentality.

The only authentic ending is the one provided here:

John and Mary die. John and Mary die. John and Mary die.

So much for endings. Beginnings are always more fun. True connoisseurs, however, are known to favor the stretch in between, since it's the hardest to do anything with.

That's about all that can be said for plots, which anyway are just one thing after another, a what and a what and a what.

Now try How and Why.

CHRISTMAS EVE AT JOHNSON'S DRUGS N GOODS

Toni Cade Bambara

I was probably the first to spot them cause I'd been watching the entrance to the store on the lookout for my daddy, knowing that if he didn't show soon, he wouldn't be coming at all. His new family would be expecting him to spend the holidays with them. For the first half of my shift, I'd raced the cleaning cart down the aisles doing a slapdash job on the signs and glass cages, eager to stay in view of the doorway. And look like Johnson's kept getting bigger, swelling, sprawling itself all over the corner lot, just to keep me from the door, to wear me out in the marathon vigil.

In point of fact, Johnson's Drugs N Goods takes up less than one-third of the block. But it's laid out funny in crisscross aisles so you get to feeling like a rat in an endless maze. Plus the ceilings are high and the fluorescents a blazing white. And Mrs. Johnson's got these huge signs sectioning off the spaces—TOBACCO DRUGS HOUSEWARES, etc.—like it was some big-time department store. The thing is, till the two noisy women came in, it felt like a desert under a blazing sun. Piper in Tobacco even had on shades. The new dude in Drugs looked like he was at the end of a wrong-way telescope. I got to feeling like a nomad with the cleaning cart, trekking across the sands with no end in sight, wandering. The overhead lights creating mirages and racing up my heart till I'd realize that wasn't my daddy in the parking lot, just the poster-board Santa Claus. Or that wasn't my daddy in the entrance way, just the Burma Shave man in a frozen stance. Then I'd tried to make out pictures of Daddy getting off the bus at the terminal, or driving a rented car past the Chamber of Commerce building, or sitting jammed-leg in one of them DC point-o-nine brand X planes, coming to see me.

By the time the bus pulled into the lot and the two women in their big-city clothes hit the door, I'd decided Daddy was already at the house waiting for me, knowing that for a mirage too, since Johnson's is right across from the railroad and bus terminals and the house is a dollar-sixty cab away. And I know he wouldn't feature going to the house on the off chance of running into Mama. Or even if he escaped that fate, having to sit in the parlor with his hat in his lap while Aunt Harriet looks him up and down grunting, too busy with the latest crossword puzzle contest to offer the man some supper. And Uncle Henry talking a blue streak bout how he outfoxed the city council or somethin and nary a cold beer in sight for my daddy.

But then the two women came banging into the store and I felt better. Right away the store stopped sprawling, got fixed. And we all got pulled together from our various zones to one focal point—them. Changing up the whole atmosphere of the place fore they even got into the store proper. Before we knew it, we were all smiling, looking halfway like you supposed to on Christmas Eve, even if you do got to work for ole lady Johnson, who don't give you no slack whatever the holiday.

"What the hell does this mean, Ethel?" the one in the fur coat say, talking loud and fast, yanking on the rails that lead the way into the store. "What are we, cattle? Being herded into the blankety-blank store and in my fur coat," she grumbles, boosting herself up between the rails, swinging her body along like the kids do in the park.

Me and Piper look at each other and smile. Then Piper moves down to the edge of the counter right under the Tobacco sign so as not to miss nothing. Madeen over in Housewares waved to me to ask what's up and I just shrug. I'm fascinated by the women.

"Look here," the one called Ethel say, drawing the words out lazy slow. "Do you got a token for this sucker?" She's shoving hard against the turnstile folks supposed to exit through. Pushing past and grunting, the turnstile crank cranking like it gonna bust, her Christmas corsage of holly and bells just ajingling and hanging by a thread. Then she gets through and stumbles toward the cigar counter and leans back against it, studying the turnstile hard. It whips back around in place, making scrunching noises like it's been abused.

"You know one thing," she say, dropping her face onto her coat collar so Piper'd know he's being addressed.

"Ma'am?"

"That is one belligerent bad boy, that thing right there."

Piper laughs his prizewinning laugh and starts touching the stacks of gift-wrapped stuff, case the ladies in the market for pipe tobacco or something. Two or three of the customers who'd been falling asleep in the magazines coming to life now, inching forward. Phototropism, I'd call it, if somebody asked me for a word.

The one in the fur coat's coming around now the right way—if you don't count the stiff-elbow rail-walking she was doing—talking about "Oh, my God, I can walk, I can walk, Ethel, praise de lawd."

The two women watching Piper touch the cigars, the humidors, the gift-wrapped boxes. Mostly he's touching himself, cause George Lee Piper love him some George Lee Piper. Can't blame him. Piper be fine.

"You work on commissions, young man?" Fur Coat asking.

"No, ma'am."

The two women look at each other. They look over toward the folks inching forward. They look at me gliding by with the cleaning cart. They look back at each other and shrug.

"So what's his problem?" Ethel says in a stage whisper. "Why he so hot to sell us something?"

"Search me." Fur Coat starts flapping her coat and frisking herself. "You know?" she asking me.

"It's a mystery to me," I say, doing my best to run ole man Samson over. He sneaking around trying to jump Madeen in Housewares. And it is a mystery to me how come Piper always so eager to make a sale. You'd think he had half interest in the place. He says it's because it's his job, and after all, the Johnsons are Black folks. I guess so, I guess so. Me, I just clean the place and stay busy in case Mrs. J is in the prescription booth, peeking out over the top of the glass.

When I look around again, I see that the readers are suddenly very interested in cigars. They crowding around Ethel and Fur Coat. Piper kinda embarrassed by all the attention, though fine as he is, he oughta be used to it. His expression's cool but his hands give him away, sliding around the counter like he shuffling a deck of slippery cards. Fur Coat nudges Ethel and they bend over to watch the hands, doing these chicken-head jerkings. The readers take up positions just like a director was hollering "Places" at em. Piper, never one to disappoint an audience, starts zipping around these invisible walnut shells. Right away Fur Coat whips out a little red change purse and slaps a dollar bill on the counter. Ethel dips deep into her coat pocket, bending her knees and being real comic, then plunks down some change. Ole man Sampson tries to boost up on my cleaning cart to see the shells that ain't there.

"Scuse me, Mr. Sampson," I say, speeding the cart up sudden so that quite naturally he falls off, the dirty dog.

Piper is snapping them imaginary shells around like nobody's business, one of the readers leaning over another's shoulder, staring pop-eyed.

"All right now, everybody step back," Ethel announces. She waves the crowd back and pushes up one coat sleeve, lifts her fist into the air and jerks out one stiff finger from the bunch, and damn if the readers don't lift their heads to behold in amazement this wondrous finger.

"That, folks," Fur Coat explains, "is what is known as the indicator finger. The indicator is about to indicate the indicatee."

"Say wha?" Dirty ole man Sampson decides he'd rather sneak up on Madeen than watch the show.

"What's going on over there?" Miz Della asks me. I spray the watch case and make a big thing of wiping it and ignoring her. But then the new dude in Drugs hollers over the same thing.

"Christmas cheer gone to the head. A coupla vaudevillians," I say. He smiles, and Miz Della says "Ohhh" like I was talking to her.

"This one," Ethel says, planting a finger exactly one-quarter of an inch from the countertop.

Piper dumb-shows a lift of the shell, turning his face away as though he can't bear to look and find the elusive pea ain't there and he's gonna have to take the ladies' money. Then his eyes swivel around and sneak a peek and widen, lighting up his whole face in a prizewinning grin.

"You got it," he shouts.

The women grab each other by the coat shoulders and jump each other up and down. And I look toward the back cause I know Mrs. J got to be hearing all this carrying-on, and on payday if Mr. J ain't handing out the checks, she's going to give us some long lecture about decorum and what it means to be on board at Johnson's Drugs N Goods. I wheel over to the glass jars and punch bowls, wanting alibi distance just in case. And also to warn Madeen about Sampson gaining on her. He's ducking down behind the coffeepots, walking squat and shameless.

"Pay us our money, young man," Fur Coat is demanding, rapping her knuckles on the counter.

"Yeah, what kind of crooked shell game is you running here in this joint?" say Ethel, finding a good foil character to play.

"We should hate to have to turn the place out, young man."

"It out," echoes Ethel.

The women nod to the crowd and a coupla folks giggle. And Piper tap-taps on the cash register like he shonuff gonna give em they money. I'd rather they turned the place out myself. I want to call my daddy. Only way any of us are going to get home in time to dress for the Christmas dance at the center is for the women to turn it out. Like I say, Piper ain't too clear about the worker's interest versus management's, as the dude in Drugs would say it. So he's light-tapping and quite naturally the cash drawer does not come out. He's yanking some unseen dollar from the not-there drawer and handing it over. Damn if Fur Coat don't snatch it, deal out the bills to herself and her friend and then make a big production out of folding the money flat and jamming it in that little red change purse.

"I wanna thank you," Ethel says, strolling off, swinging her pocket-book so that the crowd got to back up and disperse. Fur Coat spreads her coat and curtsies.

"A pleasure to do business with you ladies," Piper says, tipping his hat, looking kinda disappointed that he didn't sell em something. Tipping his hat the way he tipped the shells, cause you know Mrs. J don't allow no hats indoors. I came to work in slacks one time and she sent me home to change and docked me too. I wear a gele some times just to mess her around, and you can tell she trying to figure out if she'll go for it or not. The woman is crazy. Not Uncle Henry type crazy, but Black property owner type crazy. She thinks this is a museum, which is why folks don't hardly come in here to shop. That's okay cause we all get to know each other well. It's not okay cause it's a drag to look busy. If you look like you ain't buckling under a weight of work, Mrs. J will have you count the Band-Aids in the boxes to make sure the company ain't pulling a fast one. The woman crazy.

Now Uncle Henry type crazy is my kind of crazy. The type crazy to get you a job. He march into the "saloon" as he calls it and tells Leon D that he is not an equal opportunity employer and that he, Alderman Henry Peoples, is going to put some fire to his ass. So soon's summer comes, me and Madeen got us a job at Leon D. Salon. One of them hushed, funeral type shops with skinny models parading around for customers corseted and strangling in their seats, huffin and puffin.

Madeen got fired right off on account of the pound of mascara she wears on each lash and them weird dresses she designs for herself (with less than a yard of cloth each if you ask me). I did my best to hang in there so's me and Madeen'd have hang-around money till Johnson started hiring again. But it was hard getting back and forth from the stockroom to this little kitchen to fix the espresso to the showroom. One minute up to your ass in carpet, the next skidding across white linoleum, the next making all this noise on ceramic tile and people looking around at you and all. Was there for two weeks and just about had it licked by stationing different kind of shoes at each place that I could slip into, but then Leon D stumbled over my bedroom slippers one afternoon.

But to hear Uncle Henry tell it, writing about it all to Daddy, I was working at a promising place making a name for myself. And Aunt Harriet listening to Uncle Henry read the letter, looking me up and down and grunting. She know what kind of name it must be, cause my name in the family is Miss Clumsy. Like if you got a glass-top coffee table with doodads on em, or a hurricane lamp sitting on a mantel anywhere near a door I got to come through, or an antique jar you brought all the way from Venice the time you won the crossword puzzle contest—you can rest assure I'll demolish them by and by. I ain't vicious, I'm just clumsy. It's my gawky stage, Mama says. Aunt Harriet cuts her eye at Mama and grunts.

My daddy advised me on the phone not to mention anything to the Johnsons about this gift of mine for disaster or the fact that I worked at Leon D. Salon. No sense the Johnson's calling up there to check on me and come to find I knocked over a perfume display two times in the same day. Like I say—it's a gift. So when I got to clean the glass jars and punch bowls at Johnson's, I take it slow and pay attention. Then I take up my station relaxed in Fabrics, where the worst that can happen is I upset a box of pins.

Mrs. J is in the prescription booth, and she clears her throat real loud. We all look to the back to read the smoke signals. She ain't paying Fur Coat and Ethel no attention. They over in Cosmetics messing with Miz Della's mind and her customers. Mrs. J got her eye on some young teenagers browsing around Jewelry. The other eye on Piper. But this does not mean Piper is supposed to check the kids out. It means Madeen is. You got to know how to read Mrs. J to get along.

She always got one eye on Piper. Tries to make it seem like she don't trust him at the cash register. That may be part of the reason now, now that she's worked up this cover story so in her mind. But we all know why she watches Piper, same reason we all do. Cause Piper is so fine you just can't help yourself. Tall and built up, blue-black and smooth, got the nerve to have dimples, and wears this splayed-out push-broom mustache he's always raking in with three fingers. Got a big butt too that makes you wanna hug the customer that asks for the cartoons Piper keeps behind him, two shelfs down. Mercy. And when it's slow, or when Mrs. J comes bustling over for the count, Piper steps from behind the counter and shows his self. You get to see the whole Piper from the shiny boots to the glistening fro and every inch of him fine. Enough to make you holler.

Miz Della in Cosmetics, a sister who's been passing for years but fooling nobody but herself, she always lolligagging over to Tobacco talking bout are there any new samples of those silver-tipped cigars for women. Piper don't even squander energy to bump her off any more. She mostly just ain't even there. At first he would get mad when she used to act hinkty and had these white men picking her up at the store. Then he got sorrowful about it all, saying she was a pitiful person. Now that she's going out with the blond chemist back there, he just wiped her off the map. She tries to mess with him, but Piper ain't heard the news she's been born. Sometimes his act slips, though, cause he does take a lot of unnecessary energy to play up to Madeen whenever Miz Della's hanging around. He's not consistent in his attentions, and that spurs Madeen the dress designer to madness. And Piper really oughta put brakes on that, cause Madeen subject to walk in one day in a fishnet dress and no underwear and then what he goin do about that?

Last year on my birthday my daddy got on us about dressing like hussies to attract the boys. Madeen shrugged it off and went about her business. It hurt my feelings. The onliest reason I was wearing that tight sweater and that skimpy skirt was cause I'd been to the roller rink and that's how we dress. But my daddy didn't even listen and I was really hurt. But then later that night, I come through the living room to make some cocoa and he apologized. He lift up from the couch where he always sleeps when he comes to visit, lifted up and whispered it—"Sorry." I could just make him out by the light from the refrigerator.

"Candy," he calls to make sure I heard him. And I don't want to close the frig door cause I know I'll want to remember this scene, figuring it's going to be the last birthday visit cause he fixin to get married and move outta state.

"Sir?"

He pat the couch and I come on over and just leave the frig door open so we can see each other. I forgot to put the milk down, so I got this cold milk bottle in my lap, feeling stupid.

"I was a little rough on you earlier," he say, picking something I can't see from my bathrobe. "But you're getting to be a woman now and certain things have to be said. Certain things have to be understood so you can decide what kind of woman you're going to be, ya know?"

"Sir," I nod. I'm thinking Aunt Harriet ought to tell me, but then Aunt Harriet prefers to grunt at folks, reserving words for the damn crossword puzzles. And my mama stay on the road so much with the band, when she do come home for a hot minute all she has to tell me is "My slippers're in the back closet" or "Your poor tired Ma'd like some coffee."

He takes my hand and don't even kid me about the milk bottle, just holds my hand for a long time saying nothing, just squeezes it. And I know he feeling bad about moving away and all, but what can he do, he got a life to lead. Just like Mama got her life to lead. Just like I got my life to lead and'll probably leave here myself one day and become an actress or a director. And I know I should tell him it's all right. Sitting there with that milk bottle chilling me through my bathrobe, the light from the refrigerator throwing funny shadows on the wall, I know that years later when I'm in trouble or something, or hear that my daddy died or something like that, I'm going feel real bad that I didn't tell him—it's all right, Daddy, I understand. It ain't like he'd made any promises about making a home for me with him. So it ain't like he's gone back on his word. And if the new wife can't see taking in no half-grown new daughter, hell, I understand that. I can't get the words together, neither can he. So we just squeeze each other's hands. And that'll have to do.

"When I was a young man," he says after while, "there were girls who ran around all made up in sassy clothes. And they were okay to party with, but not the kind you cared for, ya know?" I nod and he pats my hand. But I'm thinking that ain't right, to party with a person you don't care for. How come you can't? I want to ask, but he's talking. And I was raised not to interrupt folk when they talking, especially my daddy. "You and Madeen cause quite a stir down at the barbershop." He tries to laugh it, but it comes out scary. "Got to make up your mind now what kind of woman you're going to be. You know what I'm saying?" I nod and he loosens his grip so I can go make my cocoa.

I'm messing around in the kitchenette feeling dishonest. Things I want to say, I haven't said. I look back over toward the couch and know this picture is going to haunt me later. Going to regret the things left unsaid. Like a coward, like a child maybe. I fix my cocoa and keep my silence, but I do remember to put the milk back and close the refrigerator door.

"Candy?"

"Sir?" I'm standing there in the dark, the frig door closed now and we can't even see each other.

"It's not about looks anyway," he says, and I hear him settling deep into the couch and pulling up the bedclothes. "And it ain't always about attracting some man either . . . not necessarily."

I'm waiting to hear what it is about, the cup shaking in the saucer and me wanting to ask him all over again how it was when he and Mama first met in Central Park, and how it used to be when they lived in Philly and had me and how it was when the two of them were no longer making any sense together but moved down here anyway and then split up. But I could hear that breathing he does just before the snoring starts. So I hustle on down the hall so I won't be listening for it and can't get to sleep.

All night I'm thinking about this woman I'm going to be. I'll look like Mama but don't wanna be no singer. Was named after Grandma Candestine but don't wanna be no fussy old woman with a bunch of kids. Can't see myself turning into Aunt Harriet either, doing crossword puzzles all day long. I look over at Madeen, all sprawled out in her bed, tangled up in the sheets looking like the alcoholic she trying to be these days, sneaking liquor from Uncle Henry's closet. And I know I don't wanna be stumbling down the street with my boobs out and my dress up and my heels cracking off and all. I write for a whole hour in my diary trying to connect with the future me and trying not to hear my daddy snoring.

Fur Coat and Ethel in Housewares talking with Madeen. I know they must be cracking on Miz Della, cause I hear Madeen saying something about equal opportunity. We used to say that Mrs. J was an equal opportunity employer for hiring Miz Della. But then she went and hired real white folks—a blond, crew-cut chemist and a pimply-face kid for the stockroom. If you ask me, that's running equal opportunity in the ground. And running the business underground cause don't nobody round here deal with no white chemist. They used to wrinkly old folks grinding up the herbs and bark and telling them very particular things to do and not to do working the roots. So they keep on going to Mama Drear down past the pond or Doc Jessup in back of the barbershop. Don't do a doctor one bit of good to write out a prescription talking about fill it at Johnson's, cause unless it's an emergency folk stay strictly away from a white root worker, especially if he don't tell you what he doing.

Aunt Harriet in here one day when Mama Drear was too sick to counsel and quite naturally she asks the chemist to explain what all he doing back there with the mortar and pestle and the scooper and the scales. And he say something about rules and regulations, the gist of which was mind your business, lady. Aunt Harriet dug down deep into her crossword-puzzle words and pitched a natural bitch. Called that man a bunch of choicest names. But the line that got me was—"Medication without explanation is obscene." And what she say that for, we ran that in the ground for days. Infatuation without fraternization is obscene. Insemination without obligation is tyranny. Fornication without contraception is obtuse, and so forth and so on. Madeen's best line came out the night we were watching a TV special about welfare. Sterilization without strangulation and hell's damnation is I-owe-you-one-crackers. Look like every situation called for a line like that, and even if it didn't, we made it fit.

Then one Saturday morning we were locked out and we standing around shivering in our sweaters and this old white dude jumps out a pickup truck hysterical, his truck still in gear and backing out the lot. His wife had given their child an overdose of medicine and the kid was out cold. Look like everything he said was grist for the mill.

"She just administered the medicine without even reading the label," he told the chemist, yanking on his jacket so the man couldn't even get out his keys. "She never even considered the fact it might be dangerous, the medicine so old and all." We follow the two down the aisle to the prescription booth, the old white dude talking a mile a minute, saying they tried to keep the kid awake, tried to walk him, but he wouldn't walk. Tried to give him an enema, but he wouldn't stay propped up. Could the chemist suggest something to empty his stomach out and sooth his inflamed ass and what all? And besides he was breathing funny and should he administer mouth-to-mouth resuscitation? The minute he tore out of there and ran down the street to catch up with his truck, we started in.

Administration without consideration is illiterate. Irrigation without resuscitation is evacuation without ambulation is inflammation without information is execution without restitution is. We got downright silly about the whole thing till Mrs. J threatened to fire us all. But we kept it up for a week.

Then the new dude in Drugs who don't never say much stopped the show one afternoon when we were trying to figure out what to call the street riots in the sixties and so forth. He say Revolution without Transformation is Half-assed. Took me a while to ponder that one, a whole day in fact just to work up to it. After while I would listen real hard whenever he opened his mouth, which wasn't often. And I jotted down the titles of the books I'd see him with. And soon's I finish up the stack that's by my bed, I'm hitting the library. He started giving me some of the newspapers he keeps stashed in that blue bag of his we all at first thought was full of funky jockstraps and sneakers. Come to find it's full of carrots and oranges and books and stuff. Madeen say he got a gun in there too. But then Madeen all the time saying something. Like she saying here lately that the chemist's jerking off there behind the poisons and the goopher dust.

The chemist's name is Hubert Tarrly. Madeen tagged him Herbert Tareyton. But the name that stuck was Nazi Youth. Every time I look at him I hear Hitler barking out over the loudspeaker urging the youth to measure up and take over the world. And I can see these stark-eyed gray kids in short pants and suspenders doing jump-ups and scissor kicks and turning they mamas in to the Gestapo for listening to the radio. Chemist looks like he grew up like that, eating knockwurst and beating on Jews, rounding up gypsies, saying *Sieg heil* and shit. Mrs. J said something to him one morning and damn if he didn't click his heels. I like to die. She blushing all over her simple self talking bout that's Southern cavalier style. I could smell the gas. I could see the flaming cross too. Nazi Youth and then some. The dude in Drugs started calling him that too, the dude whose name I can never remember. I always wanna say Ali Baba when I talk about him with my girl friends down at the skating rink or with the older sisters at the arts center. But that ain't right. Either you call a person a name that says what they about or you call em what they call themselves, one or the other.

Now take Fur Coat, for instance. She is clearly about the fur coat. She moving up and down the aisles talking while Ethel in the cloth coat is doing all the work, picking up teapots, checking the price on the dust mops, clicking a bracelet against the punch bowl to see if it ring crystal, hollering to somebody about whether the floor wax need buffing or not. And it's all on account of the fur coat. Her work is something other than that. Like when they were in Cosmetics messing with Miz Della, some white ladies come up talking about what's the latest in face masks. And every time Miz Della pull something out the box, Ethel shake her head and say that brand is crap. Then Fur Coat trots out the sure-fire recipe for the face mask. What she tells the old white ladies is to whip us some egg white to peaks, pour in some honey, some oil of wintergreen, some oil of eucalyptus, the juice of a lemon and a half a teaspoon of arsenic. Now any fool can figure out what lemon juice do to arsenic, or how honey going make the concoction stick, and what all else the oil of this and that'll do to your face. But Fur Coat in her fur coat make you stand still and listen to this madness. Fur Coat an authority in her fur coat. The fur coat is an act of alchemy in itself, as Aunt Harriet would put it.

Just like my mama in her fur coat, same kind too—Persian lamb, bought hot in some riot or other. Mama's coat was part of the Turn the School Out Outfit. Hardly ever came out of the quilted bag cept for that. Wasn't for window-shopping, wasn't for going to rehearsal, wasn't for church teas, was for working her show. She'd flip a flap of that coat back over her hip when she strolled into the classroom to get on the teacher's case bout saying something out of the way about Black folks. Then she'd pick out the exact plank, exact spot she'd take her stand on, then plant one of them black suede pumps from the I. Miller outlet she used to work at. Then she'd lift her chin arrogant proud to start the rap, and all us kids would lean forward and stare at the cameo brooch visible now on the wide-wale wine plush corduroy dress. Then she'd work her show in her outfit. Bam-bam that black suede pocketbook punctuating the points as Mama ticked off the teacher's offenses. And when she got to the good part, and all us kids would strain up off the benches to hear every word so we could play it out in the schoolyard, she'd take both fists and brush that fur coat way back past her hips and she'd challenge the teacher to either change up and apologize or meet her for a showdown at a school-board hearing. And of course ole teacher'd apologize to all us Black kids. Then Mama'd let the coat fall back into place and she'd whip around, the coat draping like queen robes, and march herself out. Mama was baad in her fur coat.

I don't know what-all Fur Coat do in her fur coat but I can tell it's hellafyin whatever it all is. They came into Fabrics and stood around a while trying to see what shit they could get into. All they had in their baskets was a teapot and some light bulbs and some doodads from the special gift department, perfume and whatnot. I waited on a few customers wanting braid and balls of macramé twine, nothing where I could show my stuff.

Now if somebody wanted some of the silky, juicy cotton stuff I could get into something fancy, yanking off the yards, measuring it doing a shuffle-stick number, nicking it just so, then ripping the hell out the shit. But didn't nobody ask for that. Fur Coat and Ethel kinda finger some bolts and trade private jokes, then they moved onto Drugs.

"We'd like to see the latest in rubberized fashions for men, young man." Fur Coat is doing a super Lady Granville Whitmore the Third number. "If you would." She bows her head, fluttering her lashes.

Me and Madeen start messing around in the shoe-polish section so's not to miss nothing. I kind of favor Fur Coat, on account of she got my mama's coat on, I guess. On the other hand, I like the way Ethel drawl talk like she too tired and bored to go on. I guess I like em both cause they shopping the right way, having fun and all. And they got plenty of style. I wouldn't mind being like that when I am full-grown.

The dude in Drugs thinks on the request a while, sucking in his lips like he wanna talk to himself on the inside. He's looking up and down the counter, pauses at the plastic rain hats, rejects them, then squints hard at Ethel and Fur Coat. Fur Coat plants a well-heeled foot on the shelf with the tampons and pads and sighs. Something about that sigh I don't like. It's real rather than play snooty. The dude in Drugs always looks a little crumbled, a little rough dry, like he jumped straight out the hamper but not quite straight. But he got stuff to him if you listen rather than look. Seems to me ole Fur Coat is looking. She keeps looking while the dude moves down the aisle behind the counter, ducks down out of sight, reappears and comes back, dumping an armful of boxes on the counter.

"One box of Trojans and one box of Ramses," Ethel announces. "We want to do the comparison test."

"On the premises?" Lady G Fur says, planting a dignified hand on her collarbone.

"Egg-zack-lee."

"In your opinion, young man," Lady G Fur says, staying the arm of the brand tester, "which of the two is the best? Uhmm—the better of the two, that is. In your vast experience as lady-killer and cock hound, which passes the X test?" It's said kinda snotty. Me and Madeen exchange a look and dust around the cans of shoe polish.

"Well," the dude says, picking up a box in each hand, "in my opinion, Trojans have a snappier ring to em." He rattles the box against his ear, then lets Ethel listen. She nods approval. Fur Coat will not be swayed. "On the other hand, Ramses is a smoother smoke. Cooler on the throat. What do you say in your vast experience as—er—"

Ethel is banging down boxes of Kotex cracking up, screaming, "He gotcha. He gotcha that time. Old laundry bag got over on you, Helen."

Mrs. J comes out of the prescription booth and hustles her bulk to the counter. Me and Madeen clamp down hard on giggles and I damn near got to climb in with the neutral shoe polish to escape attention. Ethel and Fur Coat don't give a shit, they paying customers, so they just roar. Cept

Fur Coat's roar is phony, like she really mad and gonna get even with the dude for not turning out to be a chump. Meanwhile, the dude is standing like a robot, arms out at exactly the same height, elbows crooked just so, boxes displayed between thumb and next finger, the gears in the wrist click, clicking, turning. And not even cracking a smile.

"What's the problem here?" Mrs. J trying not to sound breathless or angry and ain't doing too good a job. She got to say it twice to be heard.

"No problem, Mrs. Johnson," the dude says straight-face. "The customers are buying condoms, I am selling condoms. A sale is being conducted, as is customary in a store."

Mrs. J looks down at the jumble of boxes and covers her mouth. She don't know what to do. I duck down, cause when folks in authority caught in a trick, the first they look for is a scapegoat.

"Well, honey," Ethel says, giving a chummy shove to Mrs. J's shoulder, "what do you think? I've heard that Trojans are ultrasensitive. They use a baby lamb brain, I understand."

"Membrane, dear, membrane," Fur Coat says down her nose. "They remove the intestines of a four-week-old lamb and use the membrane. Tough, resilient, sheer."

"Gotcha," says Ethel. "On the other hand, it is said by folks who should know that Ramses has a better box score."

"Box score," echoes Mrs. J in a daze.

"Box score. You know, honey—no splits, breaks, leaks, seeps."

"Seepage, dear, seepage," says Fur Coat, all nasal.

"Gotcha."

"The solution," says the dude in an almost robot voice, "is to take one small box of each and do the comparison test as you say. A survey. A random sampling of your friends." He says this to Fur Coat, who is not enjoying it all nearly so much as Ethel, who is whooping and hollering.

Mrs. J backs off and trots to the prescription booth. Nazi Youth peeks over the glass and mumbles something soothing to Mrs. J. He waves me and Madeen away like he somebody we got to pay some mind.

"We will take one super-duper, jumbo family size of each."

"Family size?" Fur Coat is appalled. "And one more thing, young man," she orders. "Wrap up a petite size for a small-size smart-ass acquaintance of mine. Gift-wrapped, ribbons and all."

It occurs to me that Fur Coat's going to present this to the dude. Right then and there I decide I don't like her. She's not discriminating with her stuff. Up till then I was thinking how much I'd like to trade Aunt Harriet in for either of these two, hang out with them, sit up all night while they drink highballs and talk about men they've known and towns they've been in. I always did want to hang out with women like this and listen to their stories. But they beginning to reveal themselves as not nice people, just cause the dude is rough dry on Christmas Eve. My Uncle Henry all the time telling me they different kinds of folks in the community, but when you boil it right down there's just nice and not nice. Uncle

Henry say they folks who'll throw they mamas to the wolves if the fish sandwich big enough. They folks who won't whatever the hot sauce. They folks that're scared, folks that are dumb; folks that have heart and some with heart to spare. That all boils down to nice and not nice if you ask me. It occurs to me that Fur Coat is not nice. Fun, dazzling, witty, but not nice.

"Do you accept Christmas gifts, young man?" Fur Coat asking in icy tones she ain't masking too well.

"No. But I do accept Kwanza presents at the feast."

"Quan . . . hmm. . . ."

Fur Coat and Ethel go into a huddle with the stage whispers. "I bet he thinks we don't know beans about Quantas . . . Don't he know we are The Ebony Jet Set . . . We never travel to kangaroo land except by. . . ."

Fur Coat straightens up and stares at the dude. "Will you accept a whatchamacallit gift from me even though we are not feasting, as it were?"

"If it is given with love and respect, my sister, of course." He was sounding so sincere, it kinda got to Fur Coat.

"In that case. . . ." She scoops up her bundle and sweeps out the place. Ethel trotting behind hollering, "He gotcha, Helen. Give the boy credit. Maybe we should hire him and do a threesome act." She spun the turnstile round three times for she got into the spin and spun out the store.

"Characters," says Piper on tiptoe, so we all can hear him. He laughs and checks his watch. Madeen slinks over to Tobacco to be in asking distance in case he don't already have a date to the dance. Miz Della's patting some powder on. I'm staring at the door after Fur Coat and Ethel, coming to terms with the fact that my daddy ain't coming. It's gonna be just Uncle Henry and Aunt Harriet this year, with maybe Mama calling on the phone between sets to holler in my ear, asking have I been a good girl, it's been that long since she's taken a good look at me.

"You wanna go to the Kwanza celebrations with me sometime this week or next week, Candy?"

I turn and look at the dude. I can tell my face is falling and right now I don't feel up to doing anything about it. Holidays are depressing. Maybe there's something joyous about this celebration he's talking about. Cause Lord knows Christmas is a drag. The sister who taught me how to wrap a gele asked me was I coming to the celebration down at the Black Arts Center, but I didn't know nothing bout it.

"Look here," I finally say, "would you please get a pencil and paper and write your name down for me. And write that other word down too so I can look it up."

He writes his name down and spins the paper around for me to read. "Obatale."

"Right," he says, spinning it back. "But you can call me Ali Baba if you want to." He was leaning over too far writing out Kwanza for me to see if that was a smile on his face or a smirk. I figure a smile, cause Obatale nice people.

GRYPHON

Charles Baxter

On Wednesday afternoon, between the geography lesson on ancient Egypt's hand-operated irrigation system and an art project that involved drawing a model city next to a mountain, our fourth-grade teacher, Mr. Hibler, developed a cough. This cough began with a series of muffled throat-clearings and progressed to propulsive noises contained within Mr. Hibler's closed mouth. "Listen to him," Carol Peterson whispered to me. "He's gonna blow up." Mr. Hibler's laughter—dazed and infrequent—sounded a bit like his cough, but as we worked on our model cities we would look up, thinking he was enjoying a joke, and see Mr. Hibler's face turning red, his cheeks puffed out. This was not laughter. Twice he bent over, and his loose tie, like a plumb line, hung down straight from his neck as he exploded himself into a Kleenex. He would excuse himself, then go on coughing. "I'll bet you a dime," Carol Peterson whispered, "we get a substitute tomorrow."

Carol sat at the desk in front of mine and was a bad person—when she thought no one was looking she would blow her nose on notebook paper, then crumple it up and throw it into the wastebasket—but at times of crisis she spoke the truth. I knew I'd lose the dime.

"No deal," I said.

When Mr. Hibler stood us in formation at the door just prior to the final bell, he was almost incapable of speech. "I'm sorry, boys and girls," he said. "I seem to be coming down with something."

"I hope you feel better tomorrow, Mr. Hibler," Bobby Kryzanowicz, the faultless brown-noser, said, and I heard Carol Peterson's evil giggle. Then Mr. Hibler opened the door and we walked out to the buses, a clique of us starting noisily to hawk and raugh as soon as we thought we were a few feet beyond Mr. Hibler's earshot.

Since Five Oaks was a rural community, and in Michigan, the supply of substitute teachers was limited to the town's unemployed community college graduates, a pool of about four mothers. These ladies fluttered, provided easeful class days, and nervously covered material we had mastered weeks earlier. Therefore it was a surprise when a woman we had never seen came into the class the next day, carrying a purple purse, a checkerboard lunchbox, and a few books. She put the books on one side of Mr. Hibler's desk and the lunchbox on the other, next to the Voice of

Music phonograph. Three of us in the back of the room were playing with Heever, the chameleon that lived in a terrarium and on one of the plastic drapes, when she walked in.

She clapped her hands at us. "Little boys," she said, "why are you bent over together like that?" She didn't wait for us to answer. "Are you tormenting an animal? Put it back. Please sit down at your desks. I want no cabals this time of the day." We just stared at her. "Boys," she repeated, "I asked you to sit down."

I put the chameleon in his terrarium and felt my way to my desk, never taking my eyes off the woman. With white and green chalk, she had started to draw a tree on the left side of the blackboard. She didn't look usual. Furthermore, her tree was outsized, disproportionate, for some reason.

"This room needs a tree," she said, with one line drawing the suggestion of a leaf. "A large, leafy, shady, deciduous . . . oak."

Her fine, light hair had been done up in what I would learn years later was called a chignon, and she wore gold-rimmed glasses whose lenses seemed to have the faintest blue tint. Harold Knardahl, who sat across from me, whispered, "Mars," and I nodded slowly, savoring the imminent weirdness of the day. The substitute drew another branch with an extravagant arm gesture, then turned around and said, "Good morning. I don't believe I said good morning to all of you yet."

Facing us, she was no special age—an adult is an adult—but her face had two prominent lines, descending vertically from the sides of her mouth to her chin. I knew where I had seen those lines before: *Pinocchio.* They were marionette lines. "You may stare at me," she said to us, as a few more kids from the last bus came into the room; their eyes fixed on her, "for a few more seconds, until the bell rings. Then I will permit no more staring. Looking I will permit. Staring, no. It is impolite to stare, and a sign of bad breeding. You cannot make a social effort while staring."

Harold Knardahl did not glance at me, or nudge, but I heard him whisper "Mars" again, trying to get more mileage out of his single joke with the kids who had just come in.

When everyone was seated, the substitute teacher finished her tree, put down her chalk fastidiously on the phonograph, brushed her hands, and faced us. "Good morning," she said. "I am Miss Ferenczi, your teacher for the day. I am fairly new to your community, and I don't believe any of you know me. I will therefore start by telling you a story about myself."

While we settled back, she launched into her tale. She said her grandfather had been a Hungarian prince; her mother had been born in some place called Flanders, had been a pianist, and had played concerts for people Miss Ferenczi referred to as "crowned heads." She gave us a knowing look. "Grieg," she said, "the Norwegian master, wrote a concerto for piano that was. . . "—she paused—"my mother's triumph at her debut concert in London." Her eyes searched the ceiling. Our eyes followed.

Nothing up there but ceiling tile. "For reasons that I shall not go into, my family's fortunes took us to Detroit, then north to dreadful Saginaw, and now here I am in Five Oaks, as your substitute teacher, for today, Thursday, October the eleventh. I believe it will be a good day: all the forecasts coincide. We shall start with your reading lesson. Take out your reading book. I believe it is called *Broad Horizons,* or something along those lines."

Jeannie Vermeesch raised her hand. Miss Ferenczi nodded at her. "Mr. Hibler always starts the day with the Pledge of Allegiance." Jeannie whined.

"Oh, does he? In that case," Miss Ferenczi said, "you must know it *very* well by now, and we certainly need not spend our time on it. No, no allegiance pledging on the premises today, by my reckoning. Not with so much sunlight coming into the room. A pledge does not suit my mood." She glanced at her watch. "Time *is* flying. Take out *Broad Horizons.*"

She disappointed us by giving us an ordinary lesson, complete with vocabulary and drills, comprehension questions, and recitation. She didn't seem to care for the material, however. She sighed every few minutes and rubbed her glasses with a frilly handkerchief that she withdrew, magician-style, from her left sleeve.

After reading we moved on to arithmetic. It was my favorite time of the morning, when the lazy autumn sunlight dazzled its way through ribbons of clouds past the windows on the east side of the classroom and crept across the linoleum floor. On the playground the first group of children, the kindergartners, were running on the quack grass just beyond the monkey bars. We were doing multiplication tables. Miss Ferenczi had made John Wazny stand up at his desk in the front row. He was supposed to go through the tables of six. From where I was sitting, I could smell the Vitalis soaked into John's plastered hair. He was doing fine until he came to six times eleven and six times twelve. "Six times eleven," he said, "is sixty-eight. Six times twelve is. . . " He put his fingers to his head, quickly and secretly sniffed his fingertips, and said, ". . . seventy-two." Then he sat down.

"Fine," Miss Ferenczi said, "Well now. That was very good."

"Miss Ferenczi!" One of the Eddy twins was waving her hand desperately in the air. "Miss Ferenczi! Miss Ferenczi!"

"Yes?"

"John said that six times eleven is sixty-eight and you said he was right!"

"*Did* I?" She gazed at the class with a jolly look breaking across her marionette's face. "Did I say that? Well, what *is* six times eleven?"

"It's sixty-six!"

She nodded. "Yes. So it is. But, and I know some people will not entirely agree with me, at some times it is sixty-eight."

"When? When is it sixty-eight?"

We were all waiting.

"In higher mathematics, which you children do not yet understand, six times eleven can be considered to be sixty-eight." She laughed through her nose. "In higher mathematics numbers are . . . more fluid. The only thing a number does is contain a certain amount of something. Think of water. A cup is not the only way to measure a certain amount of water, is it?" We were staring, shaking our heads. "You could use saucepans or thimbles. In either case, the water *would be the same*. Perhaps," she started again, "it would be better for you to think that six times eleven is sixty-eight only when I am in the room."

"Why is it sixty-eight," Mark Poole asked, "when you're in the room?"

"Because it's more interesting that way," she said, smiling very rapidly behind her blue-tinted glasses. "Besides, I'm your substitute teacher, am I not?" We all nodded. "Well, then, think of six times eleven equals sixty-eight as a substitute fact."

"A substitute fact?"

"Yes." Then she looked at us carefully. "Do you think," she asked, "that anyone is going to be hurt by a substitute fact?"

We looked back at her.

"Will the plants on the windowsill be hurt?" We glanced at them. There were sensitive plants thriving in a green plastic tray, and several wilted ferns in small clay pots. "Your dogs and cats, or your moms and dads?" She waited. "So," she concluded, "what's the problem?"

"But it's wrong," Janice Weber said, "isn't it?"

"What's your name, young lady?"

"Janice Weber."

"And you think it's wrong, Janice?"

"I was just asking."

"Well, all right. You were just asking. I think we've spent enough time on this matter by now, don't you, class? You are free to think what you like. When your teacher, Mr. Hibler, returns, six times eleven will be sixty-six again, you can rest assured. And it will be that for the rest of your lives in Five Oaks. Too bad, eh?" She raised her eyebrows and glinted herself at us. "But for now, it wasn't. So much for that. Let us go on to your assigned problems for today, as painstakingly outlined, I see, in Mr. Hibler's lesson plan. Take out a sheet of paper and write your names on the upper left-hand corner."

For the next half hour we did the rest of our arithmetic problems. We handed them in and then went on to spelling, my worst subject. Spelling always came before lunch. We were taking spelling dictation and looking at the clock. "Thorough," Miss Ferenczi said. "Boundary." She walked in the aisles between the desks, holding the spelling book open and looking down at our papers. "Balcony." I clutched my pencil. Somehow, the way she said those words, they seemed foreign, mis-voweled and mis-consonanted. I stared down at what I had spelled. *Balconie*. I turned the pencil upside down and erased my mistake. *Balconey*. That looked better, but still incorrect. I cursed the world of spelling and tried erasing it again and saw the paper beginning to wear away. *Balkony.* Suddenly I felt a hand on my shoulder.

"I don't like that word either," Miss Ferenczi whispered, bent over, her mouth near my ear. "It's ugly. My feeling is, if you don't like a word, you don't have to use it." She straightened up, leaving behind a slight odor of Clorets.

At lunchtime we went out to get our trays of sloppy joes, peaches in heavy syrup, coconut cookies, and milk, and brought them back to the classroom, where Miss Ferenczi was sitting at the desk, eating a brown sticky thing she had unwrapped from tightly rubber-banded waxed paper. "Miss Ferenczi," I said, raising my hand. "You don't have to eat with us. You can eat with the other teachers. There's a teacher's lounge," I ended up, "next to the principal's office."

"No, thank you," she said. "I prefer it here."

"We've got a room monitor," I said. "Mrs. Eddy." I pointed to where Mrs. Eddy, Joyce and Judy's mother, sat silently at the back of the room, doing her knitting.

"That's fine," Miss Ferenczi said. "But I shall continue to eat here, with you children. I prefer it," she repeated.

"How come?" Wayne Razmer asked without raising his hand.

"I talked to the other teachers before class this morning," Miss Ferenczi said, biting into her brown food. "There was a great rattling of the words for the fewness of the ideas. I didn't care for their brand of hilarity. I don't like ditto-machine jokes."

"Oh," Wayne said.

"What's that you're eating?" Maxine Sylvester asked, twitching her nose. "Is it food?"

"It most certainly *is* food. It's a stuffed fig. I had to drive almost down to Detroit to get it. I also brought some smoked sturgeon. And this," she said, lifting some green leaves out of her lunchbox, "is raw spinach, cleaned this morning."

"Why're you eating raw spinach?" Maxine asked.

"It's good for you," Miss Ferenczi said. "More stimulating than soda pop or smelling salts." I bit into my sloppy joe and stared blankly out the window. An almost invisible moon was faintly silvered in the daytime autumn sky. "As far as food is concerned," Miss Ferenczi was saying, "you have to shuffle the pack. Mix it up. Too many people eat . . . well, never mind."

"Miss Ferenczi," Carol Peterson said, "what are we going to do this afternoon?"

"Well," she said, looking down at Mr. Hibler's lesson plan, "I see that your teacher, Mr. Hibler, has you scheduled for a unit on the Egyptians." Carol groaned. "Yessss," Miss Ferenczi continued, "that is what we will do: the Egyptians. A remarkable people. Almost as remarkable as the Americans. But not quite." She lowered her head, did her quick smile, and went back to eating her spinach.

After noon recess we came back into the classroom and saw that Miss Ferenczi had drawn a pyramid on the blackboard close to her oak tree. Some of us who had been playing baseball were messing around in the back of the room, dropping the bats and gloves into the playground box, and Ray Schontzeler had just slugged me when I heard Miss Ferenczi's high-pitched voice, quavering with emotions. "Boys," she said, "come to order right this minute and take your seats. I do not wish to waste a minute of class time. Take out your geography books." We trudged to our desks and, still sweating, pulled out *Distant Lands and Their People*. "Turn to page forty-two." She waited for thirty seconds, then looked over at Kelly Munger. "Young man," she said, "why are you still fossicking in your desk?"

Kelly looked as if his foot had been stepped on. "Why am I what?"

"Why are you . . . burrowing in your desk like that?"

"I'm lookin' for the book, Miss Ferenczi."

Bobby Kryzanowicz, the faultless brown-noser who sat in the first row by choice, softly said, "His name is Kelly Munger. He can't ever find his stuff. He always does that."

"I don't care what his name is, especially after lunch," Miss Ferenczi said. *"Where is your book?"*

"I just found it." Kelly was peering into his desk and with both hands pulled at the book, shoveling along in front of it several pencils and crayons, which fell into his lap and then to the floor.

"I hate a mess," Miss Ferenczi said. "I hate a mess in a desk or a mind. It's . . . unsanitary. You wouldn't want your house at home to look like your desk at school, now, would you?" She didn't wait for an answer. "I should think not. A house at home should be as neat as human hands can make it. What were we talking about? Egypt. Page forty-two. I note from Mr. Hibler's lesson plan that you have been discussing the modes of Egyptian irrigation. Interesting, in my view, but not so interesting as what we are about to cover. The pyramids, and Egyptian slave labor. A plus on one side, a minus on the other." We had our books open to page forty-two, where there was a picture of a pyramid, but Miss Ferenczi wasn't looking at the book. Instead, she was staring at some object just outside the window.

"Pyramids," Miss Ferenczi said, still looking past the window. "I want you to think about pyramids. And what was inside. The bodies of the pharaohs, of course, and their attendant treasures. Scrolls. Perhaps," Miss Ferenczi said, her face gleeful but unsmiling, "these scrolls were novels for the pharaohs, helping them to pass the time in their long voyage through the centuries. But then, I am joking." I was looking at the lines on Miss Ferenczi's skin. "Pyramids," Miss Ferenczi went on, "were the repositories of special cosmic powers. The nature of a pyramid is to guide cosmic energy forces into a concentrated point. The Egyptians knew that; we have generally forgotten it. Did you know," she asked, walking to the side of the room so that she was standing by the coat closet, "that George Washington had Egyptian blood, from his grandmother? Certain features of the Constitution of the United States are notable for their Egyptian ideas."

Without glancing down at the book, she began to talk about the movement of souls in Egyptian religion. She said that when people die, their souls return to Earth in the form of carpenter ants or walnut trees, depending on how they behaved—"well or ill"—in life. She said that the Egyptians believed that people act the way they do because of magnetism produced by tidal forces in the solar system, forces produced by the sun and by its "planetary ally," Jupiter. Jupiter, she said, was a planet, as we had been told, but had "certain properties of stars." She was speaking very fast. She said that the Egyptians were great explorers and conquerors. She said that the greatest of all the conquerors, Genghis Khan, had had forty horses and forty young women killed on the site of his grave. We listened. No one tried to stop her. "I myself have been in Egypt," she said, "and have witnessed much dust and many brutalities." She said that an old man in Egypt who worked for a circus had personally shown her an animal in a cage, a monster, half bird and half lion. She said that this monster was called a gryphon and that she had heard about them but never seen them until she traveled to the outskirts of Cairo. She wrote the word out on the blackboard in large capital letters: GRYPHON. She said that Egyptian astronomers had discovered the planet Saturn but had not seen its rings. She said that the Egyptians were the first to discover that dogs, when they are ill, will not drink from rivers, but wait for rain, and hold their jaws open to catch it.

"She lies."

We were on the school bus home. I was sitting next to Carl Whiteside, who had bad breath and a huge collection of marbles. We were arguing. Carl thought she was lying. I said she wasn't, probably.

"I didn't believe that stuff about the bird," Carl said, "and what she told us about the pyramids? I didn't believe that, either. She didn't know what she was talking about."

"Oh yeah?" I had liked her. She was strange. I thought I could nail him. "If she was lying," I said, "what'd she say that was a lie?"

"Six times eleven isn't sixty-eight. It isn't ever. It's sixty-six, I know for a fact."

"She said so. She admitted it. What else did she lie about?"

"I don't know," he said. "Stuff."

"What stuff?"

"Well." He swung his legs back and forth. "You ever see an animal that was half lion and half bird?" He crossed his arms. "It sounded real fakey to me."

"It could happen," I said. I had to improvise, to outrage him. "I read in this newspaper my mom bought in the IGA about this scientist, this mad scientist in the Swiss Alps, and he's been putting genes and chromosomes and stuff together in test tubes, and he combined a human being and a hamster." I waited, for effect. "It's called a humster."

"You never." Carl was staring at me, his mouth open, his terrible bad breath making its way toward me. "What newspaper was it?"

The National Enquirer," I said, "that they sell next to the cash registers." When I saw his look of recognition, I knew I had him. "And this mad scientist," I said, "his name was, um, Dr. Frankenbush." I realized belatedly that this name was a mistake and waited for Carl to notice its resemblance to the name of the other famous mad master of permutations, but he only sat there.

"A man and a hamster?" He was staring at me, squinting, his mouth opening in distaste. "Jeez. What'd it look like?"

When the bus reached my stop, I took off down our dirt road and ran up through the backyard, kicking the tire swing for good luck. I dropped my books on the back steps so I could hug and kiss our dog, Mr. Selby. Then I hurried inside. I could smell brussels sprouts cooking, my unfavorite vegetable. My mother was washing other vegetables in the kitchen sink, and my baby brother was hollering in his yellow playpen on the kitchen floor.

"Hi, Mom," I said, hopping around the playpen to kiss her. "Guess what?"

"I have no idea."

"We had this substitute today, Miss Ferenczi, and I'd never seen her before, and she had all these stories and ideas and stuff."

"Well. That's good." My mother looked out the window in front of the sink, her eyes on the pine woods west of our house. That time of the afternoon her skin always looked so white to me. Strangers always said my mother looked like Betty Crocker, framed by the giant spoon on the side of the Bisquick box. "Listen, Tommy," she said. "Would you please go upstairs and pick your clothes off the floor in the bathroom, and then go outside to the shed and put the shovel and ax away that your father left outside this morning?"

"She said that six times eleven was sometimes sixty-eight!" I said. "And she said she once saw a monster that was half lion and half bird." I waited. "In Egypt."

"Did you hear me?" my mother asked, raising her arm to wipe her forehead with the back of her hand. "You have chores to do."

"I know," I said. "I was just telling you about the substitute."

"It's very interesting," my mother said, quickly glancing down at me, "and we can talk about it later when your father gets home. But right now you have some work to do."

"Okay, Mom." I took a cookie out of the jar on the counter and was about to go outside when I had a thought. I ran into the living room, pulled out a dictionary next to the TV stand, and opened it to the Gs. After five minutes I found it. *Gryphon:* variant of griffin. *Griffin:* "a fabulous beast with the head and wings of an eagle and the body of a lion." Fabulous was right. I shouted with triumph and ran outside to put my father's tools in their proper places.

Miss Ferenczi was back the next day, slightly altered. She had pulled her hair down and twisted it into pigtails, with red rubber bands holding them tight one inch from the ends. She was wearing a green blouse and pink scarf, making her difficult to look at for a full class day. This time there was no pretense of doing a reading lesson or moving on to arithmetic. As soon as the bell rang, she simply began to talk.

She talked for forty minutes straight. There seemed to be less connection between her ideas, but the ideas themselves were, as the dictionary would say, fabulous. She said she had heard of a huge jewel, in what she called the antipodes, that was so brilliant that when light shone into it at a certain angle it would blind whoever was looking at its center. She said the biggest diamond in the world was cursed and had killed everyone who owned it, and that by a trick of fate it was called the Hope Diamond. Diamonds are magic, she said, and this is why women wear them on their fingers, as a sign of the magic of womanhood. Men have strength, Miss Ferenczi said, but no true magic. That is why men fall in love with women but women do not fall in love with men: they just love being loved. George Washington had died because of a mistake he made about a diamond. Washington was not the first *true* President, but she didn't say who was. In some places in the world, she said, men and women still live in the trees and eat monkeys for breakfast. Their doctors are magicians. At the bottom of the sea are creatures thin as pancakes who have never been studied by scientists because when you take them up to air, the fish explode.

There was not a sound in the classroom, except for Miss Ferenczi's voice, and Donna DeShano's coughing. No one even went to the bathroom.

Beethoven, she said, had not been deaf; it was a trick to make himself famous, and it worked. As she talked, Miss Ferenczi's pigtails swung back and forth. There are trees in the world, she said, that eat meat: their leaves are sticky and close up on bugs like hands. She lifted her hands and brought them together, palm to palm. Venus, which most people think is the next closest planet to the sun, is not always closer, and, besides, it is the planet of greatest mystery because of its thick cloud cover. "I know what lies underneath those clouds," Miss Ferenczi said, and waited. After the silence, she said, "Angels. Angels live under those clouds." She said that angels were not invisible to everyone and were in fact smarter than most people. They did not dress in robes as was often claimed but instead wore formal evening clothes, as if they were about to attend a concert. Often angels *do* attend concerts and sit in the aisles, where, she said, most people pay no attention to them. She said the most terrible angel had the shape of the Sphinx. "There is no running away from that one," she said. She said that unquenchable fires burn just under the surface of the earth in Ohio, and that the baby Mozart fainted dead away in his cradle when he first heard the sound of a trumpet. She said that someone named Narzim al Harrardim was the greatest writer who ever lived. She said that planets control behavior, and anyone conceived during a solar eclipse would be born with webbed feet.

"I know you children like to hear these things," she said, "these secrets, and that is why I am telling you all this." We nodded. It was better than doing comprehension questions for the readings in *Broad Horizons*.

"I will tell you one more story," she said, "and then we will have to do arithmetic." She leaned over, and her voice grew soft. "There is no death," she said. "You must never be afraid. Never. That which is, cannot die. It will change into different earthly and unearthly elements, but I know this as sure as I stand here in front of you, and I swear it: you must not be afraid. I have seen this truth with these eyes. I know it because in a dream God kissed me. Here." And she pointed with her right index finger to the side of her head, below the mouth where the vertical lines were carved into her skin.

Absentmindedly we all did our arithmetic problems. At recess the class was out on the playground, but no one was playing. We were all standing in small groups, talking about Miss Ferenczi. We didn't know if she was crazy, or what. I looked out beyond the playground, at the rusted cars piled in a small heap behind a clump of sumac, and I wanted to see shapes there, approaching me.

On the way home, Carl sat next to me again. He didn't say much, and I didn't either. At last he turned to me. "You know what she said about the leaves that close up on bugs?"

"Huh?"

"The leaves," Carl insisted, "The meat-eating plants. I know it's true. I saw it on television. The leaves have this icky glue that the plants have got smeared all over them and the insects can't get off 'cause they're stuck. I saw it. " He seemed demoralized. "She's tellin' the truth."

"Yeah."

"You think she's seen all those angels?"

I shrugged.

"I don't think she has," Carl informed me. "I think she made that part up."

"There's a tree," I suddenly said. I was looking out the window at the farms along County Road H. I knew every barn, every broken windmill, every fence, every anhydrous ammonia tank, by heart. "There's a tree that's . . . that I've seen . . . "

"Don't you try to do it," Carl said. "You'll just sound like a jerk."

I kissed my mother. She was standing in front of the stove. "How was your day?" she asked.

"Fine."

"Did you have Miss Ferenczi again?"

"Yeah."

"Well?"

"She was fine. Mom," I asked, "can I go to my room?"

"No," she said, "not until you've gone out to the vegetable garden and picked me a few tomatoes." She glanced at the sky. "I think it's going to rain. Skedaddle and do it now. Then you come back inside and watch your brother for a few minutes while I go upstairs. I need to clean up before dinner." She looked down at me. "You're looking a little pale, Tommy." She touched the back of her hand to my forehead and I felt her diamond ring against my skin. "Do you feel all right?"

"I'm fine," I said, and went out to pick the tomatoes.

Coughing mutedly, Mr. Hibler was back the next day, slipping lozenges into his mouth when his back was turned at forty-five minute intervals and asking us how much of his prepared lesson plan Miss Ferenczi had followed. Edith Atwater took the responsibility for the class of explaining to Mr. Hibler that the substitute hadn't always done exactly what he, Mr. Hibler, would have done, but we had worked hard even though she talked a lot. About what? he asked. All kinds of things, Edith said. I sort of forgot. To our relief, Mr. Hibler seemed not at all interested in what Miss Ferenczi had said to fill the day. He probably thought it was woman's talk: unserious and not suited for school. It was enough that he had a pile of arithmetic problems from us to correct.

For the next month, the sumac turned a distracting red in the field, and the sun traveled toward the southern sky, so that its rays reached Mr. Hibler's Halloween display on the bulletin board in the back of the room, fading the pumpkin head scarecrow from orange to tan. Every three days I measured how much farther the sun had moved toward the southern horizon by making small marks with my black Crayola on the north wall, ant-sized marks only I knew were there.

And then in early December, four days after the first permanent snowfall, she appeared again in our classroom. The minute she came in the door, I felt my heart begin to pound. Once again, she was different: this time, her hair hung straight down and seemed hardly to have been combed. She hadn't brought her lunchbox with her, but she was carrying what seemed to be a small box. She greeted all of us and talked about the weather. Donna DeShano had to remind her to take her overcoat off.

When the bell to start the day finally rang, Miss Ferenczi looked out at all of us and said, "Children, I have enjoyed your company in the past, and today I am going to reward you." She held up the small box. "Do you know what this is?" She waited. "Of course you don't. It is a Tarot pack."

Edith Atwater raised her hand. "What's a Tarot pack, Miss Ferenczi?"

"It is used to tell fortunes," she said. "And that is what I shall do this morning. I shall tell your fortunes, as I have been taught to do."

"What's fortune?" Bobby Kryzanowicz asked.

"The future, young man. I shall tell you what your future will be. I can't do your whole future, of course. I shall have to limit myself to the five-card system, the wands, cups, swords, pentacles, and the higher arcanes. Now who wants to be first?"

There was a long silence. Then Carol Peterson raised her hand.

"All right," Miss Ferenczi said. She divided the pack into five smaller packs and walked back to Carol's desk, in front of mine. "Pick one card from each one of these packs," she said. I saw that Carol had a four of cups and a six of swords, but I couldn't see the other cards. Miss Ferenczi studied the cards on Carol's desk for a minute. "Not bad," she said. "I do not see much higher education. Probably an early marriage. Many children. There's something bleak and dreary here, but I can't tell what. Perhaps just the tasks of a housewife life. I think you'll do very well, for the most part." She smiled at Carol, a smile with a certain lack of interest. "Who wants to be next?"

Carl Whiteside raised his hand slowly.

"Yes," Miss Ferenczi said, "let's do a boy." She walked over to where Carl sat. After he picked his five cards, she gazed at them for a long time. "Travel," she said. "Much distant travel. You might go into the army. Not too much romantic interest here. A late marriage, if at all. But the Sun in your major arcana, that's a very good card." She giggled. "You'll have a happy life."

Next I raised my hand. She told me my future. She did the same with Bobby Kryzanowicz, Kelly Munger, Edith Atwater, and Kim Foor. Then she came to Wayne Razmer. He picked his five cards, and I could see that the Death card was one of them.

"What's your name?" Miss Ferenczi asked.

"Wayne."

"Well, Wayne," she said, "you will undergo a great metamorphosis, a change, before you become an adult. Your earthly element will no doubt leap higher, because you seem to be a sweet boy. This card, this nine of swords, tells me of suffering and desolation. And this ten of wands, well, that's a heavy load."

"What about this one?" Wayne pointed at the Death card.

"It means, my sweet, that you will die soon." She gathered up the cards. We were all looking at Wayne. "But do not fear," she said. "It is not really death. Just change. Out of your earthly shape." She put the cards on Mr. Hibler's desk. "And now, let's do some arithmetic."

At lunchtime Wayne went to Mr. Faegre, the principal, and informed him of what Miss Ferenczi had done. During the noon recess, we saw Miss Ferenczi drive out of the parking lot in her rusting green Rambler American. I stood under the slide, listening to the other kids coasting down and landing in the little depressive bowls at the bottom. I was kicking stones and tugging at my hair right up to the moment when I saw Wayne come out to the playground. He smiled, the dead fool, and with the fingers of his right hand he was showing everyone how he had told on Miss Ferenczi.

I made my way toward Wayne, pushing myself past two girls from another class. He was watching me with his little pinhead eyes.

"You told," I shouted at him. "She was just kidding."

"She shouldn't have," he shouted back. "We were supposed to be do-ing arithmetic."

"She just scared you," I said. "You're a chicken. You're a chicken, Wayne. You are. Scared of a little card," I sing-songed.

Wayne fell at me, his two fists hammering down on my nose. I gave him a good one in the stomach and then I tried for his head. Aiming my fist, I saw that he was crying. I slugged him.

"She was right," I yelled. "She was always right! She told the truth!" Other kids were whooping. "You were just scared, that's all!"

And then large hands pulled at us, and it was my turn to speak to Mr. Faegre.

In the afternoon Miss Ferenczi was gone, and my nose was stuffed with cotton clotted with blood, and my lip had swelled, and our class had been combined with Mrs. Mantei's sixth-grade class for a crowded after-noon science unit on insect life in ditches and swamps. I knew where Mrs. Mantei lived: she had a new house trailer just down the road from us, at the Clearwater Park. She was no mystery. Somehow she and Mr. Bodine, the other fourth-grade teacher, had managed to fit forty-five desks into the room. Kelly Munger asked if Miss Ferenczi had been arrested, and Mrs. Mantei said no, of course not. All that afternoon, until the buses came to pick us up, we learned about field crickets and two-striped grasshoppers, water bugs, cicadas, mosquitoes, flies, and moths. We learned about insects' hard outer shell, the exoskeleton, and the usual parts of the mouth, including the labrum, mandible, maxilla, and glossa. We learned about compound eyes, and the four-stage metamorphosis from egg to larva to pupa to adult. We learned something, but not much, about mating. Mrs. Mantei drew, very skillfully, the internal anatomy of the grasshopper on the blackboard. We learned about the dance of the honeybee, directing other bees in the hive to pollen. We found out about which insects were pests to man, and which were not. On lined white pieces of paper we made lists of insects we might actually see, then a list of insects too small to be clearly visible, such as fleas; Mrs. Mantei said that our assignment would be to memorize these lists for the next day, when Mr. Hibler would certainly return and test us on our knowledge.

HAPPY

Ann Beattie

"Your brother called," I say to my husband on the telephone. "He called to find out if he left his jumpsuit here. As though another weekend guest might have left a jumpsuit."

"As it happens, he did. I mailed it to him. He should have gotten it days ago."

"You never said anything about it. I told him. . . "

"I didn't say anything because I know you find great *significance* in what he leaves behind."

"Pictures of the two of you with your mother, and you were such unhappy little boys. . . "

"Anything you want me to bring home?" he says.

"I think I'd like some roses. Ones the color of peaches."

He clears his throat. All winter, he has little coughs and colds and irritations. The irritations are irritating. At night, he hemms over *Forbes* and I read Blake, in silence.

"I meant that could be found in Grand Central," he says.

"An éclair."

"All right," he says. He sighs.

"One banana, two banana, three banana, four . . . "

"I think you have the wrong number," I say.

"*Fifteen years,* and you still don't know my voice on the phone."

"Oh," I say. "Hi, Andy."

Andy let his secretary use his apartment during her lunch hour to have an affair with the Xerox repairman. Andy was on a diet, drinking pre-digested protein, and he had thrown everything out in his kitchen, so he wouldn't be tempted. He was allowed banana extract to flavor his formula. The secretary and the repairman got hungry and rummaged through the kitchen cabinets, and all they could find was a gallon jug of banana extract.

"I got the Coors account," Andy says. "I'm having a wall of my office painted yellow and silver."

The dog and I go to the dump. The dump permit is displayed on the back window: a drawing of a pile of rubbish, with a number underneath.

336

The dog breathes against the back window and the sticker gets bright with moisture. The dog likes the rear-view mirror and the back window equally well, and since his riding with his nose to the rear-view mirror is a clear danger, I have put three shoe boxes between the front seats as a barrier. One of the boxes has shoes inside that never fit right.

Bob Dylan is singing on the tape deck: "May God bless and keep you always, May your wishes all come true . . . "

"Back her up!" the dump man hollers. Smoke rises behind him, from something smoldering out of a pyramid into flatness. The man who runs the dump fans the smoke away, gesturing with the other hand to show me the position he wants my car to be in. The dog barks madly, baring his teeth.

"Come on, she'll get up that little incline," the dump man hollers.

The wheels whir. The dog is going crazy. When the car stops, I open my door, call "Thank you!" and tiptoe through the mush. I take the plastic bag filled with garbage and another pair of shoes that didn't work out and throw it feebly, aiming for the top of the heap. It misses by a mile, but the dump man has lost interest. Only the dog cares. He is wildly agitated.

"Please," I say to the dog when I get in the car.

"May you always be courageous," Dylan sings.

It is a bright fall day; the way the sun shines makes the edges of things radiate. When we get home, I put the dog on his lead and open the door, go into the mud room, walk into the house. When I'm away for a weekend or longer, things always look the way I expect they will when I come back. When I'm gone on a short errand, the ashtray seems to have moved forward a few inches, the plants look a little sickly, the second hand on the clock seems to be going very fast . . . I don't remember the clock having a second hand.

The third phone call of the day. "Will you trust me?" a voice says. "I need to know how to get to your house from the Whitebird Diner. My directions say go left at the fork for two miles, but I did, and I didn't pass an elementary school. I think I should have gone right at the fork. A lot of people mix up left and right; it's a form of dyslexia." Heavy breathing. "Whew," the voice says. Then: "Trust me. I can't tell you what's going on because it's a surprise."

When I don't say anything, the voice says: "Trust me. I wouldn't be some nut out in the middle of nowhere, asking whether I go right or left at the fork."

I go to the medicine cabinet and take out a brandy snifter of pills. My husband's bottle of Excedrin looks pristine. My brandy snifter is cut glass, and belonged to my grandfather. It's easy to tell my pills apart because they're all different colors: yellow Valium, blue Valium, green Donnatal. I never have to take those unless I go a whole week without eating Kellogg's All-Bran.

✿   ✿   ✿

A bear is ringing the front doorbell. There are no shades on the front windows, and the bear can see that I see it. I shake my head no, as if someone has come to sell me a raffle ticket. Could this be a bear wanting to sell me something? It does not seem to have anything with it. I shake my head no again, trying to look pleasant. I back up. The bear has left its car with the hazard light flashing, and two tires barely off Black Rock Turnpike. The bear points its paws, claws up, praying. It stands there.

I put a chain on the door and open it. The bear spreads its arms wide. It is a brown bear, with fur that looks like whatever material it is they make bathroom rugs out of. The bear sings, consulting a notebook it has pulled out from somewhere in its side:

Happy birthday to you
I know it's not the day
This song's being sung early
In case you run away

Twenty-nine was good
But thirty's better yet
Face the day with a big smile
There's nothing to regret

I wish that I could be there
But it's a question of money
A bear's appropriate instead
To say you're still my honey

The bear steps back, grandly, quite pleased with itself. It has pink rubber lips.

"From your sister," the bear says. I see the lips behind the lips. "I could really use some water," the bear says. "I came from New York. There isn't any singing message service out here. As it is, I guess this was cheaper than your sister flying in from the coast, but I didn't come cheap."

I step aside. "Perrier or tap water?" I say.

"Just regular water," the bear says.

In the kitchen, the bear removes its head and puts it on the kitchen table. The head collapses slowly, like a popover cooling. The bear has a long drink of water.

"You don't look thirty," the bear says.

The bear seems to be in its early twenties.

"Thank you," the bear says. "I hope that didn't spoil the illusion."

"Not at all," I say. "It's fine. Do you know how to get back?"

"I took the train," the bear says. "I overshot you on purpose—got my aunt's car from New Haven. I'm going back there to have dinner with her, then it doesn't take any more smarts than getting on the train to get back to the city. Thank you."

"Could I have the piece of paper?" I say.

The bear reaches in its side, through a flap. It takes out a notebook marked "American Lit. from 1850." It rips a page out and hands it to me.

I tack it on the bulletin board. The oil bill is there, as yet unpaid. My gynecologist's card, telling me that I have a 10 A.M. appointment the next day.

"Well, you don't look thirty," the bear says.

"Not only that, but be glad you were never a rabbit. I think I'm pregnant."

"Is that good news?" the bear says.

"I guess so. I wasn't trying not to get pregnant."

I hold open the front door, and the bear walks out to the porch.

"Who are you?" I say.

"Ned Brown," the bear says. "Fitting, huh? Brown? I used to work for an escort service, but I guess you know what that turned into." The bear adjusts its head. "I'm part-time at Princeton," it says. "Well," it says.

"Thank you very much," I say, and close the door.

I call the gynecologist's office, to find out if Valium has an adverse effect on the fetus.

"Mister Doctor's the one to talk to about prescription medicine," the nurse says. "Your number?"

Those photographs in *Life*, taken inside the womb. It has ears at one week, or something. If they put in a needle to do amniocentesis, it moves to the side. The horror story about the abortionist putting his finger inside, and feeling the finger grabbed. I think that it is four weeks old. It probably has an opinion on Bob Dylan, pro or con.

I have some vermouth over ice. Stand out in the back yard, wearing one of my husband's big woolly jackets. His clothes are so much more comfortable than mine. The dog has dragged down the clothesline and is biting up and down the cord. He noses, bites, ignores me. His involvement is quite erotic.

There is a pale moon in the sky. Early in the day for that. I see what they mean about the moon having a face—the eyes, at least.

From the other side of the trees, I hear the roar of the neighbors' TV. They are both deaf and have a Betamax with their favorite *Hollywood Squares* programs recorded. My husband pulled a prank and put a cassette of *Alien* in one of the boxes. He said that he found the cassette on the street. He excused himself from dinner to do it. He threw away a cassette of *Hollywood Squares* when we got home. It seemed wasteful, but I couldn't think what else to do with it, either.

Some squash are still lying on the ground. I smash one and scatter the seeds. I lose my balance when I'm bent over. That's a sign of pregnancy, I've heard: being off-kilter. I'll buy flat shoes.

"Do you know who I really love?" I say to the dog.

He turns his head. When spoken to, he always pays attention for a polite amount of time.

"I love you, and you're my dog," I say, bending to pat him.

He sniffs the squash seeds on my hand, noses my fingers but doesn't lick them.

I go in the house and get him a Hershey bar.

"What do you think about everything?" I say to the dog.

He stops eating the clothesline and devours the candy. He beats his tail. Next I'll let him off the lead, right? Wrong. I scratch behind his ears and go into the house and look for the book I keep phone numbers in. A card falls out. I see that I have missed a dentist's appointment. Another card: a man who tried to pick me up at the market.

I dial my sister. The housekeeper answers.

"Madame Villery," I say. "Her sister."

"Who?" she says, with her heavy Spanish accent.

"Which part?"

"Pardon me?"

"Madame Villery, or her sister?" I say.

"Her sister!" the housekeeper says. "One moment!"

"Madame!" I hear her calling. My sister's poor excuse for a dog, a little white yapper, starts in.

"Hello," my sister says.

"That was *some* surprise."

"What did he do?" my sister says. "Tell me about it."

It takes me back to when we were teenagers. My sister is three years younger than I am. For years, she said "Tell me about it."

"The bear rang my doorbell," I say, leaving out the part about the phone call from the diner.

"Oh, God," she says. "What were you doing? Tell me the truth."

For years she asked me to tell her the truth.

"I wasn't doing anything."

"Oh, you were—what? Just cleaning or something?"

Years in which I let her imagination work.

"Yes," I say, softening my voice.

"And then the bear was just standing there? What did you think?"

"I was amazed."

I never gave her too much. Probably not enough. She married a Frenchman that I found, and find, imperious. I probably could have told her there was no mystery there.

"Listen," I say "it was great. How are you. How's life in L.A.?"

"They're not to be equated," she says. "I'm fine, the pool is sick. It has cracked pool."

"The cement? On the bottom or—"

"Don't you love it?" she whispers. "She says, 'It has cracked pool.'"

"Am I ever going to see you?"

"He put me on a budget. I don't have the money to fly back right now. You're not on any budget. You could come out here."

"You know," I say. "Things."

"Are you holding out on me?" she says.

"What would I hold out?"

"Are you really depressed about being thirty? People get so upset—"

"It's O.K.," I say, making my voice lighter. "Hey," I say. "*Thank* you."

She blows a kiss into the phone. "Wait a minute," she says. "Remember when we played grown-up? We thought they were *twenty!* And the pillows under our nightgowns to make us pregnant? How I got pregnant after you put your finger in my stream of urine?"

"Are you?" I say, suddenly curious.

"No," she says, and doesn't ask if I am.

We blow each other a kiss. I hang up and go outside. The day is graying over. There's no difference between the way the air looks and the noncolor of my drink. I pour it on the grass. The dog gets up and sniffs it, walks away, resumes his chewing of the clothesline.

I've taken out one of the lawn chairs and am sitting in it, facing the driveway, waiting for my husband. When the car turns into the drive, I take the clothesline and toss it around the side of the house, so he won't see. The dog doesn't know what to do: be angry, or bark his usual excited greeting.

"And now," my husband says, one arm extended, car door still open, "heeeere's hubby." He thinks Ed McMahon is hilarious. He watches only the first minute of the *Tonight* show, to see Ed. He reaches behind him and takes out a cone of flowers. Inside are roses, not exactly peach-colored, but orange. Two dozen? And a white bag, smudged with something that looks like dirt; that must be the chocolate frosting of my éclair seeping through. I throw my arms around my husband. Our hipbones touch. Nothing about my body has started to change. For a second, I wonder if it might be a tumor—if that might be why I missed my period.

"Say it," he whispers, the hand holding the flowers against my left ear, the hand with the bag covering my right.

Isn't this the stereotype of the maniac in the asylum—hands clamped to both ears to . . . what? Shut out voices? Hear them more clearly? The drink has made me woozy, and all I hear is a hum. He moves his hands up and down, rubbing the sides of my head.

"Say it," he's whispering through the constant roar. "Say 'I have a nice life.'"

HEART OF A CHAMPION

T. Coraghessan Boyle

We scan the cornfields and the wheatfields winking gold and goldbrown and yellowbrown in the midday sun, on up the grassy slope to the barn redder than red against the sky bluer than blue, across the smooth stretch of the barnyard with its pecking chickens, and then right on up to the screen door at the back of the house. The door swings open, a black hole in the sun, and Timmy emerges with his corn-silk hair, corn-fed face. He is dressed in crisp overalls, stripped T-shirt, stubby blue Keds. There'd have to be a breeze—and we're not disappointed—his clean fine cup-cut hair waves and settles as he scuffs across the barnyard and out to the edge of the field. The boy stops there to gaze out over the nodding wheat, eyes unsquinted despite the sun, and blue as tinted lenses. Then he brings three fingers to his lips in a neat triangle and whistles long and low, sloping up sharp to cut off at the peak. A moment passes: he whistles again. And then we see it—way out there at the far corner of the field—the ripple, the dashing furrow, the blur of the streaking dog, white chest, flashing feet.

They're in the woods now. The boy whistling, hands in pockets, kicking along with his short baby-fat strides; the dog beside him wagging the white tip of her tail like an all-clear flag. They pass beneath an arching old black-barked oak. It creaks. And suddenly begins to fling itself down on them: immense, brutal: a panzer strike. The boy's eyes startle and then there's a blur, a smart snout clutching his pantleg, the thunderblast of the trunk, the dust and spinning leaves. "Golly, Lassie . . . I didn't even see it," says the boy sitting safe in a mound of moss. The collie looks up at him (the svelte snout, the deep gold logician's eyes), and laps at his face.

And now they're down by the river. The water is brown with angry suppurations, spiked with branches, fence posts, tires and logs. It rushes like the sides of boxcars—and chews deep and insidious at the bank under Timmy's feet. The roar is like a jetport: little wonder he can't hear the dog's warning bark. We watch the crack appear, widen to a ditch; then the halves separating (snatch of red earth, writhe of worm), the poise and pitch, and Timmy crushing down with it. Just a flash—but already he's way downstream, his head like a plastic jug, dashed and bobbed, spinning toward the nasty mouth of the falls. But there's the dog—fast as a struck match—bursting along the bank all white and gold melded in motion, hair

342

sleeked with the wind of it, legs beating time to the panting score. . . . Yet what can she hope to do?—the current surges on, lengths ahead, sure bet to win the race to the falls. Timmy sweeps closer, sweeps closer, the falls loud now as a hundred tympani, the war drums of the Sioux, Africa gone bloodlust mad! The dog strains, lashing over the wet earth like a whipcrack; strains every last ganglion and dendrite until finally she draws abreast of him. Then she's in the air, the foaming yellow water. Her paws churning like pistons, whiskers chuffing with the exertion—oh the roar!— and there, she's got him, her sure jaws clamping down on the shirt collar, her eyes fixed on the slip of rock at the falls' edge. Our blood races, organs palpitate. The black brink of the falls, the white paws digging at the rock—and then they're safe. The collie sniffs at Timmy's inert little form, nudges his side until she manages to roll him over. Then clears his tongue and begins mouth-to-mouth.

Night: the barnyard still, a bulb burning over the screen door. Inside, the family sit at dinner, the table heaped with pork chops, mashed potatoes, applesauce and peas, a pitcher of clean white milk. Home-baked bread. Mom and Dad, their faces sexless, bland, perpetually good-humored and sympathetic, poise stiff-backed, forks in midswoop, while Timmy tells his story: "So then Lassie grabbed me by the collar and golly I musta blanked out cause I don't remember anything more till I woke up on the rock—"

"Well I'll be," says Mom.

"You're lucky you've got such a good dog, son," says Dad, gazing down at the collie where she lies patiently, snout over paw, tail wapping the floor. She is combed and washed and fluffed, her lashes mascaraed and curled, her chest and paws white as dishsoap. She looks up humbly. But then her ears leap, her neck jerks round—and she's up at the door, head cocked, alert. A high yipping yowl like a stuttering fire whistle shudders through the room. And then another. The dog whines.

"Darn," says Dad. "I thought we were rid of those coyotes—next thing they'll be after the chickens again."

The moon blanches the yard, leans black shadows on the trees, the barn. Upstairs in the house, Timmy lies sleeping in the pale light, his hair fastidiously mussed, his breathing gentle. The collie lies on the throw rug beside the bed. We see that her eyes are open. Suddenly she rises and slips to the window, silent as a shadow. And looks down the long elegant snout to the barnyard below, where the coyote slinks from shade to shade, a limp pullet dangling from his jaws. He is stunted, scabious, syphilitic, his forepaw trap-twisted, his eyes running. The collie whimpers softly from behind the window. And the coyote stops in mid-trot, frozen in a cold shard of light, ears high on his head. Then drops the chicken at his feet, leers up at the window and begins a soft, crooning, sad-faced song.

The screen door slaps behind Timmy as he bolts from the house, Lassie at his heels. Mom's head emerges on the rebound. "Timmy!" (He stops as if jerked by a rope, turns to face her.) "You be home before lunch, hear?"

"Sure, Mom," he says, already spinning off, the dog by his side. We get a close-up of Mom's face: she is smiling a benevolent boys-will-be-boys smile. Her teeth are perfect.

In the woods Timmy steps on a rattler and the dog bites its head off. "Gosh," he says. "Good girl, Lassie." Then he stumbles and slips over an embankment, rolls down the brushy incline and over a sudden precipice, whirling out into the breathtaking blue space like a sky diver. He thumps down on a narrow ledge twenty feet below. And immediately scrambles to his feet, peering timorously down the sheer wall to the heap of bleached bone at its base. Small stones break loose, shoot out like asteroids. Dirt-slides begin. But Lassie yarps reassuringly from above, sprints back to the barn for a winch and cable, hoists the boy to safety.

On their way back for lunch Timmy leads them through a still and leaf-darkened copse. We remark how odd it is that the birds and crickets have left off their cheeping, how puzzling that the background music has begun to rumble so. Suddenly, round a bend in the path before them, the coyote appears. Nose to the ground, intent, unaware of them. But all at once he jerks to a halt, shudders like an epileptic, the hackles rising, tail dipping between his legs. The collie too stops short, just yards away, her chest proud and shaggy and white. The coyote cowers, bunches like a cat, glares at them. Timmy's face sags with alarm. The coyote lifts his lip. But then, instead of leaping at her adversary's throat, the collie prances up and stretches her nose out to him, her eyes soft as a leading lady's, round as a doe's. She's balsamed and perfumed; her full chest tapers a lovely S to her sleek haunches and sculpted legs. He is puny, runted, half her size, his coat like a discarded doormat. She circles him now, sniffing. She whimpers, he growls: throaty and tough, the bad guy. And stands stiff while she licks at his whiskers, noses at his rear, the bald black scrotum. Timmy is horror-struck. Then, the music sweeping off in birdtrills of flute and harpstring, the coyote slips round behind, throat thrown back, black lips tight with anticipation.

"What was she doing, Dad?" Timmy asks over his milk and sandwich.

"The sky was blue today, son," he says.

"But she had him trapped, Dad—they were stuck together end to end and I thought we had that wicked old coyote but then she went and let him go—what's got into her, Dad?"

"The barn was red today, son," he says.

Late afternoon: the sun mellow, more orange than white. Purpling clots of shadow hang from the branches, ravel out from the tree trunks. Bees and wasps and flies saw away at the wet full-bellied air. Timmy and the dog are far out beyond the north pasture, out by the old Indian burial mound, where the boy stoops now to search for arrowheads. Oddly, the collie is not watching him: instead she's pacing the crest above, whimpering softly, pausing from time to time to stare out across the forest, her eyes distant and moonstruck. Behind her, storm clouds squat on the horizon like dark kidneys or brains.

We observe the wind kicking up: leaves flapping like wash, saplings quivering, weeds whipping. It darkens quickly now, the clouds scudding low and smoky over the treetops, blotting the sun from view. Lassie's white is whiter than ever, highlighted against the dark horizon, the wind-whipped hair foaming around her. Still she doesn't look down at the boy: he digs, dirty-kneed, stoop-backed, oblivious. Then the first fat random drops, a flash, the volcanic blast of thunder. Timmy glances over his shoulder at the noise: he's just in time to watch the scorched pine plummeting toward the constellated freckles in the center of his forehead. Now the collie turns—too late!—the *swoosh-whack!* of the tree, the trembling needles. She's there in an instant, tearing at the green welter, struggling through to his side. He lies unconscious in the muddying earth, hair artistically arranged, a thin scratch painted on his cheek. The trunk lies across the small of his back like the tail of a brontosaurus. The rain falls.

Lassie tugs doggedly at a knob in the trunk, her pretty paws slipping in the wet—but it's no use—it would take a block and tackle, a crane, an army of Bunyans to shift that stubborn bulk. She falters, licks at his ear, whimpers. We observe the troubled look in her eye as she hesitates, uncertain, priorities warring: should she stand guard, or dash for help? The decision is sure and swift—her eyes firm with purpose and she's off like a shard of shrapnel, already up the hill, shooting past the dripping trees, over the river, already cleaving through the high wet banks of wheat.

A moment later she's dashing through the puddled and rain-screened barnyard, barking right on up to the back door, where she pauses to scratch daintily, her voice high-pitched and insistent. Mom swings open the door and the collie pads in, claws clacking on the shiny linoleum. "What is it girl? What's the matter? Where's Timmy?"

"Yarf! Yarfata-yarf-yarf!"

"Oh my! Dad! Dad, come quickly!"

Dad rushes in, his face stolid and reassuring as the Lincoln Memorial. "What is it, dear? . . . Why, Lassie?"

"Oh Dad, Timmy's trapped under a pine tree out by the old Indian burial ground—"

"Arpit-arp."

"—a mile and a half past the north pasture."

Dad is quick, firm, decisive. "Lassie—you get back up there and stand watch over Timmy . . . Mom and I'll go for Doc Walker. Hurry now!"

The collie hesitates at the door: "Rarf-arrar-ra!"

"Right," says Dad. "Mom, fetch the chain saw."

We're back in the woods now. A shot of the mud-running burial mound locates us—yes, there's the fallen pine, and there: Timmy. He lies in a puddle, eyes closed, breathing slow. The hiss of the rain is loud as static. We see it at work: scattering leaves, digging trenches, inciting streams to swallow their banks. It lies deep now in the low areas, and in the mid areas, and in the high areas. Then a shot of the dam, some indeterminate (but short we presume) distance off, the yellow water churning over its lip like urine, the ugly earthen belly distended, blistered with the pressure. Raindrops pock the surface like a plague.

Suddenly the music plunges to those thunderous crouching chords—we're back at the pine now—what is it? There: the coyote. Sniffing, furtive, the malicious eyes, the crouch and slink. He stiffens when he spots the boy—but then slouches closer, a rubbery dangle drooling from between his mis-meshed teeth. Closer. Right over the prone figure now, those ominous chords setting up ominous vibrations in our bowels. He stoops, head dipping between his shoulders, irises caught in the corners of his eyes: wary, sly, predatory: the vulture slavering over the fallen fawn.

But wait!—here comes the collie, sprinting out of the wheatfield, bounding rock to rock across the crazed river, her limbs contourless with sheer speed and purpose, the music racing in a mad heroic prestissimo!

The jolting front seat of a Ford. Dad, Mom and the Doctor, all dressed in rain slickers and flap-brimmed rain hats, sitting shoulder to shoulder behind the clapping wipers. Their jaws set with determination, eyes aflicker with pioneer gumption.

The coyote's jaws, serrated grinders, work at the tough bone and cartilage of Timmy's left hand. The boy's eyelids flutter with the pain, and he lifts his head feebly—but almost immediately it slaps down again, flat and volitionless, in the mud. At that instant Lassie blazes over the hill like a cavalry charge, show-dog indignation aflame in her eyes. The scrag of a coyote looks up at her, drooling blood, choking down frantic bits of flesh. Looks up at her from eyes that go back thirty million years, savage and bloodlustful and free. Looks up unmoved, uncringing, the bloody snout and steady yellow eyes less a physical challenge than philosophical. We watch the collie's expression alter in midbound—the look of offended AKC morality giving way, dissolving. She skids to a halt, drops her tail and approaches him, a buttery gaze in her golden eyes. She licks the blood from his lips.

The dam. Impossibly swollen, rain festering the yellow surface, a hundred new streams a minute rampaging in, the pressure of those millions of gallons hard-punching those millions more. There! the first gap, the water spewing out, a burst bubo. And now the dam shudders, splinters, falls to pieces like so much cheap pottery. The roar is devastating.

The two animals start at that terrible rumbling, and still working their gummy jaws, they dash up the far side of the hill. We watch the white-tipped tail retreating side by side with the hacked and tick-blistered gray one—wagging like raggled banners as they disappear into the trees at the top of the rise. We're left with a tableau: the rain, the fallen pine in the crotch of the valley's V, the spot of the boy's head. And that chilling roar in our ears. Suddenly the wall of water appears at the far end of the V, smashing through the little declivity like a god-sized fist, prickling with shattered trunks and boulders, grinding along like a quick-melted glacier, like planets in collision. We cut to Timmy: eyes closed, hair plastered, his left arm looking as though it should be wrapped in butcher's paper. How? we wonder. How will they ever get him out of this? But then we see them—Mom, Dad and the Doctor—struggling up that same rise, rushing with the frenetic music now, the torrent seething closer, booming and howling. Dad launches himself in full charge down the hillside—but the water is already sweeping over the fallen pine, lifting it like paper—there's a blur, a quick clip of a typhoon at sea (is that a flash of blond hair?), and it's over. The valley is filled to the top of the rise, the water ribbed and rushing like the Colorado in adolescence. Dad's pants are wet to the crotch.

Mom's face, the Doctor's. Rain. And then the opening strains of the theme song, one violin at first, swelling in mournful mid-American triumph as the full orchestra comes in, tearful, beautiful, heroic, sweeping us up and out of the dismal rain, back to the golden wheatfields in the midday sun. The boy cups his hands to his mouth and pipes: "Laahh-sie! Laahh-sie!" And then we see it—way out there at the end of the field—the ripple, the dashing furrow, the blur of the streaking dog, white chest, flashing feet.

CATHEDRAL

Raymond Carver

This blind man, an old friend of my wife's, he was on his way to spend the night. His wife had died. So he was visiting the dead wife's relatives in Connecticut. He called my wife from his in-laws'. Arrangements were made. He would come by train, a five-hour trip, and my wife would meet him at the station. She hadn't seen him since she worked for him one summer in Seattle ten years ago. But she and the blind man had kept in touch. They made tapes and mailed them back and forth. I wasn't enthusiastic about his visit. He was no one I knew. And his being blind bothered me. My idea of blindness came from the movies. In the movies, the blind moved slowly and never laughed. Sometimes they were led by seeing-eye dogs. A blind man in my house was not something I looked forward to.

That summer in Seattle she had needed a job. She didn't have any money. The man she was going to marry at the end of the summer was in officers' training school. He didn't have any money, either. But she was in love with the guy, and he was in love with her, etc. She'd seen something in the paper: HELP WANTED—*Reading to Blind Man,* and a telephone number. She phoned and went over, was hired on the spot. She'd worked with this blind man all summer. She read stuff to him, case studies, reports, that sort of thing. She helped him organize his little office in the county social-service department. They'd become good friends, my wife and the blind man. How do I know these things? She told me. And she told me something else. On her last day in the office, the blind man asked if he could touch her face. She agreed to this. She told me he touched his fingers to every part of her face, her nose—even her neck! She never forgot it. She even tried to write a poem about it. She was always trying to write a poem. She wrote a poem or two every year, usually after something really important had happened to her.

When we first started going out together, she showed me the poem. In the poem, she recalled his fingers and the way they had moved around over her face. In the poem, she talked about what she had felt at the time, about what went through her mind when the blind man touched her nose and lips. I can remember I didn't think much of the poem. Of course, I didn't tell her that. Maybe I just don't understand poetry. I admit it's not the first thing I reach for when I pick up something to read.

Anyway, this man who'd first enjoyed her favors, the officer-to-be, he'd been her childhood sweetheart. So okay. I'm saying that at the end of the summer she let the blind man run his hands over her face, said good-bye to him, married her childhood etc., who was now a commissioned officer, and she moved away from Seattle. But they'd kept in touch, she and the blind man. She made the first contact after a year or so. She called him up one night from an Air Force base in Alabama. She wanted to talk. They talked. He asked her to send him a tape and tell him about her life. She did this. She sent the tape. On the tape, she told the blind man about her husband and about their life together in the military. She told the blind man she loved her husband but she didn't like it where they lived and she didn't like it that he was a part of the military-industrial thing. She told the blind man she'd written a poem and he was in it. She told him that she was writing a poem about what it was like to be an Air Force officer's wife. The poem wasn't finished yet. She was still writing it. The blind man made a tape. He sent her the tape. She made a tape. This went on for years. My wife's officer was posted to one base and then another. She sent tapes from Moody AFB, McGuire, McConnell, and finally Travis, near Sacramento, where one night she got to feeling lonely and cut off from people she kept losing in that moving-around life. She got to feeling she couldn't go it another step. She went in and swallowed all the pills and capsules in the medicine chest and washed them down with a bottle of gin. Then she got into a hot bath and passed out.

But instead of dying, she got sick. She threw up. Her officer—why should he have a name? he was the childhood sweetheart, and what more does he want?—came home from somewhere, found her, and called the ambulance. In time, she put it all on a tape and sent the tape to the blind man. Over the years, she put all kinds of stuff on tapes and sent the tapes off lickety-split. Next to writing a poem every year, I think it was her chief means of recreation. On one tape, she told the blind man she'd decided to live away from her officer for a time. On another tape, she told him about her divorce. She and I began going out, and of course she told her blind man about it. She told him everything, or so it seemed to me. Once she asked me if I'd like to hear the latest tape from the blind man. This was a year ago. I was on the tape, she said. So I said okay, I'd listen to it. I got us drinks and we settled down in the living room. We made ready to listen. First she inserted the tape into the player and adjusted a couple of dials. Then she pushed a lever. The tape squeaked and someone began to talk in this loud voice. She lowered the volume. After a few minutes of harmless chitchat, I heard my own name in the mouth of this stranger, this blind man I didn't even know! And then this: "From all you've said about him, I can only conclude—" But we were interrupted, a knock at the door, something, and we didn't ever get back to the tape. Maybe it was just as well. I'd heard all I wanted to.

Now this same blind man was coming to sleep in my house.

"Maybe I could take him bowling," I said to my wife. She was at the draining board doing scalloped potatoes. She put down the knife she was using and turned around.

"If you love me," she said, "you can do this for me. If you don't love me, okay. But if you had a friend, any friend, and the friend came to visit, I'd make him feel comfortable." She wiped her hands with the dish towel.

"I don't have any blind friends," I said.

"You don't have *any* friends," she said. "Period. Besides," she said, "goddamn it, his wife's just died! Don't you understand that? The man's lost his wife!"

I didn't answer. She'd told me a little about the blind man's wife. Her name was Beulah. Beulah! That's a name for a colored woman.

"Was his wife a Negro?" I asked.

"Are you crazy?" my wife said. "Have you just flipped or something?" She picked up a potato. I saw it hit the floor, then roll under the stove. "What's wrong with you?" she said "Are you drunk?"

"I'm just asking," I said.

Right then my wife filled me in with more detail than I cared to know. I made a drink and sat at the kitchen table to listen. Pieces of the story began to fall into place.

Beulah had gone to work for the blind man the summer after my wife had stopped working for him. Pretty soon Beulah and the blind man had themselves a church wedding. It was a little wedding—who'd want to go to such a wedding in the first place?—just the two of them, plus the minister and the minister's wife. But it was a church wedding just the same. It was what Beulah had wanted, he'd said. But even then Beulah must have been carrying the cancer in her glands. After they had been inseparable for eight years—my wife's word, *inseparable*—Beulah's health went into a rapid decline. She died in a Seattle hospital room, the blind man sitting beside the bed and holding on to her hand. They'd married, lived and worked together, slept together—had sex, sure—and then the blind man had to bury her. All this without his having ever seen what the goddamned woman looked like. It was beyond my understanding. Hearing this, I felt sorry for the blind man for a little bit. And then I found myself thinking what a pitiful life this woman must have led. Imagine a woman who could never see herself as she was seen in the eyes of her loved one. A woman who could go on day after day and never receive the smallest compliment from her beloved. A woman whose husband could never read the expression on her face, be it misery or something better. Someone who could wear makeup or not—what difference to him? She could, if she wanted, wear green eye-shadow around one eye, a straight pin in her nostril, yellow slacks and purple shoes, no matter. And then to slip off into death, the blind man's hand on her hand, his blind eyes streaming tears—I'm imagining now—her last thought maybe this: that he never even knew what she looked like, and she on an express to the grave. Robert was left with a small insurance policy and half of a twenty-peso Mexican coin. The other half of the coin went into the box with her. Pathetic.

So when the time rolled around, my wife went to the depot to pick him up. With nothing to do but wait—sure, I blamed him for that—I was having a drink and watching the TV when I heard the car pull into the drive. I got up from the sofa with my drink and went to the window to have a look.

I saw my wife laughing as she parked the car. I saw her get out of the car and shut the door. She was still wearing a smile. Just amazing. She went around to the other side of the car to where the blind man was already starting to get out. This blind man, feature this, he was wearing a full beard! A beard on a blind man! Too much, I say. The blind man reached into the back seat and dragged out a suitcase. My wife took his arm, shut the car door, and, talking all the way, moved him down the drive and then up the steps to the front porch. I turned off the TV. I finished my drink, rinsed the glass, dried my hands. Then I went to the door.

My wife said, "I want you to meet Robert. Robert, this is my husband. I've told you all about him." She was beaming. She had this blind man by his coat sleeve.

The blind man let go of his suitcase and up came his hand.

I took it. He squeezed hard, held my hand, and then he let it go.

"I feel like we've already met," he boomed.

"Likewise," I said. I didn't know what else to say. Then I said, "Welcome. I've heard a lot about you." We began to move then, a little group, from the porch into the living room, my wife guiding him by the arm. The blind man was carrying his suitcase in his other hand. My wife said things like, "To your left here, Robert. That's right. Now watch it, there's a chair. That's it. Sit down right here. This is the sofa. We just bought this sofa two weeks ago."

I started to say something about the old sofa. I'd liked that old sofa. But I didn't say anything. Then I wanted to say something else, small-talk, about the scenic ride along the Hudson. How going *to* New York, you should sit on the right-hand side of the train, and coming *from* New York, the left-hand side.

"Did you have a good train ride?" I said. "Which side of the train did you sit on, by the way?"

"What a question, which side!" my wife said. "What's it matter which side?" she said.

"I just asked," I said.

"Right side," the blind man said. "I hadn't been on a train in nearly forty years. Not since I was a kid. With my folks. That's been a long time. I'd nearly forgotten the sensation. I have winter in my beard now," he said. "So I've been told, anyway. Do I look distinguished, my dear?" the blind man said to my wife.

"You look distinguished, Robert," she said. "Robert," she said. "Robert, it's just so good to see you."

My wife finally took her eyes off the blind man and looked at me. I had the feeling she didn't like what she saw. I shrugged.

I've never met, or personally known, anyone who was blind. This blind man was late forties, a heavy-set, balding man with stooped shoulders, as if he carried a great weight there. He wore brown slacks, brown shoes, a light-brown shirt, a tie, a sports coat. Spiffy. He also had this full beard. But he didn't use a cane and he didn't wear dark glasses. I'd always thought dark glasses were a must for the blind. Fact was, I wished he had a pair. At first glance, his eyes looked like anyone else's eyes. But if you looked close, there was something different about them. Too much white in the iris, for one thing, and the pupils seemed to move around in the sockets without his knowing it or being able to stop it. Creepy. As I stared at his face, I saw the left pupil turn in toward his nose while the other made an effort to keep in one place. But it was only an effort, for that eye was on the roam without his knowing it or wanting it to be.

I said, "Let me get you a drink. What's your pleasure? We have a little of everything. It's one of our pastimes."

"Bub, I'm a Scotch man myself," he said fast enough in this big voice.

"Right," I said. Bub! "Sure you are. I knew it."

He let his fingers touch his suitcase, which was sitting alongside the sofa. He was taking his bearings. I didn't blame him for that.

"I'll move that up to your room," my wife said.

"No, that's fine," the blind man said loudly. "It can go up when I go up."

"A little water with the Scotch?" I said.

"Very little," he said.

"I knew it," I said.

He said, "Just a tad. The Irish actor, Barry Fitzgerald? I'm like that fellow. When I drink water, Fitzgerald said, I drink water. When I drink whiskey, I drink whiskey." My wife laughed. The blind man brought his hand up under his beard. He lifted his beard slowly and let it drop.

I did the drinks, three big glasses of Scotch with a splash of water in each. Then we made ourselves comfortable and talked about Robert's travels. First the long flight from the West Coast to Connecticut, we covered that. Then from Connecticut up here by train. We had another drink concerning that leg of the trip.

I remembered having read somewhere that the blind didn't smoke because, as speculation had it, they couldn't see the smoke they exhaled. I thought I knew that much and that much only about blind people. But this blind man smoked his cigarette down to the nubbin and then lit another one. This blind man filled his ashtray and my wife emptied it.

When we sat down at the table for dinner, we had another drink. My wife heaped Robert's plate with cube steak, scalloped potatoes, green beans. I buttered him up two slices of bread. I said, "Here's bread and butter for you." I swallowed some of my drink. "Now let us pray," I said, and the blind man lowered his head. My wife looked at me, her mouth agape. "Pray the phone won't ring and the food doesn't get cold," I said.

We dug in. We ate everything there was to eat on the table. We ate like there was no tomorrow. We didn't talk. We ate. We scarfed. We grazed that table. We were into serious eating. The blind man had right away located his foods, he knew just where everything was on his plate. I watched with admiration as he used his knife and fork on the meat. He'd cut two pieces of meat, fork the meat into his mouth, and then go all out for the scalloped potatoes, the beans next, and then he'd tear off a hunk of buttered bread and eat that. He'd follow this up with a big drink of milk. It didn't seem to bother him to use his fingers once in a while, either.

We finished everything, including half a strawberry pie. For a few moments, we sat as if stunned. Sweat beaded on our faces. Finally, we got up from the table and left the dirty plates. We didn't look back. We took ourselves into the living room and sank into our places again. Robert and my wife sat on the sofa. I took the big chair. We had us two or three more drinks while they talked about the major things that had come to pass for them in the past ten years. For the most part, I just listened. Now and then I joined in. I didn't want him to think I'd left the room, and I didn't want her to think I was feeling left out. They talked of things that had happened to them—to them!—these past ten years. I waited in vain to hear my name on my wife's sweet lips: "And then my dear husband came into my life"—something like that. But I heard nothing of the sort. More talk of Robert. Robert had done a little of everything, it seemed, a regular blind jack-of-all-trades. But most recently he and his wife had had an Amway distributorship, from which, I gathered, they'd earned their living, such as it was. The blind man was also a ham radio operator. He talked in his loud voice about conversations he'd had with fellow operators in Guam, in the Philippines, in Alaska, and even in Tahiti. He said he'd have a lot of friends there if he ever wanted to go visit those places. From time to time, he'd turn his blind face toward me, put his hand under his beard, ask me something. How long had I been in my present position? (Three years.) Did I like my work? (I didn't.) Was I going to stay with it? (What were the options?) Finally, when I thought he was beginning to run down, I got up and turned on the TV.

My wife looked at me with irritation. She was heading toward a boil. Then she looked at the blind man and said, "Robert, do you have a TV?"

The blind man said, "My dear, I have two TVs. I have a color set and a black-and-white thing, an old relic. It's funny, but if I turn the TV on, and I'm always turning it on, I turn on the color set. It's funny, don't you think?"

I didn't know what to say to that. I had absolutely nothing to say to that. No opinion. So I watched the news program and tried to listen to what the announcer was saying.

"This is a color TV," the blind man said. "Don't ask me how, but I can tell."

"We traded up a while ago," I said.

The blind man had another taste of his drink. He lifted his beard, sniffed it, and let it fall. He leaned forward on the sofa. He positioned his ashtray on the coffee table, then put the lighter to his cigarette. He leaned back on the sofa and crossed his legs at the ankles.

My wife covered her mouth, and then she yawned. She stretched. She said, "I think I'll go upstairs and put on my robe. I think I'll change into something else. Robert, you make yourself comfortable," she said.

"I'm comfortable," the blind man said.

"I want you to feel comfortable in this house," she said.

"I am comfortable," the blind man said.

After she'd left the room, he and I listened to the weather report and then to the sports roundup. By that time, she'd been gone so long I didn't know if she was going to come back. I thought she might have gone to bed. I wished she'd come back downstairs. I didn't want to be left alone with a blind man. I asked him if he wanted another drink, and he said sure. Then I asked if he wanted to smoke some dope with me. I said I'd just rolled a number. I hadn't, but I planned to do so in about two shakes.

"I'll try some with you," he said.

"Damn right," I said. "That's the stuff."

I got our drinks and sat down on the sofa with him. Then I rolled us two fat numbers. I lit one and passed it. I brought it to his fingers. He took it and inhaled.

"Hold it as long as you can," I said. I could tell he didn't know the first thing.

My wife came back downstairs wearing her pink robe and her pink slippers.

"What do I smell?" she said.

"We thought we'd have us some cannabis," I said.

My wife gave me a savage look. Then she looked at the blind man and said, "Robert, I didn't know you smoked."

He said, "I do now, my dear. There's a first time for everything. But I don't feel anything yet."

"This stuff is pretty mellow," I said. "This stuff is mild. It's dope you can reason with," I said. "It doesn't mess you up."

"Not much it doesn't, bub," he said, and laughed.

My wife sat on the sofa between the blind man and me. I passed her the number. She took it and toked and then passed it back to me. "Which way is this going?" she said. Then she said, " I shouldn't be smoking this. I can hardly keep my eyes open as it is. That dinner did me in. I shouldn't have eaten so much."

"It was the strawberry pie," the blind man said. "That's what did it," he said, and he laughed his big laugh. Then he shook his head.

"There's more strawberry pie," I said.

"Do you want some more, Robert?" my wife said.

"Maybe in a little while," he said.

We gave our attention to the TV. My wife yawned again. She said, "Your bed is made up when you feel like going to bed, Robert. I know you must have had a long day. When you're ready to go to bed, say so." She pulled his arm. "Robert?"

He came to and said, "I've had a real nice time. This beats tapes, doesn't it?"

I said, "Coming at you," and I put the number between his fingers. He inhaled, held the smoke, and then let it go. It was like he'd been doing it since he was nine years old.

"Thanks, bub," he said. "But I think this is all for me. I think I'm beginning to feel it," he said. He held the burning roach out for my wife.

"Same here," she said. "Ditto. Me, too." She took the roach and passed it to me. "I may just sit here for a while between you two guys with my eyes closed. But don't let me bother you, okay? Either one of you. If it bothers you, say so. Otherwise, I may just sit here with my eyes closed until you're ready to go to bed," she said. "Your bed's made up, Robert, when you're ready. It's right next to our room at the top of the stairs. We'll show you up when you're ready. You wake me up now, you guys, if I fall asleep." She said that and then she closed her eyes and went to sleep.

The news program ended. I got up and changed the channel. I sat back down on the sofa. I wished my wife hadn't pooped out. Her head lay across the back of the sofa, her mouth open. She'd turned so that her robe had slipped away from her legs, exposing a juicy thigh. I reached to draw her robe back over her, and it was then that I glanced at the blind man. What the hell! I flipped the robe open again.

"You say when you want some strawberry pie," I said.

"I will," he said.

I said, "Are you tired? Do you want me to take you up to your bed? Are you ready to hit the hay?"

"Not yet," he said. "No, I'll stay up with you, bub. If that's all right. I'll stay up until you're ready to turn in. We haven't had a chance to talk. Know what I mean? I feel like me and her monopolized the evening." He lifted his beard and he let it fall. He picked up his cigarettes and his lighter.

"That's all right," I said. Then I said, "I'm glad for the company."

And I guess I was. Every night I smoked dope and stayed up as long as I could before I fell asleep. My wife and I hardly ever went to bed at the same time. When I did go to sleep, I had these dreams. Sometimes I'd wake up from one of them, my heart going crazy.

Something about the church and the Middle Ages was on the TV. Not your run-of-the-mill TV fare. I wanted to watch something else. I turned to the other channels. But there was nothing on them, either. So I turned back to the first channel and apologized.

"Bub, it's all right," the blind man said. "It's fine with me. Whatever you want to watch is okay. I'm always learning something. Learning never ends. It won't hurt me to learn something tonight. I got ears," he said.

We didn't say anything for a time. He was leaning forward with his head turned at me, his right ear aimed in the direction of the set. Very disconcerting. Now and then his eyelids drooped and then they snapped open again. Now and then he put his fingers into his beard and tugged, like he was thinking about something he was hearing on the television.

On the screen, a group of men wearing cowls was being set upon and tormented by men dressed in skeleton costumes and men dressed as devils. The men dressed as devils wore devil masks, horns, and long tails. This pageant was part of a procession. The Englishman who was narrating the thing said it took place in Spain once a year. I tried to explain to the blind man what was happening.

"Skeletons," he said. "I know about skeletons," he said, and he nodded.

The TV showed this one cathedral. Then there was a long, slow look at another one. Finally, the picture switched to the famous one in Paris, with its flying buttresses and its spires reaching up to the clouds. The camera pulled away to show the whole of the cathedral rising above the skyline.

There were times when the Englishman who was telling the thing would shut up, would simply let the camera move around over the cathedrals. Or else the camera would tour the countryside, men in fields walking behind oxen. I waited as long as I could. Then I felt I had to say something. I said, "They're showing the outside of this cathedral now. Gargoyles. Little statues carved to look like monsters. Now I guess they're in Italy. Yeah, they're in Italy. There's paintings on the walls of this one church."

"Are those fresco paintings, bub?" he asked, and he sipped from his drink.

I reached for my glass. But it was empty. I tried to remember what I could remember. "You're asking me are those frescoes?" I said. "That's a good question. I don't know."

The camera moved to a cathedral outside Lisbon. The differences in the Portuguese cathedral compared with the French and Italian were not that great. But they were there. Mostly the interior stuff. Then something occurred to me, and I said, "Something has occurred to me. Do you have any idea what a cathedral is? What they look like, that is? Do you follow me? If somebody says cathedral to you, do you have any notion what they're talking about? Do you know the difference between that and a Baptist church, say?"

He let the smoke dribble from his mouth. "I know they took hundreds of workers fifty or a hundred years to build," he said. "I just heard the man say that, of course. I know generations of the same families worked on a cathedral. I heard him say that, too. The men who began their life's work on them, they never lived to see the completion of their work. In that wise, bub, they're no different from the rest of us, right?" He laughed. Then his eyelids drooped again. His head nodded. He seemed to be snoozing. Maybe he was imagining himself in Portugal. The TV was showing another cathedral now. This one was in Germany. The Englishman's voice droned on. "Cathedrals," the blind man said. He sat up and rolled his head back and forth. "If you want the truth, bub, that's about all I know. What I just said. What I heard him say. But maybe you could describe one to me? I wish you'd do it. I'd like that. If you want to know, I really don't have a good idea."

I stared hard at the shot of the cathedral on the TV. How could I even begin to describe it? But say my life depended on it. Say my life was being threatened by an insane guy who said I had to do it or else.

I stared some more at the cathedral before the picture flipped off into the countryside. There was no use. I turned to the blind man and said, "To begin with, they're very tall." I was looking around the room for clues. "They reach way up. Up and up. Toward the sky. They're so big, some of them, they have to have these supports. To help hold them up, so to speak. These supports are called buttresses. They remind me of viaducts, for some reason. But maybe you don't know viaducts, either? Sometimes the cathedrals have devils and such carved into the front. Sometimes lords and ladies. Don't ask me why this is," I said.

He was nodding. The whole upper part of his body seemed to be moving back and forth.

"I'm not doing so good, am I?" I said.

He stopped nodding and leaned forward on the edge of the sofa. As he listened to me, he was running his fingers through his beard. I wasn't getting through to him, I could see that. But he waited for me to go on just the same. He nodded, like he was trying to encourage me. I tried to think what else to say. "They're really big," I said. "They're massive. They're built of stone. Marble, too, sometimes. In those olden days, when they built cathedrals, men wanted to be close to God. In those olden days, God was an important part of everyone's life. You could tell this from their cathedral-building. I'm sorry," I said, "but it looks like that's the best I can do for you. I'm just no good at it."

"That's all right, bub," the blind man said. "Hey, listen. I hope you don't mind my asking you. Can I ask you something? Let me ask you a simple question, yes or no. I'm just curious and there's no offense. You're my host. But let me ask if you are in any way religious? You don't mind my asking?"

I shook my head. He couldn't see that, though. A wink is the same as a nod to a blind man. "I guess I don't believe in it. In anything. Sometimes it's hard. You know what I'm saying?"

"Sure, I do," he said.

"Right," I said.

The Englishman was still holding forth. My wife sighed in her sleep. She drew a long breath and went on with her sleeping.

"You'll have to forgive me," I said. "But I can't tell you what a cathedral looks like. It just isn't in me to do it. I can't do any more than I've done."

The blind man sat very still, his head down, as he listened to me.

I said, "The truth is, cathedrals don't mean anything special to me. Nothing. Cathedrals. They're something to look at on late-night TV. That's all they are."

It was then that the blind man cleared his throat. He brought something up. He took a handkerchief from his back pocket. Then he said, "I get it, bub. It's okay. It happens. Don't worry about it," he said. "Hey, listen to me. Will you do me a favor? I got an idea. Why don't you find us some heavy paper? And a pen. We'll do something. We'll draw one together. Get us a pen and some heavy paper. Go on, bub, get the stuff," he said.

So I went upstairs. My legs felt like they didn't have any strength in them. They felt like they did after I'd done some running. In my wife's room, I looked around. I found some ballpoints in a little basket on her table. And then I tried to think where to look for the kind of paper he was talking about.

Downstairs, in the kitchen, I found a shopping bag with onion skins in the bottom of the bag. I emptied the bag and shook it. I brought it into the living room and sat down with it near his legs. I moved some things, smoothed the wrinkles from the bag, spread it out on the coffee table.

The blind man got down from the sofa and sat next to me on the carpet.

He ran his fingers over the paper. He went up and down the sides of the paper. The edges, even the edges. He fingered the corners.

"All right," he said. "All right, let's do her."

He found my hand, the hand with the pen. He closed his hand over my hand. "Go ahead, bub, draw," he said. "Draw. You'll see. I'll follow along with you. It'll be okay. Just begin now like I'm telling you. You'll see. Draw," the blind man said.

So I began. First I drew a box that looked like a house. It could have been the house I lived in. Then I put a roof on it. At either end of the roof, I drew spires. Crazy.

"Swell," he said. "Terrific. You're doing fine," he said. "Never thought anything like this could happen in your lifetime, did you, bub? Well, it's a strange life, we all know that. Go on now. Keep it up."

I put in windows with arches. I drew flying buttresses. I hung great doors. I couldn't stop. The TV station went off the air. I put down the pen and closed and opened my fingers. The blind man felt around over the paper. He moved the tips of his fingers over the paper, all over what I had drawn, and he nodded.

"Doing fine," the blind man said.

I took up the pen again, and he found my hand. I kept at it. I'm no artist. But I kept drawing just the same.

My wife opened up her eyes and gazed at us. She sat up on the sofa, her robe hanging open. She said, "What are you doing? Tell me, I want to know."

I didn't answer her.

The blind man said, "We're drawing a cathedral. Me and him are working on it. Press hard," he said to me. "That's right. That's good," he said. "Sure. You got it, bub. I can tell. You didn't think you could. But you can, can't you? You're cooking with gas now. You know what I'm saying? We're going to really have us something here in a minute. How's the old arm?" he said. "Put some people in there now. What's a cathedral without people?"

My wife said, "What's going on? Robert, what are you doing? What's going on?"

"It's all right," he said to her. "Close your eyes now," the blind man said to me.

I did it. I closed them just like he said.

"Are they closed?" he said. "Don't fudge."

"They're closed," I said.

"Keep them that way," he said. He said, "Don't stop now. Draw."

So we kept on with it. His fingers rode my fingers as my hand went over the paper. It was like nothing else in my life up to now.

Then he said, "I think that's it. I think you got it," he said. "Take a look. What do you think?"

But I had my eyes closed. I thought I'd keep them that way for a little longer. I thought it was something I ought to do.

"Well?" he said. "Are you looking?"

My eyes were still closed. I was in my house. I knew that. But I didn't feel like I was inside anything.

"It's really something," I said.

HARD FEELINGS

Joseph Connolly

From the outside, a pick-up basketball game looks like nothing more than a bunch of guys playing a game, but if you've been in there, especially in there under the basket where most of the bumping and pushing go on, you know that every game is a jumble of little animosities and petty jealousies, and that at least two guys on the court flat out hate each other. It comes out in the banter and the force of the collisions and in whether a guy helps another guy up after knocking him down.

In our Sunday morning game at the King school in Cambridge, the two guys who hate each other are Neil Prentice and Frank Reposa. If they were closer in size, things might get ugly, but Neil is a little guy, about five-eight and skinny. Reposa is around six-four, two-twenty-five, and he does most of his banging on me. I'm not crazy about either of them, but I get caught in the middle because I invited Neil into the game. The only weapon he brings to the game is an ugly, old-fashioned set-shot. He holds the ball over his right shoulder, as if he wants you to compare it to his head, and then he pushes it up with his whole arm. Kevin Wolfe says he looks like he's trying to throw a pumpkin over a fence. It goes in with irritating frequency, and occasionally you'll hear some guy mutter that a shot that ugly shouldn't count.

Neil is a relative newcomer to our game. He's been playing with us for about a year and a half, and the rest of us have been at it for twelve. My wife, Sally, has suggested a few times that, at thirty-six, I'm going to have to start thinking about putting away the sneakers for good. I tell her I'll quit when she gets pregnant or when I blow out my other knee, whichever comes first. "Thanks, Mark," she says, "I'm glad to see I fit into the equation." Maybe I shouldn't joke about Sally getting pregnant, not when we're thinking about going to a doctor for help. Sally is thirty-five, and getting anxious. I'm not quite as eager as she is, I guess. Having a child would astonish me. Sometimes I feel like I'm still a kid myself, that being an adult is just a face I put on in the morning with my jacket and tie. Even with a job that takes me all over the country and a house that Sally and I own, it all feels like a big game, like I'm playing grown-up. Sally thinks that's why I still play ball, because I don't want to admit I'm an adult.

Neil's girlfriend's name is Madelyn, but I call her the Madwoman. She met Sally at the food co-op and latched onto her the way unstable people sometimes do when they meet someone who is stable, patient, and kind. Madelyn thinks that anyone who hasn't been through therapy must be as screwed up as she was before she started. Sally is all right, I guess, because she saw a counselor for a while in high school after her parents were killed in a traffic accident. Madelyn is always using words like "wellness" and "empowerment," and she and Neil jump on every New Age or self-help bandwagon that comes along. Sally told me that Madelyn and Neil have masks they wear when they have arguments, real masks they made themselves with paint and papier-maché. They call them the Masks of Anger. I almost fell off my chair laughing, picturing the two of them wearing Punch and Judy masks and bitching at each other about who didn't balance the checkbook or whose underwear was all over the floor. Sally said it wasn't such a crazy idea; it was just a way of putting anger behind them when they were through fighting. Nothing's that simple, I said, and Sally agreed. Sally and I deal with anger in more traditional ways, which sometimes means we don't deal with it at all. We just get quiet for long stretches of time, then we get over it. Anyway, I made my own mask by cutting a Jack-o-lantern face out of a paper plate. I keep it on my bedside table, and I pick it up any time I want to announce a change in my state of mind. "This is the Mask of Horniness," I say, or "This is the Mask of Having to go to the Bathroom Real Bad." Sally laughs and tells me I'm mean.

I first met Neil and Madelyn at dinner at their place. In the car on the way over, Sally gave me a brief lecture about how Neil and Madelyn were different from the people I'm used to, and why certain kinds of humor might not go over. She should have said *any* kind of humor. Their apartment is decorated in the style I call Early College-kid. They say they don't care about material things, and it shows. There isn't much furniture, and what there is looks second-hand. The dining room itself, which doubles as a library, has brick-and-board bookshelves along one wall filled with every book on self-esteem ever written. The table is rectangular, like a conference table, and looming over it is the world's ugliest light fixture. A single white globe hangs from a wide, clear plastic bell that reminds me of the Cone of Silence on the old T.V. show *Get Smart*. Someone on the show would say, "Lower the Cone of Silence" and this thing would come down over them. It was supposed to prevent eavesdropping on their conversations, but instead it made them unable to hear each other, and they would sit there trying to shout and no noise would come out. We all sat down at the table, and I looked up at the light fixture and said "Lower the Cone of Silence." Neil and Madelyn both turned puzzled stares on me, and Sally wrinkled up her nose and shook her head.

Dinner was the predictable vegetable stir-fry with rice and herbal tea, during which Neil and Madelyn eagerly told us their whole emotional histories, their never-ending quest for what I believe they called "integration." After my Cone of Silence blunder I retreated into nod-and-smile mode. Sally, as usual, was gracious and engaged, and acted as if nothing could have fascinated her more than the dependencies and degradations of Madelyn's romantic history. Madelyn's hair is wild, reddish, and frizzy, and I couldn't help thinking it got that way from being so close to her brain. I don't mean to be callous; it's just that she seems so smug about her suffering. She believes we all have the same wounds, but that she and Neil are special because they *know* they are suffering, and the rest of us are kidding ourselves.

At one point, Madelyn asked Sally—not me, but Sally—whether I was "in touch with my feelings."

"I'm in touch with my parents," I said. "Does that count?"

Neil smiled, but Madelyn just kept looking at Sally, waiting for an answer. Sally, whose hair is straight and brown, and whose brown eyes are always calm, looked right at me and smiled.

"Mark thinks he can tough out emotional problems the way he toughs out his sports injuries," she said.

All three of them looked at me. I felt like I was on display, like a patient in a teaching hospital. They were all wondering if I could be cured. "I hate sports analogies," I said to Madelyn. "Don't you?" I succeeded in changing the subject; Madelyn began talking about how sports and sports talk are used to oppress women in the workplace.

Despite her professed dislike of sports, it was Madelyn's idea that Neil should join our Sunday game. She asked Sally to ask me to invite him, and I did, and I've been sorry ever since. He acts like he's an anthropologist among savages, analyzing every move on the court in terms of power relationships, psychic wounds, and lost connections to our fathers. The other guys don't have to listen to this stuff, but I get it when I pick him up before games and when I drive him home and on the too frequent occasions when Sally and I get together with the two of them.

"I've noticed," he said once, just before I dropped him off, "that you say 'My fault' a lot during the game." His little pop-psych lectures always begin with "I've noticed."

I said, "Yeah, what about it?"

"Well, I don't want to make a big deal of this, but it seems to me that 'fault' is a highly charged word."

"Oh, please," I said. "Look, if I start to cut to a spot, and my teammate passes to that spot and the ball goes out of bounds because I stopped cutting, my teammate looks bad because he's thrown the ball out of bounds. I say 'My fault' to acknowledge that my teammate has done the right thing. It's a courtesy."

He considered for a moment. Then he said, "Nobody else says it."

I pulled to the curb in front of his apartment and kept my foot on the clutch while I waited for him to get out. "I'm an exceptionally courteous person," I said.

I told Kevin about the sensitive-male spin Neil puts on everything, and soon Neil was being subjected to some fairly friendly ribbing from some of the brighter guys on the court. After a flagrant foul, Kevin might say "I sensed some hostility in that foul" or "You guys should hug now, to show there's no hard feelings." Reposa is not one of the brighter guys on the court, and it took him a while to figure out what was going on. Occasionally he would mutter something like "You guys have all turned into faggots all of the sudden." When he finally realized that Neil was the butt of these jokes he jumped in with both feet, and he wasn't friendly or subtle.

Reposa is simply an offensive person. Every Sunday morning, we go through the ritual of trying to make fair teams out of whoever's shown up that day, and every Sunday morning Reposa says we should play "guineas versus micks." I once made the mistake of pointing out that Neil is a WASP, and Reposa said, "The little fruit looks like a mick to me. You keep him." He goes out of his way to set illegal picks and knock Neil to the floor; if Neil's glasses stay on he'll say "Damn, I'll have to hit him harder next time." Even the other guys, who don't like Neil either, have told Reposa to lay off.

What puzzles me is why Neil keeps showing up. It's clear he hasn't been playing basketball his whole life, as the rest of us have, and I don't think he gets out of it what we get out of it. He wants to analyze everything, and I play to get away from analyzing, to get out of my brain. During the week, work piles up, bills come due, somebody cuts me off in traffic or some smelly drunk leans over me in the subway, maybe Sally and I get testy with each other over some little thing, and my brain takes all these little set-backs and passes them on to my muscles for storage. That's the way I see it. I don't know how it works, but I swear it's true: muscles have their own memory. Sometimes when Sally is giving me a back-rub she sticks her strong thumbs into a certain spot between my shoulder blades and tears well up in my eyes, tears Sally can't see because I'm face down on the bed, and I know she's disturbed the hiding place of some old, forgotten grief. For a moment, I get that lost-child feeling, like something dark and sad is looming over me, and I say "Not there" and she says "Does that hurt too much?" and I say "Yes." So when I play basketball, I'm trying to empty the week's tensions out of my muscles. It starts with the stretching I do before the game, bending and pulling until the knots come out and I feel loose enough to play. Then I put on the battle gear I need to hold my thirty-six year old body together—a leather brace for my right ankle, a leather and metal brace for my left knee, hundred and fifty dollar leather shoes. Sometimes some guy will shake his head and remind us of the cheap canvas shoes we all played in back in high school, when our bodies were light and quick and we moved up and down the court like a cluster of sparrows. Now we have thicker bodies and thinner hair, and our game is an earthbound game of cunning and collisions.

It's not a game for Neil. He doesn't have the strength, or the experience he needs to make up for his lack of strength. But every week he shows up, takes his punishment, hits a couple of his ugly set-shots, and presents me with his post-game psychoanalysis on the way home. He seems to enjoy it, so what the hell.

This Sunday morning I pulled my car into Neil and Madelyn's driveway and they both came out of the house, and Neil climbed into the back seat and Madelyn got in front.

"I'm coming to watch," she said, and smiled. I glanced back at Neil, and he gave me a kind of what-can-I-do shrug. I didn't say anything. There was no rule, spoken or otherwise, about bringing wives or girlfriends to watch our game. It's just that nobody ever did. If someone had to break that pattern, it didn't seem like Neil was the right person to do it. I also couldn't think of anyone who would be more out of place at our game than Madelyn. Our games aren't very pretty, and sometimes the talk gets a little raw. It was hard to imagine her having a good time.

The court in the downstairs gym at the King School is considerably shorter than regulation, but it's plenty long enough for a bunch of weekend athletes like us. There are no bleachers, so Madelyn had to sit in a little plastic chair that was probably designed for a fourth grader. Things were quieter than usual during our pre-game warm-up. Guys were making furtive glances at Madelyn. Reposa, who was red-eyed and surly, kept looking back and forth between Neil and Madelyn, and you could almost see his little brain working, trying to find something obnoxious to say. The best he could do was "Bet she doesn't shave her legs."

"Why should she?" Neil said.

"Let's go," Kevin said. "Let's pick teams." In a minute, we were lined up, guineas versus micks, with Neil an honorary mick on our side. I don't know why, but suddenly I felt good. My first couple of shots went down, and I started to get that elated feeling you get sometimes when everything is coming together. Neil would probably say it was biorhythms. Reposa was covering me, and as soon as he broke a sweat a stale, boozy smell came off him. He smelled like a rug at a frat party. When you're in your twenties, you can stay out late and get hammered and still get up in the morning and make your body go, but the body of a man approaching forty is less forgiving. I decided to torture him. I ran everywhere, sprinting on transitions, running him off picks and through crowds, bumping him in the low post and then stepping out and hitting little ten-foot jumpers. When we weren't running, I was needling him about his smell.

"Jesus, Frank," I said, "when did they make Jack Daniels the breakfast of champions?"

"Shut the fuck up," he said.

"Hey," I shouted, "don't anybody light a match near Frank!" He started taking me under the basket and pounding me with his elbows, but his legs were pretty rubbery and he couldn't put much into it. We took a break after the first hour, and Reposa left the gym, probably to find a bathroom.

Neil spent the break sitting on the floor next to Madelyn, while the rest of us gathered around Mike Costa's cooler. Mike always brought a cooler full of juice and ice water. Madelyn was whispering something to Neil, and he was nodding and smiling. I couldn't help feeling we'd all just been reduced to caricatures—hulking, tribal males in a ritual of dominance. I wanted to walk over there and say "Look, it's a game. It's fun."

When we started again, Reposa was covering Eddie Monahan, and Mike Costa was on me. Mike is rangy and quick, and I knew I was going to have trouble scoring for the rest of the day. The guy who took up the scoring slack, to everyone's surprise, was Neil. He was hitting his shot, and he even started cutting through the lane like I'd been urging him to do for months. We started setting picks for him and feeding him the ball, giving him a chance to show off for his girlfriend. With about ten minutes left, I had the ball on the right side and Neil ran his man off a pick near the top of the circle and headed for the basket. I hit him with the pass, and as he turned to put the ball up, Reposa stepped over from the left side and clotheslined him—raked his forearm across Neil's face and laid him out flat. The lenses of Neil's glasses skittered across the floor.

"What the hell was that?" I shouted at Reposa.

"Weak side help," he said, and grinned.

It was Kevin, surprisingly, who went after Reposa, shoving him repeatedly and swearing at him. I ran over to get between them, but Reposa turned and walked away. "Fuck all you guys," he said.

Meanwhile, Mike Costa was tending to Neil. Neil's nose was bleeding, and Mike had gotten him up on his knees, bent over with his face in his hands. His hands were full of blood, and blood spilled over onto the floor. Mike kneaded Neil's shoulders and whispered to him. I walked over, and Mike looked up at me. "There's a towel in my bag," he said.

I jogged over to Mike's bag to get the towel. Madelyn was standing with her toes on the out-of-bounds line, watching the scene on the court with an expression I couldn't quite pin down. It could have been fear, or anger, or contempt, and it might have been all three.

"It's just a nosebleed," I said. "He's all right." She turned her strange expression on me for a full second, then looked back out at the court. Hell, I thought, she looks that way most of the time.

The game was over. Reposa grabbed his stuff quickly and left without saying anything else. Neil had to stop up his nose with toilet paper, but other than that he seemed fine. Our games usually end with handshakes, and Neil isn't always included in the ritual, but on this day everybody shook his hand or patted his butt and said "Good game." He'd had a good game, too. It was probably the best he ever played.

When Neil went over to Madelyn to pick up his stuff, she put a hand on his chin and gave his face a good looking over, but the look on her face didn't change and she didn't offer any sympathy or express any concern. The drive home was quiet. Madelyn sat in back this time, and Neil sat up front with me.

"You had your shot going today," I said, to break the silence.

"Yeah," he said. "Yeah, it felt good."

I stopped the car in front of their house and they both opened their doors and got out. Neil looked back in at me.

"Good game," I said.

"Yeah," he said. "Good game." Madelyn closed her door without saying anything and went ahead of him to the house.

When I got home, I took four Tylenol capsules and sat down on the edge of the bathtub to take off my shoes and the braces on my ankle and knee. Sally stood in the doorway, leaning against the frame, and I told her what happened between Neil and Reposa, and about Madelyn's silence in the car.

"Why is Reposa such a jerk?" she said.

"I don't know. He's just a little man in a big man's body."

"Why don't you just tell him not to come anymore?"

I peeled off the knee brace and ran a finger along my surgery scar. "I'd love to," I said. "But he's been in the game from the beginning. It would be an awfully unpleasant scene."

"More unpleasant than what happened this morning?" This question was an example of what I once would have called "oversimplifying the situation" and Sally called "cutting through the crap." I had as much as admitted I'd rather confront Reposa physically on the court than emotionally off the court, and as long I was on my post-game adrenaline high, that attitude felt right to me. I also knew the rightness of it would fade as the post-game ache invaded my muscles and joints. "No," I said. "You're right."

Then we just looked at each other. Women, it seems to me, aren't satisfied with just being right. Once they've established that they're right, they expect you to do something about it. Sally and I both knew I wasn't going to say anything to Reposa, that there would have to be more, and greater, violence before anybody thought to try to kick him out of the game.

"You're right, you're right," I said.

"Take your shower," she said, and she left.

About an hour and a half later, Sally and I were in the living room, reading the Sunday paper, when the doorbell rang. Sally got up to answer it. It was Madelyn, and she was crying. Right away, Sally was comforting her, stroking her hair and asking her what was wrong.

"Neil hit me," she said, staring accusingly at me.

Sally steered Madelyn to the couch and sat her down. After a moment of silence, Madelyn announced that she wanted to be alone with Sally.

"Okay," I said, quietly, pushing myself with some effort out of my chair. I was sore now, and my knee crackled as I stood. "I guess I'll go for a drive." Sally just nodded at me, and I walked out the still-open front door, and closed it gently behind me.

I drove back to Neil and Madelyn's apartment. Neil didn't seem surprised to see me. His eyes were puffy and red, but I couldn't tell if it was from crying or from the shot he took from Reposa. He had a bit of a mouse under his left eye. We sat down at the dining room table, under the Cone of Silence, and Neil apologized for not having any beer.

"Madelyn says you hit her," I said.

He started to say something, then stopped. He looked defeated, which was not unusual for Neil, but now it was worse than ever. He shook his head and stared out the window.

"Did you hit her?" I said. I thought of the tee-shirt Neil sometimes wore at basketball, a shirt with "Another Man Against Violence Against Women" emblazoned on the front. It always struck me as a kind of shallow boast, like saying you were against child molesting or something.

Neil seemed to be gathering the strength to make an assertion. It appeared to be difficult for him to paint a picture of reality different from the one Madelyn painted. I had to push him.

"Yes or no," I said.

"I did not hit her," he said.

"Why does she say you did?"

"Look," he said, and then he started to blush. "Look, Mark, do you know about the Masks of Anger?"

Oh Jesus, I thought Yes, I told him, I knew about the Masks of Anger.

"Well," he said, "when I got out of the shower this afternoon, Madelyn was sitting here at the table, wearing the Mask of Anger."

I didn't laugh, and I didn't roll my eyes. I kept my face fixed in a look of seriousness and concern, but the scene was comic to me, comic and sad. The poor bastard was not having a good day. First a big moron tried to rip his head off, then he'd had to stuff his nose full of toilet paper to keep from bleeding to death, and finally he gets out of the shower to find his girlfriend sitting at the dining room table with a damn mask on her face, a mask that, to him, meant he was in trouble.

"What was she mad about?"

"She said," he began, and then he had to take a deep breath. "She said she was disappointed in me for not standing up to Reposa."

"That's ridiculous," I said. Neil's face brightened. "What did she want you to do, take a swing at him?"

"She said I have to stop being a victim."

I sat there a moment, gazing up at the Cone of Silence. Then I remembered that my own paper plate mask was propped up against the lamp on my bedside table. Please God, I thought, keep Madelyn out of the bedroom. To Neil, I said "I take it Madelyn doesn't have a Mask of Mild Disappointment, and that's why she had to go straight to anger?"

Now Neil smiled. "That's what I said. I mean, that's not what I said exactly, but I said that I didn't feel that anger was an appropriate response. I asked her to remove the Mask of Anger." The careful language Neil always used made it sound like he was feeling his way through life on emotional training wheels. "She said she wouldn't," he continued, "because she was angry. She was angry with me for being a victim and angry with herself, she said, because all the men she ever gets involved with are victims. Do you want some water?"

"Yes," I said. "Please." Neil popped out of his chair and went into the kitchen. Suddenly he was energetic and almost cheerful. I seemed to have offered him the opportunity to believe he might not be in the wrong, a belief I'm not sure he allowed himself. From the kitchen I heard the *shoosh* sound of bottled water being opened. He came back into the dining room with two glasses of water with ice and little lemon wedges in them. I drank half of mine, then set it down on the table.

"Look, Neil," I said, "if you didn't hit her, why is she saying you did?"

The phone rang. Neil jumped out of his chair again, this time looking nervous. Madelyn's suggested presence filled the room. Neil excused himself and answered the bedroom phone with a tentative hello. After a minute or so I heard him say that he was not a homeowner. "No, really," he said. While Neil struggled to get off the phone, I looked at the shelf full of self-help books and wondered what it would be like to be Neil. He has to walk pretty softly around Madelyn to make sure he doesn't tread too heavily on any of her emotional tender-spots. No wonder he seems nervous. One of the remarkable things about Sally is her tolerance. I don't have to feel like I'm living my life on tip-toe, the way Neil does. Then again, I don't always know when I've let Sally down. Neil finally got off the phone, and when he returned to the living room he apologized for the interruption. I asked him again why Madelyn said he hit her.

"I was just coming to that," he said. He sipped at his water. "I asked her again to take off the mask. In fact, what I said was—" He put down his glass with a thump. "Hell, I didn't feel like a victim today, you know? I played real well today. With her there watching, I played one of the best games I've ever played in my life. And just because some jerk whacks me over the head, I mean—I mean *screw* him! Screw Reposa! He's not worth the trouble."

"Right," I said. "Right on all counts." Neil gave me a look that seemed to ask if I really meant it, and I nodded yes, and he went on.

"So what I said to her—I said, 'I can't talk to you if you're going to wear that stupid mask,' and I reached out to take it off her face and she kind of moved her head to one side and—and I guess it could have seemed to her like I hit her, but I was only reaching for the stupid mask." He was crying now, not sobbing, just letting the tears run down his face. "I was only reaching for the mask." After another pause, he said, very softly, "I broke its nose."

I clapped my hand over my mouth and looked at the floor. I was going to lose it any second. I took a deep breath, then looked up at Neil and said, as solemnly as I could, "You broke the nose on the Mask of Anger?"

There was a short silence. Then a little smirk appeared behind the tears on Neil's face, and we both broke out laughing, Neil mixing his laughter with what might have been little sobs. We laughed for what seemed like half a minute, longer than we would normally laugh over a little thing like a broken mask. Then we were quiet for a while. Neil got up and found himself some tissues. When he sat down again, he said "What would you have done? I mean about Reposa, if he'd hit you like he hit me?"

The truth was that Reposa would never pull a stunt like that on me, because he's a coward who picks on little guys. "I'd have done exactly what you did," I said.

Neil nodded. It was what he'd hoped to hear. "You know," he said, "it's easier for guys like you."

"I beg your pardon?"

"For big guys," he said. He was settling down now, and I was afraid he was about to give one of his wounded-male lectures. I was right.

He launched into a lengthy and obviously well thought out speech about how, on the playgrounds and in the gym classes and locker rooms of our youth, where guys like me were in training to become what our society calls real men, guys like him were in training to become our victims. He told me about the teasing and the torture he'd been through because he was small, because his arms and legs could never seem to come together to work in concert, because a ball thrown to him was as likely to hit him in the face as to land in his hands. I usually try to deflect or break up his lectures with jokes, but he'd had a tough day, and I figured he deserved a break. It struck me, as I sat there listening, that he wasn't using his usual ready-made phrases and other psycho-props. What he was saying didn't come from the bookshelf or from something Madelyn told him. He was talking about his life.

He got up in the middle of it to get us some more water. He handed me a glass and asked me whether what he was saying made sense. It wasn't a question he normally asked.

"It does," I said.

He went on to say that we—we, the big guys—always made it clear to everyone else that the world was ours, that all the women were ours, and that guys like Neil were lesser creatures who would be left with nothing but the things we didn't want. He even started to tell me there was a price I must pay for staying in the brotherhood of the big and the tough and the cool. Then I interrupted him, and said something that startled us both.

"It's fear," I said.

Neil had been looking out the window throughout much of his speech, but now he looked at me. "What's fear?" he said.

I put my glass down on the table and looked at the floor. I wasn't sure why I'd said what I'd said. I wasn't even entirely sure what I meant.

"Fear of emotion?" Neil said.

That wasn't it, and I felt a flicker of anger go through me at the suggestion. Then I realized what it was. It wasn't fear of emotion. It was fear of being treated the way Neil was treated, by Madelyn, by the guys on the basketball court, even by me. It was fear of having the woman you love scrutinizing your inadequacies and comparing you to other men whose inadequacies she can't see because she doesn't know them like she knows you. I had looked at Neil for a moment without the lens of contempt through which I generally saw him, and I'd found him sympathetic and, when he dropped the pop-psych talk, even insightful. But I didn't want to be him, or to live with the constant threat of humiliation he lived with. We—the big guys, as he called us—did what we did out of fear that at the first sign of weakness the whole world would turn on us and treat us the way we treated him.

"Fear of emotion?" I said. "I guess you could say that."

"Yeah," he said. "That's what I thought."

We sat quietly for a while. Finally I muttered something about how he and Madelyn needed to talk, and he said all they ever did was talk, and we both laughed. Then I got up to leave.

"If Madelyn's still at your place," he began, then shrugged. I offered to tell her his side of the story, and he thanked me. I wanted to ask him if she was worth the trouble, but it didn't seem like a nice question to ask, so I kept my mouth shut. As we walked to the door, I asked him if he hurt as bad as I did.

"How do you mean?"

"I mean your body," I said. "After we play, I feel like I've been hit by a truck."

"No," he said. "Actually, I feel pretty good." We stopped at the door and faced each other. "And I'm the one who got hit by a truck."

We laughed again, and then I shook his hand and wished him luck.

"You're a lucky guy," he said. "Sally is so easy to get along with."

"That's true," I said. I felt I should say something positive about his situation, something positive about Madelyn, and my mind raced through everything I knew about her. "Well," I said after a moment, "at least Madelyn's pretty clear about what she wants."

"Sally isn't?"

For God's sake, I thought, this is supposed to be a good-bye, and he's ready to open up another round of emotional show-and-tell. He was grinning the same way he does on the basketball court when he's thrown in one of his set-shots, as if finding a possible flaw in my relationship with Sally scored him a point in some little one-on-one I didn't even know we were playing. I'd actually started to like him a little, but I stopped liking him as suddenly as I'd started.

"Sally's fine," I said. "I gotta go." I opened the door and made my escape, promising to pick him up for basketball next Sunday.

I was feeling pretty irritable when I got in the car, but that's not surprising considering how my body felt. My muscles were begging me for Tylenol and sleep. I tuned the car radio to a country station. Country music seemed like the perfect antidote to Neil and Madelyn and their need to intellectualize everything, although its emphasis on tears and slamming doors is more suited to them than to Sally and me. You don't get too many good country songs about people who get along just fine. I did hear a country song, once, that fit us pretty well. It was last winter, when I was out in Ohio on business. I was driving my rental car through the dark and sleet back to my hotel, listening to some station from across the river in

Kentucky. A song came on about a man who loves his wife and his wife loves him; he dreams his wife has left him and he wakes up crying and reaches out in the darkness to touch her and she's still there. I got back to the hotel and called Sally. She said, "What's wrong? You weren't going to call until eleven." I said "Nothing's wrong," and my voice came out kind of husky and I couldn't say anything else, so she said "What's wrong?" again, and I just sat there with my eyes closed, holding the phone.

When I got back home, Madelyn was gone.

"You just missed her," Sally said.

"Rats," I said.

"I can imagine your disappointment." Sally then gave me Madelyn's side of the story; it was a fluid narrative, in which Neil started out as a vicious bully and evolved slowly into a frightened victim of male-dominated culture. If she worked at it hard enough, I figured Madelyn could eventually prove that Neil's alleged violent outburst was my fault. She still maintained that Neil hit her, but she was ready to forgive him.

"That could be tough," I said. "I'm not sure Neil's ready to be forgiven for something he claims he didn't do." I was in the bathroom, getting the Tylenol out of the cabinet. Sally stood in the doorway.

"You've been talking to Neil?"

"I was over there the whole time Madelyn was here." I washed down the Tylenol with a glass of water. "We've been doing some serious bonding."

"I'll bet."

"We hugged, we cried," I said. "We shared our wounds."

"Seriously," she said. "Tell me."

"Okay, Neil cried," I said. We went back to the living room and sat together on the couch, and I recounted the whole scene with Neil, including his speech about how tough it is to be a little guy. I almost mentioned what I'd said about fear, but I didn't feel like getting into it.

"You don't like them very much, do you?" she said.

I shrugged. "I think they're kind of silly."

"Still," she said, "it was nice of you to go over there and talk with Neil. And don't say 'a man's gotta do what a man's gotta do.'"

"I wasn't going to say that." I *was* going to say that. "Besides, how do you know I wasn't going over there to chew him out?"

"I know you better than that."

"Do you?" I said. "How well do you know me?" It was a teasing question; I wasn't really looking for an answer.

"As well as you let me," she said. "Probably a little better."

Sally was giving me an opportunity. She'd given me opportunities before, and I'd always backed away.

"Wait," I said. I went into the bedroom, took my mask from its post on the bedside table, and brought it back into the living room. I sat next to Sally, holding the mask in front of my face. She smiled and shook her head.

"All right," she said. "Who are we now?"

"This," I announced, "is the Mask of Not Letting My Wife Get to Know Me."

"Fine," she said. "Now take it off."

And I did.

SISTER

Deborah Joy Corey

I am on the cool green grass when Sister comes rolling in the driveway. Her husband is driving and when the car stops, Sister grabs the car keys and throws them to the grass. "He's pounded my legs all the way here," she cries and Daddy comes down from the porch. Sister is sobbing now and her babies are in the back seat with two brown bags of groceries, moving around as if in slow motion, rolling their fingers around their faces, and breathing tiny spots of steam on the windows. Sister is still crying and I—with my good eye for shiny objects—find the keys and carry them back, using my index finger as a hook for the thick silver ring.

Daddy is talking to Sister's husband like nothing ever happened. Talking about the heat and the dry dusty air. I lean my head in the baby blue car and look down to Sister's lap; she is wrapped in a flimsy cotton dress and sure enough, all along her knee, round bruises have bunched themselves together like a cluster of old grapes, soft and tender.

The gravel driveway snaps under my pink plastic flip-flops. I am just tall enough to reach my bony arm in front of Sister and dangle the keys like bells in between her and her man, just tall and brave enough, and he grabs those keys and stares at Sister like she is a moving dartboard, and he is intent on making his point. I move away and Sister pushes open her door and pulls away from his grabbing hand. She runs across the lawn and her man jumps out of the car and follows her. He is taking long giant steps behind Sister. He grabs her hair which is short and has no give, he grabs it tight and drops her down on her back. His arm comes down like a half-moon and his fist bangs her face. "Oh," I hear the wind push out of her and Daddy moves toward them hollering, "Lydia, get out here."

Mama comes out of the house waving her white dish cloth in the air. "No," she screams, "not in my yard, not my girl." She runs to them, then stops and puts her hands on her hips. Her bigness makes Sister's man look small. "No," she says firm-like.

Sister stands up and the blood spits out like a red waterfall. She covers her face and walks funny. Daddy turns away and goes into the house, his whole body drooping like a wet rag. The girl baby starts to cry—wide open-mouthed cries—and everyone looks toward the car and they are all quiet on the sunburnt lawn. Then Sister's man makes his move. He runs to the car and drives away. The babies' faces look like melted masks against the windows. When their car pulls away, things are unusually close

373

and quiet. We watch them until all that is left is a swirling circle of powder over the parched road and Sister begins to cry, not a likely cry, but a cry like a moose's call, all whiny and low.

In the night, I wake tossing and crying because I feel crowded in my sleep. The day's heat is still trapped under my skin. I hear a train roll by two or three fields away and I listen until I can hear no more whistle. The silence blends in just right with my brother's wheezing; he sleeps in the hallway outside my door. I move to the window and play with the dark curl that hides on the back of my neck. Clover smell is rushing around outside and I push my face against the black screen to breathe a deeper breath. I think, "Oh, Sister, I hope your face is okay. I hope your man learns to keep his temper down." I watch the fireflies that cover the fields and light on and off like snow sparkles. I watch the fields and heavens, flies and stars, all bright, first one, then the other and I say, "Jesus, don't blame me for giving those keys. I don't want Sister here, Jesus. . . " Brother wheezes louder. Wheezy Weasel, I call him when his chest gets heavy. I go to him and he is fast asleep. His eyes cross furiously under his thin lids. I whisper his name. His front teeth rest on his fat bottom lip. "Wheezy," I say, "get up quick, the whole world's on fire."

On Sunday Wheezy is sicker than ever. His face swells red and Mama puts a mustard pack on his chest and head until his entire bed and body stains yellow. Mama hums him a hymn. She's humming *Glory Glory Hallelujah*. She sings it over and over until my brother says, "Mama." He lifts his head and he says, "Mama, please no more." Mama stops her singing right up quick and sends me away. I go down the crooked steps and walk to where Daddy sits on the porch. His face is as long and as brown as an Indian's. He and Sister are talking about getting the babies back. Daddy is whittling a man's head out of a smooth piece of wood. There are thin white shavings dropping between his shoes. I go out to the grass where I have worn a patch from sitting. I sit in that patch and watch the ghosts of dandelions blow through the air until Mama comes and gets me for church.

We walk down the dusty road and Mama's presence is as big as the sun itself. She says Daddy will take care of things at home. She says my brother is feeling better. Her skin is as white and thin as papier mache and I wish I could smell like her, all clean and freshly brushed with dusting powder.

The touch of Mama's cool hand as I lie across her lap during the sermon comforts me. The preacher's voice is soft, but the *amens* echo around us like gunfire. "Amen," I say under my breath as I chew the thumbnail which I have saved especially for this time alone with Mama. Even now, we are not really alone. Even now, I share Mama with her interest in what's being said.

When we get home, Sister and her babies are on the porch with Daddy. You can tell by the way they are sitting that they are not discussing anything important. The babies stick their faces out through the slats of the railing and chew at the wood. Wheezy sits on the porch step all covered with dry mustard; his eyes are like green marbles in the sun. Mama checks his face for fever and pats the top of his head. I sit down beside him, twisting my hair around my fingers.

"Mama," Sister says, "Daddy went and got the babies back. He says there was nothing to it 'cause their father was laid out cold on the couch." She says this very proud of Daddy, and Mama picks up one of the babies and looks into its face. Mama clicks her tongue and the baby smiles.

"Mama, I just gotta move back home. I can't take being scared all the time. I gotta get me and the babies out of that trailer before he kills us," Sister says. "Mama, can I come back home?"

Daddy stands up. He looks out over the lawn and taps the whittled man's head against the railing, then walks down to the old well house, which is no longer a well house, but a storage space for his beer bottles. Daddy is not bad, he only drinks when things get too much for him, bills or my brother's wheezes. Sister sits up and watches Mama's face. She is as alert and nervous as a caged dog. "Mama?" she snaps.

"You know we got nothing extra," Mama says and Sister begins this long plea. Twisting her voice to match her words and saying she'll sleep on the floor, she won't eat much, she'll do anything just to get away from *him*. I shrink into my body when I hear her talk about staying forever. I think how Mama will be all tied up with Wheezy and Sister and her babies, and how Daddy will stay drunk, and I'll be nothing. I'll be the shriveled up pea in the corner of the pod. I think how Sister is like a long sticky fly-catch blowing in the wind and we are all the flies sticking to her troubles.

"What about your Daddy?" Mama says. "You know he hasn't had any work for a month." She bounces the baby in her arms, up and down, swaying her hips like she's in a hula hoop.

"I'll do Tupperware parties and I'll pay rent," Sister says looking big-eyed like she has already had a glimpse of her new life.

Mama takes the baby into the kitchen and the screen door bangs behind her. Sister picks up her other baby and balances him on her hip bone.

"Can I or can't I?" she asks and Mama says something back that makes the worried lines go out of Sister's face.

The door of the well house is slightly open and the cool from the darkness pushes out. There are empty brown bottles all along the walls and it takes my eyes a while to adjust without the sun. Daddy is sitting in one corner with a piece of hay dangling from his mouth. When he drinks, the hay remains in his mouth, unchanged. I sit down in the opposite corner beside an old milk can and roll an empty around the palms of my hand. "Well, I guess she's gonna stay," I say and Daddy just watches me and drinks. When he guzzles, his adam's apple bobs in and out like a horse's heartbeat. I stare down at the musty floor boards. Mama says Daddy drinks because his soul is troubled. She also says if we could see our soul we'd see that it is in the shape of wings and I believe her, because sometimes when I sit on the lawn and stare out at the green mountain ridges that surround our home, I can feel my soul wanting to get loose to see what lies beyond those high slopes. Daddy chugs a whole beer before he sees my thumb stuck in the top of the beer bottle. The thumb is swelling blue from my tugging to get it out. "What in hell?" Daddy staggers over toward me. He grabs my arm and smashes the bottle against the old milk can. The brown glass makes a sharp obstacle course all around me and I struggle with words in my throat, but they don't come up. Daddy pushes me out into the light. "Get out," he says and slams the door behind me.

I know Daddy's anger with me is just the beginning of things to come with Sister being around. I wander down the long road and take a turn at the crossing toward the old folk's home that Mama calls heaven's waiting room. I stop at the black bridge and let my feet hang out over the edge and stare down where the clear creek water rushes by like a jet. I can see the round rocks in the creek's bottom and I wonder about my kazoo. I wonder if maybe it's hidden between those rocks getting all rusty. I dropped it over when I was thinking about a boy and Mama would proba- bly say that was good punishment for me. His name is Lenny Moore and he's the only boy in the whole fourth grade. He sits at the desk in front of me. He's jiggly and nervous, and he's always sending me scrawly notes about how he likes me and would like to kiss me someday, and for a while I liked the notes and the thoughts I had of Lenny. I liked him a lot un- til the day he accidentally wet his pants and his yellow water ran back un- der his chair to my new white sneakers. It's hard to forget that smell and the yellow stains and besides the rest of the kids call him Leaky Moore, which keeps us both cringing and blushing at the memory. The smell of melting tar comes out around the dark boards of the bridge, and the smell is so strong you'd think it came in a black cloud. I swing my legs and for- get about my thumb and Daddy and all the broken glass, but I still have a clear picture of Sister and her babies.

At the old folk's home, I crawl up on Mrs. Harris's bed and rest my- self. Her room smells of plastic and fly repellent. She is wandering around the room touching all her things and saying, "I've got to get ready, I've got to get ready." Mama's been letting me come to visit Mrs. Harris all sum- mer and she is always like this, not quite sure of where she belongs any- more. She says her old man sleeps up in the attic and bakes molasses cookies all day. She says the mosquitos sneak in through her screen at night and bite her to death. I tell Mrs. Harris there is no screen on the window, but she just keeps on talking and smiling like I've never said a word. She takes some old crochet work out of a plastic bag and rubs her wrinkled fingers over it. I tell her all about the gall of Sister and her ba- bies, and she is so happy for me, having family and all, and she puts the crochet work back in the bag, sniffing and trying to hide her sad joy. Be- fore I leave, Mrs. Harris combs the snarls from my hair. She combs it one hundred times and I count the mosquito bites on her legs which are really too many to count.

On the way home I find Daddy wading around in the creek. He is pushing his legs against the current and staring down through the water in a panic. I lean out over the water as far as I dare and I say, "Daddy, what are you doing?" He looks up, his mouth all wilted and opened and he squints his eyes at me. He screams my name and his scream bounces under the bridge and back to the water. He rubs his face, then slaps at the current like he's disgusted. He whispers my name, all worn out.

Daddy takes me home by the arm and his wet self makes spots of mud on the dirt road. He hangs on to my arm like he's afraid I'll get away, like I'm some shiny slippery trout and I know what he thinks. He's thinking back to the black bridge. He's thinking that I might have been lying under the water, still, and in another world. He's thinking it over and over.

We're almost home and I can see Mama standing in the doorway wagging the fly swatter and I know what I'm in for. Daddy keeps pulling me along and when we step on the porch, Mama takes one big step toward us. She grabs my arm and I begin to circle around her like a human Maypole. "Don't *slap* you *slap* ever *slap* go *slap* away *slap* without *slap* telling *slap* us *slap* where *slap* you're *slap* going *SLAP SLAP*." I run upstairs to my room and bury my wet face in the feather pillow and for a long time I don't look at the red marks on my legs.

When Mama wakes me, the sun has gone down. She takes me into her room where everyone except Daddy is sitting in the dark on the bed. They are listening to the voice in the yard. Sister says her man is as drunk as a hoot. His words are running all together like unsettled Jell-O. "Give me my babies, I want my kids back. Give 'em back or I'll shoot all of you. I'll blow you all to kingdom come." Things get real still and you can feel the fear running through each of us as if we were all hanging on to an electric fence. I can feel it pushing right out to the end of my fingers. Wheezy is shaking like a dried up leaf and just to watch him makes me shake. Sister wraps one arm around me and I think about the story Daddy tells about the crazy man who went to a farmer's house and shot his whole family while they slept. Daddy said he'd never seen such a sight, all those bodies bled dry in their beds. I can see us all slumped over in this bed in a pool of blood, and right away everything that I've thought or felt these last few days seems stupid.

We hear the screen door slam and Mama moves to the hall window. I go right behind her. Sister's man is sitting on the hood of his car with a bottle in one hand and a gun in the other. He's loose and wiry like a Slinky toy. Daddy stands right in front of him. I close my eyes. "Give me the gun," Daddy says. "Go home and get yourself sober." There is a tiny little click and then stillness like the whole world has disappeared. I open my eyes and Sister's man points the gun right at Daddy's chest. Mama and I both pull our breath back through our mouths in a gasp. And Daddy reaches out and takes the gun from him in one clean sweep, smooth as honey, and Mama says, "Put the babies to bed." Sister's man rolls himself into a ball. He says he has lost everything and starts to cry. He cries so hard and so loud that I believe he is crying for all of us. It seems like all of our hurts have snuck down inside of him and are now pouring out on the top of his car in tears and wet noises.

Later, Daddy comes into my room and looks down at me and Sister's baby. The baby has its face shoved into the mattress and is sound asleep. Daddy makes a moon shadow across my white sheets. He says he wanted to make sure the bed is big enough for the baby and me. I say it is. Daddy is just one big dark spot in the middle of my room. He drops his hand down and I touch it. I feel the red metal of my kazoo hidden away in his palm like a lost treasure. Daddy doesn't say anything, he just lets the kazoo go and goes back to his room. I blow it once to see if it still works and the girl baby turns and snuggles up to my side. Her breath is sour and small and wispy. I listen to it go in and out of her like clockwork and I imagine the flapping of wings around me, in the night.

WHITE ANGEL

Michael Cunningham

We lived then in Cleveland, in the middle of everything. It was the sixties—our radios sang out love all day long. This of course is history. It was
before the city of Cleveland went broke, before its river caught fire. We
were four. My mother and father, Carlton, and me. Carlton turned sixteen the year I turned nine. Between us were several brothers and sisters,
weak flames quenched in our mother's womb. We are not a fruitful or
many-branched line. Our family name is Morrow.

Our father was a high school music teacher. Our mother taught children called "exceptional," which meant that some could name the day
Christmas would fall in the year 2000 but couldn't remember to take
down their pants when they peed. We lived in a tract called Woodlawn—
neat one- and two-story houses painted optimistic colors. The tract bor-
dered a cemetery. Behind our back yard was a gully choked with brush
and, beyond that, the field of smooth, polished stones. I grew up with the
cemetery and didn't mind it. It could be beautiful. A single stone angel,
small-breasted and determined, rose amid the more conservative markers
close to our house. Farther away, in a richer section, miniature mosques
and Parthenons spoke silently to Cleveland of man's enduring accom-
plishments. Carlton and I played in the cemetery as children and, with a
little more age, smoked joints and drank Southern Comfort there. I was,
thanks to Carlton, the most criminally advanced nine-year-old in my
fourth-grade class. I was going places. I made no move without his counsel.

Here is Carlton several months before his death, in an hour so alive
with snow that earth and sky are identically white. He labors among the
markers, and I run after, stung by snow, following the light of his red knitted cap. Carlton's hair is pulled back into a ponytail, neat and economical,
a perfect pine cone of hair. He is thrifty, in his way.

We have taken hits of acid with our breakfast juice. Or, rather, Carlton
has taken a hit, and I, in consideration of my youth, have been allowed
half. This acid is called windowpane. It is for clarity of vision, as Vicks is
for decongestion of the nose. Our parents are at work, earning the daily
bread. We have come out into the cold so that the house, when we reenter
it, will shock us with its warmth and righteousness. Carlton believes in
shocks.

"I think I'm coming on to it," I call out. Carlton has on his buckskin jacket, which is worn down to the shine. On the back, across his shoulder blades, his girlfriend has stitched an electric blue eye. As we walk I speak into the eye. "I think I feel something," I say.

"Too soon," Carlton calls back. "Stay loose, Frisco. You'll know when the time comes."

I am excited and terrified. We are into serious stuff. Carlton has done acid half a dozen times before, but I am new at it. We slipped the tabs into our mouths at breakfast, while our mother paused over the bacon. Carlton likes taking risks.

Snow collects in the engraved letters on the headstones. I lean into the wind, trying to decide whether everything around me seems strange because of the drug or just because everything truly is strange. Three weeks earlier, a family across town had been sitting at home, watching television, when a single-engine plane fell on them. Snow swirls around us, seeming to fall up as well as down.

Carlton leads the way to our spot, the pillared entrance to a society tomb. This tomb is a palace. Stone cherubs cluster on the peaked roof, with their stunted, frozen wings and matrons' faces. Under the roof is a veranda, backed by cast-iron doors that lead to the house of the dead proper. In summer this veranda is cool. In winter it blocks the wind. We keep a bottle of Southern Comfort here.

Carlton finds the bottle, unscrews the cap, and takes a good, long draw. He is studded with snowflakes. He hands me the bottle, and I take a more conservative drink. Even in winter, the tomb smells mossy. Dead leaves and a yellow M&M's wrapper, worried by the wind, scrape on the marble floor.

"Are you scared?" Carlton asks me.

I nod. I never think of lying to him.

"Don't be, man," he says. "Fear will screw you right up. Drugs can't hurt you if you feel no fear."

I nod.

We stand sheltered, passing the bottle. I lean into Carlton's certainty as if it gave off heat.

"We can do acid all the time at Woodstock," I say.

"Right on. Woodstock Nation. Yow!"

"Do people really *live* there?" I ask.

"Man, you've got to stop asking that. The concert's over, but people are still there. It's a new nation. Have faith."

I nod again, satisfied. There is a different country for us to live in. I am already a new person, renamed Frisco. My old name was Robert.

"We'll do acid all the time," I say.

"You better believe we will." Carlton's face, surrounded by snow and marble, is lit. His eyes are vivid as neon. Something in them tells me he can see the future, a ghost that hovers over everybody's head. In Carlton's future we all get released from our jobs and schooling. Awaiting us all, and soon, is a bright, perfect simplicity. A life among the trees by the river.

"How are you feeling, man?" he asks me.

"Great," I tell him, and it is purely the truth. Doves clatter up out of a bare tree and turn at the same instant, transforming themselves from steel to silver in snow-blown light. I know then that the drug is working. Everything before me has become suddenly, radiantly itself. How could Carlton have known this was about to happen? "Oh," I whisper. His hand settles on my shoulder.

"Stay loose, Frisco," he says. "There's not a thing in this pretty world to be afraid of. I'm here."

I am not afraid. I am astonished. I had not realized until this moment how real everything is. A twig lies on the marble at my feet, bearing a cluster of hard brown berries. The broken-off end is raw, white, fleshy. Trees are alive.

"I'm here," Carlton says again, and he is.

Hours later, we are sprawled on the sofa in front of the television, ordinary as Wally and the Beav. Our mother makes dinner in the kitchen. A pot lid clangs. We are undercover agents. I am trying to conceal my amazement.

Our father is building a grandfather clock from a kit. He wants to have something to leave us, something for us to pass along. We can hear him in the basement, sawing and pounding. I know what is laid out on his sawhorses—a long, raw wooden box, onto which he glues fancy moldings. A pearl of sweat meanders down his forehead as he works. Tonight I discovered my ability to see every room of the house at once, to know every single thing that goes on. A mouse nibbles inside the wall. Electrical wires curl behind the plaster, hidden and patient as snakes.

"Sh-h-h," I say to Carlton, who has not said anything. He is watching television through his splayed fingers. Gunshots ping. Bullets raise chalk dust on a concrete wall. I have no idea what we are watching.

"Boys?" our mother calls from the kitchen. I can, with my new ears, hear her slap hamburger into patties. "Set the table like good citizens," she calls.

"O.K., Ma," Carlton replies, in a gorgeous imitation of normality. Our father hammers in the basement. I can feel Carlton's heart ticking. He pats my hand, to assure me that everything's perfect.

We set the table, fork knife spoon, paper napkins triangled to one side. We know the moves cold. After we are done I pause to notice the dining room wallpaper: a golden farm, backed by mountains. Cows graze, autumn trees cast golden shade. This scene repeats itelf three times, on three walls. "Zap," Carlton whispers. "Zzzzzoom."

"Did we do it right?" I ask him.

"We did everything perfect, little son. How are you doing in there, anyway?" He raps lightly on my head.

"Perfect, I guess." I am staring at the wallpaper as if I were thinking of stepping into it.

"You guess. You guess? You and I are going to other planets, man. Come over here."

"Where?"

"Here. Come here." He leads me to the window. Outside, snow skitters under the street lamps. Ranch-style houses hoard their warmth but bleed light into the gathering snow.

"You and I are going to fly, man," Carlton whispers, close to my ear. He opens the window. Snow blows in, sparking on the carpet. "Fly," he says, and we do. For a moment we strain up and out, the black night wind blowing in our faces—we raise ourselves up off the cocoa-colored deep-pile wool-and-polyester carpet by a sliver of an inch. I swear it to this day. Sweet glory. The secret of flight is this: You have to do it immediately, before your body realizes it is defying the laws.

We both know we have taken momentary leave of the earth. It does not strike either of us as remarkable, any more than does the fact that airplanes sometimes fall from the sky, or that we have always lived in Ohio and will soon leave for a new nation. We settle back down. Carlton touches my shoulder.

"You wait, Frisco," he says. "Miracles are happening. Goddam miracles."

I nod. He pulls down the window, which reseals itself with a sucking sound. Our own faces look back at us from the cold, dark glass. Behind us, our mother drops the hamburgers into the skillet. Our father bends to his work under a hooded light bulb, preparing the long box into which he will lay clockwork, pendulum, a face. A plane drones by overhead, invisible in the clouds. I glance nervously at Carlton. He smiles his assurance and squeezes the back of my neck.

March. After the thaw. I am walking through the cemetery, thinking about my endless life. One of the beauties of living in Cleveland is that any direction feels like progress. I've memorized the map. We are by my calculations 350 miles shy of Woodstock, New York. On this raw new day I am walking east, to the place where Carlton and I keep our bottle. I am going to have an early nip, to celebrate my bright future.

When I get to our spot I hear low moans coming from behind the tomb. I freeze, considering my options. The sound is a long, drawn-out agony with a whip at the end, a final high C, something like "ooooooOw." A wolf's cry run backward. What decides me on investigation rather than flight is the need to create a story. In the stories Carlton likes best, people always do the foolish, risky thing. I find I can reach decisions this way—by thinking of myself as a character in a story told by Carlton.

I creep around the side of the monument, cautious as a badger, pressed up close to the marble. I peer over a cherub's girlish shoulder. What I find is Carlton on the ground with his girlfriend, in a jumble of clothes and bare flesh. Carlton's jacket, the one with the embroidered eye, is draped over the stone, keeping watch.

I hunch behind the statue. I can see the girl's naked arms, and the familiar bones of Carlton's spine. The two of them moan together in the brown winter grass. Though I can't make out the girl's expression, Carlton's face is twisted and grimacing, the cords of his neck pulled tight. I had never thought the experience might be painful. I watch, trying to learn. I hold on to the cherub's cold wings.

It isn't long before Carlton catches sight of me. His eyes rove briefly, ecstatically skyward, and what do they light on but his brother's small head, sticking up next to a cherub's. We lock eyes and spend a moment in mutual decision. The girl keeps on clutching at Carlton's skinny back. He decides to smile at me. He decides to wink.

I am out of there so fast I tear up divots. I dodge among the stones, jump the gully, clear the fence into the swing-set-and-picnic-table sanctity of the back yard. Something about that wink. My heart beats fast as a sparrow's.

I go into the kitchen and find our mother washing fruit. She asks what's going on. I tell her nothing is. Nothing at all.

She sighs over an apple's imperfection. The curtains sport blue teapots. Our mother works the apple with a scrub brush. She believes they come coated with poison.

"Where's Carlton?" she asks.

"Don't know," I tell her.

"Bobby?"

"Huh?"

"What exactly is going on?"

"Nothing," I say. My heart works itself up to a hummingbird's rate, more buzz than beat.

"I think something is. Will you answer a question?"

"O.K."

"Is your brother taking drugs?"

I relax a bit. It's only drugs. I know why she is asking. Lately police cars have been cruising past our house like sharks. They pause, take note, glide on. Some neighborhood crackdown. Carlton is famous in these parts.

"No," I tell her.

She faces me with the brush in one hand, an apple in the other. "You wouldn't lie to me, would you?" She knows something is up. Her nerves run through this house. She can feel dust settling on the tabletops, milk starting to turn in the refrigerator.

"No," I say.

"Something's going on," she sighs. She is a small, efficient woman who looks at things as if they gave off a painful light. She grew up on a farm in Wisconsin and spent her girlhood tying up bean rows, worrying over the sun and rain. She is still trying to overcome her habit of modest expectations.

I leave the kitchen, pretending sudden interest in the cat. Our mother follows, holding her brush. She means to scrub the truth out of me. I follow the cat, his erect black tail and pink anus.

"Don't walk away when I'm talking to you," our mother says.

I keep walking, to see how far I'll get, calling "Kittykittykitty." In the front hall, our father's homemade clock chimes the half hour. I make for the clock. I get as far as the rubber plant before she collars me.

"I told you not to walk away," she says, and cuffs me a good one with the brush. She catches me on the ear and sets it ringing. The cat is out of there quick as a quarter note.

I stand for a minute, to let her know I've received the message. Then I resume walking. She hits me again, this time on the back of the head, hard enough to make me see colors. "Will you *stop?*" she screams. Still, I keep walking. Our house runs west to east. With every step I get closer to Yasgur's farm.

Carlton comes home whistling. Our mother treats him like a guest who's overstayed. He doesn't care. He is lost in optimism. He pats her cheek and calls her "Professor." He treats her as if she were harmless, and so she is.

She never hits Carlton. She suffers him the way farm girls suffer a thieving crow, with a grudge so old it borders on reverence. She gives him a scrubbed apple and tells him what she'll do if he tracks mud on the carpet.

I am waiting in our room. He brings the smell of the cemetery with him—its old snow and wet pine needles. He rolls his eyes at me, takes a crunch of his apple. "What's happening, Frisco?" he says.

I have arranged myself loosely on my bed, trying to pull a Dylan riff out of my harmonica. I have always figured I can bluff my way into wisdom. I offer Carlton a dignified nod.

He drops onto his own bed. I can see a crushed crocus stuck to the black rubber sole of his boot.

"Well, Frisco," he says. "Today you are a man."

I nod again. Is that all there is to it?

"*Yow,*" Carlton says. He laughs, pleased with himself and the world. "That was so perfect."

I pick out what I can of "Blowin' in the Wind."

Carlton says, "Man, when I saw you out there spying on us I thought to myself, *Yes.* Now *I'm* really here. You know what I'm saying?" He waves his apple core.

"Uh-huh," I say.

"Frisco, that was the first time her and I ever did it. I mean, we'd talked. But when we finally got down to it, there you were. My brother. Like you *knew.*"

I nod, and this time for real. What happened was an adventure we had together. All right. The story is beginning to make sense.

"Aw, Frisco," Carlton says. "I'm gonna find you a girl, too. You're nine. You been a virgin too long."

"Really?" I say.

"*Man.* We'll find you a woman from the sixth grade, somebody with a little experience. We'll get stoned and all make out under the trees in the boneyard. I want to be present at your deflowering, man. You're gonna need a brother there."

I am about to ask, as casually as I can manage, about the relationship between love and bodily pain, when our mother's voice cuts into the room. "You did it," she screams. "You tracked mud all over the rug."

A family entanglement follows. Our mother brings our father, who comes and stands in the doorway with her, taking in evidence. He is a formerly handsome man. His face has been worn down by too much patience. He has lately taken up some sporty touches—a goatee, a pair of calfskin boots.

Our mother points out the trail of muddy half-moons that lead from the door to Carlton's bed. Dangling over the end of the bed are the culprits themselves, voluptuously muddy, with Carlton's criminal feet still in them.

"You see?" she says. "You see what he thinks of me?"

Our father, a reasonable man, suggests that Carlton clean it up. Our mother finds that too small a gesture. She wants Carlton not to have done it in the first place. "I don't ask for much," she says. "I don't ask where he goes. I don't ask why the police are suddenly so interested in our house. I ask that he not track mud all over the floor. That's all." She squints in the glare of her own outrage.

"Better clean it right up," our father says to Carlton.

"And that's it?" our mother says. "He cleans up the mess and all is forgiven?"

"Well, what do you want him to do? Lick it up?"

"I want some consideration," she says, turning helplessly to me. "That's what I want."

I shrug, at a loss. I sympathize with our mother but am not on her team.

"All right," she says. "I just won't bother cleaning the house anymore. I'll let you men handle it. I'll sit and watch television and throw my candy wrappers on the floor."

She starts out, cutting the air like a blade. On the way she picks up a jar of pencils, looks at it, and tosses the pencils on the floor. They fall like fortune-telling sticks, in pairs and criss-crosses.

Our father goes after her, calling her name. Her name is Isabel. We can hear them making their way across the house, our father calling "Isabel, Isabel, Isabel," while our mother, pleased with the way the pencils looked, dumps more things onto the floor.

"I hope she doesn't break the TV," I say.

"She'll do what she needs to do," Carlton says.

"I hate her," I say. I am not certain about that. I want to test the sound of it, to see if it's true.

"She's got more balls than any of us, Frisco," he says. "Better watch what you say about her."

I keep quiet. Soon I get up and start gathering pencils, because I prefer that to lying around and trying to follow the shifting lines of allegiance. Carlton goes for a sponge and starts in on the mud.

"You get shit on the carpet, you clean it up," he says. "Simple."

The time for all my questions about love has passed, and I am not so unhip as to force a subject. I know it will come up again. I make a neat bouquet of pencils. Our mother rages through the house.

Later, after she has thrown enough and we three have picked it all up, I lie on my bed thinking things over. Carlton is on the phone to his girlfriend, talking low. Our mother, becalmed but still dangerous, cooks dinner. She sings as she cooks, some slow forties number that must have been all over the jukes when her first husband's plane went down in the Pacific. Our father plays his clarinet in the basement. That is where he goes to practice, down among his woodworking tools, the neatly hung hammers and awls that throw oversized shadows in the light of the single bulb. If I put my ear to the floor, I can hear him, pulling a long, low tomcat moan out of that horn. There is some strange comfort in pressing my ear to the carpet and hearing our father's music leaking up through the floorboards. Lying down, with my ear to the floor, I join in on my harmonica.

That spring our parents have a party to celebrate the sun's return. It has been a long, bitter winter, and now the first wild daisies are poking up on the lawns and among the graves.

Our parents' parties are mannerly affairs. Their friends, schoolteachers all, bring wine jugs and guitars. They are Ohio hip. Though they hold jobs and meet mortgages, they think of themselves as independent spirits on a spying mission. They have agreed to impersonate teachers until they write their novels, finish their dissertations, or just save up enough money to set themselves free.

Carlton and I are the lackeys. We take coats, fetch drinks. We have done this at every party since we were small, trading on our precocity, doing a brother act. We know the moves. A big, lipsticked woman who has devoted her maidenhood to ninthgrade math calls me Mr. Right. An assistant vice principal in a Russian fur hat asks us both whether we expect to vote Democratic or Socialist. By sneaking sips I manage to get myself semicrocked.

The reliability of the evening is derailed halfway through, however, by a half dozen of Carlton's friends. They rap on the door and I go for it, anxious as a carnival sharp to see who will step up next and swallow the illusion that I'm a kindly, sober nine-year-old child. I'm expecting callow adults, and what do I find but a pack of young outlaws, big-booted and wild-haired. Carlton's girlfriend stands in front, in an outfit made up almost entirely of fringe.

"Hi, Bobby," she says confidently. She comes from New York, and is more than just locally smart.

"Hi," I say. I let them all in despite a retrograde urge to lock the door and phone the police. Three are girls, four boys. They pass me in a cloud of dope smoke and sly-eyed greeting.

What they do is invade the party. Carlton is standing on the far side of the rumpus room, picking the next album, and his girl cuts straight through the crowd to his side. She has the bones and the loose, liquid moves some people consider beautiful. She walks through that room as if she'd been sent to teach the whole party a lesson.

Carlton's face tips me off that this was planned. Our mother demands to know what's going on here. She is wearing a long, dark red dress that doesn't interfere with her shoulders. When she dresses up, you can see what it is about her, or what it was. She is the source of Carlton's beauty. I have our father's face.

Carlton does some quick talking. Though it is against our mother's better judgment, the invaders are suffered to stay. One of them, an Eddie Haskell for all his leather and hair, tells her she is looking good. She is willing to hear it.

So the outlaws, house-sanctioned, start to mingle. I work my way over to Carlton's side, the side unoccupied by his girlfriend. I would like to say something ironic and wised-up, something that will band Carlton and me against every other person in the room. I can feel the shape of the comment I have in mind, but, being a tipsy nine-year-old, can't get my mouth around it. What I say is "Shit, man."

Carlton's girl laughs. I would like to tell her what I have figured out about her, but I am nine, and three-quarters gone on Tom Collinses. Even sober, I can only imagine a sharp-tongued wit.

"Hang on, Frisco," Carlton tells me. "This could turn into a real party."

I can tell by the light in his eyes what is going down. He has arranged a blind date between our parents' friends and his own. It's a Woodstock move—he is plotting a future in which young and old have business together. I agree to hang on, and go to the kitchen, hoping to sneak a few knocks of gin.

There I find our father leaning up against the refrigerator. A line of butterfly-shaped magnets hovers around his head. "Are you enjoying this party?" he asks, touching his goatee. He is still getting used to being a man with a beard.

"Uh-huh."

"I am, too," he says sadly. He never meant to be a high school music teacher. The money question caught up with him.

"What do you think of this music?" he asks. Carlton has put the Stones on the turntable. Mick Jagger sings "19th Nervous Breakdown." Our father gestures in an openhanded way that takes in the room, the party, the whole house—everything the music touches.

"I like it," I say.

"So do I." He stirs his drink with his finger, and sucks on the finger.

"I *love* it," I say, too loud. Something about our father leads me to raise my voice. I want to grab handfuls of music out of the air and stuff them into my mouth.

"I'm not sure I could say I love it," he says. "I'm not sure if I could say that, no. I would say I'm friendly to its intentions. I would say that if this is the direction music is going in, I won't stand in its way."

"Uh-huh," I say. I am already anxious to get back to the party but don't want to hurt his feelings. If he senses he's being avoided, he can fall into fits of apology more terrifying than our mother's rages.

"I think I may have been too rigid with my students," our father says. "Maybe over the summer you boys could teach me a few things about the music young people are listening to these days."

"Sure," I say loudly. We spend a minute waiting for the next thing to say.

"You boys are happy, aren't you?" he asks. "Are you enjoying this party?"

"We're having a great time," I say.

"I thought you were. I am, too."

I have by this time gotten myself to within jumping distance of the door. I call out, "Well, goodbye," and dive back into the party.

Something has happened in my absence. The party has started to roll. Call it an accident of history and the weather. Carlton's friends are on decent behavior, and our parents' friends have decided to give up some of their wine-and-folksong propriety to see what they can learn. Carlton is dancing with a vice principal's wife. Carlton's friend Frank, with his ancient-child face and I.Q. in the low sixties, dances with our mother. I see that our father has followed me out of the kitchen. He positions himself at the party's edge; I leap into its center. I invite the fuchsia-lipped math teacher to dance. She is only too happy. She is big and graceful as a parade float, and I steer her effortlessly out into the middle of everything. My mother, who is known around school for Sicilian discipline, dances freely, which is news to everybody. There is no getting around her beauty.

The night rises higher and higher. A wildness sets in. Carlton throws new music on the turntable—Janis Joplin, the Doors, the Dead. The future shines for everyone, rich with the possibility of more nights exactly like this. Even our father is pressed into dancing, which he does like a flightless bird, all flapping arms and potbelly. Still, he dances. Our mother has a kiss for him.

Finally I nod out on the sofa, blissful under the drinks. I am dreaming of flight when our mother comes and touches my shoulder. I smile up into her flushed, smiling face.

"It's hours past your bedtime," she says, all velvet motherliness. I nod. I can't dispute the fact.

She keeps on nudging my shoulder. I am a moment or two apprehending the fact that she actually wants me to leave the party and go to bed. "No," I tell her.

"Yes," she smiles.

"No," I say cordially, experimentally. This new mother can dance, and flirt. Who knows what else she might allow?

"Yes." The velvet motherliness leaves her voice. She means business of the usual kind. I get myself off the sofa and I run to Carlton for protection. He is laughing with his girl, a sweaty question mark of hair plastered to his forehead. I plow into him so hard he nearly goes over.

"Whoa, Frisco," he says. He takes me up under the arms and swings me a half turn. Our mother plucks me out of his hands and sets me down, with a good, farm-style hold on the back of my neck.

"Say good night, Bobby," she says. She adds, for the benefit of Carlton's girl, "He should have been in bed before this party started."

"*No*," I holler. I try to twist loose, but our mother has a grip that could crack walnuts.

Carlton's girl tosses her hair and says, "Good night, baby." She smiles a victor's smile. She smooths the stray hair off Carlton's forehead.

"*No*," I scream again. Something about the way she touches his hair. Our mother calls our father, who comes and scoops me up and starts out of the room with me, holding me like a live bomb. Before I go, I lock eyes with Carlton. He shrugs and says, "Night, man." Our father hustles me out. I do not take it bravely. I leave flailing, too furious to cry, dribbling a thread of spittle.

Later I lie alone on my narrow bed, feeling the music hum in the coiled springs. Life is cracking open right there in our house. People are changing. By tomorrow, no one will be quite the same. How can they let me miss it? I dream up revenge against our parents, and worse for Carlton. He is the one who could have saved me. He could have banded with me against them. What I can't forgive is his shrug, his mild-eyed "Night, man." He has joined the adults. He has made himself bigger and taken size from me. As the Doors thump "Strange Days," I hope something awful happens to him. I say so to myself.

Around midnight, dim-witted Frank announces he has seen a flying saucer hovering over the back yard. I can hear his deep, excited voice all the way in my room. He says it is like a blinking, luminous cloud. I hear half the party struggling out through the sliding glass door in a disorganized whooping knot. By that time everyone is so delirious a flying saucer would be just what was expected. That much celebration would logically attract an answering happiness from across the stars.

I get out of bed and sneak down the hall. I will not miss alien visitors for anyone, not even at the cost of our mother's wrath or our father's disappointment. I stop at the end of the hallway, though, embarrassed to be in pajamas. If there really are aliens, they will think I am the lowest member of the house. While I hesitate over whether to go back to my room to change, people start coming back inside, talking about a trick of the mist and an airplane. People resume their dancing.

Carlton must have jumped the back fence. He must have wanted to be there alone, singular, in case they decided to take somebody with them. A few nights later I will go out and stand where he could have been standing. On the far side of the gully, now a river swollen with melted snow, the cemetery will gleam like a lost city. The moon will be full. I will hang around just as Carlton must have, hypnotized by the silver light on the stones, the white angel raising her arms across the river.

According to our parents the mystery is why he ran back to the house full tilt. Something in the graveyard may have scared him, he may have needed to break its spell, but I think it's more likely that when he came back to himself he just couldn't wait to return to the music and the people, the noisy disorder of continuing life.

Somebody has shut the sliding glass door. Carlton's girlfriend looks lazily out, touching base with her own reflection. I look, too. Carlton is running toward the house. I hesitate. Then I figure he can bump his nose. It will be a good joke on him. I let him keep coming. His girlfriend sees him through her own reflection, starts to scream a warning just as Carlton hits the glass.

It is an explosion. Triangles of glass fly brightly through the room. I think that for him, it must be more surprising than painful, like hitting water from a great height. He stands blinking for a moment. The whole party stops, stares, getting its bearings. Bob Dylan sings "Just Like a Woman." Carlton reaches up curiously to take out the shard of glass that is stuck in his neck, and that is when the blood starts. It shoots out of him. Our mother screams. Carlton steps forward into his girlfriend's arms and the two of them fall together. Our mother throws herself down on top of him and the girl. People shout their accident wisdom. Don't lift him. Call an ambulance. I watch from the hallway. Carlton's blood spurts, soaking into the carpet, spattering people's clothes. Our mother and father both try to plug the wound with their hands, but the blood just shoots between their fingers. Carlton looks more puzzled than anything, as if he can't quite follow this turn of events. "It's all right," our father tells him, trying to stop the blood. "It's all right, just don't move, it's all right." Carlton nods, and holds our father's hand. His eyes take on an astonished light. Our mother screams, "Is anybody *doing* anything?" What comes out of Carlton grows darker, almost black. I watch. Our father tries to get a hold on Carlton's neck while Carlton keeps trying to take his hand. Our mother's hair is matted with blood. It runs down her face. Carlton's girl holds him to her breasts, touches his hair, whispers in his ear.

He is gone by the time the ambulance gets there. You can see the life drain out of him. When his face goes slack our mother wails. A part of her flies wailing through the house, where it will wail and rage forever. I feel our mother pass through me on her way out. She covers Carlton's body with her own.

He is buried in the cemetery out back. Years have passed—we are living in the future, and it has turned out differently from what we'd planned. Our mother has established her life of separateness behind the guest room door. Our father mutters his greetings to the door as he passes.

One April night, almost a year to the day after Carlton's accident, I hear cautious footsteps shuffling across the living room floor after midnight. I run out eagerly, thinking of ghosts, but find only our father in moth-colored pajamas. He looks unsteadily at the dark air in front of him.

"Hi, Dad," I say from the doorway.

He looks in my direction. "Yes?"

"It's me. Bobby."

"Oh, Bobby," he says. "What are you doing up, young man?"

"Nothing," I tell him. "Dad?"

"Yes, son."

"Maybe you better come back to bed. O.K.?"

"Maybe I had," he says. "I just came out here for a drink of water, but I seem to have gotten turned around in the darkness. Yes, maybe I better had."

I take his hand and lead him down the hall to his room. The grandfather clock chimes the quarter hour.

"Sorry," our father says.

I get him into bed. "There," I say. "O.K.?"

"Perfect. Could not be better."

"O.K. Good night."

"Good night. Bobby?"

"Uh-huh?"

"Why don't you stay a minute?" he says. "We could have ourselves a talk, you and me. How would that be?"

"O.K.," I say. I sit on the edge of his mattress. His bedside clock ticks off the minutes.

I can hear the low rasp of his breathing. Around our house, the Ohio night chirps and buzzes. The small gray finger of Carlton's stone pokes up among the others, within sight of the angel's white eyes. Above us, airplanes and satellites sparkle. People are flying even now toward New York or California, to take up lives of risk and invention.

I stay until our father has worked his way into a muttering sleep.

Carlton's girlfriend moved to Denver with her family a month before. I never learned what it was she'd whispered to him. Though she'd kept her head admirably during the accident, she lost it afterward. She cried so hard at the funeral that she had to be taken away by her mother—an older, redder-haired version of her. She started seeing a psychiatrist three times a week. Everyone, including my parents, talked about how hard it was for her, to have held a dying boy in her arms at that age. I'm grateful to her for holding my brother while he died, but I never once heard her mention the fact that though she had been through something terrible, at least she was still alive and going places. At least she had protected herself by trying to warn him. I can appreciate the intricacies of her pain. But as long as she was in Cleveland, I could never look her straight in the face. I couldn't talk about the wounds she suffered. I can't even write her name.

COMMUNIST

Richard Ford

My mother once had a boyfriend named Glen Baxter. This was in 1961. We—my mother and I—were living in the little house my father had left her up the Sun River, near Victory, Montana, west of Great Falls. My mother was thirty-two at the time. I was sixteen. Glen Baxter was somewhere in the middle, between us, though I cannot be exact about it.

We were living then off the proceeds of my father's life insurance policies, with my mother doing some part-time waitressing work up in Great Falls and going to the bars in the evenings, which I know is where she met Glen Baxter. Sometimes he would come back with her and stay in her room at night, or she would call up from town and explain that she was staying with him in his little place on Lewis Street by the GN yards. She gave me his number every time, but I never called it. I think she probably thought that what she was doing was terrible, but simply couldn't help herself. I thought it was all right, though. Regular life it seemed, and still does. She was young, and I knew that even then.

Glen Baxter was a Communist and liked hunting, which he talked about a lot. Pheasants. Ducks. Deer. He killed all of them, he said. He had been to Vietnam as far back as then, and when he was in our house he often talked about shooting the animals over there—monkeys and beautiful parrots—using military guns just for sport. We did not know what Vietnam was then, and Glen, when he talked about that, referred to it only as "the Far East." I think now he must've been in the CIA and been disillusioned by something he saw or found out about and been thrown out, but that kind of thing did not matter to us. He was a tall, dark-eyed man with short black hair, and was usually in a good humor. He had gone halfway through college in Peoria, Illinois, he said, where he grew up. But when he was around our life he worked wheat farms as a ditcher, and stayed out of work winters and in the bars drinking with women like my mother, who had work and some money. It is not an uncommon life to lead in Montana.

What I want to explain happened in November. We had not been seeing Glen Baxter for some time. Two months had gone by. My mother knew other men, but she came home most days from work and stayed inside watching television in her bedroom and drinking beers. I asked about Glen once, and she said only that she didn't know where he was, and I assumed they had had a fight and that he was gone off on a flyer back to Illinois or Massachusetts, where he said he had relatives. I'll admit that I liked him. He had something on his mind always. He was a labor man as well as a Communist, and liked to say that the country was poisoned by the rich, and strong men would need to bring it to life again, and I liked that because my father had been a labor man, which was why we had a house to live in and money coming through. It was also true that I'd had a few boxing bouts by then—just with town boys and one with an Indian from Choteau—and there were some girlfriends I knew from that. I did not like my mother being around the house so much at night, and I wished Glen Baxter would come back, or that another man would come along and entertain her somewhere else.

At two o'clock on a Saturday, Glen drove up into our yard in a car. He had had a big brown Harley-Davidson that he rode most of the year, in his black-and-red irrigators and a baseball cap turned backwards. But this time he had a car, a blue Nash Ambassador. My mother and I went out on the porch when he stopped inside the olive trees my father had planted as a shelter belt, and my mother had a look on her face of not much pleasure. It was starting to be cold in earnest by then. Snow was down already onto the Fairfield Bench, though on this day a chinook was blowing, and it could as easily have been spring, though the sky above the Divide was turning over in silver and blue clouds of winter.

"We haven't seen you in a long time, I guess," my mother said coldly.

"My little retarded sister died," Glen said, standing at the door of his old car. He was wearing his orange VFW jacket and canvas shoes we called wino shoes, something I had never seen him wear before. He seemed to be in a good humor. "We buried her in Florida near the home."

"That's a good place," my mother said in a voice that meant she was a wronged party in something.

"I want to take this boy hunting today, Aileen," Glen said. "There're snow geese down now. But we have to go right away, or they'll be gone to Idaho by tomorrow."

"He doesn't care to go," my mother said.

"Yes I do," I said, and looked at her.

My mother frowned at me. "Why do you?"

"Why does he need a reason?" Glen Baxter said and grinned.

"I want him to have one, that's why." She looked at me oddly. "I think Glen's drunk, Les."

"No, I'm not drinking," Glen said, which was hardly ever true. He looked at both of us, and my mother bit down on the side of her lower lip and stared at me in a way to make you think she thought something was being put over on her and she didn't like you for it. She was very pretty, though when she was mad her features were sharpened and less pretty by a long way. "All right, then I don't care," she said to no one in particular. "Hunt, kill, maim. Your father did that too." She turned to go back inside.

"Why don't you come with us, Aileen?" Glen was smiling still, pleased.

"To do what?" my mother said. She stopped and pulled a package of cigarettes out of her dress pocket and put one in her mouth.

"It's worth seeing."

"See dead animals?" my mother said.

"These geese are from Siberia, Aileen," Glen said. "They're not like a lot of geese. Maybe I'll buy us dinner later. What do you say?"

"Buy what with?" my mother said. To tell the truth, I didn't know why she was so mad at him. I would've thought she'd be glad to see him. But she just suddenly seemed to hate everything about him.

"I've got some money," Glen said. "Let me spend it on a pretty girl tonight."

"Find one of those and you're lucky," my mother said, turning away toward the front door.

"I already found one," Glen Baxter said. But the door slammed behind her, and he looked at me then with a look I think now was helplessness, though I could not see a way to change anything.

My mother sat in the backseat of Glen's Nash and looked out the window while we drove. My double gun was in the seat between us beside Glen's Belgian pump, which he kept loaded with five shells in case, he said, he saw something beside the road he wanted to shoot. I had hunted rabbits before, and had ground-sluiced pheasants and other birds, but I had never been on an actual hunt before, one where you drove out to some special place and did it formally. And I was excited. I had a feeling that something important was about to happen to me, and that this would be a day I would always remember.

My mother did not say anything for a long time, and neither did I. We drove up through Great Falls and out the other side toward Fort Benton, which was on the benchland where wheat was grown.

"Geese mate for life," my mother said, just out of the blue, as we were driving. "I hope you know that. They're special birds."

"I know that," Glen said in the front seat. "I have every respect for them."

"So where were you for three months?" she said. "I'm only curious."

"I was in the Big Hole for a while," Glen said, "and after that I went over to Douglas, Wyoming."

"What were you planning to do there?" my mother asked.

"I wanted to find a job, but it didn't work out."

"I'm going to college," she said suddenly, and this was something I had never heard about before. I turned to look at her, but she was staring out her window and wouldn't see me.

"I knew French once," Glen said. "*Rosé's* pink. *Rouge's* red." He glanced at me and smiled. "I think that's a wise idea, Aileen. When are you going to start?"

"I don't want Les to think he was raised by crazy people all his life," my mother said.

"Les ought to go himself," Glen said.

"After I go, he will."

"What do you say about that, Les?" Glen said, grinning.

"He says it's just fine," my mother said.

"It's just fine," I said.

Where Glen Baxter took us was out onto the high flat prairie that was disked for wheat and had high, high mountains out to the east, with lower heart-break hills in between. It was, I remember, a day for blues in the sky, and down in the distance we could see the small town of Floweree, and the state highway running past it toward Fort Benton and the Hi-line. We drove out on top of the prairie on a muddy dirt road fenced on both sides, until we had gone about three miles, which is where Glen stopped.

"All right," he said, looking up in the rearview mirror at my mother. "You wouldn't think there was anything here, would you?"

"*We're* here," my mother said. "You brought us here."

"You'll be glad though," Glen said, and seemed confident to me. I had looked around myself but could not see anything. No water or trees, nothing that seemed like a good place to hunt anything. Just wasted land. "There's a big lake out there, Les," Glen said. "You can't see it now from here because it's low. But the geese are there. You'll see."

"It's like the moon out here, I recognize that," my mother said, "only it's worse." She was staring out at the flat wheatland as if she could actually see something in particular, and wanted to know more about it. "How'd you find this place?"

"I came once on the wheat push," Glen said.

"And I'm sure the owner told you just to come back and hunt anytime you like and bring anybody you wanted. Come one, come all. Is that it?"

"People shouldn't own land anyway," Glen said. "Anybody should be able to use it."

"Les, Glen's going to poach here," my mother said. "I just want you to know that, because that's a crime and the law will get you for it. If you're a man now, you're going to have to face the consequences."

"That's not true," Glen Baxter said, and looked gloomily out over the steering wheel down the muddy road toward the mountains. Though for myself I believed it was true, and didn't care. I didn't care about anything at that moment except seeing geese fly over me and shooting them down.

"Well, I'm certainly not going out there," my mother said. "I like towns better, and I already have enough trouble."

"That's okay," Glen said. "When the geese lift up you'll get to see them. That's all I wanted. Les and me'll go shoot them, won't we, Les?"

"Yes," I said, and I put my hand on my shotgun, which had been my father's and was heavy as rocks.

"Then we should go on," Glen said, "or we'll waste our light."

We got out of the car with our guns. Glen took off his canvas shoes and put on his pair of black irrigators out of the trunk. Then we crossed the barbed wire fence, and walked out into the high, tilled field toward nothing. I looked back at my mother when we were still not so far away, but I could only see the small, dark top of her head, low in the backseat of the Nash, staring out and thinking what I could not then begin to say.

On the walk toward the lake, Glen began talking to me. I had never been alone with him, and knew little about him except what my mother said—that he drank too much, or other times that he was the nicest man she had ever known in the world and that someday a woman would marry him, though she didn't think it would be her. Glen told me as we walked that he wished he had finished college, but that it was too late now, that his mind was too old. He said he had liked the Far East very much, and that people there knew how to treat each other, and that he would go back some day but couldn't go now. He said also that he would like to live in Russia for a while and mentioned the names of people who had gone there, names I didn't know. He said it would be hard at first, because it was so different, but that pretty soon anyone would learn to like it and wouldn't want to live anywhere else, and that Russians treated Americans who came to live there like kings. There were Communists everywhere now, he said. You didn't know them, but they were there. Montana had a large number, and he was in touch with all of them. He said that Communists were always in danger and that he had to protect himself all the time. And when he said that he pulled back his VFW jacket and showed me the butt of a pistol he had stuck under his shirt against his bare skin. "There are people who want to kill me right now," he said, "and I would kill a man myself if I thought I had to." And we kept walking. Though in a while he said, "I don't think I know much about you, Les. But I'd like to. What do you like to do?"

"I like to box," I said. "My father did it. It's a good thing to know."

"I suppose you have to protect yourself too," Glen said.

"I know how to," I said.

"Do you like to watch TV," Glen asked, and smiled.

"Not much."

"I love to," Glen said. "I could watch it instead of eating if I had one."

I looked out straight ahead over the green tops of sage that grew to the edge of the disked field, hoping to see the lake Glen said was there. There was an airishness and a sweet smell that I thought might be the place we were going, but I couldn't see it. "How will we hunt these geese?" I said.

"It won't be hard," Glen said. "Most hunting isn't even hunting. It's only shooting. And that's what this will be. In Illinois you would dig holes in the ground and hide and set out your decoys. Then the geese come to you, over and over again. But we don't have time for that here." He glanced at me. "You have to be sure the first time here."

"How do you know they're here now," I asked. And I looked toward the Highwood Mountains twenty miles away, half in snow and half dark blue at the bottom. I could see the little town of Floweree then, looking shabby and dimly lighted in the distance. A red bar sign shone. A car moved slowly away from the scattered buildings.

"They always come November first," Glen said.

"Are we going to poach them?"

"Does it make any difference to you," Glen asked.

"No, it doesn't."

"Well then, we aren't," he said.

We walked then for a while without talking. I looked back once to see the Nash far and small in the flat distance. I couldn't see my mother, and I thought that she must've turned on the radio and gone to sleep, which she always did, letting it play all night in her bedroom. Behind the car the sun was nearing the rounded mountains southwest of us, and I knew that when the sun was gone it would be cold. I wished my mother had decided to come along with us, and I thought for a moment of how little I really knew her at all.

Glen walked with me another quarter-mile, crossed another barbed wire fence where sage was growing, then went a hundred yards through wheatgrass and spurge until the ground went up and formed a kind of long hillock bunker built by a farmer against the wind. And I realized the lake was just beyond us. I could hear the sound of a car horn blowing and a dog barking all the way down in the town, then the wind seemed to move and all I could hear then and after then were geese. So many geese, from the sound of them, though I still could not see even one. I stood and listened to the high-pitched shouting sound, a sound I had never heard so close, a sound with size to it—though it was not loud. A sound that meant great numbers and that made your chest rise and your shoulders tighten with expectancy. It was a sound to make you feel separate from it and everything else, as if you were of no importance in the grand scheme of things.

"Do you hear them singing," Glen asked. He held his hand up to make me stand still. And we both listened. "How many do you think, Les, just hearing?"

"A hundred," I said. "More than a hundred."

"Five thousand," Glen said. "More than you can believe when you see them. Go see."

I put down my gun and on my hands and knees crawled up the earthwork through the wheatgrass and thistle, until I could see down to the lake and see the geese. And they were there, like a white bandage laid on the water, wide and long and continuous, a white expanse of snow geese, seventy yards from me, on the bank, but stretching far onto the lake, which was large itself—a half-mile across, with thick tules on the far side and wild plums farther and the blue mountain behind them.

"Do you see the big raft?" Glen said from below me, in a whisper.

"I see it," I said, still looking. It was such a thing to see, a view I had never seen and have not since.

"Are any on the land?" he said.

"Some are in the wheatgrass," I said, "but most are swimming."

"Good," Glen said. "They'll have to fly. But we can't wait for that now."

And I crawled backwards down the heel of land to where Glen was, and my gun. We were losing our light, and the air was purplish and cooling. I looked toward the car but couldn't see it, and I was no longer sure where it was below the lighted sky.

"Where do they fly to?" I said in a whisper, since I did not want anything to be ruined because of what I did or said. It was important to Glen to shoot the geese, and it was important to me.

"To the wheat," he said. "Or else they leave for good. I wish your mother had come, Les. Now she'll be sorry."

I could hear the geese quarreling and shouting on the lake surface. And I wondered if they knew we were here now. "She might be," I said with my heart pounding, but I didn't think she would be much.

It was a simple plan he had. I would stay behind the bunker, and he would crawl on his belly with his gun through the wheatgrass as near to the geese as he could. Then he would simply stand up and shoot all the ones he could close up, both in the air and on the ground. And when all the others flew up, with luck some would turn toward me as they came into the wind, and then I could shoot them and turn them back to him, and he would shoot them again. He could kill ten, he said, if he was lucky, and I might kill four. It didn't seem hard.

"Don't show them your face," Glen said. "Wait till you think you can touch them, then stand up and shoot. To hesitate is lost in this."

"All right," I said. "I'll try it."

"Shoot one in the head, and then shoot another one," Glen said. "It won't be hard." He patted me on the arm and smiled. Then he took off his VFW jacket and put it on the ground, climbed up the side of the bunker, cradling his shotgun in his arms, and slid on his belly into the dry stalks of yellow grass out of my sight.

Then, for the first time in that entire day, I was alone. And I didn't mind it. I sat squat down in the grass, loaded my double gun and took my other two shells out of my pocket to hold. I pushed the safety off and on to see that it was right. The wind rose a little, scuffed the grass and made me shiver. It was not the warm chinook now, but a wind out of the north, the one geese flew away from if they could.

Then I thought about my mother, in the car alone, and how much longer I would stay with her, and what it might mean to her for me to leave. And I wondered when Glen Baxter would die and if someone would kill him, or whether my mother would marry him and how I would feel about it. And though I didn't know why, it occurred to me that Glen Baxter and I would not be friends when all was said and done, since I didn't care if he ever married my mother or didn't.

Then I thought about boxing and what my father had taught me about it. To tighten your fists hard. To strike out straight from the shoulder and never punch backing up. How to cut a punch by snapping your fist inwards, how to carry your chin low, and to step toward a man when he is falling so you can hit him again. And most important, to keep your eyes open when you are hitting in the face and causing damage, because you need to see what you're doing to encourage yourself, and because it is when you close your eyes that you stop hitting and get hurt badly. "Fly all over your man, Les," my father said. "When you see your chance, fly on him and hit him till he falls." That, I thought, would always be my attitude in things.

And then I heard the geese again, their voices in unison, louder and shouting, as if the wind had changed again and put all new sounds in the cold air. And then a *boom*. And I knew Glen was in among them and had stood up to shoot. The noise of geese rose and grew worse, and my fingers burned where I held my gun too tight to the metal, and I put it down and opened my fist to make the burning stop so I could feel the trigger when the moment came. *Boom*, Glen shot again, and I heard him shuck a shell, and all the sounds out beyond the bunker seemed to be rising—the geese, the shots, the air itself going up. *Boom*, Glen shot another time, and I knew he was taking his careful time to make his shots good. And I held my gun and started to crawl up the bunker so as not to be surprised when the geese came over me and I could shoot.

From the top I saw Glen Baxter alone in the wheatgrass field, shooting at a white goose with black tips of wings that was on the ground not far from him, but trying to run and pull into the air. He shot it once more, and it fell over dead with its wings flapping.

Glen looked back at me and his face was distorted and strange. The air around him was full of white rising geese and he seemed to want them all. "Behind you, Les," he yelled at me and pointed. "They're all behind you now." I looked behind me, and there were geese in the air as far as I could see, more than I knew how many, moving so slowly, their wings wide out and working calmly and filling the air with noise, though their voices were not as loud or as shrill as I had thought they would be. And they were so close! Forty feet, some of them. The air around me vibrated and I could feel the wind from their wings and it seemed to me I could kill as many as the times I could shoot—a hundred or a thousand—and I raised my gun, put the muzzle on the head of a white goose, and fired. It shuddered in the air, its wide feet sank below its belly, its wings cradled out to hold back air, and it fell straight down and landed with an awful sound, a noise a human would make, a thick, soft, *hump* noise. I looked up again and shot another goose, could hear the pellets hit its chest, but it didn't fall or even break its pattern for flying. *Boom*, Glen shot again. And then again. "Hey," I heard him shout, "Hey, hey." And there were geese flying over me, flying in line after line. I broke my gun and reloaded, and thought to myself as I did: I need confidence here, I need to be sure with this. I pointed at another goose and shot it in the head, and it fell the way the first one had, wings out, its belly down, and with the same thick noise of hitting. Then I sat down in the grass on the bunker and let geese fly over me.

By now the whole raft was in the air, all of it moving in a slow swirl above me and the lake and everywhere, finding the wind and heading out south in long wavering lines that caught the last sun and turned to silver as they gained a distance. It was a thing to see, I will tell you now. Five thousand white geese all in the air around you, making a noise like you have never heard before. And I thought to myself then: this is something I will never see again. I will never forget this. And I was right.

Glen Baxter shot twice more. One he missed, but with the other he hit a goose flying away from him, and knocked it half falling and flying into the empty lake not far from shore, where it began to swim as though it was fine and make its noise.

Glen stood in the stubby grass, looking out at the goose, his gun lowered. "I didn't need to shoot that one, did I, Les?"

"I don't know," I said, sitting on the little knoll of land, looking at the goose swimming in the water.

"I don't know why I shoot 'em. They're so beautiful." He looked at me.

"I don't know either," I said.

"Maybe there's nothing else to do with them." Glen stared at the goose again and shook his head. "Maybe this is exactly what they're put on earth for."

I did not know what to say because I did not know what he could mean by that, though what I felt was embarrassment at the great numbers of geese there were, and a dulled feeling like a hunger because the shooting had stopped and it was over for me now.

Glen began to pick up his geese, and I walked down to my two that had fallen close together and were dead. One had hit with such an impact that its stomach had split and some of its inward parts were knocked out. Though the other looked unhurt, its soft white belly turned up like a pillow, its head and jagged bill-teeth, its tiny black eyes looking as they would if they were alive.

"What's happened to the hunters out here?" I heard a voice speak. It was my mother, standing in her pink dress on the knoll above us, hugging her arms. She was smiling though she was cold. And I realized that I had lost all thought of her in the shooting. "Who did all this shooting? Is this your work, Les?"

"No," I said.

"Les is a hunter, though, Aileen," Glen said. "He takes his time." He was holding two white geese by their necks, one in each hand, and he was smiling. He and my mother seemed pleased.

"I see you didn't miss too many," my mother said and smiled. I could tell she admired Glen for his geese, and that she had done some thinking in the car alone. "It *was* wonderful, Glen," she said. "I've never seen anything like that. They were like snow."

"It's worth seeing once, isn't it?" Glen said. "I should've killed more, but I got excited."

My mother looked at me then. "Where's yours, Les?"

"Here," I said and pointed to my two geese on the ground beside me.

My mother nodded in a nice way, and I think she liked everything then and wanted the day to turn out right and for all of us to be happy. "Six, then. You've got six in all."

"One's still out there," I said, and motioned where the one goose was swimming in circles on the water.

"Okay," my mother said and put her hand over her eyes to look. "Where is it?"

Glen Baxter looked at me then with a strange smile, a smile that said he wished I had never mentioned anything about the other goose. And I wished I hadn't either. I looked up in the sky and could see the lines of geese by the thousands shining silver in the light, and I wished we could just leave and go home.

"That one's my mistake there," Glen Baxter said and grinned. "I shouldn't have shot that one, Aileen. I got too excited."

My mother looked out on the lake for a minute, then looked at Glen and back again. "Poor goose." She shook her head. "How will you get it, Glen?"

"I can't get that one now," Glen said.

My mother looked at him. "What do you mean?"

"I'm going to leave that one," Glen said.

"Well, no. You can't leave one," my mother said. "You shot it. You have to get it. Isn't that a rule?"

"No," Glen said.

And my mother looked from Glen to me. "Wade out and get it, Glen," she said in a sweet way, and my mother looked young then, like a young girl, in her flimsy short-sleeved waitress dress and her skinny, bare legs in the wheatgrass.

"No." Glen Baxter looked down at his gun and shook his head. And I didn't know why he wouldn't go, because it would've been easy. The lake was shallow. And you could tell that anyone could've walked out a long way before it got deep, and Glen had on his boots.

My mother looked at the white goose, which was not more than thirty yards from the shore, its head up, moving in slow circles, its wings settled and relaxed so you could see the black tips. "Wade out and get it, Glenny, won't you, please?" she said. "They're special things."

"You don't understand the world, Aileen," Glen said. "This can happen. It doesn't matter."

"But that's so cruel, Glen," she said, and a sweet smile came on her lips.

"Raise up your own arms, 'Leeny," Glen said. "I can't see any angel's wings, can you, Les?" He looked at me, but I looked away.

"Then you go on and get it, Les," my mother said. "You weren't raised by crazy people." I started to go, but Glen Baxter suddenly grabbed me by my shoulder and pulled me back hard, so hard his fingers made bruises in my skin that I saw later.

"Nobody's going," he said. "This is over with now."

And my mother gave Glen a cold look then. "You don't have a heart, Glen," she said. "There's nothing to love in you. You're just a son of a bitch, that's all."

And Glen Baxter nodded at my mother, then, as if he understood something he had not understood before, but something that he was willing to know. "Fine," he said, "that's fine." And he took his big pistol out from against his belly, the big blue revolver I had only seen part of before and that he said protected him, and he pointed it out at the goose on the water, his arm straight away from him, and shot and missed. And then he shot and missed again. The goose made its noise once. And then he hit it dead, because there was no splash. And then he shot it three times more until the gun was empty and the goose's head was down and it was floating toward the middle of the lake where it was empty and dark blue. "Now who has a heart?" Glen said. But my mother was not there when he turned around. She had already started back to the car and was almost lost from sight in the darkness. And Glen smiled at me then and his face had a wild look on it. "Okay, Les?" he said.

"Okay," I said.

"There're limits to everything, right?"

"I guess so," I said.

"Your mother's a beautiful woman, but she's not the only beautiful woman in Montana." And I did not say anything. And Glen Baxter suddenly said, "Here," and he held the pistol out at me. "Don't you want this? Don't you want to shoot me? Nobody thinks they'll die. But I'm ready for it right now." And I did not know what to do then. Though it is true that what I wanted to do was to hit him, hit him as hard in the face as I could, and see him on the ground bleeding and crying and pleading for me to stop. Only at that moment he looked scared to me, and I had never seen a grown man scared before—though I have seen one since—and I felt sorry for him, as though he was already a dead man. And I did not end up hitting him at all.

A light can go out in the heart. All of this happened years ago, but I still can feel now how sad and remote the world was to me. Glen Baxter, I think now, was not a bad man, only a man scared of something he'd never seen before—something soft in himself—his life going a way he didn't like. A woman with a son. Who could blame him there? I don't know what makes people do what they do, or call themselves what they call themselves, only that you have to live someone's life to be the expert.

My mother had tried to see the good side of things, tried to be hopeful in the situation she was handed, tried to look out for us both, and it hadn't worked. It was a strange time in her life then and after that, a time when she had to adjust to being an adult just when she was on the thin edge of things. Too much awareness too early in life was her problem, I think.

And what I felt was only that I had somehow been pushed out into the world, into the real life then, the one I hadn't lived yet. In a year I was gone to hard-rock mining and no-paycheck jobs and not to college. And I have thought more than once about my mother saying that I had not been raised by crazy people, and I don't know what that could mean or what difference it could make, unless it means that love is a reliable commodity, and even that is not always true, as I have found out.

Late on the night that all this took place I was in bed when I heard my mother say, "Come outside, Les. Come and hear this." And I went out onto the front porch barefoot and in my underwear, where it was warm like spring, and there was a spring mist in the air. I could see the lights of the Fairfield Coach in the distance, on its way up to Great Falls.

And I could hear geese, white birds in the sky, flying. They made their high-pitched sound like angry yells, and though I couldn't see them high up, it seemed to me they were everywhere. And my mother looked up and said, "Hear them?" I could smell her hair wet from the shower. "They leave with the moon," she said. "It's still half wild out here."

And I said, "I hear them," and I felt a chill come over my bare chest, and the hair stood up on my arms the way it does before a storm. And for a while we listened.

"When I first married your father, you know, we lived on a street called Bluebird Canyon, in California. And I thought that was the prettiest street and the prettiest name. I suppose no one brings you up like your first love. You don't mind if I say that, do you?" She looked at me hopefully.

"No," I said.

"We have to keep civilization alive somehow." And she pulled her little housecoat together because there was a cold vein in the air, a part of the cold that would be on us the next day. "I don't feel part of things tonight, I guess."

"It's all right," I said.

"Do you know where I'd like to go?"

"No," I said. And I suppose I knew she was angry then, angry with life, but did not want to show me that.

"To the Straits of Juan de Fuca. Wouldn't that be something? Would you like that?"

"I'd like it," I said. And my mother looked off for a minute, as if she could see the Straits of Juan de Fuca out against the line of mountains, see the lights of things alive and a whole new world.

"I know you liked him," she said after a moment. "You and I both suffer fools too well."

"I didn't like him too much," I said. "I didn't really care."

"He'll fall on his face. I'm sure of that," she said. And I didn't say anything because I didn't care about Glen Baxter anymore, and was happy not to talk about him. "Would you tell me something if I asked you? Would you tell me the truth?"

"Yes," I said.

And my mother did not look at me. "Just tell the truth," she said.

"All right," I said.

"Do you think I'm still very feminine? I'm thirty-two years old now. You don't know what that means. But do you think I am?"

And I stood at the edge of the porch, with the olive trees before me, looking straight up into the mist where I could not see geese but could still hear them flying, could almost feel the air move below their white wings. And I felt the way you feel when you are on a trestle all alone and the train is coming, and you know you have to decide. And I said, "Yes, I do." Because that was the truth. And I tried to think of something else then and did not hear what my mother said after that.

And how old was I then? Sixteen. Sixteen is young, but it can also be a grown man. I am forty-one years old now, and I think about that time without regret, though my mother and I never talked in that way again, and I have not heard her voice now in a long, long time.

CRAZY, CRAZY, NOW SHOWING EVERYWHERE

Ellen Gilchrist

IT is fall again, or what passes for fall in Alexandria. Sultry October days that drift into a brief wet winter without even changing the leaves on the trees.

I sit here two blocks from Fanny's house, gazing out my window. I sit here nearly every afternoon, listening to jazz on the radio, waiting for Duncan to come home and ruin my day. And two blocks away his revered ideal idol, Fanny's husband, Gabe, Gabe Yellin, the gorgeous ageless archconservative, by which means he means with Duncan's help to conserve whatever made and keeps him a millionaire, Greedy Gabe, as Fanny calls him, her stormtrooper, lugs his briefcase up her stairs and hands her the pills.

And no one knows and no one wants to know and no one wants to talk about it anymore. There is nothing anyone can do, they say. No one can help her unless she helps herself. It's nice of you to be concerned, Lilly. It's nice of you to care. It's nice of you to visit her.

"Twin beds," Fanny is saying. "Twin beds all over the house. Darling, when I first met those people, when Gabe took me to visit them, I thought they must be real old. I didn't know married people slept in twin beds. I thought to myself, what is the matter with these people?"

She is talking about my in-laws. That's what Fanny and I do when I visit. We say terrible things about my in-laws and her in-laws and my husband and her husband and Yellin-Kase, the water heater factory that makes us all that dough. Yellin-Kase, The World's Largest Manufacturer Of Water Heaters.

At the moment Fanny and I are working over my mother-in-law. "I kept looking around the house for evidence of life," she is saying. "For something that wasn't put away. It was all put away. It was all in cabinets. Even the pillows had these plastic covers. We spent the night, and I said, Gabe, can I take the cover off the pillow while I sleep? Of course, that was the beginning, when they had just begun the factory. When it was all a dream. But she had money, your mother-in-law. Even then. But it was put away. Everything was put away."

"Look at her sons," I say. "Donny has ulcers, Jerry has asthma and Duncan's practically impotent. The perfect mother. They kiss without touching. I swear they do. I never saw such armor."

"Hush," Fanny says. "You know this room is bugged." She laughs her wonderful laugh, wishing it really were.

"I forgot," I say in a whisper, laughing back into her beautiful ruined face, hypnotized by her great black eyes, her musical voice, forgetting she is crazy, forgetting I am crazy to be there.

I am seated on a soft flowered chair, my feet propped up on her bed. I have been for a walk in the park and stopped by for a cup of chicory coffee and cookies from the tall glass jars on the nightstand. Who else but Fanny keeps Oreos and Lorna Doones and Hershey's Kisses out in the open for anyone to see? Usually I do not sit in the chair. Usually I get my cookies and jump right into bed, kiss her soft welcoming cheeks, hold her in my arms. But today the bed is full of dogs. There are six or seven of them, spaniels and terriers and Irish setters.

"Goddamn these dogs," I say. One of them is licking me.

"Bribe them," she says. "They can be bribed." I take dog biscuits from the package she hands me and lead them out into the hall.

"Go for a walk with me," I say, returning to the room. "It's a glorious day. You can't afford to miss this day."

"I can see it," she says. "It's outside the windows. I've been watching it."

"Aren't you ever going to leave the room again?"

"Oh, I go down to dinner. I go nearly every evening. It's the new game. We have dinner. Then we have dessert."

"Who cooks now?"

"Gabe does. Since his cook died." Everything is his with Fanny. His house, his children, his dogs, his factory, his game. Only the room is hers. "Or we send out for things. It doesn't matter. It's all right, Lilly. I know what I'm doing."

"You don't know what you're doing." I stand up, starting to walk around the room. "You can't take those pills without seeing a psychiatrist."

"He goes for me. I told you all about it. I told Treadway that if he liked me so much he could just come over here and see me. I was tired of going over there. Get dressed. Get in the car. Go see Treadway. Come back home." She laughed, falling back against the pillows. "Now Gabe goes. They're crazy about each other. They give each other things. Gabe gives him money and he gives Gabe pills." She looked away.

"I'm sorry. I don't mean to make you unhappy. I know what you're afraid of. I just don't like the idea of you staying here forever taking those pills. . . ."

"They'll lock me up again if I don't take them."

"They can't lock you up unless you let them. There's a new law. Oh, God, Fanny, why won't you believe me? Or go to a good psychiatrist and believe him. There are good psychiatrists. They aren't all like Treadway. They don't lock people up anymore."

"You don't understand," she says. "You just don't understand."

I am staring at the open drawer of the nightstand. The drawer is always open, the bottles are always there for us to see, Elavil and Stelazine and lithium. Her little maids, she calls them. They travel day and night around her bloodstream, destroying the muscles, doing God knows what to the liver and kidney and spleen, to the will and desire and ambition and rage. Not the intelligence. Her intelligence is beyond the reach of chemicals. Who knows? Perhaps she is right to believe this bed, these pills, this childlike life are her only refuge.

"Oh, Fanny, I love you," I say, knocking the dogs off the bed, for they have come back in, cuddling up in her arms. This morning light is pouring in the tall windows of the famous room.

"I will save you," she says. "I will save you if I can. I cannot bear it if they have you too."

It is Friday, the worst day of my week. On Friday nights we dine with Duncan's family. Two black women cook all afternoon in the Kases' kitchen, making stuffed artichokes and oyster soup and rack of lamb and au gratin potatoes and creamed spinach, setting the long table with finger bowls and heavy silver and crystal wineglasses.

At six-thirty we assemble in the den, all the Kase sons and their wives. We talk about taxes and crime and corruption and society people who are deadbeats or hippies or drunks. I do not speak of Mrs. Kase's sister's suicide. They do not speak of my childlessness.

At seven one of the black women calls us to dinner and we file into the dining room and light the Sabbath candles.

"I saw Fanny today," I say. "She looks wonderful. She's the wisest person I've ever known."

"I'm glad to hear that," my father-in-law says. "That's nice."

"It's criminal what Gabe is doing to her," I say. "I think all the time about reporting him to the police."

"It's such a shame," my mother-in-law says, not daring to tell me to shut up.

My father-in-law sighs and attends to the lamb. Gabe is his business partner in the factory. My husband, Duncan, is third in command, the golden boy, the one they hope can hold it all together. They think of themselves as being in a state of siege, from the government and its meddling, from the labor unions' constant attempts to unionize the plant, from competitors in other states and foreign countries. It is hard staying rich. At any moment it could all fall apart. Meanwhile, their alliance is all that holds it together.

"She must have been beautiful when she was young," I say. "The paintings De Laureal did of her are wonderful. She put them back up. Did I tell you that?"

"That's nice," Mrs. Kase says. "It's such a shame what Gabe's been through."

"She's the one to pity," I say. "She might have been a great artist. She's the one to feel sorry for."

Duncan coughs, gets up, and starts pouring the Bordeaux. His mother and father exchange a long look.

"What in the world does Fanny say to Lilly?" the Yellins ask each other.

"What on earth is Lilly telling Fanny?" the Kases sigh.

"*You are next*," Fanny said to me the night we met. "Come to see me. Come right away. *I will save you if I can. You have to come to see me.*"

That was the night I met her, a New Year's Eve, the year I married Duncan for his money and came to live in Alexandria. I am from Monroe. My parents are school-teachers. I thought I would have a more exotic life. I was raised to worship money. I was raised to get money any way I could. I met Duncan at Tulane. He couldn't even ask me to marry him without asking his parents' permission. I married him in spite of that. I married him to have his money. Now I have to pay for that. I have to pay and pay and pay. I am a cliché. Except for Fanny. She makes my life different from the lives around me.

That New Year's Eve I was wearing a black and white satin evening suit I ordered from a magazine. My hair was long and loose and shiny. I was Duncan's dream girl that winter, his bride, and he was taking me around to pay New Year's duty calls.

Fanny still went downstairs back then. She was seated on a loveseat before the fireplace watching her youngest son roast chestnuts. She was wearing a wrinkled red silk dress and her legs were folded under her. No stockings, no shoes. She looked up at me, smiling a wonderful mysterious smile. She was the most interesting person I had ever met. I sat down beside her and told her anything she wanted to know, drinking martinis as fast as Gabe could bring them from the kitchen.

"I've just come home from Mandeville," she said. She was laughing, holding my hand. "You know, the Loony Bin."

"Oh, sure," I said. Of course I had not known. I had never known anyone who had been locked up for being crazy.

"It's wonderful," she said. "I never wanted to leave. I made a lot of friends."

"We have to be going, Lilly," Duncan said. "Mother wants us to go to the Durnings' with them."

"Come back," Fanny said, still holding on to my hand. "Promise you'll come. Promise you'll visit me *every* New Year's Eve of your life."

I promised. How could I stay away?

That was the year she painted the room, the famous, much talked about room, her "madness museum," as she called it.

"Crazy, Crazy, Now Showing Everywhere," it said on the door in two-inch letters.

Below that, in God forgive me, *my* handwriting, "Lilly says, spit in one hand and worry in the other and see which one fills up the fastest." She *made* me write it there. At that time, the first year I knew her, the year she was painting the room, you had to be very careful what you said around her as she might seize on *anything* and make you write it on the wall.

From the door the mural spread inward onto the four walls of the high-ceilinged, rectangular room. Water colors, crayons, oils, acrylics, long sections marked "Conspiracies" and "Swindles," names and dates and anecdotes from her fifty years' war with the wealthy Jewish world into which she was born.

There were crossword puzzles made of jargon cut from newspapers. WHOSE LIFE IS IT ANYWAY was glued to a chair. There were quotations from thick books on psychiatry. The east wall was devoted to R. D. Laing. The floor was littered with paintbrushes and jars of paint and hundreds of Marks-A-Lot pens.

All this frightened me, but I could not stay away. Fanny's room was the most exciting place in Alexandria. Anyone was likely to be there, a museum director, a painter, a journalist, a poet, one of her former inmates from Mandeville, visitors from New Orleans.

Sometimes I would not see her for weeks. Then, suddenly, there would be her voice on the phone, soft, conspiratorial. "Hurry," she would say. "Come as soon as he leaves for work. I have a present for you. Please come. I need you."

I would go. It was impossible to stay away. She would be waiting, propped up in bed cutting words and slogans from magazines and newspapers. "My work," she called it. "I have to find the words, when I find the right words I will expose them. You'll see. I will have it all out in the open where everyone can see. Then they will not be able to deny it. Then everyone will know."

She would be working away, a music box playing her favorite song over and over. "Raindrops Keep Falling on My Head," that was the one she liked that year.

"Look," she said one morning, taking a jeweler's box out from underneath a pillow, putting it into my hand. "Keep this. In case you need to call me."

I opened it and found a beautiful pearl and diamond earring, just one. She showed me how to twist the pearl that hung like a drop from a diamond stem. "Just turn it," she said. "Like this. I'll hear you. No matter where I am I'll hear you."

"Sure," I said, going along with the joke.

"Tell me what's going on," she said. "What are those Kase people doing to you?"

"Oh, nothing. Everything's fine. I'm going to take some classes this fall, maybe go into the real estate business with Duncan's cousin. I'm fine. I'm getting used to being here. It's fine. I'm starting to like it here."

"You're going to be the scapegoat," she said. "They are going to use you for the scapegoat. They can't forgive you for being pretty. You know that, don't you?"

"Oh, it's not like that. I knew what I was getting into. I met them before I married him. I knew what it was going to be like."

"Be careful, Lilly, they are going to eat you alive."

"It's not like that. It isn't that bad. When I get worried I just go to the park and run as fast as I can."

"Write it down," she said, handing me a pen. "Here, take this. Write it on the wall."

"Oh, no, I don't want to write it."

"Write, 'When I worry I run as fast as I can.' Please write it. Please write it down for me." I took the pen and wrote it on the wall beside the door. It seemed like a perfectly reasonable thing to say until she made me write it down.

That spring, that April, that May, were bad times in both our lives. I played tennis all day long. She worked on the room.

"The black apes are on their way," she told me one morning on the phone. "They leave messages on my easel. I have put my paints away. Now it must all be in words. You have to help me, Lilly. You have to bring me words."

"Are you spitting out the pills?" I said. At that time I believed they were good for her. "Don't spit out the pills. Please don't spit out the pills."

"I have to," she said. "Gabe is after me to sign papers again. They are bringing me papers to sign. Will you come to me? Will you come this morning?"

"I don't know. I have to play tennis. I have to play tennis every day this week."

"Please come," she said. "And bring me words. I need more words. I need all the words I can get."

She was too crazy for me that summer. I stayed away. I was trying to make my marriage work. I decorated the house, studied recipe books, had dinner parties, worked on my body. I had recurrent dreams about Fanny. I dreamed we were on a sailboat in the islands, sailing through clear blue Caribbean waters. I was at the tiller and Fanny was tied to the mast so she couldn't fall overboard. We sailed and sailed, laughing and talking, drinking endless cups of coffee. The journey was pleasant and I was happy at the tiller, but *I did not know where we were going.*

There was a destination, someplace I was supposed to deliver her to but she could not tell me where it was. I sailed to port after port but no one was waiting on the piers or they would not let us disembark. At the end of the dream I thought I saw our harbor in the distance and I set the sails and started for it through an open sea.

Then slowly, terribly, great whales began to surface before the prow. Great, brown whales rising up like uncharted shoals all around us. They wore harnesses around their bellies. They had riders. The black apes of Fanny's terrors were riding them. I would wake covered with sweat, shaking and terrified, determined to stay away from her.

Duncan and I went off to the real Caribbean in July. While I was gone Fanny finished the room and moved out into the hall and bathroom.

"Oh, did you ever see the bathroom?" she said to me later. "Oh, I could never make it again. I painted on the bathtub, on the toilet, on the washstand, on the floor. 'Oh, dear, we have to lock Mother up again,' I heard Gloria saying.

"You should have seen the tub. They could not deny it now. Now they knew what they were doing. I had dumped the whole thing in their laps. They bought off Clark. They bought off Treadway. But I showed them. They had no way of not knowing anymore. 'Oh, dear, we have to lock poor old Mother up again,' Gloria said. 'Oh, dear, oh dear.' "

The day before they came to get her she wrote MURDER over the bed in three-foot letters.

"Gibberish," Doctor Treadway said when he saw it.

"Generalities," Gabe added. And as soon as Fanny was safely back in Mandeville he called the painters. They painted the room light blue with white trim. How could I have stopped them? I was sailing from Petit Saint Vincent to Mustique, locked up on a fifty-foot sailboat watching Duncan drink beer and brood over the unions and the government coming to take his money away.

"Oh, I could never make the room again," she said the other day, safe at home once more, safe in the arms of her wonderful keepers, Stelazine and lithium and Elavil. The little bottles standing guard beside her bed, the little maids. The room is so clean and cheerful, there is a blue silk quilt on the bed, a clean rug on the floor. The paintings are hanging on the wall, the dresser drawers are shut, the books are on the shelves.

"I would have photographed it. If I had been here I would have stopped him. I can't believe he let them paint it all away."

"Here," she said, taking a sketch pad from a drawer beside the bed. "This is what I'm doing now. I'm going to play their game. I'm going to put them on paper and have them framed and nail nails into the wall and hang them up. That's what they told me at the Loony Bin. You have to play their game. That's the new idea. So I played their game. And now I'm home. Here, look at what I'm doing." She opened the pad. It was a scale drawing of her house, everything very precise like an architect's sketch. In front of the house were seven garbage cans, all in a row with the tops down nice and tight. "I'm going to do a series of these drawings," she said. "Won't they love it when they see it? Won't Gabe be surprised?"

"Oh, God, you're so subtle," I said. I gave her a kiss. "I have to get home now. I have to go cook dinner. I'll see you soon. I'll talk to you later."

"Bring me a present," she said. "Bring me words. I need some words. I want you to bring me words every day this week."

What words would I take her? What words could set her free? Could words undo the words that put her there? *Love is all you need.* I could tell her what the Beatles say. *Hey, Jude, don't be afraid. I want to hold your hand. Remember to let it out of your head.*

I could tear in there some morning and drag her out of bed and put her into the car and start driving. I would drive northwest into the mountains. I would drive all night. I would go up into the mountains until we were at fourteen thousand feet. I would make her get out and look at where she was. *Think how far she would see. How far I would see.*

"You're crazy," Duncan says. "You're as crazy as she is to even go over there, Lilly. There's nothing anyone can do. She's a pain in the ass, that's what she is. A terrible embarrassment. No one makes her stay in that room. No one makes her take those pills. Now quit worrying about it. Quit talking about it all the time."

"You're wrong," I say. "It's Gabe. It's his fault. He gives her the pills. He hands them to her. He's the one that does it."

"They do it together, Lilly. It's their life. It's what they do. It's what they like to do. Mind your own business, would you? Stop driving me crazy with this nonsense."

I go out and sit on the front steps. It's a beautiful old neighborhood, especially this time of year, in early fall. It's almost dark now, first dark, dusk some people call it. I like to sit here this time of day, watching the jays and nightjars fight above the city roofs, turning and swooping and diving, calling, caw, caw, caw, calling good news, good news, good news, calling hunger, hunger, hunger.

413

HOW TO TALK TO A HUNTER

Pam Houston

When he says "Skins or blankets?" it will take you a moment to realize that he's asking which you want to sleep under. And in your hesitation he'll decide that he wants to see your skin wrapped in the big black moose hide. He carried it, he'll say, soaking wet and heavier than a dead man, across the tundra for two—was it hours or days or weeks? But the payoff, now, will be to see it fall across one of your white breasts. It's December, and your skin is never really warm, so you will pull the bulk of it around you and pose for him, pose for his camera, without having to narrate this moose's death.

You will spend every night in this man's bed without asking yourself why he listens to top-forty country. Why he donated money to the Republican Party. Why he won't play back his messages while you are in the room. You are there so often the messages pile up. Once you noticed the bright green counter reading as high as fifteen.

He will have lured you here out of a careful independence that you spent months cultivating; though it will finally be winter, the dwindling daylight and the threat of Christmas, that makes you give in. Spending nights with this man means suffering the long face of your sheepdog, who likes to sleep on your bed, who worries when you don't come home. But the hunter's house is so much warmer than yours, and he'll give you a key, and just like a woman, you'll think that means something. It will snow hard for thirteen straight days. Then it will really get cold. When it is sixty below there will be no wind and no clouds, just still air and cold sunshine. The sun on the windows will lure you out of bed, but he'll pull you back under. The next two hours he'll devote to your body. With his hands, with his tongue, he'll express what will seem to you like the most eternal of loves. Like the house key, this is just another kind of lie. Even in bed; especially in bed, you and he cannot speak the same language. The machine will answer the incoming calls. From under an ocean of passion and hide and hair you'll hear a woman's muffled voice between the beeps.

Your best female friend will say, "So what did you think? That a man who sleeps under a dead moose is capable of commitment?"

This is what you learned in college: A man desires the satisfaction of his desire; a woman desires the condition of desiring.

The hunter will talk about spring in Hawaii, summer in Alaska. The man who says he was always better at math will form the sentences so carefully it will be impossible to tell if you are included in these plans. When he asks you if you would like to open a small guest ranch way out in the country, understand that this is a rhetorical question. Label these conversations future perfect, but don't expect the present to catch up with them. Spring is an inconceivable distance from the December days that just keep getting shorter and gray.

He'll ask you if you've ever shot anything, if you'd like to, if you ever thought about teaching your dog to retrieve. Your dog will like him too much, will drop the stick at his feet every time, will roll over and let the hunter scratch his belly.

One day he'll leave you sleeping to go split wood or get the mail and his phone will ring again. You'll sit very still while a woman who calls herself something like Janie Coyote leaves a message on his machine: She's leaving work, she'll say, and the last thing she wanted to hear was the sound of his beautiful voice. Maybe she'll talk only in rhyme. Maybe the counter will change to sixteen. You'll look a question at the mule deer on the wall, and the dark spots on either side of his mouth will tell you he shares more with this hunter than you ever will. One night, drunk, the hunter told you he was sorry for taking that deer, that every now and then there's an animal that isn't meant to be taken, and he should have known that deer was one.

Your best male friend will say, "No one who needs to call herself Janie Coyote can hold a candle to you, but why not let him sleep alone a few nights, just to make sure?"

The hunter will fill your freezer with elk burger, venison sausage, organic potatoes, fresh pecans. He'll tell you to wear your seat belt, to dress warmly, to drive safely. He'll say you are always on his mind, that you're the best thing that's ever happened to him, that you make him glad that he's a man.

Tell him it don't come easy, tell him freedom's just another word for nothing left to lose.

These are the things you'll know without asking: The coyote woman wears her hair in braids. She uses words like "howdy." She's man enough to shoot a deer.

A week before Christmas you'll rent *It's a Wonderful Life* and watch it together, curled on your couch, faces touching. Then you'll bring up the word "monogamy." He'll tell you how badly he was hurt by your predecessor. He'll tell you he couldn't be happier spending every night with you. He'll say there's just a few questions he doesn't have the answers for.

He'll say he's just scared and confused. Of course this isn't exactly what he means. Tell him you understand. Tell him you are scared too. Tell him to take all the time he needs. Know that you could never shoot an animal; and be glad of it.

Your best female friend will say, "You didn't tell him you loved him, did you?" Don't even tell her the truth. If you do you'll have to tell her that he said this: "I feel exactly the same way."

Your best male friend will say, "Didn't you know what would happen when you said the word 'commitment'?"
But that isn't the word that you said.
He'll say, "Commitment, monogamy, it all means just one thing."
The coyote woman will come from Montana with the heavier snows. The hunter will call you on the day of the solstice to say he has a friend in town and can't see you. He'll leave you hanging your Christmas lights; he'll give new meaning to the phrase "longest night of the year." The man who has said he's not so good with words will manage to say eight things about his friend without using a gender-determining pronoun. Get out of the house quickly. Call the most understanding person you know who will let you sleep in his bed.

Your best female friend will say, "So what did you think? That he was capable of living outside his gender?"

When you get home in the morning there's a candy tin on your pillow. Santa, obese and grotesque, fondles two small children on the lid. The card will say something like "From your not-so-secret admirer." Open it. Examine each carefully made truffle. Feed them, one at a time, to the dog. Call the hunter's machine. Tell him you don't speak chocolate.

Your best female friend will say, "At this point, what is it about him that you could possibly find appealing?"

Your best male friend will say, "Can't you understand that this is a good sign? Can't you understand that this proves how deep he's in with you?" Hug your best male friend. Give him the truffles the dog wouldn't eat.

Of course the weather will cooperate with the coyote woman. The highways will close, she will stay another night. He'll tell her he's going to work so he can come and see you. He'll even leave her your number and write "Me at Work" on the yellow pad of paper by his phone. Although you shouldn't, you'll have to be there. It will be you and your nauseous dog and your half-trimmed tree all waiting for him like a series of questions.

This is what you learned in graduate school: In every assumption is contained the possibility of its opposite.

In your kitchen he'll hug you like you might both die there. Sniff him for coyote. Don't hug him back.

He will say whatever he needs to to win. He'll say it's just an old friend. He'll say the visit was all the friend's idea. He'll say the night away from you has given him time to think about how much you mean to him. Realize that nothing short of sleeping alone will ever make him realize how much you mean to him. He'll say that if you can just be a little patient, some good will come out of this for the two of you after all. He still won't use a gender-specific pronoun.

Put your head in your hands. Think about what it means to be patient. Think about the beautiful, smart, strong, clever woman you thought he saw when he looked at you. Pull on your hair. Rock your body back and forth. Don't cry.

He'll say that after holding you it doesn't feel right holding anyone else. For "holding," substitute "fucking." Then take it as a compliment.

He will get frustrated and rise to leave. He may or may not be bluffing. Stall for time. Ask a question he can't immediately answer. Tell him you want to make love on the floor. When he tells you your body is beautiful say, "I feel exactly the same way." Don't, under any circumstances, stand in front of the door.

Your best female friend will say, "They lie to us, they cheat on us, and we love them more for it." She'll say, "It's our fault; we raise them to be like that."

Tell her it can't be your fault. You've never raised anything but dogs.

The hunter will say it's late and he has to go home to sleep. He'll emphasize the last word in the sentence. Give him one kiss that he'll remember while he's fucking the coyote woman. Give him one kiss that ought to make him cry if he's capable of it, but don't notice when he does. Tell him to have a good night.

Your best male friend will say, "We all do it. We can't help it. We're self-destructive. It's the old bad-boy routine. You have a male dog, don't you?"

The next day the sun will be out and the coyote woman will leave. Think about how easy it must be for a coyote woman and a man who listens to top-forty country. The coyote woman would never use a word like "monogamy"; the coyote woman will stay gentle on his mind.

If you can, let him sleep alone for at least one night. If you can't, invite him over to finish trimming your Christmas tree. When he asks how you are, tell him you think it's a good idea to keep your sense of humor during the holidays.

Plan to be breezy and aloof and full of interesting anecdotes about all the other men you've ever known. Plan to be hotter than ever before in bed, and a little cold out of it. Remember that necessity is the mother of invention. Be flexible.

First, he will find the faulty bulb that's been keeping all the others from lighting. He will explain, in great detail, the most elementary electrical principles. You will take turns placing the ornaments you and other men, he and other women, have spent years carefully choosing. Under the circumstances, try to let this be a comforting thought.

He will thin the clusters of tinsel you put on the tree. He'll say something ambiguous like "Next year you should string popcorn and cranberries." Finally, his arm will stretch just high enough to place the angel on the top of the tree.

Your best female friend will say, "Why can't you ever fall in love with a man who will be your friend?"

Your best male friend will say, "You ought to know this by now: Men always cheat on the best women."

This is what you learned in the pop psychology book: Love means letting go of fear.

Play Willie Nelson's "Pretty Paper." He'll ask you to dance, and before you can answer he'll be spinning you around your wood stove, he'll be humming in your ear. Before the song ends he'll be taking off your clothes, setting you lightly under the tree, hovering above you with tinsel in his hair. Through the spread of the branches the all-white lights you insisted on will shudder and blur, outlining the ornaments he brought: a pheasant, a snow goose, a deer.

The record will end. Above the crackle of the wood stove and the rasp of the hunter's breathing you'll hear one long low howl break the quiet of the frozen night: your dog, chained and lonely and cold. You'll wonder if he knows enough to stay in his doghouse. You'll wonder if he knows that the nights are getting shorter now.

SHILOH

Bobbie Ann Mason

Leroy Moffitt's wife, Norma Jean, is working on her pectorals. She lifts three-pound dumbbells to warm up, then progresses to a twenty-pound barbell. Standing with her legs apart, she reminds Leroy of Wonder Woman.

"I'd give anything if I could just get these muscles to where they're real hard," says Norma Jean. "Feel this arm. It's not as hard as the other one."

"That's 'cause you're right-handed," says Leroy, dodging as she swings the barbell in an arc.

"Do you think so?"

"Sure."

Leroy is a truckdriver. He injured his leg in a highway accident four months ago, and his physical therapy, which involves weights and a pulley, prompted Norma Jean to try building herself up. Now she is attending a body-building class. Leroy has been collecting temporary disability since his tractor-trailer jackknifed in Missouri, badly twisting his left leg in its socket. He has a steel pin in his hip. He will probably not be able to drive his rig again. It sits in the backyard, like a gigantic bird that has flown home to roost. Leroy has been home in Kentucky for three months, and his leg is almost healed, but the accident frightened him and he does not want to drive any more long hauls. He is not sure what to do next. In the meantime, he makes things from craft kits. He started by building a miniature log cabin from notched Popsicle sticks. He varnished it and placed it on the TV set, where it remains. It reminds him of a rustic Nativity scene. Then he tried string art (sailing ships on black velvet), a macramé owl kit, a snap-together B-17 Flying Fortress, and a lamp made out of a model truck, with a light fixture screwed in the top of the cab. At first the kits were diversions, something to kill time, but now he is thinking about building a full-scale log house from a kit. It would be considerably cheaper than building a regular house, and besides, Leroy has grown to appreciate how things are put together. He has begun to realize that in all the years he was on the road he never took time to examine anything. He was always flying past scenery.

"They won't let you build a log cabin in any of the new subdivisions," Norma Jean tells him.

"They will if I tell them it's for you," he says, teasing her. Ever since they were married, he has promised Norma Jean he would build her a new home one day. They have always rented, and the house they live in is small and nondescript. It does not even feel like a home, Leroy realizes now.

Norma Jean works at the Rexall drugstore, and she has acquired an amazing amount of information about cosmetics. When she explains to Leroy the three stages of complexion care; involving creams, toners, and moisturizers, he thinks happily of other petroleum products—axle grease, diesel fuel. This is a connection between him and Norma Jean. Since he has been home, he has felt unusually tender about his wife and guilty over his long absences. But he can't tell what she feels about him. Norma Jean has never complained about his traveling; she has never made hurt re-marks, like calling his truck a "widow-maker." He is reasonably certain she has been faithful to him, but he wishes she would celebrate his perma-nent homecoming more happily. Norma Jean is often startled to find Leroy at home, and he thinks she seems a little disappointed about it. Per-haps he reminds her too much of the early days of their marriage, before he went on the road. They had a child who died as an infant, years ago. They never speak about their memories of Randy, which have almost faded, but now that Leroy is home all the time, they sometimes feel awk-ward around each other, and Leroy wonders if one of them should men-tion the child. He has the feeling that they are waking up out of a dream together—that they must create a new marriage, start afresh. They are lucky they are still married. Leroy has read that for most people losing a child destroys the marriage—or else he heard this on *Donahue*. He can't always remember where he learns things anymore.

At Christmas, Leroy bought an electric organ for Norma Jean. She used to play the piano when she was in high school. "It don't leave you," she told him once. "It's like riding a bicycle."

The new instrument had so many keys and buttons that she was be-wildered by it at first. She touched the keys tentatively, pushed some but-tons, then pecked out "Chopsticks." It came out in an amplified fox-trot rhythm, with marimba sounds.

"It's an orchestra!" she cried.

The organ had a pecan-look finish and eighteen preset chords, with optional flute, violin, trumpet, clarinet, and banjo accompaniments. Norma Jean mastered the organ almost immediately. At first she played Christmas songs. Then she bought *The Sixties Songbook* and learned every tune in it, adding variations to each with the rows of brightly colored but-tons.

"I didn't like these old songs back then," she said. "But I have this crazy feeling I missed something."

"You didn't miss a thing," said Leroy.

Leroy likes to lie on the couch and smoke a joint and listen to Norma Jean play "Can't Take My Eyes Off You" and "I'll Be Back." He is back again. After fifteen years on the road, he is finally settling down with the woman he loves. She is still pretty. Her skin is flawless. Her frosted curls resemble pencil trimmings.

Now that Leroy has come home to stay, he notices how much the town has changed. Subdivisions are spreading across western Kentucky like an oil slick. The sign at the edge of town says "Pop: 11,500"—only seven hundred more than it said twenty years before. Leroy can't figure out who is living in all the new houses. The farmers who used to gather around the courthouse square on Saturday afternoons to play checkers and spit tobacco juice have gone. It has been years since Leroy has thought about the farmers, and they have disappeared without his noticing.

Leroy meets a kid named Stevie Hamilton in the parking lot at the new shopping center. While they pretend to be strangers meeting over a stalled car, Stevie tosses an ounce of marijuana under the front seat of Leroy's car. Stevie is wearing orange jogging shoes and a T-shirt that says CHATTAHOOCHEE SUPER-RAT. His father is a prominent doctor who lives in one of the expensive subdivisions in a new white-columned brick house that looks like a funeral parlor. In the phone book under his name there is a separate number, with the listing "Teenagers."

"Where do you get this stuff?" asks Leroy. "From your pappy?"

"That's for me to know and you to find out," Stevie says. He is slit-eyed and skinny.

"What else you got?"

"What you interested in?"

"Nothing special. Just wondered."

Leroy used to take speed on the road. Now he has to go slowly. He needs to be mellow. He leans back against the car and says, "I'm aiming to build me a log house, soon as I get time. My wife, though, I don't think she likes the idea."

"Well, let me know when you want me again," Stevie says. He has a cigarette in his cupped palm, as though sheltering it from the wind. He takes a long drag, then stomps it on the asphalt and slouches away.

Stevie's father was two years ahead of Leroy in high school. Leroy is thirty-four. He married Norma Jean when they were both eighteen, and their child Randy was born a few months later, but he died at the age of four months and three days. He would be about Stevie's age now. Norma Jean and Leroy were at the drive-in, watching a double feature (*Dr. Strangelove* and *Lover Come Back*), and the baby was sleeping in the back seat. When the first movie ended, the baby was dead. It was the sudden infant death syndrome. Leroy remembers handing Randy to a nurse at the emergency room, as though he were offering her a large doll as a present. A dead baby feels like a sack of flour. "It just happens sometimes," said the doctor, in what Leroy always recalls as a nonchalant tone. Leroy can hardly remember the child anymore, but he still sees vividly a scene from *Dr. Strangelove* in which the President of the United States was talking in a folksy voice on the hot line to the Soviet premier about the bomber accidentally headed toward Russia. He was in the War Room, and the world map was lit up. Leroy remembers Norma Jean standing catatonically beside him in the hospital and himself thinking: Who is this strange girl? He had forgotten who she was. Now scientists are saying that crib death is caused by a virus. Nobody knows anything, Leroy thinks. The answers are always changing.

When Leroy gets home from the shopping center, Norma Jean's mother, Mabel Beasley, is there. Until this year, Leroy has not realized how much time she spends with Norma Jean. When she visits, she inspects the closets and then the plants, informing Norma Jean when a plant is droopy or yellow. Mabel calls the plants "flowers," although there are never any blooms. She always notices if Norma Jean's laundry is piling up. Mabel is a short, overweight woman whose tight, brown-dyed curls look more like a wig than the actual wig she sometimes wears. Today she has brought Norma Jean an off-white dust ruffle she made for the bed; Mabel works in a custom-upholstery shop.

"This is the tenth one I made this year," Mabel says. "I got started and couldn't stop."

"It's real pretty," says Norma Jean.

"Now we can hide things under the bed," says Leroy, who gets along with his mother-in-law primarily by joking with her. Mabel has never really forgiven him for disgracing her by getting Norma Jean pregnant. When the baby died, she said that fate was mocking her.

"What's that thing?" Mabel says to Leroy in a loud voice, pointing to a tangle of yarn on a piece of canvas.

Leroy holds it up for Mabel to see. "It's my needlepoint," he explains. "This is a *Star Trek* pillow cover."

"That's what a woman would do," says Mabel. "Great day in the morning!"

"All the big football players on TV do it," he says.

"Why, Leroy, you're always trying to fool me. I don't believe you for one minute. You don't know what to do with yourself—that's the whole trouble. Sewing!"

"I'm aiming to build us a log house," says Leroy, "Soon as my plans come."

"Like *heck* you are," says Norma Jean. She takes Leroy's needlepoint and shoves it into a drawer. "You have to find a job first. Nobody can afford to build now anyway."

Mabel straightens her girdle and says, "I still think before you get tied down y'all ought to take a little run to Shiloh."

"One of these days, Mama," Norma Jean says impatiently.

Mabel is talking about Shiloh, Tennessee. For the past few years, she has been urging Leroy and Norma Jean to visit the Civil War battleground there. Mabel went there on her honeymoon—the only real trip she ever took. Her husband died of a perforated ulcer when Norma Jean was ten, but Mabel, who was accepted into the United Daughters of the Confederacy in 1975, is still preoccupied with going back to Shiloh.

"I've been to kingdom come and back in that truck out yonder," Leroy says to Mabel, "but we never yet set foot in that battleground. Ain't that something? How did I miss it?"

"It's not even that far," Mabel says.

After Mabel leaves, Norma Jean reads to Leroy from a list she has made. "Things you could do," she announces. "You could get a job as a guard at Union Carbide, where they'd let you set on a stool. You could get on at the lumberyard. You could do a little carpenter work, if you want to build so bad. You could—"

"I can't do something where I'd have to stand up all day."

"You ought to try standing up all day behind a cosmetics counter. It's amazing that I have strong feet, coming from two parents that never had strong feet at all." At the moment Norma Jean is holding on to the kitchen counter, raising her knees one at a time as she talks. She is wearing two-pound ankle weights.

"Don't worry," says Leroy. "I'll do something."

"You could truck calves to slaughter for somebody. You wouldn't have to drive any big old truck for that."

"I'm going to build you this house," says Leroy. "I want to make you a real home."

"I don't want to live in any log cabin."

"It's not a cabin. It's a house."

"I don't care. It looks like a cabin."

"You and me together could lift those logs. It's just like lifting weights."

Norma Jean doesn't answer. Under her breath, she is counting. Now she is marching through the kitchen. She is doing goose steps.

Before his accident, when Leroy came home he used to stay in the house with Norma Jean, watching TV in bed and playing cards. She would cook fried chicken, picnic ham, chocolate pie—all his favorites. Now he is home alone much of the time. In the mornings, Norma Jean disappears, leaving a cooling place in the bed. She eats a cereal called Body Buddies, and she leaves the bowl on the table, with the soggy tan balls floating in a milk puddle. He sees things about Norma Jean that he never realized before. When she chops onions, she stares off into a corner, as if she can't bear to look. She puts on her house slippers almost precisely at nine o'clock every evening and nudges her jogging shoes under the couch. She saves bread heels for the birds. Leroy watches the birds at the feeder. He notices the peculiar way goldfinches fly past the window. They close their wings, then fall, then spread their wings to catch and lift themselves. He wonders if they close their eyes when they fall. Norma Jean closes her eyes when they are in bed. She wants the lights turned out. Even then, he is sure she closes her eyes.

He goes for long drives around town. He tends to drive a car rather carelessly. Power steering and an automatic shift make a car feel so small and inconsequential that his body is hardly involved in the driving process. His injured leg stretches out comfortably. Once or twice he has almost hit something, but even the prospect of an accident seems minor in a car. He cruises the new subdivisions, feeling like a criminal rehearsing for a robbery. Norma Jean is probably right about a log house being inappropriate here in the new subdivisions. All the houses look grand and complicated. They depress him.

One day when Leroy comes home from a drive he finds Norma Jean in tears. She is in the kitchen making a potato and mushroom-soup casserole, with grated-cheese topping. She is crying because her mother caught her smoking.

"I didn't hear her coming. I was standing here puffing away pretty as you please," Norma Jean says, wiping her eyes.

"I knew it would happen sooner or later," says Leroy, putting his arm around her.

"She don't know the meaning of the word 'knock,'" says Norma Jean. "It's a wonder she hadn't caught me years ago."

"Think of it this way," Leroy says. "What if she caught me with a joint?"

"You better not let her!" Norma Jean shrieks. "I'm warning you, Leroy Moffitt!"

"I'm just kidding. Here, play me a tune. That'll help you relax."

Norma Jean puts the casserole in the oven and sets the timer. Then she plays a ragtime tune, with horns and banjo, as Leroy lights up a joint and lies on the couch, laughing to himself about Mabel's catching him at it. He thinks of Stevie Hamilton—a doctor's son pushing grass. Everything is funny. The whole town seems crazy and small. He is reminded of Virgil Mathis, a boastful policeman Leroy used to shoot pool with. Virgil recently led a drug bust in a back room at a bowling alley, where he seized ten thousand dollars' worth of marijuana. The newspaper had a picture of him holding up the bags of grass and grinning widely. Right now, Leroy can imagine Virgil breaking down the door and arresting him with a lungful of smoke. Virgil would probably have been alerted to the scene because of all the racket Norma Jean is making. Now she sounds like a hard-rock band. Norma Jean is terrific. When she switches to a Latin-rhythm version of "Sunshine Superman," Leroy hums along. Norma Jean's foot goes up and down, up and down.

"Well, what do you think?" Leroy says, when Norma Jean pauses to search through her music.

"What do I think about what?"

His mind has gone blank. Then he says, "I'll sell my rig and build us a house." That wasn't what he wanted to say. He wanted to know what she thought—what she *really* thought—about them.

"Don't start in on that again," says Norma Jean. She begins playing "Who'll Be the Next in Line?"

Leroy used to tell hitchhikers his whole life story—about his travels, his hometown, the baby. He would end with a question: "Well, what do you think?" It was just a rhetorical question. In time, he had the feeling that he'd been telling the same story over and over to the same hitchhikers. He quit talking to hitchhikers when he realized how his voice sounded—whining and self-pitying, like some teenage-tragedy song. Now Leroy has the sudden impulse to tell Norma Jean about himself, as if he had just met her. They have known each other so long they have forgotten a lot about each other. They could become reacquainted. But when the oven timer goes off and she runs to the kitchen, he forgets why he wants to do this.

The next day, Mabel drops by. It is Saturday and Norma Jean is cleaning. Leroy is studying the plans of his log house, which have finally come in the mail. He has them spread out on the table—big sheets of stiff blue paper, with diagrams and numbers printed in white. While Norma Jean runs the vacuum, Mabel drinks coffee. She sets her coffee cup on a blueprint.

"I'm just waiting for time to pass," she says to Leroy, drumming her fingers on the table.

As soon as Norma Jean switches off the vacuum, Mabel says in a loud voice, "Did you hear about the datsun dog that killed the baby?"

Norma Jean says, "The word is 'dachshund.'"

"They put the dog on trial. It chewed the baby's legs off. The mother was in the next room all the time." She raises her voice. "They thought it was neglect."

Norma Jean is holding her ears. Leroy manages to open the refrigerator and get some Diet Pepsi to offer Mabel. Mabel still has some coffee and she waves away the Pepsi.

"Datsuns are like that," Mabel says. "They're jealous dogs. They'll tear a place to pieces if you don't keep an eye on them."

"You better watch out what you're saying, Mabel," says Leroy.

"Well, facts is facts."

Leroy looks out the window at his rig. It is like a huge piece of furniture gathering dust in the backyard. Pretty soon it will be an antique. He hears the vacuum cleaner. Norma Jean seems to be cleaning the living room rug again.

Later, she says to Leroy, "She just said that about the baby because she caught me smoking. She's trying to pay me back."

"What are you talking about?" Leroy says, nervously shuffling blueprints.

"You know good and well," Norma Jean says. She is sitting in a kitchen chair with her feet up and her arms wrapped around her knees. She looks small and helpless. She says, "The very idea, her bringing up a subject like that! Saying it was neglect."

"She didn't mean that," Leroy says.

"She might not have *thought* she meant it. She always says things like that. You don't know how she goes on."

"But she didn't really mean it. She was just talking."

Leroy opens a king-sized bottle of beer and pours it into two glasses, dividing it carefully. He hands a glass to Norma Jean and she takes it from him mechanically. For a long time, they sit by the kitchen window watching the birds at the feeder.

Something is happening. Norma Jean is going to night school. She has graduated from her six-week body-building course and now she is taking an adult-education course in composition at Paducah Community College. She spends her evenings outlining paragraphs.

"First you have a topic sentence," she explains to Leroy. "Then you divide it up. Your secondary topic has to be connected to your primary topic."

To Leroy, this sounds intimidating. "I never was any good in English," he says.

"It makes a lot of sense."

"What are you doing this for, anyhow?"

She shrugs. "It's something to do." She stands up and lifts her dumbbells a few times.

"Driving a rig, nobody cared about my English."

"I'm not criticizing your English."

Norma Jean used to say, "If I lose ten minutes' sleep, I just drag all day." Now she stays up late, writing compositions. She got a B on her first paper—a how-to theme on soup-based casseroles. Recently Norma Jean has been cooking unusual foods—tacos, lasagna, Bombay chicken. She doesn't play the organ anymore, though her second paper was called "Why Music Is Important to Me." She sits at the kitchen table, concentrating on her outlines, while Leroy plays with his log house plans, practicing with a set of Lincoln Logs. The thought of getting a truckload of notched, numbered logs scares him, and he wants to be prepared. As he and Norma Jean work together at the kitchen table, Leroy has the hopeful thought that they are sharing something, but he knows he is a fool to think this. Norma Jean is miles away. He knows he is going to lose her. Like Mabel, he is just waiting for time to pass.

One day, Mabel is there before Norma Jean gets home from work, and Leroy finds himself confiding in her. Mabel, he realizes, must know Norma Jean better than he does.

"I don't know what's got into that girl," Mabel says. "She used to go to bed with the chickens. Now you say she's up all hours. Plus her a-smoking. I like to died."

"I want to make her this beautiful home," Leroy says, indicating the Lincoln Logs. "I don't think she even wants it. Maybe she was happier with me gone."

"She don't know what to make of you, coming home like this."

"Is that it?"

Mabel takes the roof off his Lincoln Log cabin. "You couldn't get *me* in a log cabin," she says: "I was raised in one. It's no picnic, let me tell you."

"They're different now," says Leroy.

"I tell you what," Mabel says, smiling oddly at Leroy.

"What?"

"Take her on down to Shiloh. Y'all need to get out together, stir a little. Her brain's all balled up over them books."

Leroy can see traces of Norma Jean's features in her mother's face. Mabel's worn face has the texture of crinkled cotton, but suddenly she looks pretty. It occurs to Leroy that Mabel has been hinting all along that she wants them to take her with them to Shiloh.

"Let's all go to Shiloh," he says. "You and me and her. Come Sunday."

Mabel throws up her hands in protest. "Oh, no, not me. Young folks want to be by theirselves."

When Norma Jean comes in with groceries, Leroy says excitedly, "Your mama here's been dying to go to Shiloh for thirty-five years. It's about time we went, don't you think?"

"I'm not going to butt in on anybody's second honeymoon," Mabel says.

"Who's going on a honeymoon, for Christ's sake?" Norma Jean says loudly.

"I never raised no daughter of mine to talk that-a-way," Mabel says.

"You ain't seen nothing yet," says Norma Jean. She starts putting away boxes and cans, slamming cabinet doors.

"There's a log cabin at Shiloh," Mabel says. "It was there during the battle. There's bullet holes in it."

"When are you going to *shut up* about Shiloh, Mama?" asks Norma Jean.

"I always thought Shiloh was the prettiest place, so full of history," Mabel goes on. "I just hoped y'all could see it once before I die, so you could tell me about it." Later, she whispers to Leroy, "You do what I said. A little change is what she needs."

"Your name means 'the king,'" Norma Jean says to Leroy that evening. He is trying to get her to go to Shiloh, and she is reading a book about another century.

"Well, I reckon I ought to be right proud."

"I guess so."

"Am I still king around here?"

Norma Jean flexes her biceps and feels them for hardness. "I'm not fooling around with anybody, if that's what you mean," she says.

"Would you tell me if you were?"

"I don't know."

"What does *your* name mean?"

"It was Marilyn Monroe's real name."

"No kidding!"

"Norma comes from the Normans. They were invaders," she says. She closes her book and looks hard at Leroy. "I'll go to Shiloh with you if you'll stop staring at me."

On Sunday, Norma Jean packs a picnic and they go to Shiloh. To Leroy's relief, Mabel says she does not want to come with them. Norma Jean drives, and Leroy, sitting beside her, feels like some boring hitchhiker she has picked up. He tries some conversation, but she answers him in monosyllables. At Shiloh, she drives aimlessly through the park, past bluffs and trails and steep ravines. Shiloh is an immense place, and Leroy cannot see it as a battleground. It is not what he expected. He thought it would look like a golf course. Monuments are everywhere, showing through the thick clusters of trees. Norma Jean passes the log cabin Mabel mentioned. It is surrounded by tourists looking for bullet holes.

"That's not the kind of log house I've got in mind," says Leroy apologetically.

"I know *that.*"

"This is a pretty place. Your mama was right."

"It's O.K.," says Norma Jean. "Well, we've seen it. I hope she's satisfied."

They burst out laughing together.

At the park museum, a movie on Shiloh is shown every half hour, but they decide that they don't want to see it. They buy a souvenir Confederate flag for Mabel, and then they find a picnic spot near the cemetery. Norma Jean has brought a picnic cooler, with pimiento sandwiches, soft drinks, and Yodels. Leroy eats a sandwich and then smokes a joint, hiding it behind the picnic cooler. Norma Jean has quit smoking altogether. She is picking cake crumbs from the cellophane wrapper, like a fussy bird.

Leroy says, "So the boys in gray ended up in Corinth. The Union soldiers zapped 'em finally. April 7, 1862."

They both know that he doesn't know any history. He is just talking about some of the historical plaques they have read. He feels awkward, like a boy on a date with an older girl. They are still just making conversation.

"Corinth is where Mama eloped to," says Norma Jean.

They sit in silence and stare at the cemetery for the Union dead and, beyond, at a tall cluster of trees. Campers are parked nearby, bumper to bumper, and small children in bright clothing are cavorting and squealing. Norma Jean wads up the cake wrapper and squeezes it tightly in her hand. Without looking at Leroy, she says, "I want to leave you."

Leroy takes a bottle of Coke out of the cooler and flips off the cap. He holds the bottle poised near his mouth but cannot remember to take a drink. Finally he says, "No, you don't."

"Yes, I do."

"I won't let you."

"You can't stop me."

"Don't do me that way."

Leroy knows Norma Jean will have her own way. "Didn't I promise to be home from now on?" he says.

"In some ways, a woman prefers a man who wanders," says Norma Jean. "That sounds crazy, I know."

"You're not crazy."

Leroy remembers to drink from his Coke. Then he says, "Yes, you *are* crazy. You and me could start all over again. Right back at the beginning."

"We *have* started all over again," says Norma Jean. "And this is how it turned out."

"What did I do wrong?"

"Nothing."

"Is this one of those women's lib things?" Leroy asks.

"Don't be funny."

The cemetery, a green slope dotted with white markers, looks like a subdivision site. Leroy is trying to comprehend that his marriage is breaking up, but for some reason he is wondering about white slabs in a graveyard.

"Everything was fine till Mama caught me smoking," says Norma Jean, standing up. "That set something off."

"What are you talking about?"

"She won't leave me alone—*you* won't leave me alone." Norma Jean seems to be crying, but she is looking away from him. "I feel eighteen again. I can't face that all over again." She starts walking away. "No, it *wasn't* fine. I don't know what I'm saying. Forget it."

Leroy takes a lungful of smoke and closes his eyes as Norma Jean's words sink in. He tries to focus on the fact that thirty-five hundred soldiers died on the grounds around him. He can only think of that war as a board game with plastic soldiers. Leroy almost smiles, as he compares the Confederates' daring attack on the Union camps and Virgil Mathis's raid on the bowling alley. General Grant, drunk and furious, shoved the Southerners back to Corinth, where Mabel and Jet Beasley were married years later, when Mabel was still thin and good-looking. The next day, Mabel and Jet visited the battleground, and then Norma Jean was born, and then she married Leroy and they had a baby, which they lost, and now Leroy and Norma Jean are here at the same battleground. Leroy knows he is leaving out a lot. He is leaving out the insides of history. History was always just names and dates to him. It occurs to him that building a house out of logs is similarly empty—too simple. And the real inner workings of a marriage, like most of history, have escaped him. Now he sees that building a log house is the dumbest idea he could have had. It was clumsy of him to think Norma Jean would want a log house. It was a crazy idea. He'll have to think of something else, quickly. He will wad the blueprints into tight balls and fling them into the lake. Then he'll get moving again. He opens his eyes. Norma Jean has moved away and is walking through the cemetery, following a serpentine brick path.

Leroy gets up to follow his wife, but his good leg is asleep and his bad leg still hurts him. Norma Jean is far away, walking rapidly toward the bluff by the river, and he tries to hobble toward her. Some children run past him, screaming noisily. Norma Jean has reached the bluff, and she is looking out over the Tennessee River. Now she turns toward Leroy and waves her arms. Is she beckoning to him? She seems to be doing an exercise for her chest muscles. The sky is unusually pale—the color of the dust ruffle Mabel made for their bed.

FIVE POINTS

Alice Munro

While they drink vodka and orange juice in the trailer park on the cliffs above Lake Huron, Neil Bauer tells Brenda a story. It happened a long way away, in Victoria, British Columbia, where Neil grew up. Neil is not much younger than Brenda—less than three years—but it sometimes feels to her like a generation gap, because she grew up here, and stayed here, marrying Cornelius Zendt when she was twenty years old, and Neil grew up on the West Coast, where things were very different, and he left home at sixteen to travel and work all over.

What Brenda has seen of Victoria, in pictures, is flowers and horses. Flowers spilling out of baskets hanging from old-fashioned lampposts, filling grottoes and decorating parks; horses carrying wagonloads of people to look at the sights.

"That's all just tourist shit," Neil says. "About half the place is nothing but tourist shit. That's not where I'm talking about."

He is talking about Five Points, which was—is—a section, or maybe just a corner, of the city, where there was a school and a drugstore and a Chinese grocery and a candy store. When Neil was in public school, the candy store was run by a grouchy old woman with painted-on eyebrows. She used to let her cat sprawl in the sun in the window. After she died, some new people, Europeans, not Poles or Czechs but from some smaller country—Croatia; is that a country?—took over the candy store and changed it. They cleared out all the stale candy and the balloons that wouldn't blow up and the ballpoint pens that wouldn't write and the dead Mexican jumping beans. They painted the place top to bottom and put in a few chairs and tables. They still sold candy—in clean jars now, instead of cat-pissed cardboard boxes—and rulers and erasers. But they also started to operate as a kind of neighborhood café, with coffee and soft drinks and homemade cakes.

The wife, who made the cakes, was very shy and fussy, and if you came up and tried to pay her she would call for her husband in Croatian, or whatever—let's say it was Croatian—in such a startled way you'd think that you'd broken into her house and interrupted her private life. The husband spoke English pretty well. He was a little bald guy, polite and nervous, a chain-smoker, and she was a big, heavy woman with bent shoulders, always wearing an apron and a cardigan sweater. He washed the windows and swept off the sidewalk and took the money, and she baked the buns and cakes and made things that people had never seen before but that quickly became popular, like pierogi and poppy-seed loaf.

Their two daughters spoke English just like Canadians, and went to the convent school. They showed up in their school uniforms in the late afternoon and got right to work. The younger one washed the coffee cups and glasses and wiped the tables, and the older one did everything else. She waited on customers, worked the cash register, filled the trays, and shooed away the little kids who were hanging around not buying anything. When the younger one finished washing up, she would sit in the back room doing her homework, but the older one never sat down. If there was nothing to do at the moment, she just stood by the cash register, watching.

The younger one was called Lisa, the older one Maria. Lisa was small and nice enough looking—just a little kid. But Maria, by the age of maybe thirteen, had big, saggy breasts and a rounded-out stomach and thick legs. She wore glasses, and her hair was done in braids around her head. She looked about fifty years old.

And she acted it, the way she took over the store. Both parents seemed willing to take a back seat to her. The mother retreated to the back room, and the father became a handyman-helper. Maria understood English and money and wasn't fazed by anything. All the little kids said, "Ugh, that Maria—isn't she *gross?*" But they were scared of her. She looked like she already knew all about running a business.

Brenda and her husband also run a business. They bought a farm just south of Logan and filled the barn with used appliances (which Cornelius knows how to fix) and secondhand furniture and all the other things—the dishes, pictures, knives and forks and ornaments and jewelry—that people like to poke through and think they're buying cheap. It's called Zendt's Furniture Barn. Locally, a lot of people refer to it as the Used Furniture on the Highway.

They didn't always do this. Brenda used to teach nursery school, and Cornelius, who is twelve years older than she is, worked in the salt mine at Walley, on the lake. After his accident they had to think of something he could do sitting down most of the time, and they used the money they got to buy a worn-out farm with good buildings. Brenda quit her job, because there was too much for Cornelius to handle by himself. There are hours in the day and sometimes whole days when he has to lie down and watch television, or just lie on the living room floor, coping with the pain.

In the evenings Cornelius likes to drive over to Walley. Brenda never offers—she waits for him to say, "Why don't you drive?" if he doesn't want the movement of his arms or legs to jar his back. The kids used to go along, but now that they're in high school—Lorna in grade eleven and Mark in grade nine—they usually don't want to. Brenda and Cornelius sit in the parked van and look at the sea gulls lining up out on the breakwater, the grain elevators, the great green-lighted shafts and ramps of the mine where Cornelius used to work, the pyramids of coarse gray salt. Sometimes there is a long lake boat in port. Of course, there are pleasure boats in the summer, wind surfers out on the water, people fishing off the pier. The time of the sunset is posted daily on a board on the beach then; people come especially to watch it. Now, in October, the board is bare and the lights are turned on along the pier—one or two diehards are still fishing—and the water is choppy and cold-looking, the harbor entirely businesslike.

There is still work going on on the beach. Since early last spring, boulders have been set up in some places, sand has been poured down in others, a long rocky spit has been constructed, all making a protected curve of beach, with a rough road along it, on which they drive. Never mind Cornelius's back—he wants to see. Trucks, earthmovers, bulldozers have been busy all day, and they are still sitting there, temporarily tame and useless monsters, in the evening. This is where Neil works. He drives these things—he hauls the rocks around, clears the space, and makes the road for Brenda and Cornelius to drive on. He works for the Fordyce Construction Company, from Logan, which has the contract.

Cornelius looks at everything. He knows what the boats are loading (soft wheat, salt, corn) and where they're going, he understands how the harbor is being deepened, and he always wants to get a look at the huge pipe running at an angle onto the beach and crossing it, finally letting out water and sludge and rocks from the lake bottom that have never before seen the light of day. He goes and stands beside this pipe to listen to the commotion inside it, the banging and groaning of the rocks and water rushing on their way. He asks what a rough winter will do to all this changing and arranging if the lake just picks up the rocks and beach and flings them aside and eats away at the clay cliffs, as before.

Brenda listens to Cornelius and thinks about Neil. She derives pleasure from being in the place where Neil spends his days. She likes to think of the noise and the steady strength of these machines and of the men in the cabs bare-armed, easy with this power, as if they knew naturally what all this roaring and chomping up the shore was leading to. Their casual, good-humored authority. She loves the smell of work on their bodies, the language of it they speak, their absorption in it, their disregard of her. She loves to get a man fresh from all that.

When she is down there with Cornelius and hasn't seen Neil for a while, she can feel uneasy and forlorn, as if this might be a world that could turn its back on her. Just after she has been with Neil, it's her kingdom—but what isn't, then? The night before they are to meet—last night, for instance—she should be feeling happy and expectant, but to tell the truth the last twenty-four hours, even the last two or three days, seem too full of pitfalls, too momentous, for her to feel anything much but caution and anxiety. It's a countdown—she actually counts the hours. She has a tendency to fill them with good deeds—cleaning jobs around the house that she was putting off, mowing the lawn, doing a reorganization at the

Furniture Barn, even weeding the rock garden. The morning of the day it-self is when the hours pass most laggingly and are full of dangers. She al-ways has a story about where she's supposed to be going that afternoon, but her expedition can't be an absolutely necessary one—that would be calling too much attention to it—so there's the chance, always, that some-thing will come up to make Cornelius say, "Can't you put that off till later in the week? Can't you do it some other day?" It's not so much that she wouldn't then be able to get in touch with Neil that bothers her. Neil would wait an hour or so, then figure out what had happened. It's that she thinks she couldn't bear it. To be so close, then have to do without. Yet she doesn't feel any physical craving during those last torturing hours; even her secret preparations—her washing, shaving, oiling, and perfum-ing—don't arouse her. She stays numb, harassed by details, lies, arrange-ments, until the moment when she actually sees Neil's car. The fear that she won't be able to get away is succeeded, during the fifteen-minute drive, by the fear that he won't show up, in that lonely, dead-end spot in the swamp which is their meeting place. What she's looking forward to, during those last hours, gets to be less of a physical thing—so that missing it would be like missing not a meal you're hungry for but a ceremony on which your life or salvation depended.

By the time Neil was an older teenager—but not old enough to get into bars, still hanging around at the Five Points Confectionery (the Croa-tians kept the old name for it)—the change had arrived, which everybody who was alive then remembers. (That's what Neil thinks, but Brenda says, "I don't know—as far as I was concerned, all that was just sort of going on someplace else.") Nobody knew what to do about it, nobody was pre-pared. Some schools were strict about long hair (on boys), some thought it best to let that go and concentrate on serious things. Just hold it back with an elastic band was all they asked. And what about clothes? Chains and seed beads, rope sandals, Indian cotton, African patterns, everything all of a sudden soft and loose and bright. In Victoria the change may not have been contained so well as in some other places. It spilled over. Maybe the climate softened people up, not just young people. There was a big burst of paper flowers and marijuana fumes and music (the stuff that seemed so wild then, Neil says, and seems so tame now), and that music rolling out of downtown windows hung with dishonored flags, over the flowers beds in Beacon Hill Park to the yellow broom on the sea cliffs to the happy beaches looking over at the magic peaks of the Olympics. Everybody was in on the act. University professors wandered around with flowers behind their ears, and people's mothers turned up in those outfits. Neil and his friends had contempt for these people, naturally—these hip oldsters, toe-dippers. Neil and his friends took the world of drugs and music seriously.

When they wanted to do drugs, they went outside the Confectionery. Sometimes they went as far as the cemetery and sat on the seawall. Some-

times they sat beside the shed that was in back of the store. They couldn't
go in; the shed was locked. Then they went back inside the Confectionery
and drank Cokes and ate hamburgers and cheeseburgers and cinnamon
buns and cakes, because they got very hungry. They leaned back on their
chairs and watched the patterns move on the old pressed-tin ceiling,
which the Croatians had painted white. Flowers, towers, birds, and monsters detached themselves, swam overhead.

"What were you taking?" Brenda says.

"Pretty good stuff, unless we got sold something rotten. Hash, acid,
mescaline sometimes. Combinations sometimes. Nothing too serious."

"All I ever did was smoke about a third of a joint on the beach when at
first I wasn't even sure what it was, and when I got home my father
slapped my face."

(That's not the truth. It was Cornelius. Cornelius slapped her face. It
was before they were married, when Cornelius was working nights in the
mine and she would sit around on the beach after dark with some friends
of her own age. Next day she told him, and he slapped her face.)

All they did in the Confectionery was eat, and moon around, happily
stoned, and play stupid games, such as racing toy cars along the tabletops.
Once, a guy lay down on the floor and they squirted ketchup at him. Nobody cared. The daytime customers—the housewives buying bakery
goods and the pensioners killing time with a coffee—never came in at
night. The mother and Lisa had gone home on the bus, to wherever they
lived. Then even the father started going home, a little after suppertime.
Maria was left in charge. She didn't care what they did, as long as they
didn't do damage and as long as they paid.

This was the world of drugs that belonged to the older boys, that they
kept the younger boys out of. It was a while before they noticed that the
younger ones had something, too. They had some secret of their own.
They were growing insolent and self-important. Some of them were always pestering the older boys to let them buy drugs. That was how it became evident that they had quite a bit of unexplained money.

Neil had—he has—a younger brother named Jonathan. Very straight
now, married, a teacher. Jonathan began dropping hints; other boys did
the same thing, they couldn't keep the secret to themselves, and pretty
soon it was all out in the open. They were getting their money from
Maria. Maria was paying them to have sex with her. They did it in the
back shed after she closed the store up at night. She had the key to the
shed.

She also had the day-to-day control of the money. She emptied the till
at night, she kept the books. Her parents trusted her to do this. Why not?
She was good at arithmetic, and she was devoted to the business. She understood the whole operation better than they did. It seemed that they
were very uncertain and superstitious about money, and they did not want
to put it in the bank. They kept it in a safe or maybe just a strongbox
somewhere, and got it as they needed it. They must have felt they couldn't

trust anybody, banks or anybody, outside of the family. What a godsend Maria must have seemed to them—steady and smart, not pretty enough to be tempted to put her hopes or energies into anything but the business. A pillar, Maria.

She was a head taller and thirty or forty pounds heavier than those boys she paid.

There are always a few bad moments after Brenda turns off the highway—where she has some excuse to be driving, should anyone see her—and onto the side road. The van is noticeable, unmistakable. But once she has taken the plunge, driving where she shouldn't be, she feels stronger. When she turns onto the dead-end swamp road, there's no excuse possible. Spotted here, she's finished. She has about half a mile to drive out in the open before she gets to the trees. She'd hoped that they would plant corn, which would grow tall and shelter her, but they hadn't, they'd planted beans. At least the roadsides here hadn't been sprayed; the grass and weeds and berry bushes had grown tall, though not tall enough to hide a van. There was goldenrod and milkweed, with the pods burst open, and dangling bunches of bright, poisonous fruit, and wild grapevine flung over everything, even creeping onto the road. And finally she was in, she was into the tunnel of trees. Cedar, hemlock, farther back in the wetter ground the wispy-looking tamarack, lots of soft maples with leaves spotty yellow and brown. No standing water, no black pools, even far back in the trees. They'd had luck, with the dry summer and fall. She and Neil had had luck, not the farmers. If it had been a wet year, they could never have used this place. The hard ruts she eases the van through would have been slick mud and the turnaround spot at the end a soggy sinkhole.

That's about a mile and a half in. There are some tricky spots to drive—a couple of bumpy little hills rising out of the swamp, and a narrow log bridge over a creek where she can't see any water, just choking, yellowy cress and nettles, sucking at dry mud.

Neil drives an old blue Mercury—dark blue that can turn into a pool, a spot of swampy darkness under the trees. She strains to see it. She doesn't mind getting there a few minutes ahead of him, to compose herself, brush out her hair and check her face and spray her throat with purse cologne (sometimes between her legs as well). More than a few minutes makes her nervous. She isn't afraid of wild dogs or rapists or eyes watching her out of thickets—she used to pick berries in here when she was a child; that's how she knew about the place. She is afraid of what may not be there, not what is. The absence of Neil, the possibility of his defection, his sudden denial of her. That can turn any place, any thing, ugly and menacing and stupid. Trees or gardens or parking meters or coffee tables—it wouldn't matter. Once, he didn't come; he was sick: food poisoning or the most incredible hangover of his life—something terrible, he told her on the phone that night—and she had to pretend it was somebody calling to sell them a sofa. She never forgot the wait, the draining of hope, the heat and the bugs—it was in July—and her body oozing sweat, here on the seat of the van, like some sickly admission of defeat.

He is there, he's there first; she can see one eye of the Mercury in the deep cedar shade. It's like hitting water when you're dead of heat and scratched and bitten all over from picking berries in the summer bush— the lapping sweetness of it, the cool kindness soaking up all your troubles in its sudden depths. She gets the van parked and fluffs out her hair and jumps out, tries the door to show it's locked, else he'll send her running back, just like Cornelius—are you sure you locked the van? She walks across the little sunny space, the leaf-scattered ground, seeing herself walk, in her tight white pants and turquoise top and low-slung white belt and high heels, her bag over her shoulder. A shapely woman, with fair, freckled skin and blue eyes rimmed with blue shadow and liner, screwed up appealingly against any light. Her reddish-blond hair—touched up yesterday—catching the sun like a crown of petals. She wears heels just for this walk, just for this moment of crossing the road with his eyes on her, the extra bit of pelvic movement and leg length they give her.

Often, often, they've made love in his car, right here at their meeting place, though they always keep telling each other to wait. Stop; wait till we get to the trailer. "Wait" means the opposite of what it says, after a while. Once, they started as they drove. Brenda slipped off her pants and pulled up her loose summer skirt, not saying a word, looking straight ahead, and they ended up stopping beside the highway, taking a shocking risk. Now when they pass this spot, she always says something like "Don't go off the road here," or "Somebody should put up a warning sign."

"Historical marker," Neil says.

They have a history of passion, the way families have a history, or people who have gone to school together. They don't have much else. They've never eaten a meal with each other, or seen a movie. But they've come through some complicated adventures together, and dangers—not just of the stopping-on-the-highway kind. They've taken risks, surprising each other, always correctly. In dreams you can have the feeling that you've had this dream before, that you have this dream over and over again, and you know that it's really nothing that simple. You know that there's a whole underground system that you call "dreams," having nothing better to call them, and that this system is not like roads or tunnels but more like a live body network, all coiling and stretching, unpredictable but finally familiar—where you are now, where you've always been. That was the way it was with them and sex, going somewhere like that, and they understood the same things about it and trusted each other, so far.

Another time on the highway, Brenda saw a white convertible approaching, an old white Mustang convertible with the top down—this was in the summer—and she slid to the floor.

"Who's in that car?" she said. "Look! Quick! Tell me."

"Girls," Neil said. "Four or five girls. Out looking for guys."

"My daughter," Brenda said, scrambling up again. "Good thing I wasn't wearing my seat belt."

"You got a daughter old enough to drive? You got a daughter owns a convertible?"

"Her friend owns it. Lorna doesn't drive yet. But she could—she's sixteen."

She felt there were things in the air then that he could have said, that she hoped he wouldn't. The things men feel obliged to say about young girls.

"You could have one that age yourself," she said. "Maybe you do and don't know it. Also, she lied to me. She said she was going to play tennis."

Again he didn't say anything she hoped not to hear, any sly reminder about lies. A danger past.

All he said was, "Easy. Take it easy. Nothing happened."

She had no way of knowing how much he understood of her feelings at that moment, or if he understood anything. They almost never mentioned that part of her life. They never mentioned Cornelius, though he was the one Neil talked to the first time he came to the Furniture Barn. He came to look for a bicycle—just a cheap bike to ride on the country roads. They had no bikes around at that time, but he stayed and talked to Cornelius for a while, about the kind he wanted, ways of repairing or improving that kind, how they should watch out for one. He said he would drop by again. He did that, very soon, and only Brenda was there. Cornelius had gone to the house to lie down; it was one of his bad days. Neil and Brenda made everything clear to each other then, without saying anything definite. When he phoned and asked her to have a drink with him, in a tavern on the lakeshore road, she knew what he was asking and she knew what she would answer.

She told him she hadn't done anything like this before. That was a lie in one way and in another way true.

During store hours, Maria didn't let one sort of transaction interfere with another. Everybody paid as usual. She didn't behave any differently; she was still in charge. The boys knew that they had some bargaining power, but they were never sure how much. A dollar. Two dollars. Five. It wasn't as if she had to depend on one or two of them. There were always several friends outside, waiting and willing, when she took one of them into the shed before she caught the bus home. She warned them that she would stop dealing with them if they talked, and for a while they believed her. She didn't hire them regularly at first, or all that often.

That was at first. Over a few months' time, things began to change. Maria's needs increased. The bargaining got to be more open and obstreperous. The news got out. Maria's powers were being chipped, then hammered, away.

Come on, Maria, give me a ten. Me, too. Maria, give me a ten, too. Come on, Maria, you know me.

Twenty, Maria. Give me twenty. Come on. Twenty bucks. You owe me, Maria. Come on, now. You don't want me to tell. Come on, Maria.

A twenty, a twenty, a twenty. Maria is forking over. She is going to the shed every night. And if that isn't bad enough for her, some boys start refusing. They want the money first. They take the money and then they say no. They say she never paid them. She paid them, she paid them in front of witnesses, and all the witnesses deny that she did. They shake their heads, they taunt her. *No. You never paid him. I never saw you. You pay me now and I'll go. I promise I will. I'll go. You pay me twenty, Maria.*

And the older boys, who have learned from their younger brothers what is going on, are coming up to her at the cash register and saying, "How about me, Maria? You know me, too. Come on, Maria, how about a twenty?" Those boys never go to the shed with her, never. Did she think they would? They never even promise, they just ask her for money. *You know me a long time, Maria.* They threaten, they wheedle. *Aren't I your friend, too, Maria?*

Nobody was Maria's friend.

Maria's matronly, watchful calm was gone—she looked wild and sullen and mean. She gave them looks full of hate, but she continued giving them money. She kept handing over the bills. Not even trying to bargain, or to argue or refuse, anymore. In a rage she did it—a silent rage. The more they taunted her, the more readily the twenty-dollar bills flew out of the till. Very little, perhaps nothing, was done to earn them now.

They're stoned all the time, Neil and his friends. All the time, now that they have this money. They see sweet streams of atoms flowing in the Formica tabletops. Their colored souls are shooting out under their fingernails. Maria has gone crazy, the store is bleeding money. How can this go on? How is it going to end? Maria must be into the strongbox now; the till at the end of the day wouldn't have enough for her. And all the time her mother keeps on baking buns and making pierogi, and the father keeps sweeping the sidewalk and greeting the customers. Nobody has told them. They go on just the same.

They had to find out on their own. They found a bill that Maria hadn't paid—something like that, somebody coming in with an unpaid bill—and they went to get the money to pay it, and they found that there was no money. The money wasn't where they kept it, in the safe or strongbox or wherever, and it wasn't anywhere else—the money was gone. That was how they found out.

Maria had succeeded in giving away everything. All they had saved, all their slowly accumulated profits, all the money on which they operated their business. Truly, everything. They could not pay the rent now, they could not pay the electricity bill or their suppliers. They could not keep on running the Confectionery. At least they believed they couldn't. Maybe they simply had not the heart to go on.

The store was locked. A sign went up on the door: "CLOSED UNTIL FURTHER NOTICE." Nearly a year went by before the place was reopened. It had been turned into a laundromat.

People said it was Maria's mother, that big, meek, bentover woman, who insisted on bringing charges against her daughter. She was scared of the English language and the cash register, but she brought Maria into court. Of course, Maria could only be charged as a juvenile, and she could only be sent to a place for young offenders, and nothing could be done about the boys at all. They all lied anyway—they said it wasn't them. Maria's parents must have found jobs, they must have gone on living in Victoria, because Lisa did. She still swam at the Y, and in a few years she was working at Eaton's, in Cosmetics. She was very glamorous and haughty by that time.

Neil always has vodka and orange juice for them to drink. That's Brenda's choice. She read somewhere that orange juice replenishes the vitamin C that the liquor leeches away, and she hopes the vodka really can't be detected on your breath. Neil tidies up the trailer, too—or so she thinks, because of the paper bag full of beer cans leaning against the cupboard, a pile of newspapers pushed together, not really folded, a pair of socks kicked into a corner. Maybe his housemate does it. A man called Gary, whom Brenda has never met or seen a picture of, and wouldn't know if they met on the street. Would he know her? He knows she comes here, he knows when; does he even know her name? Does he recognize her perfume, the smell of her sex, when he comes home in the evening? She likes the trailer, the way nothing in it has been made to look balanced or permanent. Things set down just wherever they will be convenient. No curtains or placemats, not even a pair of salt and pepper shakers—just the salt box and pepper tin, the way they come from the store. She loves the sight of Neil's bed—badly made, with a rough plaid blanket and a flat pillow, not a marriage bed or a bed of illness, comfort, complication. The bed of his lust and sleep, equally strenuous and oblivious. She loves the life of his body, so sure of its rights. She wants commands from him, never requests. She wants to be his territory.

It's only in the bathroom that the dirt bothers her a bit, like anybody else's dirt, and she wishes they'd done a better job of cleaning the toilet and the washbasin.

They sit at the table to drink, looking out through the trailer window at the steely, glittering, choppy water of the lake. Here the trees, exposed to lake winds, are almost bare. Birch bones and poplars stiff and bright as straw frame the water. There may be snow in another month. Certainly in two months. The seaway will close, the lake boats will be tied up for the winter, there'll be a wild landscape of ice thrown up between the shore and the open water. Neil says he doesn't know what he'll do, once the work on the beach is over. Maybe stay on, try to get another job. Maybe go on unemployment insurance for a while, get a snowmobile, enjoy the winter. Or he could go and look for work somewhere else, visit friends. He has friends all over the continent of North America and out of it. He has friends in Peru.

"So what happened?" Brenda says. "Don't you have any idea what happened to Maria?"

Neil says no, he has no idea.

The story won't leave Brenda alone; it stays with her like a coating on the tongue, a taste in the mouth.

"Well, maybe she got married," she says. "After she got out. Lots of people get married who are no beauties. That's for sure. She might've lost weight and be looking good even."

"Sure," says Neil. "Maybe have guys paying her, instead of the other way round."

"Or she might still be just sitting in one of those places. One of those places where they put people."

Now she feels a pain between her legs. Not unusual after one of these sessions. If she were to stand up at this moment, she'd feel a throb there, she'd feel the blood flowing back down through all the little veins and arteries that have been squashed and bruised, she'd feel herself throbbing like a big swollen blister.

She takes a long drink and says, "So how much money did you get out of her?"

"I never got anything," Neil says. "I just knew these other guys who did. It was my brother Jonathan made the money off her. I wonder what he'd say if I reminded him now."

"Older guys, too—you said older guys, too. Don't tell me you just sat back and watched and never got your share."

"That's what I *am* telling you. I never got anything."

Brenda clicks her tongue, tut-tut, and empties her glass and moves it around on the table, looking skeptically at the wet circles.

"Want another?" Neil says. He takes the glass out of her hand.

"I've got to go," she says. "Soon." You can make love in a hurry if you have to, but you need time for a fight. Is that what they're starting on? A fight? She feels edgy but happy. Her happiness is tight and private, not the sort that flows out from you and fuzzes everything up and makes you good-naturedly careless about what you say. The very opposite. She feels light and sharp and unconnected. When Neil brings her back a full glass, she takes a drink from it at once, to safeguard this feeling.

"You've got the same name as my husband," she says. "It's funny I never thought of that before."

She has thought of it before. She just hasn't mentioned it, knowing it's not something Neil would like to hear.

"Cornelius isn't the same as Neil," he says.

"It's Dutch. Some Dutch people shorten it to Neil."

"Yeah, but I'm not Dutch, and I wasn't named Cornelius, just Neil."

"Still, if his had been shortened you'd be named the same."

"His isn't shortened."

"I never said it was. I said if it had been."

"So why say that if it isn't?"

He must feel the same thing she does—the slow but irresistible rise of a new excitement, the need to say, and hear, dire things. What a sharp, releasing pleasure there is in the first blow, and what a dazzling temptation ahead—destruction. You don't stop to think why you want that destruction. You just do.

"Why do we have to drink every time?" Neil says abruptly. "Do we want to turn ourselves into alcoholics or something?"

Brenda takes a quick sip and pushes her glass away. "Who has to drink?" she says.

She thinks he means they should drink coffee, or Cokes. But he gets up and goes to the dresser where he keeps his clothes, opens a drawer, and says, "Come over here."

"I don't want to look at any of that stuff," she says.

"You don't even know what it is."

"Sure I do."

Of course she doesn't—not specifically.

"You think it's going to bite you?"

Brenda drinks again and keeps looking out the window. The sun is getting down in the sky already, pushing the bright light across the table to warm her hands.

"You don't approve," Neil says.

"I don't approve or disapprove," she says, aware of having lost some control, of not being as happy as she was. "I don't care what you do. That's you."

"I don't approve or disapprove," says Neil, in a mincing voice. "Don't care what you do."

That's the signal, which one or the other had to give. A flash of hate, pure meanness, like the glint of a blade. The signal that the fight can come out into the open. Brenda takes a deep drink, as if she very much deserved it. She feels a desolate satisfaction. She stands up and says, "Time for me to go."

"What if I'm not ready to go yet?" Neil says.

"I said me, not you."

"Oh. You got a car outside?"

"I can walk."

"That's five miles back to where the van is."

"People have walked five miles."

"In shoes like that?" says Neil. They both look at her yellow shoes, which match the appliquéd-satin birds on her turquoise sweater. Both things bought and worn for him!

"You didn't wear those shoes for walking," he says. "You wore them so every step you took would show off your fat arse."

She walks along the lakeshore road, in the gravel, which bruises her feet through the shoes and makes her pay attention to each step, lest she should twist an ankle. The afternoon is now too cold for just a sweater. The wind off the lake blows at her sideways, and every time a vehicle passes, particularly a truck, an eddy of stiff wind whirls around her and grit blows into her face. Some of the trucks slow down, of course, and some cars do, too, and men yell at her out of the windows. One car skids onto the gravel and stops ahead of her. She stands still, she cannot think what else to do, and after a moment he churns back onto the pavement and she starts walking again.

That's all right, she's not in any real danger. She doesn't even worry about being seen by someone she knows. She feels too free to care. She thinks about the first time Neil came to the Furniture Barn, how he put his arm around Samson's neck and said, "Not much of a watchdog you got here, Ma'am." She thought the "Ma'am" was impudent, phony, out of some old Elvis Presley movie. And what he said next was worse. She looked at Samson, and she said, "He's better at night." And Neil said, "So am I." Impudent, swaggering, conceited, she thought. And he's not young enough to get away with it. Her opinion didn't even change so much the second time. What happened was that all that became just something to get past. It was something she could let him know he didn't have to do. It was her job to take his gifts seriously, so that he could be serious, too, and easy and grateful. How was she sure so soon that what she didn't like about him wasn't real?

When she's in the second mile, or maybe just the second half of the first mile, the Mercury catches up to her. It pulls onto the gravel across the road. She goes over and gets in. She doesn't see why not. It doesn't mean that she is going to talk to him, or be with him any longer than the few minutes it will take to drive to the swamp road and the van. His presence doesn't need to weigh on her any more than the grit blowing beside the road.

She winds the window all the way down so that there will be a rush of chilly wind across anything he may have to say.

"I want to beg your pardon for the personal remarks," he says.

"Why?" she says. "It's true. It is fat."

"No."

"It is," she says, in a tone of bored finality that is quite sincere. It shuts him up for a few miles, until they've turned down the swamp road and are driving in under the trees.

"If you thought there was a needle there in the drawer, there wasn't."

"It isn't any of my business what there was," she says.

"All that was in there was some Percs and Quaaludes and a little hash."

She remembers a fight she had with Cornelius, one that almost broke their engagement. It wasn't the time he slapped her for smoking marijuana. They made that up quickly. It wasn't about anything to do with their own lives. They were talking about a man Cornelius worked with at the mine, and his wife, and their retarded child. This child was just a vegetable, Cornelius said; all it did was gibber away in a sort of pen in a corner of the living room and mess its pants. It was about six or seven years old, and that was all it would ever do. Cornelius said he believed that if anybody had a child like that they had a right to get rid of it. He said that was what he would do. No question about it. There were a lot of ways you could do it and never get caught, and he bet that was what a lot of people did. He and Brenda had a terrible fight about this. But all the time they were arguing and fighting Brenda suspected that this was not something Cornelius would really do. It was something he had to say he would do. To her. To her, he had to insist that he would do it. And this actually made her angrier at him than she would have been if she believed he was entirely and brutally sincere. He wanted her to argue with him about this. He wanted her protest, her horror, and why was that? Men wanted you to make a fuss, about disposing of vegetable babies or taking drugs or driving a car like a bat out of hell, and why was that? So they could have your marshmallow sissy goodness to preen against, with their hard showoff badness? So that they finally could give in to you, growling, and not have to be so bad and reckless anymore? Whatever it was, you got sick of it.

In the mine accident, Cornelius could have been crushed to death. He was working the night shift when it happened. In the great walls of rock salt an undercut is made, then there are holes drilled for explosives, and the charges are fitted in; an explosion goes off every night at five minutes to midnight. The huge slice of salt slides loose, to be started on its journey to the surface. Cornelius was lifted up in a cage on the end of the arm of the scaler. He was to break off the loose material on the roof and fix in the bolts that held it for the explosion. Something went wrong with the hydraulic controls he was operating—he stalled, tried for a little power and got a surge that lifted him, so that he saw the rock ceiling closing down on him like a lid. He ducked, the cage halted, a rocky outcrop struck him in the back.

He had worked in the mine for seven years before that and hardly ever spoke to Brenda about what it was like. Now he tells her. It's a world of its own, he says—caverns and pillars, miles out under the lake. If you get in a passage where there are no machines to light the gray walls, the salt-dusty air, and you turn your headlamp off, you can find out what real darkness is like, the darkness people on the surface of the earth never get to see. The machines stay down there forever. Some are assembled down there, taken down in parts; all are repaired there; and finally they're ransacked for usable parts, then piled into a dead-end passage that is sealed up—a tomb for these underground machines. They make a ferocious noise all the time they're working; the noise of the machines and the ventilating fans cuts out any human voice. And now there's a new machine that can do what Cornelius went up in the cage to do. It can do it by itself, without a man.

Brenda doesn't know if he misses being down there. He says he doesn't. He says he just can't look at the surface of the water without seeing all that underneath, which nobody who hasn't seen it could imagine.

Neil and Brenda drive along under the trees, where suddenly you could hardly feel the wind at all.

"Also, I did take some money," Neil says. "I got forty dollars, which, compared to what some guys got, was just nothing. I swear that's all, forty dollars. I never got any more."

She doesn't say anything.

"I wasn't looking to confess it," he says. "I just wanted to talk about it. Then what pisses me off is I lied anyway."

Now that she can hear his voice better, she notices that it's nearly as flat and tired as her own. She sees his hands on the wheel and thinks what a hard time she would have describing what he looks like. At a distance—in the car, waiting for her—he's always been a bright blur, his presence a relief and a promise. Close up, he's been certain separate areas—silky or toughened skin, wiry hair or shaved prickles, smells that are unique or shared with other men. But it's chiefly an energy, a quality of his self that she can see in his blunt, short fingers or the tanned curve of his forehead. And even to call it energy is not exact—it's more like the sap of him, rising from the roots, clear and on the move, filling him to bursting. That's what she has set herself to follow—the sap, the current, under the skin, as if that were the one true thing.

If she turned sideways now, she would see him for what he is—that tanned curved forehead, the receding fringe of curly brown hair, heavy eyebrows with a few gray hairs in them, deep-set light-colored eyes, and a mouth that enjoys itself, rather sulky and proud. A boyish man beginning to age—though he still feels light and wild on top of her, after Cornelius's bulk settling down possessively, like a ton of blankets. A responsibility, Brenda feels then. Is she going to feel the same about this one?

Neil turns the car around, he points it ready to drive back, and it's time for her to get out and go across to the van. He takes his hands off the wheel with the engine running, flexes his fingers, then grabs the wheel hard again—hard enough, you'd think, to squeeze it to pulp. "Christ, don't get out yet!" he says. "Don't get out of the car!"

She hasn't even put a hand on the door, she hasn't made a move to leave. Doesn't he know what's happening? Maybe you need the experience of a lot of married fights to know it. To know that what you think—and, for a while, hope—is the absolute end for you can turn out to be only the start of a new stage, a continuation. That's what's happening, that's what has happened. He has lost some of his sheen for her; he may not get it back. Probably the same goes for her, with him. She feels his heaviness and anger and surprise. She feels that also in herself. She thinks that up till now was easy.

ON THE RAINY RIVER

Tim O'Brien

This is one story I've never told before. Not to anyone. Not to my parents, not to my brother or sister, not even to my wife. To go into it, I've always thought, would only cause embarrassment for all of us, a sudden need to be elsewhere, which is the natural response to a confession. Even now, I'll admit, the story makes me squirm. For more than twenty years I've had to live with it, feeling the shame, trying to push it away, and so by this act of remembrance, by putting the facts down on paper, I'm hoping to relieve at least some of the pressure on my dreams. Still, it's a hard story to tell. All of us, I suppose, like to believe that in a moral emergency we will behave like the heroes of our youth, bravely and forthrightly, without thought of personal loss or discredit. Certainly that was my conviction back in the summer of 1968. Tim O'Brien: a secret hero. The Lone Ranger. If the stakes ever became high enough—if the evil were evil enough, if the good were good enough—I would simply tap a secret reservoir of courage that had been accumulating inside me over the years. Courage, I seemed to think, comes to us in finite quantities, like an inheritance, and by being frugal and stashing it away and letting it earn interest, we steadily increase our moral capital in preparation for that day when the account must be drawn down. It was a comforting theory. It dispensed with all those bothersome little acts of daily courage; it offered hope and grace to the repetitive coward; it justified the past while amortizing the future.

In June of 1968, a month after graduating from Macalester College, I was drafted to fight a war I hated. I was twenty-one years old. Young, yes, and politically naive, but even so the American war in Vietnam seemed to me wrong. Certain blood was being shed for uncertain reasons. I saw no unity of purpose, no consensus on matters of philosophy or history or law. The very facts were shrouded in uncertainty: Was it a civil war? A war of national liberation or simple aggression? Who started it, and when, and why? What really happened to the USS *Maddox* on that dark night in the Gulf of Tonkin? Was Ho Chi Minh a Communist stooge, or a nationalist savior, or both, or neither? What about the Geneva Accords? What about SEATO and the Cold War? What about dominoes? America was divided on these and a thousand other issues, and the debate had spilled out across the floor of the United States Senate and into the streets, and smart men in pinstripes could not agree on even the most fundamental matters

446

of public policy. The only certainty that summer was moral confusion. It was my view then, and still is, that you don't make war without knowing why. Knowledge, of course, is always imperfect, but it seemed to me that when a nation goes to war it must have reasonable confidence in the justice and imperative of its cause. You can't fix your mistakes. Once people are dead, you can't make them undead.

In any case those were my convictions, and back in college I had taken a modest stand against the war. Nothing radical, no hothead stuff, just ringing a few doorbells for Gene McCarthy, composing a few tedious, uninspired editorials for the campus newspaper. Oddly, though, it was almost entirely an intellectual activity. I brought some energy to it, of course, but it was the energy that accompanies almost any abstract endeavor; I felt no personal danger; I felt no sense of an impending crisis in my life. Stupidly, with a kind of smug removal that I can't begin to fathom, I assumed that the problems of killing and dying did not fall within my special province.

The draft notice arrived on June 17, 1968. It was a humid afternoon, I remember, cloudy and very quiet, and I'd just come in from a round of golf. My mother and father were having lunch out in the kitchen. I remember opening up the letter, scanning the first few lines, feeling the blood go thick behind my eyes. I remember a sound in my head. It wasn't thinking, just a silent howl. A million things all at once—I was too *good* for this war. Too smart, too compassionate, too everything. It couldn't happen. I was above it. I had the world dicked—Phi Beta Kappa and summa cum laude and president of the student body and a full-ride scholarship for grad studies at Harvard. A mistake, maybe—a foul-up in the paperwork. I was no soldier. I hated Boy Scouts. I hated camping out. I hated dirt and tents and mosquitoes. The sight of blood made me queasy, and I couldn't tolerate authority, and I didn't know a rifle from a slingshot. I was a *liberal*, for Christ sake: If they needed fresh bodies, why not draft some back-to-the-stone-age hawk? Or some dumb jingo in his hard hat and Bomb Hanoi button, or one of LBJ's pretty daughters, or Westmoreland's whole handsome family—nephews and nieces and baby grandson. There should be a law, I thought. If you support a war, if you think it's worth the price, that's fine, but you have to put your own precious fluids on the line. You have to head for the front and hook up with an infantry unit and help spill the blood. And you have to bring along your wife, or your kids, or your lover. A *law*, I thought.

I remember the rage in my stomach. Later it burned down to a smoldering self-pity, then to numbness. At dinner that night my father asked what my plans were.

"Nothing," I said. "Wait."

I spent the summer of 1968 working in an Armour meat-packing plant in my hometown of Worthington, Minnesota. The plant specialized in pork products, and for eight hours a day I stood on a quarter-mile assembly line—more properly, a disassembly line—removing blood clots from the necks of dead pigs. My job title, I believe, was Declotter. After slaughter, the hogs were decapitated, split down the length of the belly, pried open, eviscerated, and strung up by the hind hocks on a high conveyer belt. Then gravity took over. By the time a carcass reached my spot on the line, the fluids had mostly drained out, everything except for thick clots of blood in the neck and upper chest cavity. To remove the stuff, I used a kind of water gun. The machine was heavy, maybe eighty pounds, and was suspended from the ceiling by a heavy rubber cord. There was some bounce to it, an elastic up-and-down give, and the trick was to maneuver the gun with your whole body, not lifting with the arms, just letting the rubber cord do the work for you. At one end was a trigger, at the muzzle end was a small nozzle and a steel roller brush. As a carcass passed by, you'd lean forward and swing the gun up against the clots and squeeze the trigger, all in one motion, and the brush would whirl and water would come shooting out and you'd hear a quick splattering sound as the clots dissolved into a fine red mist. It was not pleasant work. Goggles were a necessity, and a rubber apron, but even so it was like standing for eight hours a day under a lukewarm blood-shower. At night I'd go home smelling of pig. It wouldn't go away. Even after a hot bath, scrubbing hard, the stink was always there—like old bacon, or sausage, a dense greasy pig-stink that soaked deep into my skin and hair. Among other things, I remember, it was tough getting dates that summer. I felt isolated; I spent a lot of time alone. And there was also that draft notice tucked away in my wallet.

In the evenings I'd sometimes borrow my father's car and drive aimlessly around town, feeling sorry for myself, thinking about the war and the pig factory and how my life seemed to be collapsing toward slaughter. I felt paralyzed. All around me the options seemed to be narrowing, as if I were hurtling down a huge black funnel, the whole world squeezing in tight. There was no happy way out. The government had ended most graduate school deferments; the waiting lists for the National Guard and Reserves were impossibly long; my health was solid; I didn't qualify for CO status—no religious grounds, no history as a pacifist. Moreover, I could not claim to be opposed to war as a matter of general principle. There were occasions, I believed, when a nation was justified in using military force to achieve its ends, to stop a Hitler or some comparable evil, and I told myself that in such circumstances I would've willingly marched off to the battle. The problem, though, was that a draft board did not let you choose your war.

Beyond all this, or at the very center, was the raw fact of terror. I did not want to die. Not ever. But certainly not then, not there, not in a wrong war. Driving up Main Street, past the courthouse and the Ben Franklin store, I sometimes felt the fear spreading inside me like weeds. I imagined myself dead. I imagined myself doing things I could not do—charging an enemy position, taking aim at another human being.

At some point in mid-July I began thinking seriously about Canada. The border lay a few hundred miles north, an eight-hour drive. Both my conscience and my instincts were telling me to make a break for it, just take off and run like hell and never stop. In the beginning the idea seemed purely abstract, the word Canada printing itself out in my head; but after a time I could see particular shapes and images, the sorry details of my own future—a hotel room in Winnipeg, a battered old suitcase, my father's eyes as I tried to explain myself over the telephone. I could almost hear his voice, and my mother's. Run, I'd think. Then I'd think, Impossible. Then a second later I'd think, *Run*.

It was a kind of schizophrenia. A moral split. I couldn't make up my mind. I feared the war, yes, but I also feared exile. I was afraid of walking away from my own life, my friends and my family, my whole history, everything that mattered to me. I feared losing the respect of my parents. I feared the law. I feared ridicule and censure. My hometown was a conservative little spot on the prairie, a place where tradition counted, and it was easy to imagine people sitting around a table down at the old Gobbler Café on Main Street, coffee cups poised, the conversation slowly zeroing in on the young O'Brien kid, how the damned sissy had taken off for Canada. At night, when I couldn't sleep, I'd sometimes carry on fierce arguments with those people. I'd be screaming at them, telling them how much I detested their blind, thoughtless, automatic acquiescence to it all, their simple-minded patriotism, their prideful ignorance, their love-it-or-leave-it platitudes, how they were sending me off to fight a war they didn't understand and didn't want to understand. I held them responsible. By God, yes, I *did*. All of them—I held them personally and individually responsible—the polyestered Kiwanis boys, the merchants and farmers, the pious churchgoers, the chatty housewives, the PTA and the Lions club and the Veterans of Foreign Wars and the fine upstanding gentry out at the country club. They didn't know Bao Dai from the man in the moon. They didn't know history. They didn't know the first thing about Diem's tyranny, or the nature of Vietnamese nationalism, or the long colonialism of the French—this was all too damned complicated, it required some reading—but no matter, it was a war to stop the Communists, plain and simple, which was how they liked things, and you were a treasonous pussy if you had second thoughts about killing or dying for plain and simple reasons.

I was bitter, sure. But it was so much more than that. The emotions went from outrage to terror to bewilderment to guilt to sorrow and then back again to outrage. I felt a sickness inside me. Real disease.

Most of this I've told before, or at least hinted at, but what I have never told is the full truth. How I cracked. How at work one morning, standing on the pig line, I felt something break open in my chest. I don't know what it was. I'll never know. But it was real, I know that much, it was a physical rupture—a cracking-leaking-popping feeling. I remember dropping my water gun. Quickly, almost without thought, I took off my apron and walked out of the plant and drove home. It was midmorning, I remember, and the house was empty. Down in my chest there was still that leaking sensation, something very warm and precious spilling out, and I was covered with blood and hog-stink, and for a long while I just concentrated on holding myself together. I remember taking a hot shower. I remember packing a suitcase and carrying it out to the kitchen, standing very still for a few minutes, looking carefully at the familiar objects all around me. The old chrome toaster, the telephone, the pink and white Formica on the kitchen counters. The room was full of bright sunshine. Everything sparkled. My house, I thought. My life. I'm not sure how long I stood there, but later I scribbled out a short note to my parents.

What it said, exactly, I don't recall now. Something vague. Taking off, will call, love Tim.

I drove north.

It's a blur now, as it was then, and all I remember is a sense of high velocity and the feel of the steering wheel in my hands. I was riding on adrenaline. A giddy feeling, in a way, except there was the dreamy edge of impossibility to it—like running a dead-end maze—no way out—it couldn't come to a happy conclusion and yet I was doing it anyway because it was all I could think of to do. It was pure flight, fast and mindless. I had no plan. Just hit the border at high speed and crash through and keep on running. Near dusk I passed through Bemidji, then turned northeast toward International Falls. I spent the night in the car behind a closed-down gas station a half mile from the border. In the morning, after gassing up, I headed straight west along the Rainy River, which separates Minnesota from Canada, and which for me separated one life from another. The land was mostly wilderness. Here and there I passed a motel or bait shop, but otherwise the country unfolded in great sweeps of pine and birch and sumac. Though it was still August, the air already had the smell of October, football season, piles of yellow-red leaves, everything crisp and clean. I remember a huge blue sky. Off to my right was the Rainy River, wide as a lake in places, and beyond the Rainy River was Canada.

For a while I just drove, not aiming at anything, then in the late morning I began looking for a place to lie low for a day or two. I was exhausted, and scared sick, and around noon I pulled into an old fishing resort called the Tip Top Lodge. Actually it was not a lodge at all, just eight or nine tiny yellow cabins clustered on a peninsula that jutted northward into the Rainy River. The place was in sorry shape. There was a dangerous wooden dock, an old minnow tank, a flimsy tar paper boathouse along the shore. The main building, which stood in a cluster of pines on high ground, seemed to lean heavily to one side, like a cripple, the roof sagging toward Canada. Briefly, I thought about turning around, just giving up, but then I got out of the car and walked up to the front porch.

The man who opened the door that day is the hero of my life. How do I say this without sounding sappy? Blurt it out—the man saved me. He offered exactly what I needed, without questions, without any words at all. He took me in. He was there at the critical time—a silent, watchful presence. Six days later, when it ended, I was unable to find a proper way to thank him, and I never have, and so, if nothing else, this story represents a small gesture of gratitude twenty years overdue.

Even after two decades I can close my eyes and return to that porch at the Tip Top Lodge. I can see the old guy staring at me. Elroy Berdahl: eighty-one years old, skinny and shrunken and mostly bald. He wore a flannel shirt and brown work pants. In one hand, I remember, he carried a green apple, a small paring knife in the other. His eyes had the bluish gray color of a razor blade, the same polished shine, and as he peered up at me I felt a strange sharpness, almost painful, a cutting sensation, as if his gaze were somehow slicing me open. In part, no doubt, it was my own sense of guilt, but even so I'm absolutely certain that the old man took one look and went right to the heart of things—a kid in trouble. When I asked for a room, Elroy made a little clicking sound with his tongue. He nodded, led me out to one of the cabins, and dropped a key in my hand. I remember smiling at him. I also remember wishing I hadn't. The old man shook his head as if to tell me it wasn't worth the bother.

"Dinner at five-thirty," he said. "You eat fish?"

"Anything," I said.

Elroy grunted and said, "I'll bet."

We spent six days together at the Tip Top Lodge. Just the two of us. Tourist season was over, and there were no boats on the river, and the wilderness seemed to withdraw into a great permanent stillness. Over those six days Elroy Berdahl and I took most of our meals together. In the mornings we sometimes went out on long hikes into the woods, and at night we played Scrabble or listened to records or sat reading in front of his big stone fireplace. At times I felt the awkwardness of an intruder, but Elroy accepted me into his quiet routine without fuss or ceremony. He took my presence for granted, the same way he might've sheltered a stray cat—no wasted sighs or pity—and there was never any talk about it. Just the opposite. What I remember more than anything is the man's willful, almost ferocious silence. In all that time together, all those hours, he never asked the obvious questions: Why was I there? Why alone? Why so preoccupied? If Elroy was curious about any of this, he was careful never to put it into words.

My hunch, though, is that he already knew. At least the basics. After all, it was 1968, and guys were burning draft cards, and Canada was just a boat ride away. Elroy Berdahl was no hick. His bedroom, I remember, was cluttered with books and newspapers. He killed me at the Scrabble board, barely concentrating, and on those occasions when speech was necessary he had a way of compressing large thoughts into small, cryptic packets of language. One evening, just at sunset, he pointed up at an owl circling over the violet-lighted forest to the west.

"Hey, O'Brien," he said. "There's Jesus."

The man was sharp—he didn't miss much. Those razor eyes. Now and then he'd catch me staring out at the river, at the far shore, and I could almost hear the tumblers clicking in his head. Maybe I'm wrong, but I doubt it.

One thing for certain, he knew I was in desperate trouble. And he knew I couldn't talk about it. The wrong word—or even the right word— and I would've disappeared. I was wired and jittery. My skin felt too tight. After supper one evening I vomited and went back to my cabin and lay down for a few moments and then vomited again; another time, in the middle of the afternoon, I began sweating and couldn't shut it off. I went through whole days feeling dizzy with sorrow. I couldn't sleep; I couldn't lie still. At night I'd toss around in bed, half awake, half dreaming, imagining how I'd sneak down to the beach and quietly push one of the old man's boats out into the river and start paddling my way toward Canada. There were times when I thought I'd gone off the psychic edge. I couldn't tell up from down, I was just falling, and late in the night I'd lie there watching weird pictures spin through my head. Getting chased by the Border Patrol—helicopters and searchlights and barking dogs—I'd be crashing through the woods, I'd be down on my hands and knees—people shouting out my name—the law closing in on all sides—my hometown draft board and the FBI and the Royal Canadian Mounted Police. It all seemed crazy and impossible. Twenty-one years old, an ordinary kid with all the ordinary dreams and ambitions, and all I wanted was to live the life I was born to—a mainstream life—I loved baseball and hamburgers and cherry Cokes—and now I was off on the margins of exile, leaving my country forever, and it seemed so impossible and terrible and sad.

I'm not sure how I made it through those six days. Most of it I can't remember. On two or three afternoons, to pass some time, I helped Elroy get the place ready for winter, sweeping down the cabins and hauling in the boats, little chores that kept my body moving. The days were cool and bright. The nights were very dark. One morning the old man showed me how to split and stack firewood, and for several hours we just worked in silence out behind his house. At one point, I remember, Elroy put down his maul and looked at me for a long time, his lips drawn as if framing a difficult question, but then he shook his head and went back to work. The man's self-control was amazing. He never pried. He never put me in a position that required lies or denials. To an extent, I suppose, his reticence was typical of that part of Minnesota, where privacy still held value, and even if I'd been walking around with some horrible deformity—four arms and three heads—I'm sure the old man would've talked about everything except those extra arms and heads. Simple politeness was part of it. But even more than that, I think, the man understood that words were insufficient. The problem had gone beyond discussion. During that long summer I'd been over and over the various arguments, all the pros and cons, and it was no longer a question that could be decided by an act of pure reason. Intellect had come up against emotion. My conscience told me to run, but some irrational and powerful force was resisting, like a weight pushing me toward the war. What it came down to, stupidly, was a sense of shame. Hot, stupid shame. I did not want people to think badly of me. Not my parents, not my brother and sister, not even the folks down at the Gobbler Café. I was ashamed to be there at the Tip Top Lodge. I was ashamed of my conscience, ashamed to be doing the right thing.

Some of this Elroy must've understood. Not the details, of course, but the plain fact of crisis.

Although the old man never confronted me about it, there was one occasion when he came close to forcing the whole thing out into the open. It was early evening, and we'd just finished supper, and over coffee and dessert I asked him about my bill, how much I owed so far. For a long while the old man squinted down at the tablecloth.

"Well, the basic rate," he said, "is fifty bucks a night. Not counting meals. This makes four nights, right?"

I nodded. I had three hundred and twelve dollars in my wallet.

Elroy kept his eyes on the tablecloth. "Now that's an on-season price. To be fair, I suppose we should knock it down a peg or two." He leaned back in his chair. "What's a reasonable number, you figure?"

"I don't know," I said. "Forty?"

"Forty's good. Forty a night. Then we tack on food—say another hundred? Two hundred sixty total?"

"I guess."

He raised his eyebrows. "Too much?"

"No, that's fair. It's fine. Tomorrow, though . . . I think I'd better take off tomorrow."

Elroy shrugged and began clearing the table. For a time he fussed with the dishes, whistling to himself as if the subject had been settled. After a second he slapped his hands together.

"You know what we forgot?" he said. "We forgot wages. Those odd jobs you done. What we have to do, we have to figure out what your time's worth. Your last job—how much did you pull in an hour?"

"Not enough," I said.

"A bad one?"

"Yes. Pretty bad."

Slowly then, without intending any long sermon, I told him about my days at the pig plant. It began as a straight recitation of the facts, but before I could stop myself I was talking about the blood clots and the water gun and how the smell had soaked into my skin and how I couldn't wash it away. I went on for a long time. I told him about wild hogs squealing in my dreams, the sounds of butchery, slaughterhouse sounds, and how I'd sometimes wake up with that greasy pig-stink in my throat.

When I was finished, Elroy nodded at me.

"Well, to be honest," he said, "when you first showed up here, I wondered about all that. The aroma, I mean. Smelled like you was awful dammed fond of pork chops." The old man almost smiled. He made a snuffling sound, then sat down with a pencil and a piece of paper. "So what'd this crud job pay? Ten bucks an hour? Fifteen?"

"Less."

Elroy shook his head. "Let's make it fifteen. You put in twenty-five hours here, easy. That's three hundred seventy-five bucks total wages. We subtract the two hundred sixty for food and lodging, I still owe you a hundred and fifteen."

He took four fifties out of his shirt pocket and laid them on the table.

"Call it even," he said.

"No."

"Pick it up. Get yourself a haircut."

The money lay on the table for the rest of the evening. It was still there when I went back to my cabin. In the morning, though, I found an envelope tacked to my door. Inside were the four fifties and a two-word note that said EMERGENCY FUND.

The man knew.

Looking back after twenty years, I sometimes wonder if the events of that summer didn't happen in some other dimension, a place where your life exists before you've lived it, and where it goes afterward. None of it ever seemed real. During my time at the Tip Top Lodge I had the feeling that I'd slipped out of my own skin, hovering a few feet away while some poor yo-yo with my name and face tried to make his way toward a future he didn't understand and didn't want. Even now I can see myself as I was then. It's like watching an old home movie: I'm young and tan and fit. I've got hair—lots of it. I don't smoke or drink. I'm wearing faded blue jeans and a white polo shirt. I can see myself sitting on Elroy Berdahl's dock near dusk one evening, the sky a bright shimmering pink, and I'm finishing up a letter to my parents that tells what I'm about to do and why I'm doing it and how sorry I am that I'd never found the courage to talk to them about it. I ask them not to be angry. I try to explain some of my feelings, but there aren't enough words, and so I just say that it's a thing that has to be done. At the end of the letter I talk about the vacations we used to take up in this north country, at a place called Whitefish Lake, and how the scenery here reminds me of those good times. I tell them I'm fine. I tell them I'll write again from Winnipeg or Montreal or wherever I end up.

On my last full day, the sixth day, the old man took me out fishing on the Rainy River. The afternoon was sunny and cold. A stiff breeze came in from the north, and I remember how the little fourteen-foot boat made sharp rocking motions as we pushed off from the dock. The current was fast. All around us, I remember, there was a vastness to the world, an unpeopled rawness, just the trees and the sky and the water reaching out toward nowhere. The air had the brittle scent of October.

For ten or fifteen minutes Elroy held a course upstream, the river choppy and silver-gray, then he turned straight north and put the engine on full throttle. I felt the bow lift beneath me. I remember the wind in my ears, the sound of the old outboard Evinrude. For a time I didn't pay attention to anything, just feeling the cold spray against my face, but then it occurred to me that at some point we must've passed into Canadian waters, across that dotted line between two different worlds, and I remember a sudden tightness in my chest as I looked up and watched the far shore come at me. This wasn't a daydream. It was tangible and real. As we came in toward land, Elroy cut the engine, letting the boat fishtail lightly about twenty yards off shore. The old man didn't look at me or speak. Bending down, he opened up his tackle box and busied himself with a bobber and a piece of wire leader, humming to himself, his eyes down.

It struck me then that he must've planned it. I'll never be certain, of course, but I think he meant to bring me up against the realities, to guide me across the river and to take me to the edge and to stand a kind of vigil as I chose a life for myself.

I remember staring at the old man, then at my hands, then at Canada. The shoreline was dense with brush and timber. I could see tiny red berries on the bushes. I could see a squirrel up in one of the birch trees, a big crow looking at me from a boulder along the river. That close—twenty yards—and I could see the delicate latticework of the leaves, the texture of the soil, the browned needles beneath the pines, the configurations of geology and human history. Twenty yards. I could've done it. I could've jumped and started swimming for my life. Inside me, in my chest, I felt a terrible squeezing pressure. Even now, as I write this, I can still feel that tightness. And I want you to feel it—the wind coming off the river, the waves, the silence, the wooded frontier. You're at the bow of a boat on the Rainy River. You're twenty-one years old, you're scared, and there's a hard squeezing pressure in your chest.

What would you do?

Would you jump? Would you feel pity for yourself? Would you think about your family and your childhood and your dreams and all you're leaving behind? Would it hurt? Would it feel like dying? Would you cry, as I did?

I tried to swallow it back. I tried to smile, except I was crying.

Now, perhaps, you can understand why I've never told this story before. It's not just the embarrassment of tears. That's part of it, no doubt, but what embarrasses me much more, and always will, is the paralysis that took my heart. A moral freeze: I couldn't decide, I couldn't act, I couldn't comport myself with even a pretense of modest human dignity.

All I could do was cry. Quietly, not bawling, just the chest-chokes.

At the rear of the boat Elroy Berdahl pretended not to notice. He held a fishing rod in his hands, his head bowed to hide his eyes. He kept humming a soft, monotonous little tune. Everywhere, it seemed, in the trees and water and sky, a great worldwide sadness came pressing down on me, a crushing sorrow, sorrow like I had never known it before. And what was so sad, I realized, was that Canada had become a pitiful fantasy. Silly and hopeless. It was no longer a possibility. Right then, with the shore so close,

I understood that I would not do what I should do. I would not swim away from my hometown and my country and my life. I would not be brave. That old image of myself as a hero, as a man of conscience and courage, all that was just a threadbare pipe dream. Bobbing there on the Rainy River, looking back at the Minnesota shore, I felt a sudden swell of helplessness come over me, a drowning sensation, as if I had toppled overboard and was being swept away by the silver waves. Chunks of my own history flashed by. I saw a seven-year-old boy in a white cowboy hat and a Lone Ranger mask and a pair of holstered six-shooters; I saw a twelve-year-old Little League shortstop pivoting to turn a double play; I saw a sixteen-year-old kid decked out for his first prom, looking spiffy in a white tux and a black bow tie, his hair cut short and flat, his shoes freshly polished. My whole life seemed to spill out into the river, swirling away from me, everything I had ever been or ever wanted to be. I couldn't get my breath; I couldn't stay afloat; I couldn't tell which way to swim. A hallucination, I suppose, but it was as real as anything I would ever feel. I saw my parents calling to me from the far shoreline. I saw my brother and sister, all the townfolk, the mayor and the entire Chamber of Commerce and all my old teachers and girlfriends and high school buddies. Like some weird sporting event: everybody screaming from the sidelines, rooting me on—a loud stadium roar. Hotdogs and popcorn—stadium smells, stadium heat. A squad of cheerleaders did cartwheels along the banks of the Rainy River; they had megaphones and pompoms and smooth brown thighs. The crowd swayed left and right. A marching band played fight songs. All my aunts and uncles were there, and Abraham Lincoln, and Saint George, and a nine-year-old girl named Linda who had died of a brain tumor back in fifth grade, and several members of the United States Senate, and a blind poet scribbling notes, and LBJ, and Huck Finn, and Abbie Hoffman, and all the dead soldiers back from the grave, and the many thousands who were later to die—villagers with terrible burns, little kids without arms or legs—yes, and the Joint Chiefs of Staff were there, and a couple of popes, and a first lieutenant named Jimmy Cross, and the last surviving veteran of the American Civil War, and Jane Fonda dressed up as Barbarella, and an old man sprawled beside a pigpen, and my grandfather, and Gary Cooper, and a kind-faced woman carrying an umbrella and a copy of Plato's *Republic,* and a million ferocious citizens waving flags of all shapes and colors—people in hard hats, people in headbands—they were all whooping and chanting and urging me toward one shore or the other. I saw faces from my distant past and distant future. My wife was there. My unborn daughter waved at me, and my two sons hopped up and down, and a drill sergeant named Blyton sneered and shot up a finger and shook his head. There was a choir in bright purple robes. There was a cabbie from the Bronx. There was a slim young man I would one day kill with a hand grenade along a red clay trail outside the village of My Khe.

The little aluminum boat rocked softly beneath me. There was the wind and the sky.

I tried to will myself overboard.

I gripped the edge of the boat and leaned forward and thought, *Now.*

I did try. It just wasn't possible.

All those eyes on me—the town, the whole universe—and I couldn't risk the embarrassment. It was as if there were an audience to my life, that swirl of faces along the river, and in my head I could hear people screaming at me. Traitor! they yelled. Turncoat! Pussy! I felt myself blush. I couldn't tolerate it. I couldn't endure the mockery, or the disgrace, or the patriotic ridicule. Even in my imagination, the shore just twenty yards away, I couldn't make myself be brave. It had nothing to do with morality. Embarrassment, that's all it was.

And right then I submitted.

I would go to the war—I would kill and maybe die—because I was embarrassed not to.

That was the sad thing. And so I sat in the bow of the boat and cried.

It was loud now. Loud, hard crying.

Elroy Berdahl remained quiet. He kept fishing, He worked his line with the tips of his fingers, patiently, squinting out at his red and white bobber on the Rainy River. His eyes were flat and impassive. He didn't speak. He was simply there, like the river and the late-summer sun. And yet by his presence, his mute watchfulness, he made it real. He was the true audience. He was a witness, like God, or like the gods, who look on in absolute silence as we live our lives, as we make our choices or fail to make them.

"Ain't biting," he said.

Then after a time the old man pulled in his line and turned the boat back toward Minnesota.

I don't remember saying goodbye. That last night we had dinner together, and I went to bed early, and in the morning Elroy fixed breakfast for me. When I told him I'd be leaving, the old man nodded as if he already knew. He looked down at the table and smiled.

At some point later in the morning it's possible that we shook hands— I just don't remember—but I do know that by the time I'd finished packing the old man had disappeared. Around noon, when I took my suitcase out to the car, I noticed that his old black pickup truck was no longer parked in front of the house. I went inside and waited for a while, but I felt a bone certainty that he wouldn't be back. In a way, I thought, it was appropriate. I washed up the breakfast dishes, left his two hundred dollars on the kitchen counter, got into the car, and drove south toward home.

The day was cloudy. I passed through towns with familiar names, through the pine forests and down to the prairie, and then to Vietnam, where I was a soldier, and then home again. I survived, but it's not a happy ending. I was a coward. I went to the war.

MAY ANGELS LEAD YOU HOME

Sharon Sheehe Stark

The day after his father's funeral Joseph Kleeve sat in his office, but not very well. "He has ants in his pants," he overhead Debbie, his secretary, tell some girlfriend over the phone. He was just wrapping up his business with Mildred Gaugler.

"Okey doke," he said. "I'll give it my best shot. Have a good day, now." A notch at a time he was nudging her out the door.

"Chust hold your horses once!" The full-bodied woman came heavily about and regarded him with bleached, unyielding eyes. "Now mindt," she said, "don't forget to make Lizzie pay for the gas it takes to come here." She shook a finger at him. "Extra yet for aggravation."

"Mildred," he said, "to the best of my knowledge, the law, God bless it, doesn't pay beans for aggravation."

"The boss is rutchy today, say not?" she said to the secretary, who looked up from *People* with a smile like the white of an apple.

When Mildred was gone, he went back to his desk, put his feet up, and tilted back. Mildred Gaugler had just retained him to recover something called a "hollyhock teapot." The object had been willed to her by her deceased mother but currently resided with her oldest sister, Lizzie. She wanted the teapot, plus gas, plus aggravation. He buzzed his secretary. She came to the doorway.

"Deb," he said, "what gets into people?"

"Beats me," she said, yawning. She went back to her desk.

The truth was, he bore a special fondness for Mrs. Gaugler and the cousinage of like clients who had been with him from the beginning—sixth-, seventh-generation Pennsylvania Dutch who saw fit to trust him despite his almost abject outsiderness. He would never adjust to their strange hybrid tongue, nor relish their doughy suppers. They got a kick out of him when he tried.

He settled their multitudinous boundary disputes, represented their drag-racing sons and disgraced daughters. Against his better judgment he drew up endlessly particularizing wills in which, for instance, one hollyhock teapot is specifically bequeathed to Mildred Gaugler. In the meantime the testator forgets and gives the teapot away, then thoughtlessly dies. Much aggrieved, Mildred decides to sue the estate; she is joined in that action by a dozen other heirs, who are missing sewing machines,

458

chocolate sets, bean dryers. The very thought of all that dusty stuff made him fidgety.

He popped out of his chair and circled his desk three times. He ate an apple, a granola bar. He took his pulse and blood pressure. Normal was boring. He set up the projector and put on his favorite reel, his son winning the district wrestling championship last year. Debbie came right away when he buzzed. She sat down, facing the screen, foot tapping the practiced beat of her tedium.

"Watch this, Deb. . . . Watch him pussyfoot out of this one. . . . You're not going to believe this pancake. . . . What a whizzer. . . . Ever see a Granby roll into a Peterson? Hold on—Christ, was that nice or was that nice? Hey, don't go, semi-finals coming up."

"Phone's ringing," she said.

"Let it."

After Michael pinned his opponent in the finals, Joseph Kleeve flicked the switch quickly, before the film moved on to the tragedy at the state tournament. He checked his watch. "I'm going for a walk," he said.

"Suit yourself."

It was not an ideal day for a stroll. A walking-stick of an old woman traversed the windy corner at Sixth and Widcombe, stepping sideways and forward at the same time. A heavy gust spun Joseph like a top, and when he came about the world stood at an angle, unfamiliar to him.

"The streets have shifted," his wife had said as she watched him dress for work. Louise always delivered difficult advice in obliquities and riddles. She wanted him to stay home another day or so. "Just until you get your bearings." Joseph lowered his head and plunged into the wind, shoulders rolled forward like wings.

Up the cold canyons now, figures whipping by, the crags of the city spiking jaggedly around him, the grays and tans and glints of brass buffed to a smoothness like marble. Joseph kept his stride deliberate, rhythmic, to encourage himself. He marched on and on, the blocks slipping by like minutes, and for one of those minutes Joseph forgot who he was and was instead the man he came from, his dad, the day they did Dog Jaw Mountain.

Through heavy winds and hailstones, hard into the boulder country, Harold Kleeve had led Troop 24, stepping high and lively long after it was clear he'd led them wrong. What Joseph remembered most about the hours they were lost was how his father saved face manually, pushing up at the corners of his mouth, reinforcing that image of a leader of men, even as his eyes reddened with the terrible strain of bravery.

Neither would he admit to finer retail than Pincus Brothers, a higher good than the quality shoes he sold there. He had spent his life preaching Naturalizers for wise women and bore only scorn for the mother who would shoe her babe in less than Buster Brown. But what happened when faith failed, when he didn't believe any of it? Monday nights and Dollar

Days and the slow, damp letdown of every January. What did he think then, varicose veins at eye level? How did he bear leading one more club-woman to the x-ray machine that showed if the feet were pinched, his doubts as crowded as the tiny white toebones. Toebones, teapots—how did a man's life attract such things?

Joseph was astonished to see that he'd already walked far beyond the business section of town. He was passing large Victorian showplaces turned into studios and offices, a renovated house with windows like ice-cube trays. Freezing, he hailed a cab to shuttle him back down to Sixth Street. Instead of going to the office, he took his car out of the lot and drove to the mall. He phoned and told Debbie not to expect him for the rest of the day. "I'm at the law library," he told her.

"Come off it," she said. "That's what *I* tell people."

"Okay," he conceded, "I'm at the mall. I'm goofing off."

He ordered a chili dog from a girl with flawless skin and eyes the green of mint. "You look like a man who make decisions all day," she said, smiling. He thought maybe she ran a consulting firm on the side. He would subscribe to her service, whatever it was. He would tell her things he never told anybody else. He wondered how his father had felt with a pretty ankle in his hand. Priestly? Like a lucky man?

"You need C, the decisive vitamin," she said, selling him a large Orange Julius, the consultation over.

At the electronics store he bought earphones for jogging and a little box named Boris. Boris could beat experts at chess. He bought the companion book on how to beat Boris.

When he ran out of quarters, he left the space-game arcade and drove out to Lum's VW. Larry Lum said, "Hey, baby, only new item on the lot is that tangerine Vanagon."

The small purchases he'd made—the hot dog, the gadgets—lay like a handful of millet at the bottom of his bereavement. He was still sucking hunger. And Lum's sound system, deft as a spider, wrapped him in sticky desire, packaged for easy handling. A Mercedes might be needed to fill him up, but a tangerine van would go a long way. "If I can take it with me," he said.

"No sweat," Larry Lum said. "I'll put the boys on it right away. Tell you what—I'll even have them drive the old one out to the house tomorrow. Or did you plan on trading her in?

"Oh, no," he said quickly. "I need them both." His dad used to chuckle over the women who put their new shoes on and carried the old pair home in a box like a coffin.

As was his wont, when in need—after losing in court or suffering affront—Joseph headed for the first point on the road to recovery. He went straight to the Improper. Before the cocktail hour a lounge was a woeful thing—naked, bereft, its cracks and shabbiness laid open, cigarette burns in the leatherette, the urine smell that such places take on after a decade or so with the same foam rubber. Always at least one boozy housewife, trying to read her watch in the dark, muttering about dinner. Waitresses standing around, still tired from the night before, always getting over someone named Rick.

At the end of the bar stood Kilray, the dining-room host, in his cerulean cutaway and frilly ecru shirt. The man looked torpid, stalled, as if his life could not possibly resume until the dinner crowd began to dribble in. Avoiding Kilray's eyes, Joseph hunched low over his Lambrusco.

When Kilray shambled over anyhow, Joseph gave him a taut sidelong look, a curt nod. The man had dank, pouched cheeks and small, insolent eyes. He put his hand on Joseph's shoulder and brought his face too close. "Liar game must be slow, you're cutting out this early."

Joseph shrugged, waiting for the inevitable "trouble with you guys" number, which, in due course, came. Stiffly polite, he endured the smug aggression masquerading as a friendly ribbing between equals. "Just as a fer instance," Kilray was saying, "what if the person on the other side is some poor orphan kid and your client's trying to grab his last dime. Whatcha gonna do counselor?"

"Punt," Joseph said.

"What if your client's up for murder and says to you, 'Kleeve, ol' boy, I did it, sure as God made popcorn, I stabbed her eighty-nine times and buried her out back.' Whatcha tellin' this clown, counselor?"

"Ribbet," Joseph said, winking at the bartender.

"Who you for, anyhow?" the man said, belligerent now. "The criminal or the victim?"

Joseph fixed him hard. "Simple," he said. "Before the crime, I'm on the victim's side. After the crime, I'm for my client." He paid for the drink and left, Kilray's breath still wet on his neck.

The way home was long but handily subdivided. If he drove straight out the old highway five or six reasonably congenial way stations dotted his route. His last regular stop within the city itself was a place called The Office. Dark hardwoods and a dignified, dyspeptic bartender contributed to its clubby atmosphere. The Office catered to a primarily professional crowd—journalists, lawyers stopping for a respectable two drinks before heading out to the suburbs, where civic-minded women waited in gleaming kitchens. These women received their husbands in rooms as tranquil as funeral parlors. They wore headbands in primary colors and had definite opinions on real subjects and kept their shoelaces tied.

Or the wives would arrive from offices of their own, their lunchtime purchases in stiff bags from tony shops. Joseph had nothing against these women, but he'd never wanted any of them. Why did he shame his wife because she was a mite irregular? He imagined Louise asleep in her antique choir gown. Louise coming home from a flea market, wearing all her new-old things at once. Should Louise reform tomorrow, he would set that new Louise against ever rarer expectations, the ideal forever revisable. She would never be right. He would never have the right wife. If he did, he would probably lose her.

Page Levingood stood over Don Briggs, one foot on the rung of the latter's stool. Joseph watched two others approach. No, he did not want their women; and he did not want their practices. The lawyers acknowledged Joseph obliquely and went on with their conversation.

They were the legal gentry, and Joseph knew that whatever scorn he bore for them was returned a hundredfold, and with a disdain more confident than his own. He knew that these men saw him as unbridled and eccentric, disgracefully got up, vulgar. They viewed his criminal clientele as the company he kept, defending felons as tantamount to accessory after the fact. His dealings with the likes of Mildred Gaugler made him practically casteless. What did he care what they thought?

He ordered another Lambrusco. Something in the air reminded him of Michael, only twice in his life his father's son. When he was a baby, his eyes were round and cobalt blue, and sometimes when you held him he would wedge his head under your chin and drive up until you cried uncle. And later—was he nine, ten?—when he set his whole self against the world, he made his teachers weep and his mother beg for clemency. For all that independent spirit, the boy could hardly bear the precariousness of the outlaw life. He would not be cast out. Joseph picked up his drink and went to crash the clique of gentlemen specialists.

"Don," he said. "Page." To the other two he gave a genial nod and raised his glass. They were young, young men. So many new lawyers had come to town that Joseph could hardly keep track. "Kleeve," he said.

"Oh, wow, hi," said the smaller of the two, thrusting out a hand. "How are you, sir? Wow, you're practically a legend. They say you're a courtroom gorer. Grrrr!" He was eager, clean, shiny as the buttons on his blazer. Waves of thick, burnished hair, neat-fitting clothes—a lawyer doll. The other young man was eager to get on with his hypothesis. "So anyhow, these two couples have a verbal agreement about the two houses, but nothing on paper, when party number one—"

Taking tiny, thoughtful sips, the shiny young man mulled the question while the two older lawyers nodded in false attentiveness, their eyes watching the secretaries straggle in. Joseph said, "Gotta run. It's a long way out to God's country."

"Yeah, take it easy, Kleeve," Page Levingood said, the questioning way you say good-bye when you haven't bothered yet to say hello.

Joseph carried his glass out with him.

Now he was passing between the trees lining a wide boulevard, his way cushioned with fallen leaves. The drive was quiet, quiet, and after a while he was riding not in his big hollow van but in the magic light inside a forties railroad car. He is six, and the box of brightness that contains him contains his father as well. They have come from a small town a few miles south, where they have made burial arrangements for his father's father, who died an indigent in the house of a patient landlady.

They are a thoughtful pair, but not sad. The old man had been a stranger to both of them. Harold Kleeve sits with a bag on his lap. The bag bulges with popcorn balls and Good n' Plenty, wax lips and moustaches and little milk bottles holding colored syrup. Bubble gum, pumpkin seeds, comic books, all things Joseph's mother would have vetoed out of hand. Harold Kleeve is a staunch upholder of parental unity, but tonight is different; tonight is an island, father and son and dark all around.

The train does not rock and sway in the jaunty, unserious style of trolley cars. So smooth, in fact, is the ride that the light seems the vehicle; they are traveling in troughs of light, and the boy thinks of the pneumatic tubes that ferry money around the store where his father works. Despite the lateness of the hour, he is saucer-eyed. His father tries to explain the principle that keeps the train tracking; Harold Kleeve is always showing and teaching.

Joseph unfolds his Fleer's Double Bubble fortune: *Keep looking: What's lost will be found.*

"Son," Harold Kleeve says, shaking tobacco into a cigarette paper. "If you don't do anything else in the world, you square it with the landlady and you bury your dead."

The boy watches his father's smoke rise and form a large blue circle under the lights, and the dark outside is the world.

Entering the Hessian Inn, he spotted a former secretary. Her name was Cathy Koolbaugh, and she was dining with a young man. Hoping to avoid her, he waved off-handedly from the foyer, pretending he'd just dashed in to buy a pack of cigarettes from the vending machine. Outside, he tossed the L&Ms into a hedge. He had no real cause for his discomfiture; the girl hadn't the faintest notion how he'd misused her name.

Once, after one of his friskier rampages, Louise and Michael had turned into a chorus of hissing indignation, ordering him to leave forever. "Get out! Get out! Get out!" they shrieked. "I'm splitting this hovel," was his response. "And don't try to stop me." Sleeping on his office couch, he'd awakened in the early hours, sodden with the incomparable grief of the spirit not yet hardened to exile. He could not survive another second without hearing their voices. Yet penitence was out of the question. Stupidly, he phoned without rehearsing first. When Louise answered, to his horror he started to cry. Humiliated, he had to think fast. "Remember Cathy Koolbaugh?" he sobbed. "I must have been crazy to let her go. I'm heartsick, heartsick. I think I'm in love with the girl." "Oh, you liar," Louise said softly, and hung up.

Joseph stayed on the old road that ran parallel to the interstate. It would carry him to within a half mile of his front door. The bars were spaced farther apart now. The inns that contained them were eighteenth-century wayfarers' stops, one in each country village. It was very lonely between towns, and the tavern lights drew Joseph like lines thrown to him in the darkness. The places had names like the Womelsdorf Tavern, the Drovers & Farmers Hotel, Lavina Stump's Place. They smelled of stale beer and dry rot and frying, the damp stone walls covered in damp blond paneling. In one of those places he shot a game of baseball darts against a guy named Ron, whose tiny daughter sat on the stool munching Slim Jims and calling Joseph a "poophead" every time he scored. The men talked about upkeep, on cars and beards. "Must you cut it much?" Ron wanted to know.

"I pretty much let'er rip," Joseph said, fondling his red bonfire of a beard.

"Now, me, I get the wife to trim it good Saturday night. Makes it nice for church." Joseph left feeling vaguely chastened.

Deeper yet into the country. He stopped at the 1780 House. He ordered a beer from an ancient, cadaverous bartender who served him and headed upstairs to bed, telling Joseph to "outen the lights" when he left.

The lot outside the next place was parked solid. Big farmers' cars—Pontiacs, Impalas, a goodly number of four-wheelers and pickups. Country music floated in the damp air, and the moon was a snippet of skin adrift in the mottled dark. The jangle of noise when he opened the door hit him in the ear like a wire brush.

Not a seat to be had in the house. Not at the bar, not at the oilcloth-draped tables laden with platters of ring bologna and American-cheese cubes and sweating pitchers of dark beer. Joseph had almost forgotten how it was on Ladies' Night at the Longswamp Hotel.

The noise grew, aggressive, excruciating, and seemed to ease off only as the din from the "boom-bas" blunted the hearing. Joseph looked for a chink in the wall of bodies pressing the bar. Even the nine or ten boom-bas players had to fight for space on the narrow strip of floor allotted them. Dozens of like instruments hung from hooks on the wall behind them or leaned against tables and laps, awaiting their owners' turns on the floor.

The players pumped and pounded and drummed to "Slap Her Down Again, Pa," and then "The More Beer Polka." The jukebox jumped and the floor shook; the sound hummed, like blood in the bones. Several bangers wore the look of serious musicians and appeared to be refining fancy mannerisms. One very tall man described a high, elegant flourish after each strike of the cymbal. Another, younger man hunched over his stick like a bass player, eyes closed, the tip of his tongue lolling.

The boom-bas itself was not unlike a pogo stick in size and function. Its heavy spring base gave it bounce, and the wealth of attached noisemakers turned it into a kind of compound percussion instrument. A band-on-a-stick. You might find bolted along its length a tambourine, a cowbell, a bicycle bell, and a musical block. Often a strap of sleighbells would appear, and a Good Humor bell, and maybe now and again, on the deluxe model, double cowbells and a shiny brass Model T horn. Set like a coolie hat on the top was a set of cymbals, and above that, covering the tip of the stick, was something akin to a hood ornament, a personal totem—maybe a beer-tap handle, a Mack bulldog, a Kiwanis K.

Two players staggered, exhausted, to their seats; two more took their places. The reconstituted crew battered through "Chattanooga Choo-choo," rallying, it seemed, around the rowdiest among them, a damp dumpling of a woman, playing with crashing abandon, all parts invested, from the flying elbows to the liquid ripple and shift of breast and belly. She had lively little foam-soled feet, and her slacks, too short, were over-stuffed peach polyesters that rode up and down as she stretched and flexed, her face florid with enjoyment. Such gusto worked like a giant mouth, sucking onlookers in; people watched with tiny, undecided smiles that reminded Joseph of screen doors cocked partway open. He found himself bopping in place, pumping his shoulders in ragged counterpoint to her looser rhythm, the flesh of her upper arms swinging, jiggling like satin sleeves.

The music stopped and Joseph's woman came off the floor, sopping with sweat, a plump hand calming her heart. When she came abreast of him, he was disappointed to see how common she was offstage. Common as Mildred Gaugler. Good grief, it *was* Mildred Gaugler!

And now it was too late to look away, because she'd already spotted him. "Ay, don't tell me!" she cried. She pinched his cheek and led him by the elbow to a table taken up by four equally vivacious late-middle-aged women. Somebody handed him a glass of beer, and Mildred Gaugler introduced him. "And this here's my Ladies' Night regklars," she said. "Myrt, Verna, Vi, and Irene."

The women had blonde or blue or pewter-toned very short perms you could see through in the light coming from the kitchen. They wore earrings of shiny plastic and startling circles of rouge drawn low on their large German faces. Each time he finished his beer, somebody replaced it, and then they'd all sit around grinning from him to one another. He might have been a kid they'd agreed to take for the day, only to find themselves at a loss as to how best to keep him entertained.

When the music started up again, Mildred hooked his arm and yanked him out of his seat. "Loan us your stick once," she said to Irene. "For Lawyer Kleeve here."

By the time they had edged their way out, the floor trembled again at full capacity. Mildred bumped a coat rack out of the way and set him up at the very edge of the players' area. She showed him how to hold the stick and then zipped around, taking a firm grip on him from behind. "Now, that there's your tempo," she said, demonstrating. He felt the heavy tides of her flesh against his as she pumped him up and down from the armpits. "Move! she cried. "Don't be s'darn poky!"

"Bounce from the knees, Mister." Verna, having joined them, was trying to make herself authoritative over the din. "Bounce, darn you!" She was wearing a short-sleeved rayon shirt that said Grundsow Lodge Auxiliary over the pocket. While Mildred operated his body from behind, Verna made his arm go, ringing here, clacking there, honking to "Knock three times on the ceiling if you wa-ant me." After a while somebody yelled, "Ease up once. Now let him go," and they released him as tenderly as they might a kid on his first bike.

The women took up their own instruments and positioned themselves on both sides of him. He began to move, woodenly at first, not bouncing so much as pitching from the waist, and when he poked his rear out too far, one of the women whacked it back with her stick. What an ingenious device it was. The more you drank the faster you learned. He began to warm to his art. In the frenzied heat his muscles loosened, liquefied. The women's boisterous enjoyment spattered him like sparks from an arc-welder. He imagined he could hear the jolly rattle of the skeleton inside his clothes.

When the record changed, he took a break and bought his table another pitcher. Then, to the grave and stately opening strains of the *1812* Overture, he sashayed back out to the floor. The players' faces turned immediately serious, then solemn, then rhapsodic, as the sound behind them swelled with fife and violin, and then guns and cannons and fireworks and extra shots of passion and madness. Joseph hammered and bashed and went crashing to crescendo with the rest; the boom-bas line was one human musical fever that broke in concert, and then they all stood, slightly dazed in dripping skin, dazed and luminous and a little embarrassed, when the music stopped.

Joseph stayed for two more considerably less affecting numbers. He began to add his own dips and furbelows; he danced around the stick. How quickly the alien way became a way of life. Then he and Verna and Vi and Myrt followed Mildred Gaugler around the room in a raucous, wobbly conga line, hammering between tables, banging the tabletops like drums as they snaked in and out.

The quiet hit hard. Looking up, he saw that the place had emptied out and a burly bartender was pulling the plug on the jukebox. Joseph's party returned to their table, where Irene was waiting, arms crossed, her lower lip shoved out. Joseph handed her boom-bas back.

"Don't do me no favors," she said.

"Oooops," he said, "Looks like I've been a bad boy."

Mildred Gaugler turned to the others. "A bad boy," she happily agreed, "but a darn good *man*, say, ladies." Verna and Vi and Myrt nodded wholeheartedly.

"Well," Joseph said, "I'll drink to that. Bring us the best you've got," he called to the waitress wiping the adjacent table with a towel.

"Last call was twenty minutes ago," she said without looking up.

He hunched his shoulders and turned up his palms. "Ooooooooch," he said. Then he bowed from the waist to the petulant one. "Good night, Irene," he said. He kissed her hand. She pushed at her curls. "Night," she replied coyly. "Nice to meetcha, I guess."

He turned to the others. "And good night, ladies."

As he headed out, Mildred called after him, "Button up, now. It's nippy out."

In the tiny town of Kemp he got out of his van. The phosphorescent clock face in the window of Groff's Garage said 3:10. A tiger tomcat crossed the street with ridiculous aplomb. Joseph tried the door of the Kemp Hotel. Resting his brow on the painted wood, he pounded and pounded. Then, stretching, he peered through the glass until he could make out the shadowy gallon jars of vinegar beets and pickled tripe. The glass canister of two-cent pretzels. Higher up, the stingy glint coming from the single shelf of bar whiskey. Joseph scanned slowly, fine-combing, as though night life were sometimes microscopic. He stopped and stared. The only action to be had was trapped in the backbar mirror. The face that flickered there frightened him, a slow-burning, bearded old man embedded deep in ice, lost in the endless perspective of things. He turned away and glanced back, turned and swiveled back, again and again, until he was sure the image would keep. Then, sighing, he gave up and stepped down from the stoop and, listing heavily, made for the only lighted building in town.

He fumbled in his pocket, found a quarter, and dropped it in. When Michael finally picked up the phone and thickly articulated "Hello," Joseph said, "Get your mother."

"See's shleep, slip . . . sleeping."

"It's okay," Louise cut in. "I'm up. I'm on the extension. Joseph, where are you?"

"Foambooth."

"Where?"

"Beau'ful downtown Kemp."

"*Our* Kemp? You're right here? Hold on a minute." He heard her scraping around. Then, "You're right!" she said. "There you are. I see you in the phone booth. I'm looking right at you!" she cried, as if he were some beatific vision. A pause, then quietly, "Why are you calling?"

"House is dark," he said.

"It's late. We were in bed."

"You sleeping in that goddamn choir robe?"

"No," she said. "First time I washed it, it fell apart."

"I'm sorry to hear that," he said.

"Where've you been?"

"Out with the ladies," he said. "Your old hubby's a killer on the boom-bas stick." He started to hum from *1812*. "Puh puh puh puhpuh-puh puh puh! puh! puh! Puh puh . . . " He stopped.

"Joseph? Joseph, what's wrong? You still there? Joseph, are you crying?"

But he could not sing and he could not speak. Nor could he bring himself to hang up. After a long time Louise said very softly, "Joseph, come home."

"Then turn on the lights," he said, raggedly.

"Michael," she called out. "Turn on the lights."

"All of them," Joseph said.

"All of them," she echoed.

He poked the phone in his pocket and waited. He blew his nose, and, tilting back, craning awkwardly over his shoulder, he tried to see up the street to his summer-yellow house with all the latticework and white porches. He squinted and swiped at the glass. But the booth was too bright and he could not see out. He occupied the box of light as he occupied his life, and for a moment he felt as discrete and unquenchable and alone as a distant star.

"Joe," she was calling from his pocket. "Joseph?"

The phone leaped out of his pocket as he lurched forward. Thrashing the door back, he hung out far enough to see for himself. Ah! All three decks were blazing to beat the band. He watched the amber bug lights come on, outlining the porches. The floods under the eaves. A bare bulb burned like God in the attic.

He stumbled back in and took up the dangling receiver. "Ay, such a sight!" he said, in tipsy imitation of Mrs. Gaugler. His laugh was sloppy, lopsided. "Ay, ay, ay, looks chust like a showboat!"

"I'm glad you like it," she said. "Now come home."

"I'll try." In the tenderest of disconnections, Joseph set the receiver back. He turned up his collar and, tugging his coat close, stomach rising, re-entered the river of time.

UNDER THE ROOF

Kate Wheeler

Moist, lead-lemon Bangkok dawn: Miss Bi Chin's Chinese alarm clock goes off, a harsh metallic sound, like tiny villagers beating pans to frighten the dragon of sleep. She opens her eyes and sees a big fire ant crawling up her yellow mosquito net; feels how the black earth's chill has penetrated her hipbones. At first she does not know where she is.

Tuk-tuks, taxis and motorbikes already roar behind the high garden wall; but the air is still sweet, yesterday's fumes brought down by the dew. She has slept outside, behind her house, under the sal tree. All around her lie pink, fleshy blossoms, fallen during the night.

She lies still on her side, allowing last night's trip to Dom Muang airport to bloom in her mind, seeing the American monk stalk from the barrier, his brown robe formally wrapped to form a collar and tight scroll down his right arm. Straight out of Burma. It delights her to remember his keen, uncertain look as he scanned the crowd for her unfamiliar face. Then she waved, and he smiled. On the way home, the taxi driver charged them only half price.

She heaves up to sitting; the monk, who is standing now at her screened upstairs window, sees her hips' awkward sideways roll, her hands pressing the small of her back. Both of them have the same thought: the body is a heap of suffering! The monk steps back quickly, lest Miss Bi Chin catch him gazing out the window—worrying about what will become of him out here in the world. As he moves into the shadow, he suddenly realizes that the worry itself is the world's first invasion, and again he is struck with gratitude for his robes. Having to be an example for others protects me, too, he thinks. It works from the outside in, the way forcing yourself to smile can make you feel happy.

Miss Bi Chin rolls up her straw sleeping mat and hurries into the house with it under her arm. Her bones ache, but she takes joy in that. Why should she rent a hotel room when she can sleep for free in her own back yard? It's not the rainy season. She will earn great merit for helping the monk to sleep as the rules require, under a roof where there is no woman. By now he must have completed his morning meditation.

In her mind she sees the Thai monks going for alms food right now all over the city: hundreds of them in bright orange robes, bare feet stepping over broken glass and black street garbage. They shave their heads only on full moon day, they have TVs and they seduce American tourists. They don't care if the tourists are women or men. Thai people crave too much for sense pleasures. Miss Bi Chin would not donate so much as an orange to Thai monks; she saves her generosity for the good, clean monks trained in Burma.

As she lights the gas under the huge aluminum teakettle, the old man comes shuffling into the dark kitchen. He pulls the light cord, searing the room with jerks of blue fluorescence. "Why do you cook in the dark, Chinese sow," he says in Malay. He is her mother's second husband's brother and lived off the family for years in Penang. Now he has come here to torture her and make her life miserable.

"Shh," she says, motioning with her head. The American monk sits cross-legged at a low table in the next room. His eyes are downcast and a small smile curves his lips. Beautifully white, he resembles the marble Buddhas they sell in Rangoon.

"So what? He doesn't understand me," the old man says. "Why don't you bring in a real man for a change? You'd be a lot less religious if you were satisfied." And I'd be happier living here, he thinks, if she were a normal woman, not lost in pious dreams.

His words roll off her mind like dew from the petals of a white lotus. "You will go to all the hells," she predicts. "First the hot and then the cold."

The old man laughs. "I am Muslim. Will I go to the same hell as you and your rag-wrapped *farang?* I am waiting for my breakfast." He walks in and shows all his teeth to the American monk. "Goo mornin sah!"

"Hey," the monk says. "Thanks for the bed. I slept great."

The old man can only nod. He doesn't understand English. Miss Bi Chin bites her tongue, deciding it is better for the monk's peace of mind not to know it was her bed that he slept in. Of course, she moved it into the sewing room.

This American monk is the favorite of the Rangoon abbot, Miss Bi Chin has heard. He's been in intensive meditation for three years, completing two levels of insight practice and the concentrations of the four heavenly abodes. But the monastery's friend in the Department of Religious Affairs lost his position in November, and the monk's last visa renewal application was rejected. He has come to Thailand to apply for re-entry into Burma; approval will take at least three months, if it comes at all. Conditions in Burma are unstable; the government has had to be very strict to maintain order, and it does not want too many foreign witnesses to its methods. Recently, they changed the country's name to Myanma, as if this would solve its problems.

If the monk cannot return, the abbot may send him back to America to found a monastery. The monk has not been told. The streams of defilements are strong in the West: all the American monks that the abbot has known disrobe soon after they go home, so they can enjoy sense pleasures. Ideally, the monk should stay in Burma a few more years; but the abbot hasn't worn robes all his life to forget that the world is not ideal. This monk is addicted to pondering, a common Western vice, but he has a devoted heart, and his practice has been good. Pork should fry in its own fat; the American devotees cry out for a monastery. This monk may be the perfect candidate.

The abbot sees no reason to make a decision yet. He's asked Miss Bi Chin, the monastery's great supporter, to report on the monk's behavior: whether living unsupervised in capitalist Bangkok becomes his downfall.

Seeing him wait for his food, so still, Miss Bi Chin has no worries. She's studied his face, too, according to Chinese physiognomy. A broad forehead means calm, the deep lines at each side of the mouth mean kindness.

"Breakfast for you." She kneels at the monk's side, offering the dishes from a cubit's distance, as the Buddha prescribed. The monk touches each plate and she sets it on the table. Wheaties, instant Nescafé with condensed milk, sliced mango, lemon cookies from England, and a bowl of instant ramen noodles.

He hasn't seen such food in three years. He smiles in gratitude at Miss Bi Chin and begins eating.

Miss Bi Chin sits on one side with her feet tucked behind her and her hands in the respectful position. Rapture arises in her mind. She has helped Western monks before, and she knows they do not do well on the diet in Rangoon—too much oil and hot pepper. This monk is bony, his skin rough. She will buy chicken extract, milk powder, and vitamins for him, she will take early lunch hours to come and cook his lunch: monks eat no solid food between noon and dawn.

She stops her ears against the sound of the old man, slurping in the kitchen like a hungry ghost.

The monk wipes his mouth. He has finished everything except the noodles, which remind him too much of Burmese food. Miss Bi Chin notices. She'll reheat them for herself with fish paste; the monk's future breakfasts will be entirely Western.

Because the monk is American, he sometimes feels unworthy of being bowed to and, living on donations, guilty about the extent to which he has learned to enjoy such treatment. Miss Bi Chin, for example, is not rich. She works as a secretary at American Express, and says she refused promotion twice so that she can feel free to neglect her job when monks need help. He'd like to thank her for the food, for everything she is going to do for him, but this is not allowed.

If he were still a carpenter, he'd build her a kitchen countertop; as a monk, example and guidance are the only returns he can offer—they're what she expects, he reminds himself, slipping again into the Asian part of his mind. Her donations bring her merit. She supports what I represent, the possibility of enlightenment: not me specifically.

He clears his throat. "Where did you learn such good English?"

"Oh! My mother sent me to a British school in Penang."

"And you speak Burmese, Thai, and what else?"

"Malay, Cantonese, a little Mandarin."

The monk shakes his head. "Amazing. You're one smart lady."

Miss Bi Chin laughs in embarrassment. "I am Chinese, but my family moved to Malaysia, and we had to learn all the languages on the way. If you had my same *kamma,* you would know them, too."

"Listen." The monk laughs. "The abbot did his best to teach me Burmese." It's hard for him to imagine that this woman is also a foreigner here.

"Better for you," Miss Bi Chin says promptly. "For a monk it is most important to maintain virtue and concentration. Learning languages is only worldly knowledge. The Burmese won't let you alone if they know you can speak. When I go to meditate at Pingyan Monastery, I have to hide in my room." She laughs.

The monk smiles, charmed. Faith makes Miss Bi Chin glow like a smooth golden cat; yet her black eyes sparkle wickedly. He will have to be careful to see her as his older sister, or even as a future corpse.

He'd be surprised to know that Miss Bi Chin thinks of herself as ugly. As a child, her mother would tweak her arm hairs and say, "No one will marry you, Black Dog. Better learn English so you can feed yourself." True, no Asian men want Miss Bi Chin, but the reason may not be her skin—there are plenty of married women as dark. No, she is too well educated, too sharp-tongued, and most of all too religious. From her own side, the only Asian men she is interested in are celibate, monks. She had a long relationship with an American, Douglas, the heir to a toy fortune who does business in Bangkok and Singapore. He smokes Dunhills in a holder, and sponsors the publication of Buddhist texts. Younger than she, he left her a year ago for a glamorous twenty-year-old Thai. She still sees him sometimes at Buddhist meetings, drawling his reactionary opinions. How she ever was involved with him is a mystery to her.

Now she cries, "What is there in this world worth talking about? Everything is only blah, blah, blah. I must go to work now and type meaningless reports so that I can sustain my life and yours. I will come back to cook your lunch. Please use my house as you wish. I have many Buddhist books in English. The old man will not bother you."

She shuffles toward the monk on her knees, to remove the plates. Not to introduce the old man as her uncle is one of her secret acts of revenge.

How terrible my life would be without monks, she thinks.

The monk paces slowly up and down Miss Bi Chin's unfurnished living room. His body feels soft and chaotic among the sharp corners, the too shiny parquet, the plastic flowers under a tinted portrait of his abbot, the most famous teacher in Burma. This photograph shows the abbot's terrifying side, when his eyes, hard and sharp, pierce into each person's heart to lay bare its secret flaws. The monk prefers his tenderness, eyes that make you want to fall over sideways.

This is the first day in three years the monk has not been surrounded by other monks, living the life called "pure and clean as a polished shell": its ten precepts, 227 rules, daily alms round, chanting at dusk. The monastery wall was like a mirror facing inward; beyond it was another barrier, the national boundary of Burma. He often used to speculate on what disasters could be happening in the outside world without his knowing. Meanwhile, cocooned within the walls, the discipline of the robes, and the fierce certainties of his teacher, the monk's mind grew dextrous, plunged into nothingnesses too subtle to remember. He was merely left with a yearning to go back to them; now ordinary happiness feels harsh and coarse.

Outside, traffic roars like storm surf. What a city! He was a different man when he passed through on the way to Rangoon, drank a Singha beer at the airport bar, defiantly toasting his future as a renunciate. Even then he'd been shocked by Bangkok—everything for sale: plastic buckets, counterfeit Rolexes, bootleg software; and of course the women, dressed as primly as third-grade teachers, hoping a client will choose to marry them.

Burma may attack your health, he thinks, but Bangkok will suck you to your doom.

What if his visa is denied?

Will he disrobe? His civilian clothes are even now in a suitcase in the monastery's strong room: they must be eaten up by mildew. He's not ready to go back home as a shaven-headed, toga-wearing freak. No way would the abbot let him stay and practice under a Thai, not down here where they've got monks running around claiming to be reincarnations of Gotama the Buddha. There's a Burmese center in Penang, which Miss Bi Chin supported before she moved up to Bangkok; but she said last night it's near a huge highway and so is unsuitable for the absorption practices; plus, she added confidentially, the head monk in Penang hates Westerners. She ought to know: he's her cousin. If I get sent to Penang, the monk thinks, I'll be able to practice patience for about two weeks and then I'll be out of the robes. I was never a lifer, anyway. Or was I?

I know this is only a form.

For sure, he isn't ready just yet to lose the peace, the certainty of being a monk; nor to be separated from the abbot, his teacher: the only man on earth, he's often told himself, he truly, deeply respects. And loves.

He catches himself planning to sneak across the border at Chiang Rai and run up to Rangoon through the forest with help from Karen insurgents. Bowing three times at the abbot's feet. Here I am. In his mind the abbot laughs at him and says, Peace is not in Burma or in Bangkok. Peace comes from dropping one's preferences. That is why we beg for our food, we take what is given.

The monk stops in front of the abbot's portrait and makes the gesture of respect, palms together.

He feels the world stretching out around him. I'm here, he thinks; suddenly he's in his body again, feeling its heaviness and insubstantiality.

He can even feel the strengthening effect of the milk in the Wheaties he just ate. Conditions in Thailand are good for healing the old bod; he can make it a project. In the States he ran and did yoga fairly regularly; in

Burma he never exercised. He was never alone, and people would gossip if they saw him in an undignified posture.

Carefully he spreads his sitting cloth, a maroon-and-orange patchwork square, on the straw mat where he ate breakfast; now he lies flat on it, easing the bunched muscles of his shoulders. Slowly he raises his legs to vertical, letting the small of his back flatten against the cool straw. His sacrum releases with a loud pop.

He tucks the skirt of his robe between his knees and raises his buttocks off the ground, until he is in full shoulder stand, the queen of poses, the great redistributor of psychic energy. His mind flies, faster than light, to Vermont.

He's lived as if he'll never go back to where people know him as Tom Perkins, a carpenter and the more or less unreliable lover of Mary Rose Cassidy, who still lives in Brattleboro, where she's a partner in a cooperative restaurant. She's known he would ordain ever since they came East together in seventy-three. They were both moved by the calm faces of monks they saw; but only he had that realization at the great dome of Borobudur in Java. Tapped it, and said, "Empty. That's it! There's nothing inside." Mary Rose saw in his face that it was a deep moment for him. After coming home, they learned to meditate together at a center in western Mass. She kept saying the tradition was sexist and stifled your *joie de vivre;* Tom wondered if she did it only to keep him from getting too far away.

And she didn't expect him to be gone this long. He's written her four letters saying: my practice is getting deep, it's fascinating, I want to renew my visa.

He should've broken up with her. A year ago he knew: but it seemed cruel to cut her off by mail, and more appropriate as a monk to be vaguely affectionate, vaguely disconnected, than to delve into his past and make a big mess. He halfway hoped she'd lose patience and break up with him herself; but she says she's had no other lover since he left, and she sends a hundred dollars every other month to the monastery treasurer for his support. It's more than enough.

She would have stopped sending money. He would've had to be supported entirely by the Burmese. God knows they have little enough to spare. Think what his plane ticket to Bangkok would have cost in kyat. Four months' salary for the average worker, even at the official rate; at the black market rate, the real value of Burmese money: three years' salary.

He lowers his legs as slowly as he can, feeling unfamiliar pulls in his belly and chest.

He turns to look out the large front window—the old man is staring in at him. He's been sweeping dead leaves off the cement courtyard. He wears ancient blue rubber thongs and a checked sarong; his fine-skinned purplish breasts sag over his ribs. His gaze is clouded and fierce, an old man's rage. The monk has assumed that he is some sort of servant, a trusted retainer of Miss Bi Chin's; he didn't quite take the old man into consideration. Now, this stare rips away all barriers between them.

Lying on the floor, his robes in disarray, he's Tom again, for the first time since he ordained.

With as much dignity as he can muster, he gets to his feet and goes out the back door, into the tiny walled garden where Miss Bi Chin slept. The old man has swept the pink sal flowers into a pile. The fresh ones look like parts of Mary Rose; the decaying ones, black and slimy, remind him of things the abbot says about sensuous desire. He watches one blossom fall, faster than he'd expect. It's heavy, the petals thick as blotting paper. He picks it up, rubs one petal into bruised transparency.

I should call Mary Rose while I've got the Thai phone system, he thinks. I need to tell the truth.

Now he wishes he'd studied the rules, for he doesn't know if using the phone would break the precept against taking what is not given. It's a subtle thing, but how impeccable does he have to be? Miss Bi Chin offered her house, but then steered him into her library. She surely expects to do all his telephoning. Surprising Mary Rose with an overseas collect charge isn't too monkly, except that she still considers him her lover. The irony of this is not lost on him.

Well, it's ten P.M. in Brattleboro. If he waits until Miss Bi Chin comes home it'll be too late, and what's more, she'll overhear everything: the phone is in the kitchen where she'll be cooking lunch. He walks around the corner of the house and asks the old man's permission to use the phone.

The old man waggles his head as if his neck had lost its bones. He says in Malay, "I don't understand you, and you don't understand me!"

The monk decides that this weird movement contains some element of affirmation. In any case, his mind is made up.

As he watches his hand travel toward the phone, he remembers the abbot talking about the gradations of defilement. Desire shakes the mind. The body moves, touches the object, touches it, causing the object to move. When he touches the receiver, he picks it up quickly and dials.

"Tom?" The satellite transmission is so clear, Mary Rose sounds like she's in the next room. "Oh, it's fantastic to hear your voice!"

When he hangs up, an hour later, he feels sick—he can't help imagining her expression when she gets the phone bill. Yet he has to admit, he's intensely alive, too, as if he'd stuck his fingers in a socket, as if someone had handed him a sword.

He thinks: Maybe this will create a vacuum that my visa will rush into.

He goes up to Miss Bi Chin's sewing room and closes the door. Cross-legged on his sitting cloth, he tries to cut off all thoughts of Mary Rose so he can send loving-kindness to the abbot, his benefactor. At first tears come, his body feels bludgeoned by emotion; but then his loving feeling strengthens, the abbot's presence hardens in his mind. Suddenly he and the abbot are welded together, a bond tighter than Krazy Glue. The monk's lips curve up: here there is no grief.

Miss Bi Chin and the old man are eating dinner, chicken and Chinese cabbage in ginger sauce; the monk is upstairs reading a list of the Twenty-Four Mental States Called Beautiful.

"Your monk talked on the phone for two hours," the old man says slyly. "He put his feet above his head and then pointed them at the portrait of Pingyan Sayadaw."

It is not true that the monk pointed his feet at the portrait, but as soon as the old man says so, he begins to believe himself. He's tired of having monks in the house, tired of the prissy, superior way his step-niece behaves when these eunuchs are about. What good do they do? They live off other people, beg for their food, they raise no children. The old man has no children either, but he can call himself a man. He was a policeman for six years in Malaysia, until a bullet lodged near his spine.

Miss Bi Chin pretends he does not exist, but he pinches her bicep, hard.

"Ow!" she cries, and jerks her arm away. "I *told* him he could use the house as he pleased." Too late, she realizes she shouldn't have descended to arguing: it causes the old man to continue.

"Well, he did that. He only waited for you to leave before changing his behavior. I think he's a very loose monk. He wandered up the stairs, down the stairs, examining this and that. Out into the garden to stare at the sky and pick up flowers. Then he got on the phone. He'll be poking in the refrigerator tomorrow, getting his own food."

"You just hate monks."

"Wait and see," the old man says lightly. "Have you noticed his lower lip? Full of lust and weakness."

Miss Bi Chin lowers her face until all she can see is her bowl of soupy cabbage. The old man is her curse for some evil deed in the past. How he abuses her, how he tries to poison her mind! She tells herself that the old man's evil speech is a sign of his own suffering, yet he seems to cause her more pain than he feels himself. Sometimes she enjoys doing battle with him—and she has developed great strength by learning to seal off her mental state so that he cannot infiltrate. This strength she uses on different occasions: on a crowded bus when an open sore is thrust beneath her nose, or when her boss at American Express overloads her with work. At other times the old man defeats her, causes her defilements to arise. Hatred. Fear. A strange sadness, like homesickness, when she thinks of him helpless in the grip of his obsessions.

She could never kick him out. Crippled, too old to learn Thai or get a job, how would he survive in Bangkok? And he does make himself useful, he tends the garden and cleans the floors and bathrooms. Even more important, without him as witness, she and her monks would not be allowed to be in the same house together. The Buddha knew human nature very well when he made those rules, she thinks.

Washing up, she hears that the old man has turned on his TV and is watching his favorite talk show, whose host gained fame after a jealous wife cut off his penis, and he had it sewn on again.

"Why do you have to watch that!" she scolds at his fat, unresponsive back.

She goes up to the sewing room in a fury, which dissipates into shame as soon as she sees the monk reading. The light from the window lies flat and weak on the side of his shaven head. His pallor makes him look as if he has just been peeled; her ex-lover Douglas had a similar look, and it gives her a shiver. She turns on the yellow electric lamp so he will not ruin his eyes and leaves the door wide open, as is necessary when a monk and a woman are together in a room.

"Hello, sister," he says. The edges of his eyelids feel burnt by tears; Miss Bi Chin notices redness, but thinks it is from ill health.

She begins to speak even before she has finished her three bows. "Please instruct me, sir, I am so hateful. I should practice meditation for many years, like you, so I can attain the *anagami* stage where anger is uprooted forever. But I am tied to my six sense doors, I cannot become a nun, I must live in this world full of low people. I think also, if I quit my job, who will support you monks when you come to Bangkok?"

As she speaks he takes the formal posture, and unconsciously sets his mouth in the same line as the abbot's in the portrait downstairs. Usually when someone bows to him, the beauty of the ancient hierarchy springs up like cool water inside him. Today he'd like to run from this woman, bunched up on the floor, getting ready to spill out her hot, messy life.

But he has to serve her, or else why give up Mary Rose?

"I'm not *anagami*. I'm just an American monk." He waggles his head from side to side, trying to look cheerful, maybe even throw her off track.

"You are so humble!" she says, looking up at him with eyes tormented and devoted as a dog's.

Oh my God, he thinks. Mary Rose. He forces himself to go on. "I understand your wish to renounce the world. Look at me, I left behind a very good woman to do this. I don't regret it," he adds quickly.

She thinks, he should not be talking about his woman; and then: who was she? He must have loved her, to look so regretful even after three years.

"Of course not. Monks enjoy a higher happiness," she says.

"But you don't need to be a nun to purify your mind. Greed, hatred, and delusion are the same whether you are in robes or not. Don't be hard on yourself. We all get angry."

"I am hard because hatred is hard." She says something in Pali, the scriptural language. But he can tell she's relieved, she's heard something that has helped her. She goes on more softly, "Sometimes I want to strike out against one person."

Miss Bi Chin feels a great relief as she confesses this, as if a rusty pin had been removed from her flesh.

"You'll also hurt yourself." The monk regrets his occasional cruelties to Mary Rose. Once, feeling perverse, he called her a cow, only because he knew she was sensitive about her big breasts. The word, the moment, the look on her face, have come back to his mind hundreds of times. And today she said that he wasted three years of her life, that he is a coward, that he insulted her by not speaking sooner.

"I know! I know!" Miss Bi Chin falls silent.

The monk tries for a better topic. "Who's the old man you have living with you? He gave me quite a look through the window."

He has the psychic powers, Miss Bi Chin thinks. "You've guessed my enemy. My step-uncle. My mother sent him to me. I cannot get rid of him." She picks like a schoolgirl at the hem of her dress, hearing the old man's mocking voice: "If you don't have the guts to throw me out, you deserve whatever you get."

The monk sees her face go deep red. That horrible old man! He sees him staring in the window again, his rheumy, cruel eyes. I'd better be careful though. Maybe they've slept together. You never know, when two people live in the same house.

"Every personal relationship brings suffering," he says cautiously.

"Better to live alone if one wants to free the mind," Miss Bi Chin quotes from the admonitions of the abbot. "Should I ask Uncle to leave?"

"Um, any reason why you can't?"

"Why not!" She giggles. She is not so much planning to kick out the old man as letting herself fall just a little in love with this monk. He is so breezy and American, like a hero in the movies; yet he has much wisdom. "Well, he has to stay here until you get your visa, because you and I would not be able to be in the house alone."

The monk smiles uncertainly. "I may not get a visa."

"Of course you will. You have good *kamma* from practice."

"Yet we never know when our *kamma* will ripen, do we. Good or bad."

They both nod slowly, looking into each other's eyes.

"What will you do if you can't go back?" She really wants to know; and it gives her a thrill to talk about this, knowing that the monk is ignorant of the abbot's intentions. Perhaps she'll report the answer to Rangoon.

"I'll try to remain in equanimity."

That's a good answer for the abbot, she thinks, but it's not enough for me. She extends herself: "Would you like to go back to your country and begin a monastery?"

"Oh, no," he says lightly.

"Why?"

"I have no interest in making others follow rules. I'm not a cop, basically."

"Don't you miss your home?"

"Yes, but. . . "

"I should have offered you to use the phone. Maybe you want to call your parents."

"I've already used it. I hope that's all right."

A shock runs down Miss Bi Chin's back. So it's true what the old man says. "You used the phone?"

"It was sort of urgent. I had to make a call. I did it collect, there'll be no charge to you. Maybe I should call Penang and confess?"

"Oh, no, no, no," she says. "I offered you to use my house as you wished. Who did you talk to?"

"Well, my old girlfriend from the States," and he finds himself describing the whole situation to Miss Bi Chin, confessing. Recklessly, he even says he might have postponed breaking up because he was afraid to lose a supporter. Because Miss Bi Chin is a stranger—and because she knows so much more about being a monk than he does—he feels compelled to expose his worst motivations. If forgiving words come out of these quietly smiling lips, he'll be exonerated. If her face turns from gold to brass and she casts him out, that will be right also.

As he speaks, Miss Bi Chin feels she is walking through a huge house, where rooms open up unexpectedly one after another. When she was in the British school, she had to read a poem about the East being East and the West being West, and never the twain shall meet. This is not true: she knows she can follow this monk far into his labyrinth, and maybe get lost. For him it is the simplest thing to say: the old man is bad, ask him to leave. But for himself, it is so complicated. In one room of his mind he is a monk, and using the phone was an error; in another room calling was the right thing to do. First he is too strict with himself, then he lets go of the rules altogether.

Should she tell the abbot? What would there be to tell? That the monk used the telephone after she had already given permission? That he was impatient to perform a wholesome act?

Miss Bi Chin has a water heart: it flows in uncontrollable sympathy toward the monk. She knows he was afraid to be forgotten when he went so far from home. That is the true reason he did not cut off this girlfriend, but he is a man and cannot admit such kind of fears.

She interrupts. "If I were Mary Rose," she tells him, "if Mary Rose were Burmese, or even Thai, as soon as you ordained, her reason for sending money would change. She would donate to earn merit for herself. You would then feel grateful but not indebted. You would feel to strive hard in meditation, to make her sacrifice worthwhile. And I think that your mind is very pure and you are trying to perform your discipline perfectly, but because you were in intensive practice you do not know in precise way what monks should do and not do when they are in ordinary life. Therefore I think you should spend your time here studying the texts in my library and learning what you did not learn."

At the end of this speech she is breathless, shocked to hear herself admonishing a monk.

"Thank you," he says. "That's great." His face is broken up by emotion; he looks as if he might weep.

Now, she thinks, should I tell the abbot that his monk is falling apart? Not yet. It's only his first day.

Within a week it is obvious to the old man that Miss Bi Chin and the monk are in love.

"I should call Rangoon," he teases Miss Bi Chin. They both know he will never do so, if only because he will not know how to introduce the topic to a person he has never met. But the threat gives him power over her. Miss Bi Chin now ignores it when he fails to sweep or clean the bathrooms. The monk sometimes sweeps away the blossoms under the sal tree; the old man stands at the window of the sewing room, enjoying this spectacle. Miss Bi Chin made loud remarks about the toilet but ended up cleaning it herself. She also serves the old man his meals before going in and prattling with the monk. The old man has never felt so satisfied since he moved in here two years ago.

Miss Bi Chin, too, is happy. These days she feels a strange new kind of freedom. She and the monk are so often in the same room—he sits in the kitchen while she cooks, and otherwise they go to the sewing room and study or meditate—that the old man has fewer opportunities to pinch or slap. In the past she even feared that the old man might kill her, but he seems calmed by the monk's purity of mind.

The monk actually wants to know what she thinks about this and that. When she comes home from work, he asks respectfully how her day was, and they discuss her problems. He sees so clearly people's motivation! Then they go to the texts and try to look behind the surface to see what is the effect on the mind of each instruction, always asking, what did the Buddha intend? When they disagree with each other, they don't let each other off the hook: sometimes their arguments are fierce, exciting.

"Why do Burmese and Thais call each other lax?" he asks one night. "The Thais accuse the Burmese because Burmese monks will take stuff straight out of a woman's hand. Then the Burmese turn around and say Thais drink milk after noon. Can't they see it's all relative?"

"You don't know Thai monks," she replies hotly. "Won't take a pencil from a woman's hand but you don't know what they take from her other parts."

"Yeah, but not all Thai monks are bad. What about those old Ajahns up north? They live under trees."

"Insects also live under trees! Burmese get good results in their meditation, in the city or in the forest. You better listen to your own teacher to know what is right. No one reaches enlightenment by saying 'it is all relative.'"

His lips go tight, but then he nods. "You're right. Pingyan Sayadaw says Western skepticism makes people sour inside. You stay at the crossroads and never go anywhere. 'I don't believe this path, I don't believe that path.' Look at the power of mind he has."

"Such a strong monk," she says joyously.

No man has ever yielded to her thinking; it fills her heart with cold, delicious fire.

"Incredible," the monk replies, his pale eyes shining.

Then they meditate together, and her mind becomes so fresh. She feels she is living in the time of the Buddha with this monk. When the old man accuses her of being in love, she retorts that she's always been in love with the truth.

The monk is getting healthy, eating Wheaties and doing yoga every day. Miss Bi Chin often asks if there's anything he needs, so he can say "A bottle of vitamin C" or "A new pair of rubber thongs" without feeling strange. He feels pleasantly glutted with conversation. In Burma, he never sifted through his thoughts, the idea was simply to take in as much as he could. At Miss Bi Chin's, he can sort, digest, refine. She helps direct his studies, she's almost as good as a monk; and in turn he's helping her figure out how to deal with daily life.

A perfect marriage would be like this, he thinks, except sex would screw it up with expectations. At times his feelings for Miss Bi Chin do grow warm, and he tosses on her bed at night; but there's no question in his mind about these feelings. They'll go away at the third stage of enlightenment. Having left Mary Rose, he feels more like a monk than ever. It's good exercise for him to see Miss Bi Chin's loveliness with detachment, as if she were a flower or a painting in a museum. When she exclaims that she's ugly and dark, he corrects her, saying, "All self-judgment reinforces the ego."

He writes the abbot every week. "Living in the world is not as difficult as I feared, but maybe this is because Miss Bi Chin's house is like a monastery. I am studying in her library. Her support is generous and her behavior is impeccable. She sleeps outside, under a tree. One night it rained and she went straight out to a hotel."

The monk has only two fears during this period. One is that the embassy of Myanma will not approve his visa. The other is that it will. When he thinks of Pingyan Monastery, he remembers its discomforts: diarrhea in the Rains, in April prickly heat.

I have my head in the sand, he thinks; or, I am asleep between my mother's breasts.

Miss Bi Chin is showing the monk a large bruise on her upper arm. It is the blue-black of an eggplant and has ugly spider's legs spreading in all directions around it. If he were not a monk, he'd touch it gently with his finger.

"I can't believe he does this to you," he says. "Don't you want him to leave? I'll be there when you say it. I'll stand over him while he packs."

"If he left, you'd have to go also. Where? He'd come back the next day. He was in the narcotics squad in Malaysia. I don't know what he would do. I think something. He has his old gun in a sack. It is broken but he could fix it."

Hearing about the gun makes the monk's stomach light with horror. Human beings, what they'll do to each other. Imagine a rapist's mind, a murderer's. Delusion, darkness, separation. How has Miss Bi Chin let this evil being stay in the house? How has she been able to live under the roof with such fear?

"He's got to go. If I'm still here he'd be less likely to bother you," the monk says. "I'm an American, after all. He'd get into big trouble if he pulled anything. Now that I can use the phone"—he laughs a little—"I can get on the horn to the embassy."

"But he is my step-uncle," Miss Bi Chin says weakly. She doesn't really want the monk to be proposing this. He sounds not like a monk, but like any other American boasting about his country's power.

"Look," the monk says. "I'll sleep outside. I'll eat outside. I'll stay outside all day. We can leave the gate open so people in the street can see us. I think this thing with the old man is more serious than you think. We can work out the monk part. The Patimokkha only talks about sleeping under the same roof and sharing a secluded seat, and in the second case a woman follower has to accuse me of seducing you."

"Okay. I'll get you a tent," Miss Bi Chin says.

"No way. You didn't have one," the monk retorts. "Why don't you find him a job instead?"

The old man knows something is wrong: when he comes back from the soda shop at six, the two of them are sitting in the patio chairs side by side, facing the gate, like judges.

"You must leave this house tomorrow," Miss Bi Chin says. The monk's face bears a look the old man knows is dangerous: determination mixed with terror, the look of a young boy about to pull a trigger. In a flash he calculates his chances. The monk is not healthy and probably knows no dirty fighting tricks, but is thirty years younger and much larger. He must have been a laborer once, his arms and chest show signs of former strength; and he's been exercising every day.

The old man makes his hands into claws. "Heugh!" he cries, and fakes a pounce: only six inches forward. Of course, the monk leaps to his feet. The old man laughs. This kind of thing brings vigor in old age.

"So you lovebirds want privacy?" he says. "Watch out I don't take the kitchen knife to you tonight. I'm old but I'm still a man."

"I got you a job guarding the Chinese market," Miss Bi Chin says. "They'll give you a room in back." She was surprised how easy this solution was, once the monk opened her mind to it. Now she owes the monk her happiness. Her house suddenly seems vast; her nostrils fill with the sweet scent of sal flowers, as if the old man were a fire emitting sharp smoke which had been put out.

The next morning she calls a taxi. All of the old man's clothes fit into a vinyl sports bag, but his TV is too big to carry on the bus.

Watching him go, old and crooked, out the gate, Miss Bi Chin feels bad. Her mother will not understand. Loyalty is important in a family.

She's been living in this house with the American monk, who tells her about the youth revolution when everyone decided their parents were wrong. This was the beginning of meditation in America; even the monk got interested in spiritual things at first because of drugs.

Now the monk meets her in the garden. He's smiling softly. "Remember the test of loving-kindness?" he asks her. "You're sitting under a tree with a neutral person, a friend, and an enemy, and a robber comes and says you have to choose who he'll kill?"

"I remember," she says dully. "I refuse the decision."

The abbot's letter has taken a month to arrive. He writes through an interpreter: "My son in robes: I hope you get a visa soon. I am glad you keep good morality. Miss Bi Chin says you are suitable to be a teacher and your speeches are refined. I praise her for sleeping outside, but maybe it is your turn. Be careful of desire and pride, and do not think too much."

Miss Bi Chin has sent several glowing reports by aerogram. Now she is not so sure. She hates sleeping in the bed, she feels she has lost her power in some obscure way. She and the monk are trying hard to keep the rules. They avoid being in the house together, but there are too many robbers in Bangkok to leave the street gate open, so they rely on the fact that they're always visible from the second floor of the elementary school across the street. They joke about their debt to one small, distracted boy who's always staring out the window; but this is almost like a lovers' joke. Miss Bi Chin feels disturbed by the monk's presence now. When he looks at her with soft eyes she feels nothing but fear. Perhaps he is in love with her. Perhaps he thinks of her at night. She dreads his quick buzz of the doorbell, announcing he's coming in to use the bathroom.

One morning at work she types an aerogram to the abbot. It makes her happy to see the clarity of the Selectric type on the thin, blue paper. "I worry about the American monk. We're alone together in my compound ever since he asked my uncle to leave my house. We try to keep his precepts, but I want your opinion. He spoke about his personal life. There was a woman in love with him at home. He said the precepts are relative, what is most important is the effect on the mind."

She tosses this in her Out box and watches the office boy take it away with her boss's letters to America. For some reason, she thinks of the gun lying in the bottom of the old man's sports bag as he walked off down the street.

"Don't you want to go home and teach your own people?" Miss Bi Chin asks again.

She's brought up this subject many times, and the monk always says no. But today his answer surprises both of them. With the old man gone, things have fallen into place. He likes sleeping under the sal tree, the same kind of tree under which the Buddha was born and died. Monks did this in ancient times, dwelt at the roots of trees. He loves its glossy green leaves and pink flowers; he imagines it is the tradition, and at night his roots go down with its roots, deep into the black soil. "Maybe I'm in a special position," he says. "Americans are hungry for truth. Our society is so materialistic."

"You don't want to be an abbot though," Miss Bi Chin says. "It is too tiring."

"I don't know," he says. "If my teacher asked me to I guess I'd have to go."

"Well, an abbot wouldn't be staying here alone with me, I can tell you that much," Miss Bi Chin bursts out.

That night he lies awake under the sal tree. Why didn't she tell him sooner, if it wasn't proper for him to stay? Is she in love with him? Or is she teaching him step by step?

He remembers the rules he's studied. Miss Bi Chin herself could be the woman follower who accuses him of seduction. Even though they haven't shared a seat, it's possible that if she brings a charge against him, there'd be no power in his denial, since they've been rather secluded together in her compound.

He understands something new: a monk's life has to be absolutely clear-cut. These rules were made for a reason. Ambiguous situations mean murky feelings, subterranean defilements. Again he can thank Miss Bi Chin for showing him how to go.

Whether he gets his visa or not is unimportant. He must go to Penang and live with other monks and prepare for the responsibilities of the future. If the Penang abbot hates Westerners, it's probably because he's never met one who appreciates the robes. If it's difficult to be there, it will develop his mental strength.

He imagines himself a monk in old age. The stubble on his head will grow out white, he'll laugh at the world like his teacher. Old Burmese monks are so very much alive, he thinks. Their bodies are light, their skin emits a glow. If you can feel free amid restrictions you truly are free.

In the morning he is quiet as Miss Bi Chin serves his breakfast on the front patio.

He is red now, not white: his blood is healthy. He keeps his eyes down as she hands him the plates. Wheaties, mango, cookies, Nescafé. Talk to me, she cries inside herself. She stares at his mouth, seeing its weakness and lust. It shows the part of him she loves, the human part.

She hasn't slept all night, and her mind is wild as an untamed elephant. Maybe the abbot will get her aerogram and make the monk disrobe. He'll stay in her house and live a lay life; they can make love after having their conversations. I could call the embassy and withdraw his visa application, she thinks. What is the worst that could happen? That I am reborn as a nun who'll be seduced by a foreigner?

At last she understands the old man, who said once he didn't care if *kamma* punished him in a future life, as long as he got to do what he wanted to in this life. How can we know who we'll be, or who we were? We can only try to be happy.

Frightened by her thoughts, she watches the monk bite a U shape out of his toast. He's being careful, moving stiffly as a wooden puppet; and he must have shaved his head this morning, it is shiny, hairless, there is a small bloody nick over his ear.

She knows she won't be able to cancel his visa application; and that her aerogram will result, not in the monk's disrobing, but in his being sent to Penang and forbidden to stay with her again. She hasn't accused him of downfall offenses, or disgusting offenses. So he'll go on with his practice and maybe become an abbot, or a fully liberated arhat. At least I was full of wholesome moral dread when I wrote that aerogram, she thinks. When the benefits come, I can enjoy them without guilt. Such as they'll be. Someone will give me a new Buddha image, I'll be offered another promotion and refuse it. She laughs under her breath. Is this what I was looking for when, as a young girl, I began running from temple to temple and lost all my friends?

"What are you laughing about," the monk says.

"I was thinking of something."

"I have to go to Penang," he says. His voice is low and hollow, so neither of them is sure he's actually spoken.

"I am sorry my house is unsuitable for you to stay."

"No, it's been wonderful to be here. But I need to be around other monks. I feel like we've been playing with the rules a little bit. We're in a gray area."

He smiles at her coaxingly, but she refuses the bait. "I'll buy you a ticket to Penang this afternoon."

How can she be so cold suddenly? She's pulling him out, compelling him to make the contact. "I'll miss you. Don't tell the abbot, okay?"

"If there is no lust, a monk may say he will miss."

"I want this to stay between us," he says. "You've been like my sister. And teacher. I'm sorry I have to go."

"Every personal relationship brings suffering," she says, but she's smiling at him, finally, a tiny complicated smile he'd never believe could appear on her golden face. Suddenly he sees her eyes are full of tears, and he knows he'll be lonely in Penang, not only for Miss Bi Chin but for Mary Rose, who also fixed things so he could ask for whatever he wanted.

Nothing changes, the old man thinks. There they are, sitting in the front courtyard, talking about nothing. He's standing at the jalousied window of the third-grade classroom, during the children's first morning recess. He knew this was the time. Bi Chin doesn't go to work until nine-thirty.

He woke up in a rage that drove him to the bus stop, still not knowing what he would do—something: he has his pistol in the sports bag. He had it fixed, and late at night he practices shooting at bottles floating in the *kh-long* past the Chinese market. His aim isn't what it was. The pistol is heavier than he remembered, his eyes are bad, his arm shakes.

He knew an idea would come when he was actually standing at the window, and it has. He sees one thing he can succeed at. He can at least hit that plate glass window, shatter it behind their heads. He sees it clearly, bursting, shower of light. They run inside and slam the door. Miss Bi Chin in her terror grabs the monk. Ha! They find themselves embracing. That'll be a good one, if he doesn't miss and blow one of their heads off.

Happy with this solution, the old man begins to hum as he unzips the sports bag. The gun's cold oil smell reaches his nostrils, making him sharp and powerful. He's always wanted to break that window, he doesn't know why. Just to see it smash. I'm an evil old man, he thinks. Good thing I became a cop.

THE LIAR

Tobias Wolff

My mother read everything except books. Advertisements on buses, entire menus as we ate, billboards; if it had no cover it interested her. So when she found a letter in my drawer that was not addressed to her she read it. "What difference does it make if James has nothing to hide?"—that was her thought. She stuffed the letter in the drawer when she finished it and walked from room to room in the big empty house, talking to herself. She took the letter out and read it again to get the facts straight. Then, without putting on her coat or locking the door, she went down the steps and headed for the church at the end of the street. No matter how angry and confused she might be, she always went to four o'clock Mass and now it was four o'clock.

It was a fine day, blue and cold and still, but Mother walked as though into a strong wind, bent forward at the waist with her feet hurrying behind in short, busy steps. My brother and sisters and I considered this walk of hers funny and we smirked at one another when she crossed in front of us to stir the fire, or water a plant. We didn't let her catch us at it. It would have puzzled her to think that there might be anything amusing about her. Her one concession to the fact of humor was an insincere, startling laugh. Strangers often stared at her.

While Mother waited for the priest, who was late, she prayed. She prayed in a familiar, orderly, firm way first for her late husband, my father, then for her parents—also dead. She said a quick prayer for my father's parents (just touching base; she had disliked them) and finally for her children in order of their ages, ending with me. Mother did not consider originality a virtue and until my name came up her prayers were exactly the same as on any other day.

But when she came to me she spoke up boldly. "I thought he wasn't going to do it any more. Murphy said he was cured. What am I supposed to do now?" There was reproach in her tone. Mother put great hope in her notion that I was cured. She regarded my cure as an answer to her prayers and by way of thanksgiving sent a lot of money to the Thomasite Indian Mission, money she had been saving for a trip to Rome. She felt cheated and she let her feelings be known. When the priest came in Mother slid back on the seat and followed the Mass with concentration. After communion she began to worry again and went straight home without stopping to talk to Frances, the woman who always cornered Mother after Mass to tell about the awful things done to her by Communists, devil-worshipers, and Rosicrucians. Frances watched her go with narrowed eyes.

Once in the house, Mother took the letter from my drawer and brought it into the kitchen. She held it over the stove with her fingernails, looking away so that she would not be drawn into it again, and set it on fire. When it began to burn her fingers she dropped it in the sink and watched it blacken and flutter and close upon itself like a fist. Then she washed it down the drain and called Dr. Murphy.

The letter was to my friend Ralphy in Arizona. He used to live across the street from us but he had moved. Most of the letter was about a tour we, the junior class, had taken of Alcatraz. That was all right. What got Mother was the last paragraph where I said that she had been coughing up blood and the doctors weren't sure what was wrong with her, but that we were hoping for the best.

This wasn't true. Mother took pride in her physical condition, considered herself a horse: "I'm a regular horse," she would reply when people asked about her health. For several years now I had been saying unpleasant things that weren't true and this habit of mine irked Mother greatly, enough to persuade her to send me to Dr. Murphy, in whose office I was sitting when she burned the letter. Dr. Murphy was our family physician and had no training in psychoanalysis but he took an interest in "things of the mind," as he put it. He had treated me for appendicitis and tonsilitis and Mother thought that he could put the truth into me as easily as he took things out of me, a hope Dr. Murphy did not share. He was basically interested in getting me to understand what I did, and lately he had been moving toward the conclusion that I understood what I did as well as I ever would.

Dr. Murphy listened to Mother's account of the letter, and what she had done with it. He was curious about the wording I had used and became irritated when Mother told him she had burned it. "The point is," she said, "he was supposed to be cured and he's not."

"Margaret, I never said he was cured."

"You certainly did. Why else would I have sent over a thousand dollars to the Thomasite mission?"

"I said that he was responsible. That means that James knows what he's doing, not that he's going to stop doing it."

"I'm sure you said he was cured."

"Never. To say that someone is cured you have to know what health is. With this kind of thing that's impossible. What do you mean by curing James, anyway?"

"You know."

"Tell me anyway."

"Getting him back to reality, what else?"

"Whose reality? Mine or yours?"

"Murphy, what are you talking about? James isn't crazy, he's a liar."

"Well, you have a point there."

"What am I going to do with him?"

"I don't think there's much you can do. Be patient."

"I've been patient."

"If I were you, Margaret, I wouldn't make too much of this. James doesn't steal, does he?"

"Of course not."

"Or beat people up or talk back."

"No."

"Then you have a lot to be thankful for."

"I don't think I can take any more of it. That business about leukemia last summer. And now this."

"Eventually he'll outgrow it, I think."

"Murphy, he's sixteen years old. What if he doesn't outgrow it? What if he just gets better at it?"

Finally Mother saw that she wasn't going to get any satisfaction from Dr. Murphy, who kept reminding her of her blessings. She said something cutting to him and he said something pompous back and she hung up. Dr. Murphy stared at the receiver. "Hello," he said, then replaced it on the cradle. He ran his hand over his head, a habit remaining from a time when he had hair. To show that he was a good sport he often joked about his baldness, but I had the feeling that he regretted it deeply. Looking at me across the desk, he must have wished that he hadn't taken me on. Treating a friend's child was like investing a friend's money.

"I don't have to tell you who that was."

I nodded.

Dr. Murphy pushed his chair back and swiveled it around so he could look out the window behind him, which took up most of the wall. There were still a few sailboats out on the Bay, but they were all making for shore. A woolly gray fog had covered the bridge and was moving in fast. The water seemed calm from this far up, but when I looked closely I could see white flecks everywhere, so it must have been pretty choppy.

"I'm surprised at you," he said. "Leaving something like that lying around for her to find. If you really have to do these things you could at least be kind and do them discreetly. It's not easy for your mother, what with your father dead and all the others somewhere else."

"I know. I didn't mean for her to find it."

"Well." He tapped his pencil against his teeth. He was not convinced professionally, but personally he may have been. "I think you ought to go home now and straighten things out."

"I guess I'd better."

"Tell your mother I might stop by, either tonight or tomorrow. And James—don't underestimate her."

While my father was alive we usually went to Yosemite for three or four days during the summer. My mother would drive and Father would point out places of interest, meadows where boom towns once stood, hanging trees, rivers that were said to flow upstream at certain times. Or he read to us; he had that grownups' idea that children love Dickens and Sir Walter Scott. The four of us sat in the back seat with our faces composed, attentive, while our hands and feet pushed, pinched, stomped, goosed, prodded, dug, and kicked.

One night a bear came into our camp just after dinner. Mother had made a tuna casserole and it must have smelled to him like something worth dying for. He came into the camp while we were sitting around the fire and stood swaying back and forth. My brother Michael saw him first and elbowed me, then my sisters saw him and screamed. Mother and Father had their backs to him but Mother must have guessed what it was because she immediately said, "Don't scream like that. You might frighten him and there's no telling what he'll do. We'll just sing and he'll go away."

We sang "Row Row Row Your Boat" but the bear stayed. He circled us several times, rearing up now and then on his hind legs to stick his nose into the air. By the light of the fire I could see his doglike face and watch the muscles roll under his loose skin like rocks in a sack. We sang harder as he circled us, coming closer and closer. "All right," Mother said, "enough's enough." She stood abruptly. The bear stopped moving and watched her. "Beat it," Mother said. The bear sat down and looked from side to side. "Beat it," she said again, and leaned over and picked up a rock.

"Margaret, don't," my father said.

She threw the rock hard and hit the bear in the stomach. Even in the dim light I could see the dust rising from his fur. He grunted and stood to his full height. "See that?" Mother shouted: "He's filthy. Filthy!" One of my sisters giggled. Mother picked up another rock. "Please, Margaret," my father said. Just then the bear turned and shambled away. Mother pitched the rock after him. For the rest of the night he loitered around the camp until he found the tree where we had hung our food. He ate it all. The next day we drove back to the city. We could have bought more supplies in the valley, but Father wanted to go and would not give in to any argument. On the way home he tried to jolly everyone up by making jokes, but Michael and my sisters ignored him and looked stonily out the windows.

Things were never easy between my mother and me, but I didn't underestimate her. She underestimated me. When I was little she suspected me of delicacy, because I didn't like being thrown into the air, and because when I saw her and the others working themselves up for a roughhouse I found somewhere else to be. When they did drag me in I got hurt, a knee in the lip, a bent finger, a bloody nose, and this too Mother seemed to hold against me, as if I arranged my hurts to get out of playing.

Even things I did well got on her nerves. We all loved puns except Mother, who didn't get them, and next to my father I was the best in the family. My speciality was the Swifty—"'You can bring the prisoner down,' said Tom condescendingly." Father encouraged me to perform at dinner, which must have been a trial for outsiders. Mother wasn't sure what was going on, but she didn't like it.

She suspected me in other ways. I couldn't go to the movies without her examining my pockets to make sure I had enough money to pay for the ticket. When I went away to camp she tore my pack apart in front of all the boys who were waiting in the bus outside the house. I would rather have gone without my sleeping bag and a few changes of underwear, which I had forgotten, than be made such a fool of. Her distrust was the thing that made me forgetful.

And she thought I was cold-hearted because of what happened the day my father died and later at his funeral. I didn't cry at my father's funeral, and showed signs of boredom during the eulogy, fiddling around with the hymnals. Mother put my hands into my lap and I left them there without moving them as though they were things I was holding for someone else. The effect was ironical and she resented it. We had a sort of reconciliation a few days later after I closed my eyes at school and refused to open them. When several teachers and then the principal failed to persuade me to look at them, or at some reward they claimed to be holding, I was handed over to the school nurse, who tried to pry the lids open and scratched one of them badly. My eye swelled up and I went rigid. The principal panicked and called Mother, who fetched me home. I wouldn't talk to her, or open my eyes, or bend, and they had to lay me on the back seat and when we reached the house Mother had to lift me up the steps one at a time. Then she put me on the couch and played the piano to me all afternoon. Finally I opened my eyes. We hugged each other and I wept. Mother did not really believe my tears, but she was willing to accept them because I had staged them for her benefit.

My lying separated us, too, and the fact that my promises not to lie any more seemed to mean nothing to me. Often my lies came back to her in embarrassing ways, people stopping her in the street and saying how sorry they were to hear that⸺. No one in the neighborhood enjoyed embarrassing Mother, and these situations stopped occurring once everybody got wise to me. There was no saving her from strangers, though. The summer after Father died I visited my uncle in Redding and when I got back I found to my surprise that Mother had come to meet my bus. I tried to slip away from the gentleman who had sat next to me but I couldn't shake him. When he saw Mother embrace me he came up and presented her with a card and told her to get in touch with him if things got any worse. She gave him his card back and told him to mind his own business. Later, on the way home, she made me repeat what I had said to the man. She shook her head. "It's not fair to people," she said, "telling them things like that. It confuses them." It seemed to me that Mother had confused the man, not I, but I didn't say so. I agreed with her that I shouldn't say such things and promised not to do it again, a promise I broke three hours later in conversation with a woman in the park.

It wasn't only the lies that disturbed Mother; it was their morbidity. This was the real issue between us, as it had been between her and my father. Mother did volunteer work at Children's Hospital and St. Anthony's Dining Hall, collected things for the St. Vincent de Paul Society. She was a lighter of candles. My brother and sisters took after her in this way. My father was a curser of the dark. And he loved to curse the dark. He was never more alive than when he was indignant about something. For this reason the most important act of the day for him was the reading of the evening paper.

Ours was a terrible paper, indifferent to the city that bought it, indifferent to medical discoveries—except for new kinds of gases that made your hands fall off when you sneezed—and indifferent to politics and art. Its business was outrage, horror, gruesome coincidence. When my father sat down in the living room with the paper Mother stayed in the kitchen and kept the children busy, all except me, because I was quiet and could be trusted to amuse myself. I amused myself by watching my father.

He sat with his knees spread, leaning forward, his eyes only inches from the print. As he read he nodded to himself. Sometimes he swore and threw the paper down and paced the room, then picked it up and began again. Over a period of time he developed the habit of reading aloud to me. He always started with the society section, which he called the parasite page. This column began to take on the character of a comic strip or a serial, with the same people showing up from one day to the next, blinking in chiffon, awkwardly holding their drinks for the sake of Peninsula orphans, grinning under sunglasses on the deck of a ski hut in the Sierras. The skiers really got his goat, probably because he couldn't understand them. The activity itself was inconceivable to him. When my sisters went to Lake Tahoe one winter weekend with some friends and came back excited about the beauty of the place, Father calmed them right down. "Snow," he said, "is overrated."

Then the news, or what passed in the paper for news: bodies unearthed in Scotland, former Nazis winning elections, rare animals slaughtered, misers expiring naked in freezing houses upon mattresses stuffed with thousands, millions: marrying priests, divorcing actresses, high-rolling oilmen building fantastic mausoleums in honor of a favorite horse, cannibalism. Through all this my father waded with a fixed and weary smile.

Mother encouraged him to take up causes, to join groups, but he would not. He was uncomfortable with people outside the family. He and my mother rarely went out, and rarely had people in, except on feast days and national holidays. Their guests were always the same. Dr. Murphy and his wife and several others whom they had known since childhood. Most of these people never saw each other outside our house and they didn't have much fun together. Father discharged his obligations as host by teasing everyone about stupid things they had said or done in the past and forcing them to laugh at themselves.

Though Father did not drink, he insisted on mixing cocktails for the guests. He would not serve straight drinks like rum-and-Coke or even Scotch-on-the-rocks, only drinks of his own devising. He gave them lawyerly names like "The Advocate," "The Hanging Judge," "The Ambulance Chaser," "The Mouthpiece," and described their concoction in detail. He told long, complicated stories in a near-whisper, making everyone lean in his direction, and repeated important lines; he also repeated the important lines in the stories my mother told, and corrected her when she got something wrong. When the guests came to the ends of their own stories he would point out the morals.

Dr. Murphy had several theories about Father, which he used to test on me in the course of our meetings. Dr. Murphy had by this time given up his glasses for contact lenses, and lost weight in the course of fasts which he undertook regularly. Even with his baldness he looked years younger than when he had come to the parties at our house. Certainly he did not look like my father's contemporary, which he was.

One of Dr. Murphy's theories was that Father had exhibited a classic trait of people who had been gifted children by taking an undemanding position in an uninteresting firm. "He was afraid of finding his limits," Dr. Murphy told me: "As long as he kept stamping papers and making out wills he could go on believing that he didn't *have* limits." Dr. Murphy's fascination with Father made me uneasy, and I felt traitorous listening to him. While he lived, my father would never have submitted himself for analysis; it seemed a betrayal to put him on the couch now that he was dead.

I did enjoy Dr. Murphy's recollections of Father as a child. He told me about something that happened when they were in the Boy Scouts. Their troop had been on a long hike and Father had fallen behind. Dr. Murphy and the others decided to ambush him as he came down the trail. They hid in the woods on each side and waited. But when Father walked into the trap none of them moved or made a sound and he strolled on without even knowing they were there. "He had the sweetest look on his face." Dr. Murphy said, "listening to the birds, smelling the flowers, just like Ferdinand the Bull." He also told me that my father's drinks tasted like medicine.

While I rode my bicycle home from Dr. Murphy's office Mother fretted. She felt terribly alone but she didn't call anyone because she also felt like a failure. My lying had that effect on her. She took it personally. At such times she did not think of my sisters, one happily married, the other doing brilliantly at Fordham. She did not think of my brother Michael, who had given up college to work with runaway children in Los Angeles. She thought of me. She thought that she had made a mess of her family.

Actually she managed the family well. While my father was dying upstairs she pulled us together. She made lists of chores and gave each of us a fair allowance. Bedtimes were adjusted and she stuck by them. She set regular hours for homework. Each child was made responsible for the next eldest, and I was given a dog. She told us frequently, predictably, that she loved us. At dinner we were each expected to contribute something, and after dinner she played the piano and tried to teach us to sing in harmony, which I could not do. Mother, who was an admirer of the Trapp family, considered this a character defect.

Our life together was more orderly, healthy, while Father was dying than it had been before. He had set us rules to follow, not much different really than the ones Mother gave us after he got sick, but he had administered them in a fickle way. Though we were supposed to get an allowance we always had to ask him for it and then he would give us too much because he enjoyed seeming magnanimous. Sometimes he punished us for no reason, because he was in a bad mood. He was apt to decide, as one of my sisters was going out to a dance, that she had better stay home and do something to improve herself. Or he would sweep us all up on a Wednesday night and take us ice-skating.

He changed after he learned about the cancer, and became more calm as the disease spread. He relaxed his teasing way with us, and from time to time it was possible to have a conversation with him which was not about the last thing that had made him angry. He stopped reading the paper and spent time at the window.

He and I became close. He taught me to play poker and sometimes helped me with my homework. But it wasn't his illness that drew us together. The reserve between us had begun to break down after the incident with the bear, during the drive home. Michael and my sisters were furious with him for making us leave early and wouldn't talk to him or look at him. He joked: though it had been a grisly experience we should grin and bear it—and so on. His joking seemed perverse to the others, but not to me. I had seen how terrified he was when the bear came into the camp. He had held himself so still that he had begun to tremble. When Mother started pitching rocks I thought he was going to bolt, really. I understood—I had been frightened too. The others took it as a lark after they got used to having the bear around, but for Father and me it got worse through the night. I was glad to be out of there, grateful to Father for getting me out. I saw that his jokes were how he held himself together. So I reached out to him with a joke. "'There's a bear outside,' said Tom intently." The others turned cold looks on me. They thought I was sucking up. But Father smiled.

When I thought of other boys being close to their fathers I thought of them hunting together, tossing a ball back and forth, making birdhouses in the basement, and having long talks about girls, war, careers. Maybe the reason it took us so long to get close was that I had this idea. It kept getting in the way of what we really had, which was a shared fear.

Toward the end Father slept most of the time and I watched him. From below, sometimes, faintly, I heard Mother playing the piano. Occasionally he nodded off in his chair while I was reading to him; his bathrobe would fall open then, and I would see the long new scar on his stomach, red as blood against his white skin. His ribs all showed and his legs were like cables.

I once read in a biography of a great man that he "died well." I assume the writer meant that he kept his pain to himself, did not set off false alarms, and did not too much inconvenience those who were to stay behind. My father died well. His irritability gave way to something else, something like serenity. In the last days he became tender. It was as though he had been rehearsing the scene, that the anger of his life had been a kind of stage fright. He managed his audience—us—with an old trouper's sense of when to clown and when to stand on his dignity. We were all moved, and admired his courage, as he intended we should. He died downstairs in a shaft of late afternoon sunlight on New Year's Day, while I was reading to him. I was alone in the house and didn't know what to do. His body did not frighten me but immediately and sharply I missed my father. It seemed wrong to leave him sitting up and I tried to carry him upstairs to the bedroom but it was too hard, alone. So I called up my friend Ralphy across the street. When he came over and saw what I wanted him for he started crying but I made him help me anyway. A couple of hours later Mother got home and when I told her that Father was dead she ran upstairs, calling his name. A few minutes later she came back down. "Thank God," she said, "at least he died in bed." This seemed important to her and I didn't tell her otherwise. But that night Ralphy's parents called. They were, they said, shocked at what I had done and so was Mother when she heard the story, shocked and furious. Why? Because I had not told her the truth? Or because she had learned the truth, and could not go on believing that Father had died in bed? I really don't know.

"Mother," I said, coming into the living room, "I'm sorry about the letter. I really am."

She was arranging wood in the fireplace and did not look at me or speak for a moment. Finally she finished and straightened up and brushed her hands. She stepped back and looked at the fire she had laid. "That's all right," she said. "Not bad for a consumptive."

"Mother, I'm sorry."

"Sorry? Sorry you wrote it or sorry I found it?"

"I wasn't going to mail it. It was a sort of joke."

"Ha ha." She took up the whisk broom and swept bits of bark into the fireplace, then closed the drapes and settled on the couch. "Sit down," she said. She crossed her legs. "Listen, do I give you advice all the time?"

"Yes."

"I do?"

I nodded.

"Well, that doesn't make any difference. I'm supposed to. I'm your mother. I'm going to give you some more advice, for your own good. You don't have to make all these things up, James. They'll happen anyway." She picked at the hem of her skirt. "Do you understand what I'm saying?"

"I think so."

"You're cheating yourself, that's what I'm trying to tell you. When you get to be my age you won't know anything at all about life. All you'll know is what you've made up."

I thought about that. It seemed logical.

She went on. "I think maybe you need to get out of yourself more. Think more about other people."

The doorbell rang.

"Go see who it is," Mother said. "We'll talk about this later."

It was Dr. Murphy. He and mother made their apologies and she insisted that he stay for dinner. I went to the kitchen to fetch ice for their drinks, and when I returned they were talking about me. I sat on the sofa and listened. Dr. Murphy was telling Mother not to worry. "James is a good boy," he said. "I've been thinking about my oldest, Terry. He's not really dishonest, you know, but he's not really honest either. I can't seem to reach him. At least James isn't furtive."

"No," Mother said, "he's never been furtive."

Dr. Murphy clasped his hands between his knees and stared at them. "Well, that's Terry. Furtive."

Before we sat down to dinner Mother said grace; Dr. Murphy bowed his head and closed his eyes and crossed himself at the end, though he had lost his faith in college. When he told me that, during one of our meetings, in just those words, I had the picture of a raincoat hanging by itself outside a dining hall. He drank a good deal of wine and persistently turned the conversation to the subject of his relationship with Terry. He admitted that he had come to dislike the boy. Then he mentioned several patients of his by name, some of them known to Mother and me, and said that he disliked them too. He used the word "dislike" with relish, like someone on a diet permitting himself a single potato chip. "I don't know what I've done wrong," he said abruptly, and with reference to no particular thing. "Then again maybe I haven't done anything wrong. I don't know what to think any more. Nobody does."

"I know what to think," Mother said.

"So does the solipsist. How can you prove to a solipsist that he's not creating the rest of us?"

This was one of Dr. Murphy's favorite riddles, and almost any pretext was sufficient for him to trot it out. He was a child with a card trick.

"Send him to bed without dinner," Mother said. "Let him create that."

Dr. Murphy suddenly turned to me. "Why do you do it?" he asked. It was a pure question, it had no object beyond the satisfaction of his curiosity. Mother looked at me and there was the same curiosity in her face.

"I don't know," I said, and that was the truth.

Dr. Murphy nodded, not because he had anticipated my answer but because he accepted it. "Is it fun?"

"No, it's not fun. I can't explain."

"Why is it all so sad?" Mother asked. "Why all the diseases?"

"Maybe," Dr. Murphy said, "sad things are more interesting."

"Not to me," Mother said.

"Not to me, either," I said. "It just comes out that way."

After dinner Dr. Murphy asked Mother to play the piano. He particularly wanted to sing "Come Home Abbie, the Light's on the Stair."

"That old thing," Mother said. She stood and folded her napkin deliberately and we followed her into the living room. Dr. Murphy stood behind her as she warmed up. Then they sang "Come Home Abbie, the Light's on the Stair," and I watched him stare down at Mother intently, as if he were trying to remember something. Her own eyes were closed. After that they sang "O Magnum Mysterium." They sang it in parts and I regretted that I had no voice, it sounded so good.

"Come on, James," Dr. Murphy said as Mother played the last chords. "These old tunes not good enough for you?"

"He just can't sing," Mother said.

When Dr. Murphy left, Mother lit the fire and made more coffee. She slouched down in the big chair, sticking her legs straight out and moving her feet back and forth. "That was fun," she said.

"Did you and Father ever do things like that?"

"A few times, when we were first going out. I don't think he really enjoyed it. He was like you."

I wondered if Mother and Father had had a good marriage. He admired her and liked to look at her; every night at dinner he had us move the candlesticks slightly to right and left of center so he could see her down the length of the table. And every evening when she set the table she put them in the center again. She didn't seem to miss him very much. But I wouldn't really have known if she did, and anyway I didn't miss him all that much myself, not the way I had. Most of the time I thought about other things.

"James?"

I waited.

"I've been thinking that you might like to go down and stay with Michael for a couple of weeks or so."

"What about school?"

"I'll talk to Father McSorley. He won't mind. Maybe this problem will take care of itself if you start thinking about other people."

"I do."

"I mean helping them, like Michael does. You don't have to go if you don't want to."

"It's fine with me. Really. I'd like to see Michael."

"I'm not trying to get rid of you."

"I know."

Mother stretched, then tucked her feet under her. She sipped noisily at her coffee. "What did that word mean that Murphy used? You know the one?"

"Paranoid? That's where somebody thinks everyone is out to get him. Like that woman who always grabs you after Mass—Frances."

"Not paranoid. Everyone knows what that means. Sol-something."

"Oh. Solipsist. A solipsist is someone who thinks he creates everything around him."

Mother nodded and blew on her coffee, then put it down without drinking from it. "I'd rather be paranoid. Do you really think Frances is?"

"Of course. No question about it."

"I mean really *sick?*"

"That's what paranoid *is,* is being sick. What do you think, Mother?"

"What are you so angry about?"

"I'm not angry." I lowered my voice. "I'm not angry. But you don't believe those stories of hers, do you?"

"Well, no, not exactly. I don't think she knows what she's saying, she just wants someone to listen. She probably lives all by herself in some little room. So she's paranoid. Think of that. And I had no idea. James, we should pray for her. Will you remember to do that?"

I nodded. I thought of Mother singing "O Magnum Mysterium," saying grace, praying with easy confidence, and it came to me that her imagination was superior to mine. She could imagine things as coming together, not falling apart. She looked at me and I shrank; I knew exactly what she was going to say. "Son," she said, "do you know how much I love you?"

The next afternoon I took the bus to Los Angeles. I looked forward to the trip, to the monotony of the road and the empty fields by the roadside. Mother walked with me down the long concourse. The station was crowded and oppressive. "Are you sure this is the right bus?" she asked at the loading platform.

"Yes."

"It looks so old."

"Mother—"

"All right." She pulled me against her and kissed me, then held me an extra second to show that her embrace was sincere, not just like everyone else's, never having realized that everyone else does the same thing. I boarded the bus and we waved at each other until it became embarrassing. Then Mother began checking through her handbag for something. When she had finished I stood and adjusted the luggage over my seat. I sat and we smiled at each other, waved when the driver gunned the engine, shrugged when he got up suddenly to count the passengers, waved again when he resumed his seat. As the bus pulled out my mother and I were looking at each other with plain relief.

I had boarded the wrong bus. This one was bound for Los Angeles but not by the express route. We stopped in San Mateo, Palo Alto, San Jose, Castroville. When we left Castroville it began to rain, hard; my window would not close all the way, and a thin stream of water ran down the wall onto my seat. To keep dry I had to stay away from the wall and lean forward. The rain fell harder. The engine of the bus sounded as though it were coming apart.

In Salinas the man sleeping beside me jumped up but before I had a chance to change seats his place was taken by an enormous woman in a print dress, carrying a shopping bag. She took possession of her seat and spilled over onto half of mine, backing me up to the wall. "That's a storm," she said loudly, then turned and looked at me. "Hungry?" Without waiting for an answer she dipped into her bag and pulled out a piece of chicken and thrust it at me. "Hey, by God," she hooted, "look at him go to town on that drumstick!" A few people turned and smiled. I smiled back around the bone and kept at it. I finished that piece and she handed me another, and then another. Then she started handing out chicken to the people in the seats near us.

Outside of San Luis Obispo the noise from the engine grew suddenly louder and just as suddenly there was no noise at all. The driver pulled off to the side of the road and got out, then got on again dripping wet. A few moments later he announced that the bus had broken down and they were sending another bus to pick us up. Someone asked how long that might take and the driver said he had no idea. "Keep your pants on!" shouted the woman next to me. "Anybody in a hurry to get to L.A. ought to have his head examined."

The wind was blowing hard around the bus, driving sheets of rain against the windows on both sides. The bus swayed gently. Outside the light was brown and thick. The woman next to me pumped all the people around us for their itineraries and said whether or not she had ever been where they were from or where they were going. "How about you?" She slapped my knee. "Parents own a chicken ranch? I hope so!" She laughed. I told her I was from San Francisco. "San Francisco, that's where my husband was stationed." She asked me what I did there and I told her I worked with refugees from Tibet.

"Is that right? What do you do with a bunch of Tibetans?"

"Seems like there's plenty of other places they could've gone," said a man in front of us. "Coming across the border like that. We don't go there."

"What do you do with a bunch of Tibetans?" the woman repeated.

"Try to find them jobs, locate housing, listen to their problems."

"You understand that kind of talk?"

"Yes."

"Speak it?"

"Pretty well. I was born and raised in Tibet. My parents were missionaries over there."

Everyone waited.

"They were killed when the Communists took over."

The big woman patted my arm.

"It's all right, " I said.

"Why don't you say some of that Tibetan?"

"What would you like to hear?"

"Say 'The cow jumped over the moon.'" She watched me, smiling, and when I finished she looked at the others and shook her head. "That was pretty. Like music. Say some more."

"What?"

"Anything."

They bent toward me. The windows suddenly went blind with rain. The driver had fallen asleep and was snoring gently to the swaying of the bus. Outside the muddy light flickered to pale yellow, and far off there was thunder. The woman next to me leaned back and closed her eyes and then so did all the others as I sang to them in what was surely an ancient and holy tongue.

SELECTED BIBLIOGRAPHY

Atchity, Kenneth. 1986. *A Writer's Time*. New York: W. W. Norton.

Booth, Wayne C. 1961. *The Rhetoric of Fiction*. Chicago: University of Chicago Press.

Borges, Jorge Luis. 1973. *Borges on Writing*. Ed. Norman Thomas di Giovanni, Daniel Halpern, and Frank MacShane. New York: E. P. Dutton.

Bowen, Elizabeth. 1950. *Collected Impressions*. New York: Alfred A. Knopf.

Brande, Dorothea. 1981. *On Becoming a Writer*. Los Angeles: Jeremy Tarcher.

Burroway, Janet. 1992. *Writing Fiction*, 3rd ed. New York: HarperCollins

Dillard, Annie. 1989. *The Writing Life*. New York: Harper and Row.

Fitzgerald, F. Scott. 1978. *The Notebooks of F. Scott Fitzgerald*. Ed. Matthew J. Bruccoli. New York: Harcourt Brace Jovanovich.

Forster, E. M. 1954. *Aspects of the Novel*. New York: Harcourt Brace & World.

Gardner, John. 1984. *The Art of Fiction*. New York: Alfred A. Knopf.

Hall, Donald. 1979. *Writing Well*. Boston: Little, Brown.

Hemingway, Ernest. 1984. *Ernest Hemingway on Writing*. Ed. Larry W. Phillips. New York: Charles Scribner's and Sons.

Hills, Rust. 1977. *Writing in General and the Short Story in Particular*. Boston: Houghton Mifflin.

Huddle, David. 1992. *The Writing Habit: Essays*. Gibbs Smith.

Hughes, Elaine Farris. 1990. *Writing from the Inner Self*. New York: Harper-Collins.

Hugo, Richard. 1979. *The Triggering Town*. New York: W. W. Norton.

James, Henry. 1947. *The Art of the Novel*. Oxford: Oxford University Press.

———. 1947. *The Notebooks of Henry James*. Oxford: Oxford University Press.

———. 1948. *The Art of Fiction*. New York: Charles Scribner's and Sons.

Lodge, David. 1992. *The Art of Fiction*. New York: Penguin Books.

Macauley, Robie, and Lanning, George. 1987. *Technique in Fiction*, 2nd ed. New York: St. Martin's Press.

Madden, David. 1988. *Revising Fiction: A Handbook for Fiction Writers*. New York: New American Library.

Minot, Stephen. 1988. *Three Genres*, 4th ed. Englewood Cliffs, N.J.: Prentice-Hall.

O'Connor, Flannery. 1969. *Mystery and Manners*. New York: Farrar, Straus & Giroux.

O'Connor, Frank. 1963. *The Lonely Voice: A Study of the Short Story*. Cleveland: World Publishing.

Pack, Robert and Parini, Jay, eds. 1991. *Writers on Writing*. Hanover, New Hampshire: University Press of New England.

Plimpton, George. 1953–1989. *Writers at Work: The Paris Review Interviews*, 8 vols., New York: Viking Penguin.

———. 1989. *The Writer's Chapbook*. New York: Viking.

Reed, Kit. 1982. *Story First. The Writer as Insider:* Englewood Cliffs, N.J. Prentice-Hall.

Shelnutt, Eve. 1989. *The Writing Room*. Atlanta, Georgia: Longstreet Press.

Stern, Jerome. 1991. *Making Shapely Fiction*. New York: W. W. Norton.

Strunk, William C., and E. B. White. 1979. *The Elements of Style,* 3rd ed. New York: Macmillan.

Welty, Eudora. 1977. *The Eye of the Story*. New York: Random House.

ABOUT THE CONTRIBUTORS

TONY ARDIZZONE is the author of two novels, *In the Name of the Father* and *Heart of the Order,* and two collections of stories, *The Evening News* and *Larabi's Ox.* His work has received the Flannery O'Connor Award for Short Fiction and the Milkweed National Fiction Prize. He teaches at Indiana University in Bloomington.

RICHARD BAUSCH is a short story writer and novelist whose most recent books are *Violence* and *Rebel Towers.* He is on the writing faculty of George Mason University in Fairfax, Virginia.

FRANÇOIS CAMOIN teaches writing at Vermont College and the University of Utah.

RON CARLSON is a fiction writer whose most recent book is the story collection *Plan B for the Middle Class.* He is Director of Creative Writing at Arizona State University.

GEORGE GARRETT is the Henry Hoyns Professor of Creative Writing at the University of Virginia and the author of twenty-five books. His most recent are: *The Sorrows of Fat City, Whistling in the Dark,* and *My Silk Purse and Yours.* In 1989 he received the T. S. Eliot Award and more recently, the PEN/Faulkner Bernard Malamud Award for Short Fiction.

PERRY GLASSER is the author of two collections of short fiction, *Suspicious Origins* and *Singing on the Titanic.* He has taught at Drake University in Iowa and Bradford College in Massachussetts.

KATHARINE HAAKE's first collection of stories, *No Reason on Earth,* was published by Dragon Gate Press. Independently, her stories have appeared in *The Iowa Review, Mississippi Review,* and *The Minnesota Review,* among others. She is finishing a novel and a book about teaching creative writing. She teaches at California State University.

CHRISTOPHER KEANE's forthcoming novel is titled *Christmas Babies.* He is currently writing a screenplay, *The Venus Coalition,* for actor Anthony Quinn, and he teaches a graduate workshop at Emerson College in Boston.

WILLIAM MELVIN KELLEY has published four novels, including the recently reissued *A Different Drummer,* and a book of stories titled *Dancers on the Shore.* He teaches at Sarah Lawrence.

THOMAS KENNEDY's books include a novel, *Crossing Borders,* and four volumes of literary criticism, most recently on Robert Coover. His stories appear widely, have been featured in the Pushcart and O. Henry prize collections, and published in Danish and Serbo-Croation. He lives and works in Denmark, serving *inter alia* as European editor of *Cimarron Review.*

ROD KESSLER, author of *Off In Zimbabwe,* a collection of stories, is completing work on a novel, *Edelman Unsung.* He teaches writing at Salem State College where he is also editor of *The Sextant* and an alternating director of the Eastern Writers' Conference. The answers to Exercise 50 are:

> (A) Ann Beattie, from "Weekend"; (B) William Faulkner, from "Barn Burning"; (C) Amy Hempel, from "Du Jour"; (D) Henry Miller, from *Tropic of Cancer;* (E) Toni Morrison, from *Beloved,* (F) Kurt Vonnegut, from "Deer in the Works"; (G) Ernest Hemingway, from "Soldier's Home"; (H) John Updike, from "The City."

WILLIAM KITTREDGE is the author of an autobiographical book titled *Hole in the Sky* and two previous books, *Owning It All* and *We Are Not in This Together.* He teaches at the University of Montana.

ELIZABETH LIBBEY has published three volumes of poetry: *The Crowd Inside, Songs of a Returning Soul,* and *All That Heat in a Cold Sky.* She teaches writing workshops at Trinity College in Hartford, Connecticut.

ALISON LURIE is the author of eight novels, the latest of which is *The Truth About Lorin Jones.* Her most recent book is *Don't Tell the Grown-Ups: Subversive Children's Literature.* She is the Frederic J. Whiton Professor of American Studies at Cornell.

ROBIE MACAULEY is the author of two novels, a collection of short stories, and two nonfiction books. His *Technique in Fiction* (with George Lanning) has been reissued by St. Martin's Press.

DAVID MADDEN is the author of *Bijou, The Suicide's Wife,* and other novels, short stories, plays, poetry, critical studies, and textbooks. He has conducted workshops in creative writing for over twenty-five years and has taught writing at Louisiana State University since 1968.

CAROL-LYNN MARRAZZO is a teacher and writer who lives in New Hampshire. She received an M.F.A from Vermont College in Montpelier and is currently completing a collection of stories titled *Closing Time.*

ALEXANDRA MARSHALL is a Boston writer whose novels include *Gus in Bronze, Tender Offer,* and *The Brass Bed.* Her work in progress is titled *Child Widow.* She is a writer-in-residence at Emerson College, Boston.

BRIDGET MAZUR's short stories and essays have appeared in *Shenandoah, Fiction,* and *The Iowa Review.* She teaches courses in fiction and nonfiction writing at Lebanon College in Lebanon, New Hampshire, and edits the college's literary magazine, *Northwoods Review.*

CHRISTOPHER NOËL published his first novel, *Hazard and the Five Delights*, in 1988 and has a collection of stories, *The Grasshopper Girl*, forthcoming. He teaches in the Vermont College Master's of Fine Arts program in Montpelier.

JOY NOLAN writes and teaches in western Massachusetts. She was a Writing Fellow at the Fine Arts Work Center in Provincetown, 1992–93. She holds an M.F.A from Vermont College.

DAVID RAY's most recent books are *Not Far from the River and The Maharani's New Wall and Other Poems. Sam's Book* won the Maurice English Poetry Award in 1988. He is a professor of English at the University of Missouri-Kansas City where he teaches both fiction and poetry workshops.

KEN RIVARD recently finished a screenplay about a mother and son coping with the son's learning disability and is currently working on a collection of stories and a novel. He teaches a fiction workshop in the Harvard Extension Program.

LORE SEGAL's best-known novel is *Her First American.* She is also the author of a book of Bible translations, *The Book of Adam to Moses,* and a new children's book, *Mrs. Lovewright and Purrless Her Cat.* She teaches at Ohio State University.

THALIA SELZ has contributed fiction to many magazines, including *Partisan Review, Antaeus, Chicago,* and *New Letters.* Her stories have been anthologized in *Best American Short Stories* and *O. Henry Prize Stories.* She has won twenty-three literary prizes and fellowships. She teaches at Trinity College in Hartford, Connecticut.

SHARON SHEEHE STARK has published two books of fiction, *The Dealer's Yard and Other Stories* and *A Wrestling Season.* She is a contributor to the *Atlantic,* a recipient of Guggenheim and National Endowment of the Arts fellowships, and is on the faculty of the Vermont College Master's of Fine Arts program in Montpelier.

EVE SHELNUTT is the author of three short story collections—*The Love Child, The Formal Voice,* and *The Musician,* and has also published the widely used text, *The Writing Room: Keys to the Craft of Fiction and Poetry,* and two collections of essays by contemporary writers. She is on the faculty of The College of the Holy Cross.

JAMES THOMAS is the author of *Pictures, Moving,* a collection of stories, and the coeditor of *Sudden Fiction, Sudden Fiction International,* and *Flash Fiction.* He teaches fiction writing at Wright State University, where he also codirects a summer writing program for public school teachers.

MELANIE RAE THON is the author of two novels, *Meteors in August* and *Iona Moon,* and a collection of stories, *Girls in the Grass.* She teaches in the graduate program of Syracuse University

ACKNOWLEDGMENTS

ELLEN GILCHRIST "Crazy, Crazy Now Showing Everywhere" from *Victory Over Japan* by Ellen Gilchrist. Copyright © 1983, 1984 by Ellen Gilchrist. By permission of Little, Brown and Company.

PAM HOUSTON "How to Talk to a Hunter" reprinted from *Cowboys Are My Weakness* by Pam Houston with the permission of W. W. Norton & Company, Inc. Copyright © 1992 by Pam Houston.

RICHARD JACKSON "The Other Day" from *Alive All Day*. Used by permission of the author.

JAMAICA KINCAID "Girl" from *At the Bottom of the River* by Jamaica Kincaid. Copyright © 1978, 1983 by Jamaica Kincaid. Reprinted by permission of Farrar, Straus & Giroux, Inc.

MOLLY LANZAROTTA "One Day Walk Through the Front Door" by Molly Lanzarotta. First published in *Sun Dog: The Southeast Review*. Copyright © 1992 by Molly Lanzarotta. Reprinted by permission of the author.

KIMBERLY M. LEAHY "The Smell of Garlic" used by permission of the author.

MARIETTE LIPPO "Confirmation Names" by Mariette Lippo. First published in *Sun Dog: The Southeast Review*. Copyright © 1991 by Mariette Lippo. Reprinted by permission of the author.

ALISON LURIE "My Pet" and "Total Recall" copyright © 1990 by Alison Lurie.

MATT MARINOVICH "Intelligence" by Matt Marinovich. First published in *The Quarterly*. Copyright © 1992 by Matt Marinovich. Reprinted by permission of the author.

BOBBIE ANN MASON "Shiloh" from *Shiloh and Other Stories* by Bobbie Ann Mason. Copyright © 1982 by Bobbie Ann Mason. Reprinted by permission of HarperCollins Publishers, Inc.

ALICE MUNRO "Five Points" from *Friend of My Youth* by Alice Munro. Copyright © 1990 by Alice Munro. Reprinted by permission of Alfred A. Knopf, Inc.

TIM O'BRIEN "On the Rainy River" from *The Things They Carried* by Tim O'Brien. Copyright © 1990 by Tim O'Brien. Reprinted by permission of Houghton Mifflin Company/Seymour Lawrence. All rights reserved.

DAVID RAY "Magnifying Conflict," "The Five-Highlighter Exercise," and "Cutting to the Bone" copyright © 1990 by David Ray.

MARY ROBISON "Yours" from *An Amateur's Guide to the Night* by Mary Robison. Copyright © 1983 by Mary Robison. Reprinted by permission of Alfred A. Knopf, Inc.

MURIEL SPARK Excerpt from *Memento Mori* by Muriel Spark, copyright 1958. Reprinted by permission of Georges Borchardt, Inc., and the author.

SHARON SHEEHE STARK "May Angels Lead You Home" by Sharon Sheehe Stark first appeared in *The Atlantic*. Copyright © 1986 by Sharon Sheehe Stark. Reprinted by permission of the author.

ELIZABETH TALLENT "No One's a Mystery" from *Time With Children* by Elizabeth Tallent. Copyright © 1986, 1987 by Elizabeth Tallent. Reprinted by permission of Alfred A. Knopf, Inc.

LUISA VALENZUELA "Vision Out of the Corner of One Eye" from *Strange Things Happen Here: Twenty-Six Short Stories and a Novel* by Luisa Valenzuela and translated by Helen Lane, copyright © 1975 by Ediciones de la Flor, English translation copyright © 1979 by Harcourt Brace & Company, reprinted by permission of the publisher.

ROBERT WATSON "Please Write; Don't Phone" from *Night Blooming Cactus* by Robert Watson, published by Atheneum Publishers. Copyright © 1980 by Robert Watson. Reprinted by permission of the author.

KATE WHEELER "Under the Roof" from *Not Where I Started From* by Kate Wheeler. First published in *Black Warrior Review*. Copyright © 1993 by Kate Wheeler. Reprinted by permission of Houghton Mifflin Company. All rights reserved.

TOBIAS WOLFF "The Liar" copyright © 1981 by Tobias Wolff. From *In the Garden of the North American Martyrs*. First published by The Ecco Press in 1981. Reprinted by permission.

INDEX